FAR EAST, DOWN SOUTH

the MODERN SOUTH

series editors
Susan Youngblood Ashmore
& Kari Frederickson

FAR EAST, DOWN SOUTH

ASIANS IN THE AMERICAN SOUTH

EDITED BY RAYMOND A. MOHL,
JOHN E. VAN SANT, AND CHIZURU SAEKI

The University of Alabama Press
Tuscaloosa

The University of Alabama Press
Tuscaloosa, Alabama 35487-0380
uapress.ua.edu

Hardcover edition published 2016.
Paperback edition published 2021.
eBook edition published 2016.

Typeface: Minion and Helvetica Neue

Cover image: Vietnamese shrimper Vui Van Nguyen on his boat in Bayou La Batre, Alabama, 2010; photo by Robin McDonald
Cover design: Erin Bradley Dangar / Dangar Design

Paperback ISBN: 978-0-8173-6038-2

A previous edition of this book has been cataloged by the Library of Congress.
ISBN: 978-0-8173-1914-4 (cloth)
E-ISBN: 978-0-8173-8989-5

For Ray

Contents

List of Illustrations ix

Preface xi

Introduction
David M. Reimers 1

1. The Astonishing History of Japanese Americans in Louisiana
Greg Robinson 11

2. Views of Japanese in Alabama, 1941–1953
Chizuru Saeki 29

3. Collective Aspirations of Japanese Americans in and beyond the WWII South
John Howard 49

4. Asian Immigration to Florida
Raymond A. Mohl 73

5. Chinese in Florida: History, Struggles, and Contributions to the Sunshine State
Wenxian Zhang 108

6. "Chinese for the South": Mississippi Delta Chinese Migration Chains
John Jung 132

7. Second-Generation Chinese Americans from Atlanta, Augusta, and Savannah Georgia: Overcoming "Otherness"
Daniel Bronstein 155

8. Immigrant Dreams and Second-Generation Realities: Indian Americans Negotiating Marriage, Culture, and Identity in North Carolina
Vincent H. Melomo 198

9. Resilient History and the Rebuilding of a Community: The Vietnamese American Community in New Orleans East
Karen J. Leong, Christopher A. Airriess, Wei Li, Angela Chia-Chen Chen, and Verna M. Keith 234

Contributors 249

Index 253

Illustrations

FIGURES

2.1. “Achille’s Heel,” Frank M. Spangler editorial cartoon 35

2.2. “To Make a Happy Day,” Frank M. Spangler editorial cartoon 35

6.1. “What Shall We Do with John Chinaman?” 133

6.2. John Gow Nue grocery store at the foot of Washington Street, Greenville, Mississippi 140

6.3. Family dinner inside the Mee Joe Grocery Store, Greenville, Mississippi 149

TABLES

4.1. Asian Population Increase in Florida, 1950–2010 75

4.2. Ten Most Numerous Asian Groups in Florida, 1970–2010 82

4.3. Asians in Florida, by Urban County, 1970–2010 83

4.4. Top Asian Groups in Florida’s Largest Metropolitan Areas, 2009 84

Preface

According to the 2010 US census, the population of the United States grew by 9.7 percent from 2000—from 281.4 million to 308.7 million.[1] However, the Asian population increased 46 percent during the same period, from 11.9 million to 17.6 million—the largest rate of growth of all race groups in the country. The largest percentage of the Asian population, 46 percent, lived in the western United States. The second largest percentage of Asians, 22 percent, lived in the South. While the number of Asians rose in every region between 2000 and 2010, the Asian population grew the fastest in the South at 72 percent. In other words, the growth rate of the Asian population in the United States is at a much higher rate than the overall growth rate of the population, and the growth rate of Asians in the South is even higher. The actual population numbers are astonishing. In 2010, for example, more than 1.1 million Asians resided in Texas, 573,000 in Florida, 522,000 in Virginia, and 365,000 in Georgia. And the South's ethnic diversity has continued rising in the current decade.

The rising growth rate of Asians in the South has been commented on previously. In the first edition of the *Encyclopedia of Southern Culture* (1989), Roger Daniels notes there were "many more [Asians in the South] than most Americans imagine." The updated *New Encyclopedia of Southern Culture: Ethnicity* (2007) concludes that Asian southerners "are increasingly laying claims to the southern landscape." The contributions to *Far East, Down South: Asians in the American South* reflect the historic patterns by which people of Asian descent became an integral part of southern society. Although many Americans still stereotypically perceive the South as divided biracially between whites and African Americans, the reality has been quite different.

The essays in this collection demonstrate that Asians have been part of southern diversity since Filipino sailors deserted Spanish galleons in the early nineteenth century and made their way to New Orleans. Asians have been part of the South ever since, with Chinese and Japanese immigrants coming to the region in the late nineteenth century as contract laborers, farmers, and shopkeepers. Asian immigration to the United States was curbed in 1882 by Congress, which responded to immigrant opposition on the West Coast and passed the Chinese Exclusion Act, prohibiting further Chinese labor immigration. Originally set for ten years, the act was renewed in 1892, made permanent in 1902, and not repealed until 1943. Hostility to Asian immigration, especially in the western states, led Congress to incorporate Oriental exclusion provisions in the 1924 Immigration Act in order to halt Japanese immigration. These anti-immigrant laws effectively limited the number of Chinese immigrants to the low thousands and Japanese immigrants to about one thousand in the South before World War II.

During the war, however, federal government policies brought thousands of Japanese people to the South, albeit temporarily. The 442nd Regimental Combat Team (including the 100th Infantry Battalion), comprised almost exclusively of Japanese American soldiers recruited from War Relocation Authority (WRA) internment camps and from Hawaii, trained at Camp Shelby in Mississippi. These brave Japanese American soldiers fought in Europe and became the most decorated unit in US military history. Meanwhile, over sixteen thousand Japanese Americans from the West Coast were interned at WRA camps at Rohwer and Jerome, Arkansas, because of wartime hysteria and racial prejudice. Following the attack on Pearl Harbor, President Franklin Roosevelt ordered the internment—imprisonment—of 120,000 people of Japanese ancestry, most of whom were American citizens and all of whom were innocent of crimes against the United States. After the war, few members of the 442nd Regimental Combat Team or Japanese Americans interned in Arkansas remained in the South; most returned to the western states and Hawaii. However, some American military men from the South, returning from the Pacific region after World War II and from the subsequent Korean War, came home with war brides from Japan, Korea, the Philippines, and China.

Four developments in the postwar era have led to significant growth in the numbers of Asians in the American South. First, the Immigration and Nationality Act of 1965 abolished the national origins quota system that had been in place since 1924, opening up significant immigration from all over the Pacific Rim. Second, the end of America's involvement in the Vietnam War in 1975 brought refugees and more war brides from Southeast Asia to the South. Third, as the South recovered from the racial troubles of the 1950s and 1960s, the newly minted Sun Belt region experienced rapid economic and demographic growth. Economic opportunity and warm climate attracted people and investment from all over the United States and the world. And finally, the economic growth of Japan, South Korea, Taiwan, China, India, and Southeast Asia has led students, business people, and family members of relatives already living in the region to come to the South for education, for investment, for work, and for tourism.

Today, in so-called white suburbs of the South, there are plenty of African Americans, Hispanic Americans, Arab Americans, and Asian Americans—Chinese, Japanese, Korean, Indian, and Vietnamese—residing in middle-class homes, sending their kids to nearby suburban schools, and driving SUVs to watch their children's soccer and Little League games. Asian students majoring in life sciences and physical sciences at large southern research universities no longer seems an exotic, foreign-student phenomenon—it is the norm. Urban areas of the South are even more diverse than the suburbs, as diverse as many urban areas in the Northeast and West. All varieties of ethnic restaurants can be found in the urban South; Asian grocery stores are popping up throughout southern metropolitan regions, as well, serving the growing Asian population. Southern governors and county economic development officials compete with each other by flying to Japan, South Korea, China, and India to offer tax breaks to Asian companies considering building factories in the American South. While many rural places in the South are still largely white or black, even these areas are becoming more ethnically diverse with rising numbers of people of Asian and Hispanic descent.

Neither black nor white, Asians often face prejudice and discrimination from both groups. Asians in the South have been considered by scholars to be "a third race," or an "in between people," because they did not fit the traditional racial binary of the region. Essays in this book, however, reveal that despite their "in-between" status, Asians in the South have demonstrated an ability to adapt to new circumstances while also retaining traditional cultures as a source of family and community strength. Nevertheless, discrimination has been and continues to be a harsh fact of life for many Asians in the southern states. The same southern governors who fly to Asia in search of investments and new factories also support strong anti-immigration legislation back at home. While recent anti-immigrant measures are directed at "illegal" Hispanic immigrants, such measures adversely affect Asians, who come under suspicion of being in the United States illegally—even though they may be American citizens or have legal immigrant status. With the recent dramatic increases in the number of Asians, the South has clearly become a multicultural landscape. Unfortunately, many elected officials—both Republican and Democrat—have yet to recognize ethnic diversity as a positive attribute.

***

This book has a history. New to the United States, Chizuru Saeki completed a PhD in history at Bowling Green State University in Ohio. She found a faculty position in Asian history at the University of North Alabama in Florence, a small town in northwest Alabama. As one of the few minorities in Florence, she was surprised and dismayed to encounter racial prejudice. As she recounted recently: "Then, I started thinking about how minority races in the Deep South managed to survive historically. At school, we learn the history of African Americans in the Deep South, and the story of the civil rights movement. But we know almost nothing about how other minority people lived—for instance, Asians, including myself. How are we categorized in southern society? To answer that question, I went on the journey of reading, corresponding, and sharing thoughts with other scholars who might be interested in similar topics." That process led ultimately to this book, as Chizuru pulled together the work of our contributors, with "the ambitious aim of seeing the life of Asians in the South more widely beyond state borders and their separate nationalities." Chizuru's early effort in bringing together our various scholars has been enormously important.

In the spring of 2013, after a first round of outside reviews, Chizuru became ill and informed contributors that she would be unable to complete the book project. At that point, the University of Alabama Press invited Raymond A. Mohl and John E. Van Sant to take over editorial responsibilities. Both were familiar with the project. Ray had an essay in the book on the history of Asian immigration to Florida, and John had been one of the original reviewers of the manuscript for the UA Press. Both Ray and John were committed to completing the project; they also share a hallway in the History Department at the University of Alabama at Birmingham. After revisions and a second round of outside reviews, the book began to take shape. We were fortunate to have David Reimers, an outstanding scholar of recent American immigration patterns, agree to contribute an introduction to the book. Our contributors have stuck with us through the months of turmoil and transition, and for that they have our thanks. We also wish to thank Jerry Smith, Jennifer Stitt, Donna Cox Baker, and three anonymous reviewers for their assistance in bringing this book to publication.

Note

1. US Department of Commerce, Economics and Statistics Administration, US Census Bureau, "The Asian Population: 2010," March 2012. Statistical information in the following paragraphs on Asian Americans is taken from this twenty-three-page census brief.

FAR EAST, DOWN SOUTH

Introduction

David M. Reimers

The South in the United States has become a population magnet, while the country as a whole grows at a slow pace due to the recent economic recession. The South's warm climate, job opportunities, and cheaper housing have continued to draw Americans from other states as well as immigrants from foreign countries. According to a census taken in 2006, more than half of the population growth in the United States in the previous year occurred in southern states.[1] The Sun Belt will gain new seats in Congress based on the southern population shift indicated in the census in 2010.[2] The Sun Belt states' populations and economies grew at faster rates than those in the Rust Belt, whose states will have to give up some seats in the Congress. The Sun Belt states have thus gained more influence. Now the South attracts as many people from other countries as the West, partly because California's appeal is waning due to the state's expensive housing. With the South becoming a rising power, new studies on the region will be urgently needed among scholars, business leaders, and government officials.

The recent trend of migration has brought many challenges to the local southern societies. With the increase of the immigrant population, the local communities have been expected to accommodate those whose religions and cultural traditions are unfamiliar to them. In the area of Buford Highway and Chamblee Dunwoody Road in Atlanta, Korean and Chinese immigrants established communities on a large scale. At a small Chinese bakery in Chinatown, the owner placed an altar for worshipping Daoist gods. While immigrants carry on their cultural traditions in the South and settle as minority groups in society, thereby increasing the region's ethnic and cultural diversity, local people are influenced to alter some of their traditions. Some will ultimately end up adopting immigrant traditions. For example, a number of southerners routinely visit the clinics of Chinese acupuncturists for chronic health problems. And on Sundays residents of local communities can be seen attending the service ceremonies of Sukyo Mahikari, a branch of Japanese Shintoism, instead of going to church. Such slow, gradual interactions between the local populations and the new immigrants have created opportunities for southern societies to become more open to cultural differences and part of a driving force behind global internationalism.

The intercourse between America's South and Asian culture has a long history. The first Asian immigrants who came to the southern states were Filipino (known as Manilamen) sailors, who worked as navigators on Spanish galleons and jumped into the sea to escape the brutality of their Spanish masters. They settled in bayous and marshes of Louisiana, possibly in the 1800s, and introduced the process of sun-drying shrimp in the United States.[3] Later, around 1840, to make up for the shortage of slaves from Africa, the British and Spanish brought over "coolies" from China, India, and the Philippines to islands in the Caribbean, Peru, Ecuador, and other countries in South America. Chinese laborers from the Caribbean were then brought into Louisiana during Reconstruction to work on the region's sugar plantations.[4] After the gold rush on the West Coast, more Chinese, Vietnamese, Koreans, and Japanese immigrants arrived in the South as peddlers, farmers, merchants, and factory workers. Some members of those groups experienced the Civil War, Reconstruction, the two World Wars, and the civil rights movement. As a "third race," they struggled to fit into the white-black societies but ultimately survived. Meanwhile they changed the South in irreversible ways.

Recent studies on Asian immigrants in the South have taken various approaches. John Jung, a former psychologist and well-known historian of the lives of Chinese immigrants in the South, published *Southern Fried Rice: Life in a Chinese Laundry in the Deep South* (Ying and Yang Press, 2008), which conveyed the experiences of his parents, the only Chinese living in Macon, Georgia, between 1928 and 1956. Jung's family led an isolated existence running a laundry, enduring loneliness as well as racial prejudice for over twenty years. Another Chinese scholar, Robert Seto Quan, recorded the firsthand stories of Chinese immigrants in the Mississippi Delta in *Lotus among the Magnolias: The Mississippi Chinese* (University Press of Mississippi, 2007). This ethnographic study shows that in the Mississippi Delta, Chinese were initially classified by whites as "colored," but later viewed as having a separate identity. Quan describes how these Chinese immigrants were able to expand their social and economic influence in the community by moving beyond the color line. In *Partly Colored: Asian Americans and Racial Anomaly in the Segregated South* (New York University Press, 2010), Leslie Bow takes a more theoretical approach. She analyzes the complex social status of Asian immigrants in the South. By elucidating the experiences of three different ethnic groups—Mexicans, Asians, and Native Americans—Bow explores how the color line accommodated or refused to accommodate other ethnicities within a binary racial system. And in *New Roots in America's Sacred Ground: Religion, Race and Ethnicity in Indian America* (Rutgers University Press, 2006), Khyati Y Joshi examines the religious influence of Indian Americans. Based on her interviews with forty-one second-generation Indian Americans, including those who live in Atlanta, Georgia, Joshi analyzes their experiences of religion, race, and ethnicity from elementary school to adulthood. She described how these Indian Americans encountered many conflicts between home and religious community, and between family obligations and school, while hoping to retain their ethnic identity.

This book provides a comparative perspective on various Asian immigrant groups, including Chinese, Japanese, Koreans, Vietnamese, and Indians, and their experiences in southern states from the nineteenth century to the contemporary period. It employs different lenses to analyze the lives of these immigrants. The chapters, written by immigration historians, cultural historians, American cultural studies scholars, and anthropologists, highlight the social, cultural, and political relations between Asia and America's southern states.

The early chapters of the book analyze how America's foreign policy toward Asia affected the corresponding Asian ethnic groups and created certain perceptions of Asians among American southerners. It also looks at how US-Asian relations influenced local governments' policies toward Asian immigrants in the South during the Pacific War, Vietnam War, and Cold War periods.

Greg Robinson's and Chizuru Saeki's essays take on the ambitious and challenging tasks of reconstructing the little-known stories of Japanese immigrants in Louisiana and Alabama. While Robinson takes an immigration historian's point of view, as a cultural historian Saeki examines the Japanese in Alabama in the context of the relationship between Alabama and Japan, emphasizing mutual perceptions created during the Pacific War and the postwar period. Despite the different angles of the two scholars, the histories of Japanese in the two states have clear similarities. As Robinson describes, Louisiana had long relations with Japan. Jokichi Takamine, the first Japanese immigrant, came to the state in 1884 and helped cement a special relationship between Louisiana and Japan. In 1896 he escorted a group of six Japanese businessmen to New Orleans, where they placed the first large orders for cotton.[5] Although in 1921 Louisiana enacted an alien land law formally barring all Asian immigrants from purchasing agricultural land, some Japanese managed to migrate to Louisiana, and by the 1930s the local Japanese community had expanded to include forty to fifty permanent residents, composed of farmers, importers, and fishermen. Alabama's relationship with Japan also has a long history, dating back to 1878 when the Satsuma orange was introduced to the state. Japanese immigrants contributed significantly to Alabama's economy and agriculture. One of the most notable of them was Kosaku Sawada, who gained a reputation as the foremost hybridizer of camellias and became one of five particularly exemplary Japanese immigrants in the nation after World War II. Compared to those in Louisiana, however, the number of Japanese immigrants in Alabama was quite small. The official census shows that only 21 of the estimated 127,000 Japanese living in the United States by the 1930s were in Alabama.

World War II hit the Japanese population hard in the both states, yet at the same time it brought Japanese Americans from all over the nation into Louisiana and Alabama. In the case of Louisiana, some 1,200 Issei men, largely from Hawaii, who had been arrested and interned after Pearl Harbor were put on ships and held during 1942–43 at Camp Livingston near Alexandria. New Orleans served as the point of disembarkation for over two thousand ethnic Japanese from Peru and other Latin American countries. By mid-1943, Japanese American soldiers from the One Hundredth Infantry battalion were detailed for training at Camp Livingston.

In Alabama, Fort McClellan became the temporary home for many captured enemy soldiers and Japanese Americans. On March 13, 1944, 608 Japanese American predetention draftees arrived at Fort McClellan; they eventually led a protest against officials in the fort by refusing to participate in combat training. Although Louisiana accommodated more than double that number of Japanese Americans in war relocation camps, due to the government's conscious effort to avoid tensions with the Japanese residents, there was no such mass protest from them.

After the war ended, both states developed strong economic relations with Japan. By the mid-1960s, Japan had become New Orleans's chief foreign trading partner. In 1972, the value of exports from New Orleans to Japan (including a booming business in soybeans) exceeded those to all of Europe. Japanese-affiliated companies invested over $3 billion in Alabama and employed over 13,700 Alabaman workers by 2008. Alabama's exports to Japan in 2008 totaled $732 million in value, making Japan its fifth largest export market.[6] Such trade relations have promoted warm cultural exchanges between Japan and both states that continue today.

John Howard's essay examines the treatment of Japanese Americans in Arkansas during World War II. He focuses on the tensions and contradictions that came to the fore in Arkansas from 1942 to 1945 and explores how Japanese there were understood as people and refugees. Sometimes they were a feared horde, other times "admired" individuals.

Howard discusses the impact of the closing of the Jerome and Rohwer war relocation camps in Arkansas in 1944 and 1945 on the over one hundred thousand Japanese Americans who had been detained under the War Relocation Authority (WRA) and the effects of their dispersal into the population. In 1944 President Franklin Roosevelt insisted on a "gradual release program designed to scatter the internees" in order to insure their "relocation into normal homes" after their loyalty had been determined. Although Roosevelt's original proposal of "one or two families per county" was unworkable, the guiding principle of dispersing the Japanese Americans remained a cornerstone of the US government's resettlement policy. WRA high schools and their social studies teachers taught students the importance of relocating families and individuals where they would find community acceptance and suitable work and be reassimilated into the social and economic order of the nation. When the camps in Arkansas were closed, those few Japanese Americans who were able to make their way home to California met innumerable incidents of violence against them there. In the South, those in mixed marriages also turned out to be vulnerable to persecution. Other Japanese American families found it difficult to send their children to local public schools because most schools were reluctant to accept Japanese American students. Thus, many of these families ended up home teaching their children. Further, after their release, Japanese American workers had few job options and were afforded few protections and little compensation at the factories.

An exceptional situation existed at the Wilson Plantation, located in the far northeast corner of Arkansas, near the Mississippi River. The plantation was a massive operation spread over sixty-three thousand acres, and Wilson officials marketed the plantation as a desirable postwar home for nearly one hundred Japanese Americans. These Japanese American workers were able to depend on the Wilson Plantation to defend their rights and privileges as citizens and loyal aliens after the war. The Wilson Plantation provided school buses to carry all Japanese American workers' children to and from the white schools. Wilson officials, however, segregated Japanese Americans from African Americans under Jim Crow. Though the Arkansas legislature in 1943 passed a racist alien land law that forbade sale or long-term lease of land to persons of Japanese descent, Wilson officials overlooked it. As early as the summer of 1943, the Jerome and Rohwer camps in Arkansas experimented with cooperative group farming among Japanese Americans so that they could share in the collective good. Howard's essay gives voice to those whose stories have been ignored in other histories of Japanese incarceration and highlights the roles of Issei and Nisei Japanese who resisted white racism.

Later chapters of the book focus more on the ethnic identity of Asian immigrants and their assimilation into southern societies, which had been hotbeds of racial tension between whites and African Americans. These chapters examine how Asian immigrants, including Chinese, Koreans, and Japanese, as a "partly colored" race, have fit into southern societies since the Jim Crow era.

Raymond Mohl and Wenxian Zhang analyze the history of Asian immigration and migration to Florida. Mohl provides an overview of such movement from the late nineteenth century to the contemporary period. Mohl's research shows that only a few hundred Chinese and Japanese resided in Florida in 1900 and that the state's Asian population grew slowly throughout much of the twentieth century, primarily because of restrictive immigration policies. By the 1990s, however, when Florida's Asian population totaled 154,302, these newcomers had become the fastest-growing racial group in Florida. Two decades later, the census of 2010 recorded an astonishing 571,244 Asians in various ethnic categories, an increase of 270 percent. Mohl's essay delves into the history of these immigrants and internal migrants in the early twentieth century, ranging from Japanese farmers in South Florida to Chinese laundrymen, citrus farmers, and grocers in Jacksonville, Miami, and central Florida. Changing immigration legislation in the 1950s and 1960s had produced new and larger Asian communities in Florida—Chinese in Miami; Filipinos in Jacksonville and Pensacola; Vietnamese in Orlando, Tampa, and Pensacola; Asian Indians in Miami-Dade and Broward Counties; and Koreans and Japanese concentrated in major urban areas of the state.

Zhang focuses specifically on the history of Chinese immigrants in Florida, which began in the nineteenth century. Among all Asians, Chinese were the first to come to Florida, in the years immediately after the Civil War. At that time, the state was struggling with the dire need to rebuild the South after the war had shattered the Confederate economy and social relationships based on slavery.[7] With the smallest population among all southern states, Florida had vast areas of uninhabited land and an almost nonexistent industrial base. Therefore, many Floridians believed that the quickest and most practical strategy for economic development was to attract a large number of industrious immigrants. This position was embraced by not only state, county, and local government officials but also railroad companies, farm groups, real estate firms, wealthy landowners, industrialists, and mine operators. Prior to 1900, open calls for immigration were issued to welcome all nationalities; Chinese were welcomed, especially since they were thought to be more industrious, thrifty, and docile than other nationalities. Despite high expectations, however, the proposed Chinese settlement in Florida never materialized. With the Democrats and Republicans fighting for control of the state, the Chinese question quickly became entangled in Reconstruction-era politics.[8] While the recruitment of Chinese was favored by Democrats, Republicans charged that Chinese immigration was not free or voluntary.

Nevertheless, quite a few Chinese did make their way to Florida, some by way of California, New York, or Boston, others from Cuba. During the early years of Chinese immigration to Florida, as in most other parts of the country, laundries accounted for the overwhelming majority of Chinese business ventures, with restaurants and groceries trailing behind. Arriving in Florida, these new immigrants faced tremendous challenges, including legislative measures imposed directly against them. When Chinese laundrymen were in direct competition with a local steam laundry, it fueled hostility toward foreign immigrants; the hostility peaked in Florida by 1892. But while the small Chinese community in Tampa declined steadily over the years due to a series of restrictions imposed on Chinese, southeast Florida saw a boom of Chinese grocery stores in the fast-growing Miami area. It is estimated that more than seventy thousand Chinese currently live in Florida. Chinese Americans have been making significant and visible contributions to the growth of the economy, the political life, and the cultural diversity of the state.

John Jung and Daniel Bronstein discuss the lives of Chinese immigrant families in the Mississippi Delta and Georgia, respectively. Both scholars use extensive oral histories, population census data, and city directories to follow first- and second-generation Chinese immigrant families as they coped with getting an education, finding employment, and establishing themselves in the segregated world of Jim Crow. Jung is a renowned oral historian who has previously investigated and written about issues confronting Chinese in Mississippi. According to his research, as early as the 1860s, a few Chinese immigrants found their way to the midsection of the country, including the southern states, where they generally lived in social and cultural isolation.[9] By 1870 some Chinese had migrated to Mississippi. The earliest probably did not come to the Mississippi Delta because it was so attractive but because they needed to escape from racial prejudice on the West Coast. By the 1870s many Chinese on the Pacific Coast and in the Rocky Mountain region faced virulent anti-Chinese sentiments, which eventually led to a law in 1882 excluding the admission of Chinese laborers into the United States. In western regions of the country, violence and threats to their physical safety in many communities forced Chinese to flee for their lives. By moving to regions where they would be few in number such as the Delta, they hoped they might appear to be a smaller threat to the local population and thus incur less hostility and violence than that inflicted on them in places like the West Coast.

The life of Chinese immigrants in the Mississippi Delta is unique in many ways. Although in the 1870s farm labor was the only work widely available for Chinese in the Delta, most Chinese immigrants did not take farm jobs.[10] There was a noticeable absence of Chinese laundries in the Delta as well. Instead of engaging in these occupations, many Chinese in the Mississippi Delta established their financial independence as merchants by opening grocery stores that primarily served African Americans. Once they had established a successful grocery store, they recruited relatives living in other parts of the country to join them in the Delta. Thus, over time, the Delta Chinese built strong family bonds that often extended across the region.

The first generation of Chinese immigrants to live in Georgia experienced isolation similar to Mississippi Chinese during the nineteenth century. As Bronstein's essay describes, however, second-generation Chinese immigrant families in Georgia enjoyed more opportunities for social mobility. Those Chinese who were born in Georgia or came to the state as children between 1905 and 1950 dealt with two national stereotypes imposed on them by European Americans, however—the "perpetual foreigner" and the "honorary white." Their situation was further complicated by the added dynamic of residing in a *biracial* state designed for people of European and African descent. But Georgia's second-generation Asian immigrants overcame both images by assuming many of the attributes of white southerners and with them the privileges of "whiteness" accumulated over several decades. Yet they also retained aspects of their Chinese heritage that did not undermine the growing perception of being near-white. The second-generation Chinese Americans, with the help of their immigrant parents, negotiated a higher status for themselves within a still highly segregated society beginning in the 1910s. For instance, Chinese parents managed to educate most of these children in white secondary and postsecondary schools, despite the fact that the state education system had separate educational facilities for white and "colored" children. Families also joined white churches and raised their children as Christians. Male children born in the 1910s and 1920s usually served in the Second World War and opened profitable retail or convenience stores like their parents, and women of the same age became housewives or unofficial partners in their spouses' enterprises. Younger children of both sexes attended university and professional schools to become white-collar professionals. Gradually, they found employment in white companies and even married local European Americans. By the late 1960s, the perception of "honorary white" had by and large replaced the "perpetual foreigner" image in Georgia.

While the second-generation Chinese in Georgia managed to cross the color line and became "honorary white," the second generation of Asian Indians in North Carolina faced a dilemma between assuming an American identity and preserving their Indian tradition. Vincent Melomo's essay discusses how the second-generation Indians negotiated the balance between meeting the hopes and expectations of their immigrant parents and coping with the pressures of American culture. It emphasizes how the struggles of growing up as a second-generation Indian American are tied up with questions of cultural/ethnic identity. Melomo argues that these identity struggles are particularly manifest as the second generation negotiates competing cultural models of the marriage process, which are associated with Indian and American identities. In short, many second-generation Indian Americans grow up with models of dating, marriage, and sexuality provided by their parents and their community, which contrast with the models presented by the more dominant American culture.

The final essay in the book brings this account of Asians in the South into the twenty-first century. In August 2005, Hurricane Katrina deluged and devastated New Orleans, including the eastern section of the city, where more than five thousand Vietnamese immigrants and Vietnamese Americans resided in an area called Village de L'Est. These people evacuated New Orleans prior to Katrina's arrival, but their homes and apartments were badly damaged by flooding. Months later, the Vietnamese of L'Est had a higher rate of return than any other group, and they quickly began rebuilding their homes and community, mostly without any government subsidies. Coauthors Leong, Airriess, Li, Chen, and Keith attribute this phenomenon primarily to the community and kinship networks established in Vietnam before becoming war refugees and immigrants. Most of the New Orleans Vietnamese came from a few areas south of Saigon, and in America the community was reconstituted and then replenished by subsequent chain migration from the same places. The Catholic Church held a central place in their community, both in Vietnam and in New Orleans. Under the leadership of their pastor, they were able to "define both a cohesive faith identity . . . and a broader refugee identity of survival and socio-cultural adjustment." With the church's encouragement, they became politically active, as well, especially in exerting pressure in preventing the City of New Orleans from locating a huge landfill adjacent to Village de L'Est. Historic patterns of community and a strong sense of collective memory enabled the New Orleans Vietnamese to mobilize to meet the crisis caused by Katrina's flooding.

Some ninety years have passed since the Asian Exclusion Act of 1924 was issued in response to the idea that Asian immigrants clung stubbornly to their own cultural traditions and customs, never assimilated into American culture, and were a threat to American society, including to white jobs and social stability. As you read the chapters of this book, however, you will realize that such generalizations about Asian immigrants, in this case those in the South, are patently untrue. Living in isolation and suffering segregation under Jim Crow, Asians in the South developed special survival skills and amazing adaptability, and they established their position between white and black. The aim of this book is to examine what made Asians in the South unique figures in southern history. It also seeks to convey additional insights into the challenges facing Asian immigrants today.

Notes

1. "Southern Growth Leads USA," *USA Today*, December 21, 2006.

2. "2010 Census Moves 12 House Districts," ABC News, December 21, 2010.

3. Asian American Nation, http://www.asian-nation.org/first.shtml.

4. Moon-Ho Jung, *Coolies and Cane: Race, Labor, and Sugar in the Age of Emancipation* (Baltimore: Johns Hopkins University Press, 2006).

5. "Notes," *Watchman and Southron*, September 16, 1896, p. 2; "The South," *Baltimore Sun*, October 19, 1896, p. 10.

6. Consulate General of Japan, http://www.atlanta.us.emb-japan.go.jp/japanalabama.html.

7. George Pozzetta, "Chinese Encounter with Florida: 1865–1920," *Chinese America: History and Perspectives* 2 (1989): 43.

8. Ibid., 47.

9. The Delta Chinese populace was spread over a large area, covering roughly one hundred miles from just below Memphis to just above Vicksburg, and roughly twenty to thirty miles from the Mississippi River on the west toward the eastern foothills. When the Arkansas side is included, the area extends another ten miles or so to the west of the river. The Chinese Delta "community" was quite diffuse, allowing less direct contact than for Chinese in or near Chinatowns.

10. James W. Loewen. *The Mississippi Chinese: Between Black and White* (Prospect Heights, IL: Waveland Press, 1988), 26.

Works Cited

Asian American Nation: Asian American History, Demographics, and Issues. http://www.asian-nation.org/first.shtml.

Consulate General of Japan. http://www.atlanta.us.emb-japan.go.jp/japanalabama.html.

Jung, Moon-Ho. *Coolies and Cane: Race, Labor, and Sugar in the Age of Emancipation*. Baltimore: Johns Hopkins University Press, 2006.

Loewen, James W. *The Mississippi Chinese: Between Black and White*. Prospect Heights, IL: Waveland Press, 1988.

Pozzetta, George. "The Chinese Encounter with Florida: 1865–1920." *Chinese America: History and Perspectives* 2 (1989).

"2010 Census Moves 12 House Districts." ABC News, December 21, 2010.

1
The Astonishing History of Japanese Americans in Louisiana

Greg Robinson

The history of Japanese settlement in Louisiana, whether in the metropolis of New Orleans or in the bayous, is obscure and discontinuous, but their presence in the state's history has been surprisingly substantial and multivalent. This is a first effort to draw together the myriad little fragments that make up the Japanese American experience in Louisiana, piece together a narrative from them, and try to tease out some larger conclusions.

Ethnic Japanese were far from being the first Asians to arrive in Louisiana. Historians have traced the story of the "Manilamen," Filipino sailors on the Spanish galleons plying the trade between the Philippines and Mexico in the early nineteenth century. Some of these sailors who jumped ship migrated to Louisiana, where they settled in Saint Malo, Louisiana.[1] As Moon-Ho Jung has described, groups of Chinese laborers from the Caribbean were then brought in during Reconstruction to work on the region's sugar plantations.[2]

Possibly the first Japanese settler in Louisiana, and certainly the most notable, was Jokichi Takamine. Takamine was only in his late twenties when he traveled to New Orleans for the Cotton States Exposition of 1884 as co-commissioner of the Japanese delegation (whose members allegedly introduced the first hyacinth plants to Louisiana), but he was already well known as a scientist.[3] He appreciated New Orleans so much, and in particular a local white woman named Caroline Hitch whom he met there, that after the exposition he and Hitch got married, and the couple remained in town part-time through 1888. While living in New Orleans, Takamine met the writer Lafcadio Hearn, who had previously settled there.[4] One story, doubtless exaggerated, has it that Takamine so intrigued Hearn with his stories of Japanese life that Hearn was inspired to move to Japan, where he subsequently achieved renown for his stories of languid Japanese citizens. Takamine himself, after returning briefly to Japan, immigrated definitively to the United States and moved with his wife to New York, where he opened his own laboratory. There, in 1901, he developed the process for isolating and synthesizing the hormone adrenaline, thereby achieving worldwide fame and a considerable fortune.[5]

Meanwhile, Takamine helped cement a special relationship between Louisiana and Japan. In 1896 he escorted a group of six Japanese businessmen to New Orleans, where they placed the first large orders for cotton.[6] The following year a local merchant, John W. Philips, was named acting Japanese consul.[7] New Orleans, as the only large city and commercial center in the Gulf region, became the principal conduit for Japanese trade and investment, especially in the mushrooming cotton trade.[8] Within two decades, relations expanded so greatly that in 1922, Japan opened a consulate building in the Crescent City, and Michio Kato (succeeded by Y. Saito) was appointed consul. In 1928, the Japan Society of New Orleans was created by local businessman Neal A. Leach, who served as its founding president. Leach declared that New Orleans did more business with Japan than with all of Central America.[9] By 1937 the society boasted 175 members.

Meanwhile, white agriculturalists, led by a planter with the delightful name of Seaman A. Knapp, turned to Japan to revive southwest Louisiana's once-proud rice industry, which had fallen on hard times.[10] With aid from the Department of Agriculture, Knapp visited Japan as an official agent and explored various rice plants. On Knapp's recommendation, the department invested $18,000 in Kyushu (AKA Kishu) rice, whose grains could stand up without breaking to the rolling mills introduced to process rice and which thus made mass mechanization possible. Knapp then recruited Japanese experts to plant Kishu rice (locally dubbed "Jap rice") and teach farmers their ancestral techniques for rice cultivation. As a result of the new techniques, plus better irrigation, rice fields in Louisiana and nearby Texas boomed. Within a space of five years, farmers increased their rice acreage threefold and the value of their lands tenfold.[11]

Although the 1900 census listed only seventeen Japanese residents in all of Louisiana, the establishment of such commercial and agricultural ties led some locals to encourage settlement by groups of Japanese farmers, and some immigrants to consider it. In 1902, the Japanese consul general in New York, Sadatsuchi Uchida, conscious of the problem of rural overpopulation in Japan, went on a fact-finding tour of the US South and wrote a glowing report on the prospects for rice growing in the Gulf area.[12] In 1904, R. Onisha, an Issei hired as the Japanese immigration agent for the Southern Pacific Railroad, led a group of prominent Japanese, who had come to America for the Louisiana Purchase Exhibition in Saint Louis, Missouri, on a tour of the rice country. Paul Daniels, a farmer in the town of Welsh, Louisiana, contracted with the Japanese representative at the exhibition, Tetsutaro Inumaro, to lease three hundred acres of his land and bring in a set of thirty Japanese farmers to experiment with vegetable growing.[13]

Yet racial prejudice and economic competition destroyed plans for mass settlement of ethnic Japanese. In March 1905, Jiro Harada, a Japanese commissioner from San Francisco and a UC Berkeley graduate, announced that he had made arrangements for the development of a large Japanese rice-growing colony in southwest Louisiana to be composed mainly of already established Issei, who had grown weary of prejudice on the Pacific Coast.[14] When town officials in Crowley announced that two hundred Japanese farmers would be settling there, influential whites statewide set up an outcry against any such "colonization" on the grounds that it would make the state's already intractable race problem even worse. The *Rice Belt Journal* editorialized that Japanese or Chinese people "can never become a part of the great American people, but will always remain a Jap or a Chink as the Negro is still a Negro and the Red Man an Indian." The editorial then added what was clearly the more important reason for its position: such migration would lead to overcultivation of rice, which had to be kept in limited quantities if it was to be raised profitably.[15] The *Lake Arthur Herald* complained that the southern railroads were bent on introducing Japanese colonists to increase population along its right of way and boost earnings, in violation of alien labor laws. Mixing economic fears with xenophobia and bigotry, the *Herald* charged that the newcomers were potential spies for Japan as well as encroachers on American industry: "There are many more objections to the Japanese for settlement in this country: they can never vote or become citizens of the United States; they are heathens and have been incorrigible heathens for thousands of years. They will depreciate the value of adjacent lands . . . for no one will want to buy or live near them."[16] A decade later after California enacted its 1913 Alien Land Act, barring Issei from land ownership on racial grounds, West Coast Issei, encouraged by real estate and railroad interests, once more began to consider establishing themselves in Louisiana. As previously, local whites protested, both openly on racial grounds and more indirectly.[17] The Saint Francisville *True Democrat*, a virulently negrophobic newspaper that had once defended lynching, decried the settlement plan as an "invasion." "It will be remembered that rabbits were imported into Australia to rid that country of some pest, but they propagated in such vast numbers that soon the government was offering a bounty on their heads. The Japanese correspond in many respects to the rabbit, but they cannot be killed when they become too numerous."[18] The Louisiana Distributing Company, an alliance of local organizations based in LaFourche County, voted an official resolution to the state assembly opposing any "invasion" of Japanese farmers on the grounds that they would not improve property once they purchased it and would "freeze-out" their white neighbors by objectionable conduct, thus forcing the white people to sell.[19] In 1921, Louisiana enacted an alien land law formally barring all Asian immigrants from purchasing agricultural land.

Ironically, in the face of hostility from Louisiana whites, many settlers ended up establishing themselves instead in Texas. Promoters envious of Louisiana's profitable rice fields attracted Japanese investors to Texas to build up the industry, and in 1903 K. Isomoto was recruited to start an agricultural station in Del Rio, Texas.[20] Eventually, a prosperous colony of Japanese-owned plantations sprang up around the Texas Gulf Coast (most famously the legendary Saibara clan, who settled in Webster), while merchants opened shops in downtown Houston.[21] Thus, as a result of their racist campaigns, Louisiana rice farmers still faced competition from their Texas neighbors but reaped none of the advantages of Japanese settlement.

Still, some Japanese people did manage to migrate to Louisiana, and by the 1930s the local community had expanded from forty to fifty permanent residents, a population composed of farmers, importers, and fishermen. (According to one source, in the later 1930s fifteen to twenty Japanese-owned shrimpers sailed the Gulf Coast, where Louisiana factories processed 80 percent of the nation's shrimp—Japanese fishermen visited Grand Isle, southwest of New Orleans, working alongside Chinese and Filipino fishermen and packers).[22] In 1904, Tomehitsu Hinata, a US Navy veteran of the Spanish-American War, arrived in New Orleans, where with his wife, Katsue, he opened a Japanese art and curio store on Royal Street in the French Quarter. Their daughters, Yuki, Toshi, and Kyo, who were the first Louisiana-born Nisei, attended Louisiana State University in the 1930s and were hired thereafter as teachers in the New Orleans public schools—by way of comparison, before World War II there was not a single teacher of Japanese ancestry in any of the Los Angeles area public school systems. Namyo Bessho, another US Navy Spanish-American War veteran who was one of the rare Issei to become naturalized before 1922, settled in the suburb of Algiers with his wife Koh and their children.[23]

By 1940, according to Tokumi Hamako, a Nisei employee at the New Orleans consulate who wrote a set of columns for the West Coast vernacular press on life in the Deep South, the local population included ten consular officials, plus "two Nisei doctors from Hawaii . . . a chick-sexer; a young Nisei girl from the good ol' city of Los Angeles; a ship chandler who has a French wife, two children and a bad case of asthma; a shrimp dealer who is a Stanford graduate, and his family; and a fisherman with a red face."[24] With assistance from the consulate and the Japan Society, in 1931 the city's first Japanese school opened in the Monteleone Hotel. Hisashi Nomasa, a Loyola University student, was the first permanent language instructor.[25] In 1937 Roger Yawata of Oakland enrolled at Loyola University, becoming the only Nisei collegian in New Orleans, and took over teaching at the language school.[26] Minoru Kimura, a Nisei from Hawaii, graduated from Tulane Medical School in 1936. In 1941, Clifford Uyeda enrolled in medical school at Tulane, and during World War II he worked as an intern at the city's charity hospital.[27]

A further handful of Issei and Nisei settled Outside of New Orleans. Sam Nagata came to the United States from Japan in 1905. After living for several years in Chicago, he moved to New Orleans, where in 1927 he opened a trucking business, hauling produce between New Orleans and New Iberia, Louisiana. His brother, who had been living in Montgomery, Alabama, relocated to the region in the mid-1930s and opened a fruit market/grocery store in Eunice, Louisiana, which is in Cajun country near Lafayette. Their son, Joe Nagata, made quite a record as a high school football player, enrolled at Louisiana State University (LSU) on a football scholarship, and played as first-string back in the 1942 Sugar Bowl.[28] In 1928, Manabu and Saki Kohara, who had run a photo studio in Omaha, Nebraska, moved to the central Louisiana town of Alexandria with their five children. After an abortive effort at truck farming, they opened a photo studio, which survived the Depression and prospered during the war, when a pair of nearby Army camps housed GIs (including Nisei soldiers). All of their children attended LSU. Their eldest daughter, Kay Kohara, received her MD and became one of the early Nisei women physicians, working as a resident physician in New Orleans's charity hospital before marrying and moving to Baltimore.[29]

One Nisei worked as a vegetable farmer in Shreveport and Monroe in the late 1930s, and there was in addition a small transient population in the countryside, notably peddlers and some transient merchants.[30] One source credits the Sawada family, who ran a nursery in Alabama and who operated a brisk trade in New Orleans flower markets, with introducing camellias to the city.

Throughout the prewar era, Japanese Americans in Louisiana occupied a liminal space (as did the more numerous Chinese population) between the white and black populations, and associated with both. As noted, there was ambient anti-Asian racism—Benjamin Wren has remarked that Louisiana's representatives in Congress all voted for exclusion of Japanese immigrants in 1924, and Louisiana remained one of the few southern states to bar intermarriage between whites and "Orientals"—yet individual residents were not treated as people of color, in contradistinction to black people.[31]

Indeed, from all accounts Louisiana was one of the few places in prewar America where Japanese were always granted courteous service in hotels and restaurants and routinely addressed as "sir" or "ma'am." Clifford Uyeda, who arrived in New Orleans in mid-1941, later recounted taking his first streetcar ride and being reproved when he unknowingly took an empty seat in the black section of the segregated car—the conductor soon settled the matter by taking the "colored" sign out from the slot in front of Uyeda's seat and sliding it in back of him, thus moving him into the "white" section! Uyeda added that when he was studying at Tulane, he was treated as just another student. He only faced discrimination on a single occasion, when a cafeteria worker raged at him that "Japs" were not allowed, upon which a white friend stepped in and firmly told the man to get lost.[32] Nisei journalists Larry and Guyo Tajiri, who visited New Orleans shortly after Pearl Harbor, reported that they were received with courtesy but were shocked by the treatment of African Americans.[33]

The war hit Louisiana's Japanese population hard. On December 8, the Japanese consulate closed its doors (after making a large bonfire to destroy documents) and its Japanese alien employees were interned. Japanese shrimp boats were grounded, and the Hinata art store closed its doors.[34] The Hinata daughters, anticipating dismissal from their teaching posts, voluntarily offered their resignations to the city school board, but their resignations were refused and they were granted certificates of commendation. When two Japanese American Citizens League (JACL) activists, Mike Masaoka and George Inagaki, visited New Orleans soon after to speak at a social work conference, they were arrested as potential spies by a deputy sheriff while sightseeing in Saint Bernard's Parish. The two languished in jail, frightened of lynching attempts, until the conference chairman, missing their presence, called the FBI and had them found and liberated.[35]

World War II brought Nikkei from all over the Americas into Louisiana. First, a group of Issei men, largely from Hawaii, who had been arrested and interned after Pearl Harbor was attacked, were shipped to Louisiana, and up to 1,200 were held during 1942–43 at Camp Livingston, near Alexandria. Meanwhile, New Orleans served as the post of debarkation for over 2,000 ethnic Japanese from Peru and other Latin American countries who were kidnapped from their home countries during 1942 as part of a deal with the US State Department and shipped for internment in the United States. Then in mid-1943, Japanese American soldiers from the One Hundredth Infantry Battalion were detailed for training at Camp Livingston. Masses of Nisei trainees visited nearby Alexandria, where the Kohara family put them up, establishing a virtual USO in their house. (In addition to patriotism, this may have been at least in part to forestall racial tension in the area—there are various secondhand reports of prejudice by locals, including a bigoted barber in town refusing to cut what he termed "Jap hair.")[36] Other Nisei soldiers at Camp Shelby visited New Orleans (many of them accompanied by Earl Finch, the white Mississippian who became a friend and unofficial "godfather" to Nisei GIs). Mike Tokunaga later recalled that, while on leave in New Orleans he took a bus, and was horrified to see a bus driver push an elderly black woman to the ground. "I grabbed the bus driver by the shirt and dragged him off the bus," recalled Tokunaga. "Six of us kicked the hell out of him for knocking that poor black woman down."[37]

In early 1944 the War Relocation Authority (WRA), the governmental agency responsible for caring for the Japanese Americans confined in camps under Executive Order 9066, opened an area relocation office on Saratoga Street (later moved to Howard Avenue) in New Orleans. Government officials saw an opportunity for successful resettlement in the Deep South, where land was cheap and well irrigated and there was room for development but where few of the inmates paroled from camp had resettled. They found a strong local booster in Roku (Dairoku) Sugahara. Sugahara, a Nisei businessman and veteran *Rafu Shimpo* columnist, had left the West Coast for Denver before mass removal, and thereafter migrated with his wife to New Orleans.[38] Sugahara was hired by the WRA to encourage migration, and he took up work in the New Orleans WRA office. Soon after, in August 1944, a Nisei social worker, Robert Tashima, escorted a group of Issei and Nisei farmers released from the Granada camp in Colorado, all of whom had previously resettled in the western states, on an inspection tour to determine the prospects for resettlement in Louisiana. The party passed through New Orleans, Buras, Baton Rouge, Ponchatula, and Lake Pontchartrain Beach.[39] In October 1944, WRA official Ray Knight brought in four more detainees from the camp at Manzanar in California on a tour of farms in the region. There they met with local rice growers (as well as with the Nagatas, whom WRA officials had been mistakenly informed were rice growers).[40] In early 1945, WRA employee R. E. Arne brought five Nisei from the Rohwer camp in Arkansas to look over land in New Orleans and in nearby Jefferson Parish.

Official accounts of all the visits indicated overall positive and friendly reactions by white residents—Robert Tashima noted warm reactions to both Issei and Nisei, especially from soldiers, on trains, in barber shops, in cafeterias, at theaters, and at beaches. However, Tashima's reports, in particular, laid out a number of less visible tensions. For instance, when he asked Katsuye Hinata and her daughters to speak about local attitudes towards Japanese Americans, she advised against any large influx of Japanese newcomers, warning that any resettlers would have to be "careful socially."[41] Tashima also counseled extreme caution on the religious question: "Southern Louisiana is primarily Catholic. The Japanese are strongly Christian (a few Catholics) and Buddhist. The writer feels that no reactions would be felt because of differences in sects as far as Christians are concerned (However, establishing Buddhist churches may cause some adverse feeling in the beginning). It would probably be best to conduct services in private groups at first without advertisement of any kind. Gradual introduction of Buddhist churches is recommended after acceptance is favorable."[42] It should be noted that the Nisei reporter was not without his own biases. In describing the people of Louisiana, he commented: "The laboring class has little education and is very easy going. The negroes seem to have little or no ambition. The naturalized Europeans are rather ambitious, but are not progressive in developing new ideas and improvements." He added that the quality of the schools was troublesome and that "the cultural standards are of some concern because of the large population of Negroes and uneducated whites. One can judge the cultural standards fairly well when in contact with the people."[43]

In the last days of 1944, the Southern Area WRA office put together a several-page English-language "letter" designed to attract Japanese American farmers to Louisiana (it was produced together with a second pamphlet, addressed to both Issei and Nisei, regarding resettlement in Texas). The Louisiana letter provided information on climate and ways of acquiring land and listed recommended crops for agricultural production (vegetables, sweet potatoes, feed crops, corn, and oats), while counseling against others (sugar cane, cotton). It also promoted dairy and poultry production and cultivation of Easter lily bulbs as profitable side enterprises.[44] A letter to "Japanese evacuee brethren," produced under the signature of Masami Hata, an Issei resettler identified as working as a gardener in Baton Rouge, presented the case for resettlement in somewhat poetic terms: "In regard to the general climate and soil of Louisiana, it is somewhat similar to that of Japan. Toward the evening we see many fireflies flying over the grassy field and hear frogs making melodies; cicadas and many other smaller bugs sing in the daytime."[45] In a matching letter, Roku Sugahara made his pitch for resettlement to Nisei in Plymouth Rock–style tones: "Many decades ago, the Acadians ostracized from Canada came to Louisiana and developed the haven known as the Evangeline country. Many groups of people have found a refuge here and a new start in life. So can the Nisei. The conditions and circumstances are ideal for the Issei and Nisei to get a new lease on life . . . to prosper and preserve in time to come; for basically all of us are productive, humble, god-fearing and loyal to this country which are the fundamental ingredients of a good pioneering American."[46]

Perhaps the most intriguing aspect of the WRA propaganda piece was the material on friendly local sentiment, which tiptoed carefully around the controversial issue of racial and religious prejudice. Masami Hata reported, "No anti-Japanese feeling has been manifested in the South. There are many colored people in this region and all of them seem to be very friendly toward us." His only comment about the treatment that those same people received, however, was to note that "wages are cheap here. A colored hand is paid $2.50 a day for an 8-hour day."[47]

Meanwhile, Roku Sugahara extolled New Orleans as a "melting pot of many races" where understanding and tolerance reigned. A note further explained, "Among [New Orleans's] residents and visitors are found people of many races, including French, Italians, and because of its nearness to South America, many Latin Americans. To date, about a score of Japanese Americans live in New Orleans, occupying homes in the finest residential sections, attending the city's university, working in its industries or commerce."[48] Left ostentatiously off the list of "races" enjoying such tolerance and understanding were the African Americans, who formed about 30 percent of the city, as well as Native Americans. An excerpt from the Robert Tashima report on religious questions was also carefully edited: "The writer feels that no reactions would be felt because of differences in sects as far as Christians are concerned."[49] The portion of Tashima's last sentence referring to prejudice against the Buddhist majority remained delicately excised.

In the end, despite all the WRA's efforts, only a few farmers actually migrated to Louisiana. In early 1945, notably, Frank Hattori took over a chicken farm in Saint Bernard Parish, just outside the city, hired three other detainees as workers, and made daily deliveries of produce to New Orleans.[50] WRA officials were frustrated by the lack of a more significant response and opined that the reluctance of inmates to resettle in Louisiana was a product of exaggerated fear of prejudice.[51]

Ironically, those fears would soon appear less than exaggerated, for despite the WRA's almost total failure to encourage Japanese American resettlement in the area, rumors quickly spread that the government was engaging in a plot to use government loans to "colonize" Japanese people in the area. In February 1945, a police jury in Jefferson Parish, near New Orleans, passed a resolution formally opposing any such settlement and called on farmers and real estate agents not to lease or sell land to Japanese of whatever citizenship. The text of the resolution eloquently reveals the envy and commercial self-interest that underlay the pretended fears for security. Not only did it assert that "the highest officials of both the Army and the Navy have referred to the Japanese people as abnormal and without honor and untrustworthy in every respect" but, the resolution continued, "it is a matter of public knowledge that the Japanese can live on one fish and a handful of rice; that they farm from daylight until midnight . . . that our farmers cannot hope to compete with the slavery of the Japanese and labor of a similar type in raising crops and marketing them."[52] Leander Perez, a New Orleans lawyer (and outspoken segregationist) who was district attorney and political boss of Saint Bernard and Plaquemines Parishes, quickly jumped on the bandwagon. Under his leadership, in May 1945 the two parishes adopted ordinances barring anyone of the "Japanese race" from owning land within their borders. The resolutions cited the "well known treachery, criminality, and debased nature of the Japanese which would make them a constant menace to the safety and welfare of the citizens of the state of Louisiana."[53] State commissioner of agriculture Harry L. Wilson then proposed that police juries in other parishes vote similar ordinances barring Japanese American resettlement. WRA officials protested the ordinances, noting that the Japanese Americans were citizens and serving in large numbers in the army. In June 1945, the newly created Louisiana League for the Preservation of Constitutional Rights, created by liberals in New

Orleans, condemned the Plaquemines and Saint Bernard ordinances.[54] Still, in the face of such hostility the WRA was forced to curtail its project. When in June 1945 the WRA's southern office produced a general newsletter on resettlement in the South, it included only a small section on Louisiana. It centered on the possibilities for resettlement of a few families on Avery Island, home of Tabasco sauce, to work as caretakers at the lush garden resort of Edward A. McIlhenny. Other employment offers were for domestics in Lake Charles or sharecroppers in Mandeville.[55]

Yet almost no sooner than the anti–Japanese American movement raised its head, the tensions dissipated. Despite the (largely symbolic) anti-Japanese ordinances, an estimated 190 Japanese Americans resettled in Louisiana during 1945–46, working in the shrimp industry, greenhouses, or as chick sexers, although many ultimately left.[56] James Imahara, a Nisei farmer, opened up a landscaping and greenhouse business near Baton Rouge and ultimately became a millionaire.[57] New Orleans housed resettlers with a variety of occupations. Kyokuzo Tomoda, an Issei from Stockton, moved to town with two daughters and started up the K. T. Manufacturing Co., a business selling roach powder and bug repellent.[58] Another Stockton Issei, Tetsuo Ijuin, opened a sandwich and coffee shop on Tulane Avenue near the Charity Hospital but died suddenly only a month later, following which his wife Kiyo and three daughters took the shop over and ran it for several years.[59] Yamato Kikuchi, who came from Topaz with his three sons, worked in a supermarket. Some Nisei took jobs in flower markets.

The Crescent City slowly resumed its status as a magnet for accomplished Nisei, and an estimated fourteen families were in residence by 1950. Soprano Tomi Kanazawa spent a season in New Orleans singing *Madama Butterfly* for a local opera company. Roku Sugahara, after a stint in the army, returned to New Orleans part-time, where he operated a real estate appraisal business and served as local correspondent for the *Pacific Citizen* until his untimely death in 1952. The Yenari family settled in the suburb of Gretna. Hajime Yenari, a jeweler and watchmaker, would be decorated by the emperor of Japan for his service to US-Japanese relations. His wife Katsu Oikawa Yenari, a physician, undertook a residency in pediatric medicine at Tulane and then opened up a private practice in Gretna.[60] Hajime's brother Ted Yenari, a Nisei optometrist and former G2 staffer in Tokyo during the Japanese occupation, set up shop in New Orleans, where he praised the calmer lifestyle.[61] Another ex-GI, George Asaichi Hieshima, enrolled at Tulane medical school in 1945, bringing his wife and son, and remained there until graduation in 1949.[62] Kazuo Watanabe, a former MIS officer, graduated from Tulane University Law School in the early 1950s.

As before the war, Japanese Americans in Louisiana were treated with courtesy, and accepted as "white." One local Nisei resident, an ex-GI, described in 1949 how Japanese Americans were seated in the "white" section of streetcars and accepted in "whites only" areas, while black Americans were relegated to the most undesirable jobs and barred from all public employment.[63] When a theatrical touring company with a largely Nisei cast played in New Orleans in the mid-1950s, members of the troupe were able to rent accommodations in the French Quarter.[64] However, not all Japanese Americans accepted this. Francophile artist Hideo Date, anxious to travel to Europe but unable to leave the United States, instead traveled on several visits to New Orleans to absorb its French flavor. The segregated society he experienced disturbed him. "Everything I saw was 'black and white' and 'black and white.' I got tired of it and went back to New York."[65]

Sometime around 1950, the Japanese consulate in New Orleans reopened its doors, further boosting the size of the regional ethnic population—the 1960 census listed 519 ethnic Japanese statewide—and their prestige. By the mid-1960s, Japan had become New Orleans's chief foreign trading partner—in 1972, for example, New Orleans had a higher value of exports to Japan (including a booming business in soybeans) than to all of Europe. During the decade ending in 1976, an average of two hundred Japanese ships a year called in New Orleans. Japanese tourists became a common sight on the city's streets, even as the city remained a spiritual home (and pilgrimage center) for Japanese and Nisei jazzman.[66] Such trade relations led to warm cultural exchanges between Japan and Louisiana. The author experienced this when he stayed in Kyoto and discovered that there are some twenty branches of the iconic Cafe du Monde in Japan serving chicory coffee and beignets—the only branches in the world outside Louisiana.

That said, Nikkei residents in the state long remained for the most part under the social and media radar screen. There are some exceptions. Former all-state running back Sam Nagata returned home to Louisiana following a stint in the army, serving in the famous all-Nisei 442nd Regimental Combat Team, and spent thirty years coaching local high school football teams in and around Eunice.[67] In 2003 he was elected to the Louisiana Sports Hall of Fame. Linebacker Scott Fujita of the New Orleans Saints earned even greater fame in recent years, both for his playing and community activism. Dr. Akira Arimura was named professor of medicine at Tulane University in 1965 and served there for thirty years, leading a circle of Japanese endocrinologists working in the Nobel Prize–winning medical research team of Dr. Andrew Schally. Charles H. Shindo, a California native, has served as professor of history at Louisiana State University for over a decade.

Still, not every aspect of the Japanese presence in Louisiana was so positive. In 1992, a sixteen-year-old Japanese exchange student, Yoshihiro Hattori, was shot dead in Baton Rouge by meat market manager Rodney Peairs, after Hattori and a white friend knocked mistakenly on Peairs's door in search of a Halloween party. The national JACL inquired in vain why Peairs had shot only at the Japanese boy and not his white companion. At his trial, Peairs claimed the right of self-defense, raising the image of Japanese as "out of control," and was acquitted of manslaughter, though the student's family subsequently won a large award for civil damages from Peairs.[68] Local trade with Japan declined sharply after the bursting of Japan's economic boom in the early 1990s. In 2007, New Orleans's Japanese consulate closed its doors, citing lack of business, and relocated to Texas. The move, coming at a time when the city was struggling to rebuild after the devastation wrought by Hurricane Katrina, was a major blow to the city, and it attracted fierce criticism and unsuccessful petitions.

So what conclusions can we draw from this historical sketch of the Japanese presence in Louisiana? First, the Japanese community has remained tiny in comparison to Vietnamese Americans, the state's largest Asian ethnic population, or even to South Asian, Chinese, or Filipino Americans. Nevertheless, Issei and Nisei have been present and active in state affairs for over one hundred years. While there have been incidents of hostility, especially when large numbers of outside Nikkei threatened to resettle, natives have generally been exempted from everyday racial bias. This has been partly because of their exceptional qualifications, notably as doctors and skilled merchants but also because of the important trading links between Japan and New Orleans. During the war years, when these were not present, greater prejudice was unleashed. Even before 1960 Issei and Nisei were not so much situated between black and white (as James Loewen famously termed the Mississippi Delta Chinese) as they were "probationary whites" tolerated in small numbers.[69] Over the decades a few Nisei, generally transients, helped dramatize or combat racial injustice against black Americans and other minorities. Most notably, in the summers of 1965 and 1966, following passage of the 1964 civil rights act, JACL lawyer William Marutani set up operations in the northeastern town of Bogalusa, near the Arkansas border, assisting on civil rights lawsuits and advising on voter registration.[70] In contrast, ethnic Japanese permanent residents have most often conformed to local customs and not challenged institutionalized discrimination.

Notes

1. See, for example, the Philippine History site, http://opmanong.ssc.hawaii.edu/filipino/filmig.html, accessed June 4, 2011. While some historians have theorized that Filipinos began arriving as of 1763, when Spain colonized "Luisiana," the most reliable evidence dates the community as being founded around 1812.

2. Moon-Ho Jung, *Coolies and Cane: Race, Labor, and Sugar in the Age of Emancipation* (Baltimore: Johns Hopkins University Press, 2006).

3. "Louisiana Declares War on Hyacinths," *Danville (Va.) Bee*, September 17, 1945, p. 2.

4. On Takamine and Hearn, see for example Old New Orleans, http://old-new-orleans.com/NO_Denis_Esplanade.html.

5. On Takamine, see for example *Kiyoshi Karl Kawakami, Jokichi Takamine: A Record of His American Achievements* (New York: E. W. Rudge, 1928).

6. "Notes," *Watchman and Southron*, September 16, 1896, p. 2; "The South," *Baltimore Sun*, October 19, 1896, p. 10.

7. "Recognition of Consuls," *Washington Times*, August 21, 1897, p. 4. Philips would later receive the order of the Rising Sun from the emperor of Japan for his efforts in encouraging international commerce.

8. "Japanese Capital Finances Louisiana Cotton Company," *Christian Science Monitor*, December 24, 1921, p. 4. On Japanese trade with New Orleans, see Benjamin Lee Wren, "A History of Trade Relations between Japan and the United States in the New Orleans Area," PhD thesis, University of Arizona, 1973.

9. "New Orleans Has Japanese Language Class," *Nichi Bei Shimizu*, July 15, 1931.

10. Henry C. Dethloff, *A History of the American Rice Industry, 1685–1985* (College Station: Texas A&M University Press, 1988), 78–79.

11. "Experiments in Seeds Paying Big Dividends", *Minneapolis Journal*, July 22, 1906, p. 15.

12. "A Japanese Colony," *Rice Belt Journal* (Welsh, LA), May 30, 1902, p. 1; Thomas K. Walls, *The Japanese Texans* (San Antonio: University of Texas Institute of Texan Cultures at San Antonio, 1987, 1996), 39–41.

13. "Japs to Stay," *Paducah Evening Sun*, May 18, 1904, p. 8; "Jap Colony Delayed in Coming," *Rice Belt Journal* (Welsh, LA), February 10, 1905, p. 1. African American editor Horace Cayton Sr. reported (erroneously) that fifty Japanese families had already settled in Louisiana, adding sardonically that they were welcomed by local whites who were admirers of colored men—if they were from the Orient! *Seattle Republican*, September 30, 1904, p. 2.

14. "Japanese to Move to South," *Hawaiian Gazette*, March 26, 1905, p. 1; "Woman Will Describe New Sort of Work," *San Francisco Call*, March 16, 1905, p. 6.

15. "Danger from Japanese Immigrants," *Rice Belt Journal* (Welsh, LA), April 20, 1906, p. 2.

16. "Important to Japanese," *Lake Arthur Herald*, 1906, reprinted in *Rice Belt Journal*, July 20, 1906, p. 1.

17. "Louisianians Fear Japanese," *Washington Post*, April 7, 1915, p. 6; See also, for example, "Japanese Colonies in Louisiana," *Era-Leader*, (Franklinton, LA), May 6, 1915, p. 2; "Japanese in Louisiana," *True Democrat*, (Saint Francisville, LA), April 1, April 22, 1915.

18. "Japanese in Louisiana," *True Democrat*, May 1, 1915, p. 2.

19. "Opposes the Yellow Peril," *True Democrat*, May 22, 1915, p. 2.

20. "Will Raise Rice in Texas on a Large Scale," *Richmond Times-Dispatch*, June

23, 1903, p. 9. Isomoto expressed his belief that within a few years the rice fields of Texas and Louisiana would be filled with Japanese farmers.

21. Walls, *Japanese Texans*, 44 passim; Fred R. von der Mehden, ed., *The Ethnic Groups of Houston* (Houston: Rice University Press, 1984).

22. Roku Sugahara, "A Nisei in Manhattan," *Pacific Citizen*, February 5, 1949. p. 3.

23. Roku Sugahara, "Pioneer in the Southland," *Pacific Citizen*, December 23, 1947, p. 16; "New Orleans Has Japanese Language Class", *Nichi Bei Shimizu*, July 15, 1931.

24. Tokumi Hamako, "Southern Accent . . . ," *Kashu Mainichi*, February 3, 1940.

25. "New Orleans Has Japanese Language Class."

26. "Roger Yawata," *Rafu Shimpo*, April 11, 1937.

27. Dr. Clifford I. Uyeda, *Suspended: Growing Up Asian in America* (San Francisco: National Japanese American Historical Society, 2000), 184–85.

28. War Relocation Authority photos of resettlement, collection at Bancroft Library, http://content.cdlib.org/ark:/13030/ft095002v1/?brand=calisphere, searched June 5, 2011.

29. Roku Sugahara, "The Koharas of Louisiana," *Pacific Citizen*, December 24, 1949, pp. 18, 21.

30. Tokumi Hamako, "Southern Accent," *Kashu Mainichi*, April 14, 1940; April 28, 1940.

31. Benjamin Wren, "The Rising Sun on the Mississippi," *Louisiana History: The Journal of the Louisiana Historical Association* 17, no. 3 (Summer 1976): 321–33.

32. Uyeda, *Suspended*, 78, 139–40. Uyeda notes that a Nisei soldier also related his experience of being courteously asked by a conductor to move from the black to the white section of the streetcar. Ibid., 155

33. Guyo Tajiri, interview with author, Berkeley, CA, June 2004.

34. Roku Sugahara, "A Nisei in Manhattan," *Pacific Citizen*, November 1, 1947, p. 3.

35. Bill Hosokawa, *Nisei: The Quiet Americans* (New York: William Morrow, 1969), 380.

36. Robert Martens, "The Impatient Warrior," in *We All Have a Story to Tell*, Book 2, ed. Robert H. Wells (Bloomington, IN: AuthorHouse, 2006), 268; Paul Yamada, letter to author, March 11, 2011.

37. Mike T. Tokunaga, "Building behind the Scenes," in *Japanese Eyes, American Heart: Personal Reflections of Hawaii's World War II Nisei Soldiers*, compiled by Hawaii Nikkei History Editorial Board (Honolulu: Tendai Educational Foundation, 1998), 372. In another interview, Tokunaga told a different version of the story. In the alternate version he and his buddies were riding a bus, and the white bus driver ordered a black soldier to move to the back of the bus. When the soldier refused, the driver grabbed him by the shirt, whereupon Tokunaga and his buddies tore the driver off, threw him outside, and drove off in the bus. Tom Coffman, *The Island*

Edge of America: A Political History of Hawai'i (Honolulu: University of Hawaii Press, 2003), 94. While it is difficult to decide how much credence to give either version of the story, Tokunaga's overall spirit of opposition to racism is believable.

38. Togo Tanaka, "Post Script," *Colorado Times*, February 8, 1950.

39. Robert Tashima, "Report on Trip to New Orleans," September 1944, Section 11.103, War Relocation Authority New Orleans office, WRA Papers, RG 210, National Archives. (henceforth WRA Papers).

40. [Ray Knight], "Report on Visit of Evacuees from Manzanar," October 1944[?], WRA Papers.

41. [Robert Tashima], "Report on Trip to New Orleans," September 1944, WRA papers. While the nature of such caution was not specified, it may well have had to do not only with counseling Issei and Nisei to keep a low profile but also not to disturb the regional social and racial status quo.

42. [Robert Tashima], "Committee Report on Trip to Louisiana, August 29 to September 11," WRA papers.

43. Ibid.

44. Southern Area Office, War Relocation Authority, "Letter to Issei about the South: Facts about Farming in Louisiana" undated, [December 1944?], Southern Relocation files, War Relocation Authority papers, Bancroft Library, University of California, Berkeley (henceforth "Letter").

45. Masami Hata, "Message from an Issei Living in Louisiana," December 16, 1944, in "Letter," p. 4.

46. Dairoku Sugahara, "Message from a Nisei Living in Louisiana," December 16, 1944, in "Letter," p. 5.

47. Masami Hata, "Message from an Issei."

48. Dairoku Sugahara, "Message from a Nisei."

49. "Evacuee Visitors to Louisiana Say about . . . Religion," in "Letter", p. 8.

50. War Relocation Authority Press Release, Release No. 8, April 17, 1945, Southern Relocation files, War Relocation Authority papers, Bancroft Library, University of California, Berkeley. R. E. Arne to Rex Lee, letter, June 6, 1945, WRA papers. Frank Hattori would later achieve modest attention for his hybrid tomatoes. See "Develops New Tomato," *New Canadian*, August 8, 1951, p. 8.

51. Report, June 1945, WRA papers.

52. Roku Sugahara, "A Nisei in Manhattan," *Pacific Citizen*, June 25, 1949.

53. Ibid.

54. "Mr. Wilson's Bad Counsel," *New Orleans Item*, June 29, 1945, cited in "Louisiana Group Protests Ban on Nisei Urged by State Official," *Pacific Citizen*, June 30, 1945, p. 3.

55. "Down South," WRA Southern Area Bulletin, June 15, 1945, Southern Relocation files, War Relocation Authority papers, Bancroft Library, University of California, Berkeley.

56. Roku Sugahara, "A Nisei in Manhattan," *Pacific Citizen*, September 3, 1949, p. 3. See also Hikaru Iwasaki's photo of Ted Iwai, a chick sexer at the Louisiana Hatchery, in Lane Hirabayashi et al. *Japanese American Resettlement through the Lens* (Boulder: University Press of Colorado, 2009), 120.

57. James M. Imahara and Anne Butler Hamilton, *James Imahara, Son of Immigrants* (Baton Rouge: James Imahara, 1982). See also website, "Imahara's Timeless Gardens," http://imaharas.com/about/james/, searched June 6, 2011.

58. War Relocation Authority Press Release, July 7, 1945, Southern Relocation files, War Relocation Authority papers, Bancroft Library, University of California, Berkeley.

59. Roku Sugahara, "A Sandwich Shop in New Orleans," *New Canadian*, October 13, 1948, p. 3.

60. Obituary notices, Hajime Yenari, Katsu Oikawa Yenari, *New Orleans Times Picayune*, June 5, 1997; July 3, 1998.

61. Togo Tanaka, "Post Script," *Colorado Times*, February 8, 1950.

62. "Ex-Angeleno Earns Doctor Degree," *Rafu Shimpo*, June 14, 1949, p. 1.

63. "Japanese Down in New Orleans Are Considered as Whites Says U.S. Nisei Visitor to Toronto," *New Canadian*, July 23, 1949, p. 1.

64. Sanae Kawaguchi Moorehead, telephone interview with author, April 2011.

65. Karin M. Higa, *Living in Color: The Art of Hideo Date* (Berkeley, CA: Heyday Books, 2001), 22.

66. In one case, the city became literally a place of pilgrimage. Yoichi Kimura, drummer with the Japanese Dixieland band New Orleans Rascals, moved to the Crescent City in 1966 to nurse the celebrated drummer Joe Watkins. "Japanese Musician Nurses His Dixieland Idol," *New Canadian*, September 17, 1966, p. 1.

67. "Sidelights," *Pacific Citizen*, January 12, 1946; Tom Dodge, "Legendary Coaches Helped Build Tradition," *Teche News*, August 28, 2010.

68. Peter Applebomes, "Verdict in Death of Student Reverberates across Nation," *New York Times*, May 26, 1993, p. A14; "U.S. Civil Rights Inquiry Is Sought in Louisiana Slaying," *New York Times*, May 28, 1993, p. B5; Adam Nossiter, "Japanese Boy's Kin Win Suit over Death," *New York Times*, September 16, 1994, p. A1.

69. James W. Loewen, *The Mississippi Chinese; Between Black and White* (Cambridge, MA: Harvard University Press, 1972).

70. Bill Marutani, "Nisei Lawyer in KKK Land," *New Canadian*, November 10, 1965, pp. 1, 8.

Works Cited

Arne, R. E., to Rex Lee. Letter, June 6, 1945. War Relocation Authority New Orleans office, WRA Papers, RG 210, National Archives.

Coffman, Tom. *The Island Edge of America: A Political History of Hawai'i*. Honolulu: University of Hawaii Press, 2003.

Dethloff, Henry C. *A History of the American Rice Industry, 1685–1985*. College Station: Texas A&M University Press, 1988.

"Down South." WRA Southern Area Bulletin, June 15, 1945. Southern Relocation files, War Relocation Authority papers, Bancroft Library, University of California, Berkeley.

Higa, Karin M. *Living in Color: The Art of Hideo Date*. Berkeley, CA: Heyday Books, 2001.

Hirabayashi, Lane, with Kenichiro Shimada, photographs by Hikaru Carl Iwaksaki. *Japanese American Resettlement through the Lens: Hikaru Iwasaki and the WRA's Photographic Section, 1943–1945*. Boulder: University Press of Colorado, 2009.

Hosokawa, Bill. *Nisei: The Quiet Americans*. New York: William Morrow, 1969.

Imahara, James M., and Anne Butler Hamilton. *James Imahara, Son of Immigrants*. Baton Rouge: James Imahara, 1982.

Jung, Moon-Ho. *Coolies and Cane: Race, Labor, and Sugar in the Age of Emancipation*. Baltimore: Johns Hopkins University Press, 2006.

[Knight, Ray]. "Report on Visit of Evacuees from Manzanar," October 1944[?].War Relocation Authority, New Orleans office, WRA Papers, RG 210, National Archives.

Loewen, James W. *The Mississippi Chinese: Between Black and White*. Cambridge, MA: Harvard University Press, 1972.

Martens, Robert. "The Impatient Warrior." In *We All Have a Story to Tell*, Book 2, edited by Robert H. Wells. Bloomington, IN: AuthorHouse, 2006.

Report. June 1945. War Relocation Authority, New Orleans office, WRA Papers, RG 210, National Archives.

Southern Area Office, War Relocation Authority. "Letter to Issei about the South: Facts about Farming in Louisiana," undated, [December 1944?]. Southern Relocation files, War Relocation Authority papers, Bancroft Library, University of California, Berkeley.

Tashima, Robert. "Report on Trip to New Orleans," September 1944, Section 11.103. War Relocation Authority New Orleans office, WRA Papers, RG 210, National Archives.

———. "Committee Report on Trip to Louisiana, August 29 to September 11." War Relocation Authority, New Orleans office, WRA Papers, RG 210, National Archives.

Tokunaga, Mike T. "Building behind the Scenes." in *Japanese Eyes, American Heart: Personal Reflections of Hawaii's World War II Nisei Soldiers*, compiled by Hawaii Nikkei History Editorial Board. Honolulu: Tendai Educational Foundation, 1998.

Uyeda, Clifford I. *Suspended: Growing Up Asian in America*. San Francisco: National Japanese American Historical Society, 2000.

von der Mehden, Fred R., ed. *The Ethnic Groups of Houston*. Houston: Rice University Press, 1984.

Walls, Thomas K. *The Japanese Texans*. San Antonio: University of Texas Institute of Texan Cultures at San Antonio, 1987, 1996.

War Relocation Authority Press Release. Release No. 8, April 17, 1945. Southern Relocation files. War Relocation Authority papers, Bancroft Library, University of California, Berkeley.

———. July 7, 1945. Southern Relocation files, War Relocation Authority papers, Bancroft Library, University of California, Berkeley.

Wren, Benjamin. "The Rising Sun on the Mississippi." *Louisiana History: The Journal of the Louisiana Historical Association* 17, no. 3 (Summer 1976): 321–33.

2
Views of Japanese in Alabama, 1941–1953

Chizuru Saeki

This chapter examines the history of Japan-Alabama relations during World War II and the postwar period. In this time span, political and social conflicts between Japan and the United States helped shape images of Japanese in Alabama. The chapter takes the point of view of cultural historians to analyze these perceptions. It looks at how Alabamians responded in the wake of the Pearl Harbor attack and how their views of Japan and Japanese culture changed over the following decades.

The Satsuma orange and camellia symbolize Alabama-Japan relations. In 1878 the Satsuma orange, which originated in Kagoshima Prefecture, Japan, was introduced to the area then known as Fig Tree Island (today's Satsuma, Alabama). The orange was originally introduced to Florida by the wife of the US minister resident to Japan, Robert B. Van Valkenburg, who sent some orange trees back to Florida that same year. By 1910 the epidemic of "Satsuma Madness" had taken over the Gulf Coast from Florida to Louisiana. Groves and groves of Satsumas were planted in Satsuma, Alabama. Many thought this was a get-rich-quick scheme due to the extraordinarily high demand and popularity of the orange in the US market. Alabama's economic relations with Japan had expanded so rapidly that in 1902 Japan established its honorary consul's position in Mobile.[1]

Meanwhile, the number of Japanese immigrants to southern Alabama started appearing in the US census in 1900, and they continued to increase through the 1920s.[2] One of the early Japanese immigrants was Kosaku Sawada. Born in Moni-mura in Osaka Prefecture, Sawada, the youngest child in a large family, came to the United States at the age of twenty-four. Japanese government officials at that time were promoting rice farming in Texas. The Ministry of Agriculture of the Japanese government recruited four young men from Japan to attend the 1904 World Exposition in Saint Louis, Missouri. Sawada was one of them.[3] After the exposition, they worked on rice cultivation in Texas, but their venture was unsuccessful due to poor weather conditions and insufficient knowledge of Texas soil factors. Then, Sawada and his fellow countrymen, including Saeki Imura, formed the Alvin Nursery Company and specialized in the development of pecan and Satsuma orange trees, which they imported from Japan. The nursery venture was successful, and in 1910 as part of their expansion program, they set up a branch office in Grand Bay, Alabama. In 1916, after staying six years with the Grand Bay nursery men, Sawada returned to Japan, where he married his wife, Nobu, and brought her back to Alabama. Rejoining the Alvin Nursery people, Sawada worked with them until 1919, when a severe freeze and an attack of citrus canker killed all the trees and plants of this Japanese firm and wiped them out. While other Issei (the first generation of Japanese immigrants) returned to Texas, Sawada decided to move north, about twenty-five miles, to Mobile and start a flower nursery business. By the 1920s Sawada achieved fame nationally as the foremost hybridizer of camellias, the state flower of Alabama, and was eventually regarded as one of five exemplary Japanese immigrants who had made extraordinary contributions to American society.[4] Because of men like Sawada, Mobile is now recognized as the camellia and azalea center of the country.

Life in the southern states in the early twentieth century was challenging for African Americans and other ethnic minorities, including the Japanese immigrants, due to Jim Crow laws. Since the 1890s, southern states had passed laws that prevented black citizens from achieving equality. Finally, in 1964, Pres. Lyndon Johnson managed to persuade Congress to pass the Civil Rights Act, which officially ended racial discrimination in public places. Previously the restrictions in Alabama dictated that all passenger stations operated by motor transportation companies had to have separate waiting rooms or space and separate ticket windows for whites and "colored" people. The segregation also led to the creation of separate toilets for African Americans, who were not allowed to sit with whites at restaurants either. In racially segregated Alabama, Japanese Americans were regarded as the third race between whites and blacks, though they generally associated with whites. For instance, Japanese were allowed to sit in the front seats with white passengers in public transportation vehicles.[5] In 1915 seventeen citizens of Satsuma, Alabama, including three Japanese citizens, founded the Satsuma United Methodist Church,[6] which showed that Japanese residents in the Mobile area were accepted as members of the white community and as Christian brothers and sisters. Such friendly relations between Alabamians and Japanese residents, however, were hampered by Japan's Pearl Harbor attack.

From Pearl Harbor to Enemy Sabotage

At 7:55 on Sunday morning, December 7, 1941, Japanese planes laid siege to Pearl Harbor, Hawaii. One day later, Pres. Franklin D. Roosevelt declared war against Japan and the bloody struggle between the United States and Japan begun. The attack had greatly disturbed Alabamians just like other Americans. In Florence, a small town in north Alabama with a population of only fifteen thousand, people held an urgent universitywide meeting at Florence State Teacher's College (today's University of North Alabama) and discussed how to prepare for Japan's potential bombing of the city.[7] Given the political turmoil, Mobile canceled the annual Mardi Gras Carnival celebrations that year, which were planned for February 17.[8]

The Japanese unleashed quick, triumphant invasions throughout the Pacific, taking control of European and American colonies within the first six months after the Pearl Harbor attack, while the United States was still giving priority to the European front. Fear of enemy sabotage swept the nation as Japan continued to move its forces in the Pacific, occupying Manila by January 2, 1942. The military crisis intensified racism and hatred toward Japanese across the United States. That February, Roosevelt issued Executive Order 9066, which forced the relocation of all persons of Japanese ancestry to outside of the Pacific military zone in order to prevent espionage. On the West Coast, nearly 120,000 Japanese Americans were taken to relocation centers situated in such remote and desolate locations as Jerome, Arkansas, and Heart Mountain in Wyoming.[9]

Compared with the West Coast, Alabama had few resident aliens from Axis nations. Only 21 of the estimated 127,000 Japanese living in the United States by the 1930s resided in Alabama. Nonetheless, the war intensified racial hatred there too. Immediately following the Pearl Harbor attack, Gov. Frank Dixon warned Axis aliens in the state that they had to register for an identification certificate by January 28, 1942, and the Federal Bureau of Investigation placed alien residents from Axis nations under surveillance. On December 10, 1941, one Italian and three German aliens were taken into custody in Mobile. In February 1942, federal agents raided the homes of eighteen resident alien families in that city. Alabamians were warned to be on the lookout for aliens who they had reason to believe were a threat to public peace and safety. In particular, they were instructed to notify the nearest office of the FBI of all suspicious "Japs."[10] By this time, however, many of the Japanese immigrants in Alabama had left the state because the once-thriving Satsuma orange industry had been crippled during the 1930s by freezing weather and the Depression.[11]

But those few who remained suffered greatly. In north Alabama, where only a tiny number of Japanese people settled, local Alabamians were extremely alert to finding potentially dangerous enemies in their community. For instance, soldiers from Camp Forest were dispatched to the Wilson Dam to prevent sabotage. They searched every car before letting it pass across the bridge.[12] In Athens, less than twelve hours after Pearl Harbor, the police arrested a Japanese citizen who was suspected of terrorist intentions. When it turned out that the alleged saboteur was a thirty-three-year-old Presbyterian minister from Hokkaido, Japan, and a temporary guest of Prof. J. T. Wright, the director of Trinity School, Mr.

Matsumoto was finally released.[13] In Florence, to "tear the dirty Jap apart," an American resident jumped on a Chinese man who came into a store.[14] Since some Americans had a hard time distinguishing between Japanese and other East Asians, often Chinese residents became the victims of physical assaults. To prevent such misunderstandings, *Life* magazine published an article on how to tell Japanese from Chinese people according to their physical appearances.[15]

Japanese immigrants in south Alabama, however, were treated differently during the war from those in north Alabama. When the "Jap" search started in the state, local Dauphin Way Methodist Church members and friends rushed into the Kosaku Sawada family's nursery shop in Mobile to defend the family and prove their loyalty.[16] Kosaku's son Ben Sawada was a student at Murphy High School during the war and elected to a number of offices at the school. He recalled no prejudice against their family in the Mobile community.[17] Local churches and their members contributed to Mobile's acceptance of Japanese Americans during the war, an acceptance that stood in sharp contrast to their treatment in north Alabama. In 1948 when Sawada Kosaku was interviewed in the Japanese American newspaper *Pacific Citizen*, he looked back through the years with great satisfaction because of the warmth of his friends he had made in the Mobile community, where Japanese residents were few. Sawada told the reporter that the Japanese immigrants and even the Nisei, the second generation of Japanese immigrants, were reluctant to come South due to their erroneous impression that the South was poor and conditions were dismal. However, Sawada said, "it was not certainly the richest part of the country but it was much easier and comfortable to make a living down here." Sawada's four children grew up in Mobile, Alabama, and graduated from college. The eldest son, Tom, was a graduate of Spring Hill College and spent four and half years in the army. The next son, George, was a graduate of Auburn University and Cornell University. Daughter Lurie was a graduate of Huntington College. All three operated the nursery in 1948. The youngest son, Ben, was at Emory University, where he was studying for the ministry.[18]

Tsukasa Kiyono and his family were also among the earliest Japanese immigrants in Alabama. Like the story of the Sawada family, Kiyono came to the United States in 1907 at the age of nineteen from Okayama Prefecture, Japan. He tried growing Satsuma oranges in Texas, but when the frost killed his trees, he moved to Alabama. In 1921 Kiyono returned to Japan for a visit, met and married his wife, Tomoe, and brought her back to his nursery in Mobile, where they started growing camellias and azaleas on a commercial scale. Being Japanese, both Sawada and Kiyono were barred from American citizenship by the naturalization laws during the war time, but they settled down to a new life in their adopted land, while their businesses were booming.[19]

The longtime relations between Japanese and other residents in the Mobile area and the contribution of the Japanese to the local agricultural business had shown their loyalty to the state. On the other hand, Alabamians in north Alabama had almost never dealt with Japanese residents in their community before the war, and thus they had strong prejudices.

Fort McClellan and the Japanese

The US Army had established Fort McClellan north of Anniston, Alabama, after the end of the First World War. During the Second World War, the Twenty-Seventh infantry division from New York was trained at the fort, and after Pearl Harbor it was one of the first units to depart for combat. The division trained nearly five hundred thousand men who fought in the Marshall Islands, Gilbert Islands, Saipan, Guam, and the Philippines.[20]

Fort McClellan was also the temporary home for many captured enemy soldiers and Japanese Americans. The presence of Japanese Americans, who had been drafted before or immediately after the Pearl Harbor attack, constantly reminded US military officials that their loyalty was in question. As a result of their uncertain allegiance, their weapons were removed, their posts were frequently reassigned, and they were often transferred to medical and engineer corps. However, in February 1943, the War Department lifted the "4C" classification in order to permit Japanese Americans to volunteer for any service; the draft of Japanese Americans was resumed in January 1944. The decision to reinstate the draft was the result of "the high casualty rate of the volunteers who served in the 442nd and the 100th."[21] As an immediate solution, the department began to draw soldiers from the pool of predetention inductees who had been scattered to various inland areas of the United States. The War Department thus ordered the transfer of 825 of the 1,440 Japanese American predetention soldiers to army ground forces at Camp Blanding, Florida, and Fort McClellan, Alabama.[22]

On March 13, 1944, 608 Japanese American predetention draftees arrived at Fort McClellan. Among them was Walter H. Miyao, a graduate of the University of California at Berkeley with a degree in public health. He had been denied a job with the public health department in California because of his Japanese heritage. At the fort, he was trained in the medical corps and the infantry.[23] He also oversaw a meeting of Japanese soldiers when the leaders of the Japanese soldiers at McClellan, such as Hakubun Nozawa and Tow Hori, both of whom had been transferred to McClellan from Fort Riley, Kansas, were circulating a petition to Roosevelt and Gen. Wallace C. Philoon at the fort. The petition informed the president and general of examples of racial discrimination in the army, including those they had experienced while serving in a segregated unit, and complained about the treatment of Japanese Americans in the internment camps. On March 20, 1944, hundreds of Japanese American soldiers at the fort refused to participate in combat training in protest of their treatment at the fort and the treatment of their families in the internment camps. Eventually, 106 were arrested for their refusal, and 21 were convicted and sentenced to five to thirty years in prison. The incident at McClellan was one of the major protests by Japanese Americans at US military forts during the war.[24] In 1947 President Truman pardoned those former soldiers and they were released.[25]

Toward the End of the War and Racial Images

After the battle of Midway in June 1942, the tide of the war clearly changed in the Pacific. In late 1943 the warship *Mobile* joined US naval operations in the Pacific and helped destroy Truk, Japan's major anchorage and center of communications in the Carolines. The warship also fought in Leyte Gulf in the battles to retake the Philippines.[26] Alabamian political cartoonist Frank M. Spangler depicted Japan's early course in the war in his cartoon titled "Achille's Heel," which shows an admiral labeled "Pacific Fleet" riding on the back of a turtle labeled "Jap Fleet." The admiral is saying, "Come on out and show your stuff!" and his feet are labeled "Over" and "Confidence."[27] The cartoon criticizes American overconfidence. Another cartoon by Spangler, "To Make a Happy Day," has Hitler, Hirohito, and Mussolini floating in a wooden tub labeled "Axis" and looking through telescopes labeled with the names of countries invaded by the Axis Powers. It portrays the Axis Powers' fading strength and leadership in the war.[28]

By the early summer of 1945, Japan's homeland was being subjected to merciless bombing. Newly developed napalm, mostly manufactured in Huntsville's Redstone Arsenal in Alabama, turned Tokyo and Osaka into fiery and desolated places. But, seeing that the Japanese were still reluctant to surrender, the United States used its new weapon, the atomic bomb, on Hiroshima on August 6 and Nagasaki on August 9. The Soviet Union meanwhile declared war on Japan on August 8. The devastation wreaked by the atomic bombs, combined with the Soviet Union's entry into the Pacific theater, persuaded Japanese Emperor Hirohito and the Japanese government in Tokyo to surrender on August 15.

The Pacific War changed the political face of the world, with the rise of the Allied Powers, especially the United States and the Soviet Union, and the decline of the Axis Powers, including Japan. The war also exposed racial hatred between Japanese people and Alabamians. The Pettus Museum in Killen, Alabama, for example, proudly displayed Japanese soldiers' thousand stitch belts taken by Alabamian soldiers during the Pacific War as a symbol of US victory. Japanese people believed that when one thousand stitches had been added to a belt, the belt would have special power to protect the bearer from the hazards of battle. Thus, all Japanese soldiers were sent to the battlefield with these belts. Other Alabamian soldiers brought back gold teeth of Japanese soldiers as war trophies.

Figure 2.1. "Achille's Heel," Frank M. Spangler editorial cartoon (Alabama Department of Archives and History)

Figure 2.2. "To Make a Happy Day," Frank M. Spangler editorial cartoon (Alabama Department of Archives and History)

The racist imagery that accompanied the war was contemptuous. Americans consistently emphasized the subhuman nature of the Japanese, routinely turning them into apes and vermin in films and cartoons. The Japanese were portrayed as inherently inferior, primitive, and cruel. Similarly, Americans and Europeans existed in the wartime Japanese imagination as monsters, devils, and demons that only cared about their material wealth.[29] There is no doubt that such cultural wartime propaganda fueled anti-American and anti-Japanese sentiment in the two countries. In response to a Gallup poll question in 1944 that asked, "What do you think we should do with Japan after the war?," 13 percent of Americans said that we should kill off the Japanese people, 33 percent indicated that we should destroy Japan as a nation, and only 28 percent advocated supervising Japan.[30]

Embracing the War's End in Alabama and Japan

Two weeks after Emperor Hirohito's announcement of Japan's surrender, a flotilla of Allied warships, including the battleship *Alabama*, sailed into Tokyo Bay for formal surrender ceremonies. William Venice Tingle, an Alabama soldier who participated as part of the occupation forces in Japan, recorded the scene: "We had four Jap officers on board our ship today signing. . . . They are lousy looking people. Personally I think my uniform is better 'quality' than [the one] the Jap admiral had on today."[31]

Alabamians and the people of Japan welcomed the war's end very differently. Within minutes of news of Japan's surrender, crowds poured into the streets of Alabama's towns, celebrating with great excitement and joy. A resident of Florence, Alabama, recounted: "Everyone congratulated [each other] on Court Street. There was a mob laughing, hugging, kissing, shouting and drinking. I think everyone was happy. Jimmy Gilbert started a snake dance that went all the way down Court Street at least two blocks long."[32] In Mobile, mere seconds after the official surrender news was flashed, Bienville Square was filled with laughing soldiers and civilians. Tears of happiness streamed down the cheeks of many Mobile women, who thought of their loved ones overseas. An elevator operator at the federal building was so happy that she could hardly speak. She smiled and said: "At least my two brothers will get to come home. I am so happy, that I could dance for joy."[33] In Montgomery, cars and pedestrians surged up and down Dexter Avenue, and a boy climbed to the top of the fountain on Court Square and put up an American flag.[34]

But across the Pacific, the people in Japan were devastated and fearful. They heard the voice of their emperor for the first time as he broadcast his decision to terminate the war. The emperor's announcement of the nation's defeat shook the whole nation. On that day, more than five hundred military and naval personnel committed suicide, including General Anami, who committed seppuku in true samurai fashion. The neighborhood associations started preparing for hand-to-hand fighting, and women were given sharpened bamboo stalks to use as spears since people expected that Americans would treat them badly. Virtually all the major cities of Japan, including Osaka, Nagoya, and Tokyo, lay in ruin. Hiroshima and Nagasaki simply vanished. Estimates run that at least eighty thousand died immediately after the explosion of the A-bomb in Hiroshima, and that forty thousand died of atomic bomb–caused radiation illness, which destroyed people's healthy cells and immune systems. The second bomb, on Nagasaki, killed at least forty thousand immediately.[35] Nationally, over eight million people had become homeless. Japanese industrial production stood at barely 10 percent of the normal prewar level. Julius Frank Hardeman, an Alabamian G.I who stayed in Japan, wrote: "This Japan is like nothing I have ever seen before. The trains are [only] about 25 feet long. The children are looking for you to give them something. The old are brave and laugh but the young, my age don't say much."[36] Children and adults alike suffered serious starvation. The official food rations for each person per day came to 1,050 calories, fewer than 30 percent of the amount required for a person's well-being.[37] The Japanese people were quite anxious about the future of their nation. They had never experienced a war defeat and had never been occupied by foreign countries.

From 1945 till 1952, Japan was under US occupation. In general, the years of the occupation were a period of peaceful reconstruction, one that changed US-Japan bilateral relations from those between enemies to those between allies in the Cold War.

How could hated enemies turn into trusted allies in less than seven years? One reason was Gen. Douglas MacArthur's occupation policies, which gained the understanding and support of the majority of Japanese, particularly those policies retaining the emperor's throne and instituting democratic reforms. Another reason was the calls for reconciliation in US-Japan relations, which came from not only atomic bomb victims in Hiroshima but the Methodist church in Mobile, Alabama.

US-Japan Relations through the Hiroshima Maiden Project

Americans in Alabama probably heard the real voice of a Hiroshima A-bomb victim for the first time in 1948 when Kiyoshi Tanimoto, a Japanese minister and alumnus of Emory University, talked about his experience during his speaking tour across the United States. Tanimoto was one of the six Hiroshima survivors introduced in John Hersey's "Hiroshima," the famous thirty-one-thousand-word article that appeared in the August 31, 1946, issue of *New Yorker*. The story dealt with the A-bomb dropped on that Japanese city and its effects on the six Japanese citizens. Moved by Tanimoto, who had dashed into Hiroshima amid the flames to rescue the wounded, his former classmates from Emory University began sending money and supplies to him. They also petitioned the overseas Methodist Mission Board to invite him to the United States for a speaking tour. In both 1948 and 1950, Tanimoto went on extensive speaking tours of the United States. He raised funds for the establishment of a Hiroshima Peace Center as an international educational institution to publicize the Hiroshima bombing as an omen of what could happen elsewhere if people failed to work toward global peace. He also campaigned for funds for the Hiroshima women who were injured by the A-bomb. In 1950 he appeared on the popular television program *This Is Your Life*, where he and his family met with Robert A. Lewis, copilot of the *Enola Gay*, the plane that dropped the A-bomb on Hiroshima. He appeared on three TV shows and fifteen radio programs calling for Americans to help Hiroshima victims.[38]

In May 1955 with enthusiastic support from his friend Norman Cousins, the editor of the *Saturday Review of Literature* and a well-known antinuclear advocate, Tanimoto was able to bring a group of twenty-five young Japanese women who were seriously disfigured as a result of the atomic bomb to the United States to undergo multiple reconstructive plastic surgeries. "The face of every girl was terribly scarred," Rodney Barker wrote. "One had an eye burned out. The flesh of another's throat had the corded appearance of mania hemp. The nose of another was all but burned off and the mouths of many were like twisted and distorted livid gashes."[39] The horrible scars from radiation burns had marred their chances for a normal life and marriage. Cousins and Tanimoto secured beds at Mount Sinai Hospital and convinced Quakers in the New York area to be host families for the Hiroshima women. Cousins's *Saturday Review of Literature* gave extensive coverage to the Hiroshima maiden project. It published many heartwarming stories, including tales of postwar friendship between the Hiroshima women and their American host families. The courage and cheerfulness of the Hiroshima maidens won the hearts of Americans and created an unforgettable public image of Hiroshima among Americans.[40]

Creating the Nagasaki Maiden Project in Mobile, Alabama

The Hiroshima maiden project was so inspirational that community leaders from Mobile, Alabama, tried to set up a similar project. They wanted to bring maidens from Nagasaki, where the second A-bomb was dropped, to Mobile for treatment. The Nagasaki maiden project was proposed by Dr. Carl Adkins, the minister of the Dauphin Way Methodist Church of Mobile, who hoped to mitigate Alabama's racist image through the project.

Unfortunately, that image, of course, had a basis in fact. Asian residents in postwar Alabama attested to the odd racial hierarchy there. Yao Chuang from Taiwan and his Japanese wife, Yoko Suzuki, encountered it when they took a bus from Chicago to Alabama and North Carolina in 1962. As soon as the bus crossed the Mason-Dixon line, Chuang later recalled, the bus had segregated seats. Whites entered from the front door and sat in the front seats, while blacks entered from the rear door and sat in the back seats. As "yellow," Chuang was confused about which seats he and his wife should take, so he asked the driver, who eventually directed him to the seats for whites. After he took a seat, a couple of people from India and Vietnam tried to follow him, but they were guided to the back seats for blacks. When Chuang and his wife had a daughter, her birth certificate stated that she was "white." They thought it was a mistake, so they called the state office and pointed out that their daughter was "Asian," not "white." The person they spoke to in the office responded that there were only two categories, white and black. Therefore, people from East Asia belonged to the white category, while those from South and Southeast Asia belonged to the black category.[41]

Local government officials in Alabama tried to keep East Asians on the white side of the color line by giving them some privileges of whiteness to isolate them from African Americans. But some whites feared that this third race would undermine white supremacy, and thus they discriminated against Asians.[42] By 1957 in Jacksonville and Anniston, Alabama, there were several Japanese war brides married to American GIs. One of them, Kay Takayama, remembered her early days in Anniston: "Although we came [from a] so far-away place, I never felt lonely because we Japanese women all lived close [to] each other and regularly met. We all had American husbands." Once they stepped out of the community, however, things were different. In Jacksonville, her three children faced enormous challenges on the bus and in their classrooms at public schools at the height of the Jim Crow era. Their Alabamian classmates teased them as "Japs with slant eyes and yellow skin." Her youngest son often came home with his clothes torn.[43]

Such racial conflicts in Alabama affected the image of the United States held by Japanese residents and even led some to feel contempt toward American society. According to a US survey of Japanese public opinion taken in 1956, 25 percent of Japanese respondents had negative impressions of the United States, which were attributed in part to the treatment of African Americans in the South. Some indicated agreement with the statement that "I do not like the U.S. because it does not treat colored races equally." Others pointed out the hypocrisy of US advocacy of freedom and democracy around the world while African Americans were discriminated against at home.[44]

Living in the center of Alabama's racial conflict, Minister Adkins of the Dauphin Way Methodist Church in Mobile hoped that a Nagasaki maiden project would increase awareness and understanding of racial and ethnic diversity among Alabama citizens. Adkins approached many community and church leaders in Mobile and encountered a unanimously enthusiastic response. The administrators and executive board of both the Providence hospital and the Mobile Infirmary assured him that they would do everything in their power to help his project. In particular, the Mobile Infirmary, which was the city's new $5.5-million Protestant hospital, promised Adkins that they would underwrite the expenses for all the hospital care and hospital services for the Nagasaki women. Adkins was confident that his project could take care of a group of ten to twelve girls for four to six months. He and his committee members organized a temporary steering committee to decide upon the program; by the end of a ninety-day period, the project would be carried out by a citizens committee.[45]

Adkins then approached Norman Cousins about the Nagasaki maiden project. Cousins, Dr. Hitzig, who was the head surgeon at Mount Sinai Hospital in New York, and Dr. Harada, the Japanese doctor who had accompanied the girls from Hiroshima, promised to come to Mobile for the project kickoff. They would speak to the Mobile County Medical Association and a joint meeting of all the luncheon clubs in the city. Adkins also planned to appear on a TV program to talk about the Nagasaki project and to issue a news release. In a letter to the State Department, Adkins asked for the government's permission to pursue his project and explained its significance. Above all, he pointed out, they were motivated by a desire to alleviate the image of southern racism: "We believe this program would be particularly significant for two reasons. First, Mobile is in the center of a section of our nation which no doubt in the minds of the Japanese is synonymous with race prejudice, and for us to bring these girls into the homes of the citizens of this community would be a tremendous gesture of good will. Second, the possibility of training two Japanese doctors to return home with whatever skills they are able to acquire in a six month period to continue with this plastic surgery in Japan seems to me to justify all that any of us might be able to do in working out this program."[46]

When Adkins's proposal reached the State Department, however, alarm bells went off. A memorandum from Max Bishop of the Under Secretary of State's office expressed strong concern that there might be "a rush of Hiroshima girl projects in major American cities," which might potentially "undermine U.S. nuclear policy," "reawaken anti-American sentiment overseas," and eventually "embarrass [the] U.S. government." Bishop also stated in his memorandum that "in all fairness to the persons who had to make the decision to drop the atomic bomb, we should avoid any intimation of apologizing or feeling of national guilt." Bishop informed Adkins that "the sooner the Hiroshima anniversary is forgotten or at least ignored, the sooner we can bring about a solid foundation for good relations between the United States and Japan.[47] The State Department attempted to convince Adkins that there were a significant number of competent plastic surgeons in Japan and that adequate medical care was available there, although according to Cousins such facilities in Nagasaki were only of "fair" quality.[48]

Adkins tried to negotiate with the State Department. He went to Washington, DC, and met with Walter Robertson, the assistant secretary of state for the Far East, and Richard B. Finn, the acting officer for Japanese Affairs in the department, on September 22, 1955. In the meeting, Adkins spoke first. He had not come to ask Robertson or the State Department to do anything, he said, but simply wanted to inform them of the plans that were now under consideration by the Nagasaki group in Mobile. He told them that he could understand the anxiety of the State Department over his project; therefore, his group would not do anything that might embarrass the US government. He also promised that his group would avoid publicity such as TV shows that had featured the arrival of the Hiroshima girls. Robertson responded to Adkins coldly, however. He stated that President Truman himself had decided that the atomic bombs should be dropped on Japan, and that it was done in order to shorten the war and thereby save lives. Robertson asked Adkins to defer action on the Nagasaki project and said that the project was undesirable.[49] Adkins now had no choice but to withdraw his proposal for the Nagasaki project. As a result, the Mobile project on the Nagasaki maidens never materialized.

Why was the Hiroshima maiden project able to take place when Adkins's Nagasaki project was denied by the State Department? In the case of the Hiroshima maiden project, Americans picked up a program that the Japanese had already developed for several years. Minister Tanimoto had not only started his speaking tours in 1948 but had assembled women at his church in Hiroshima before they came to the United States. In addition, the State Department did not take immediate action to stop Norman Cousins and Tanimoto's campaign for the Hiroshima maiden project; rather, it spent years asking the FBI for background checks on Cousins and his groups, only to find that they were not politically radical and were associated with only a few leftist organizations. Thirdly, at the last moment, when the State Department did try to quash the Hiroshima project by telegramming an order to stop the women's flight from Japan to New York, Gen. John W. Hull, who had authorized the military plane for the project, ignored the order. He believed that turning back the already departed flight would be a political embarrassment.[50] Fourthly, Adkins's project was planned when Japanese anti-American sentiment was peaking after the *Lucky Dragon* incident. In March 1954, a Japanese fishing boat, the *Lucky Dragon*, sailed close to the site of an American atomic bomb test in the Marshall Islands. Within three days, the crew members started showing the symptoms of radiation sickness. Japanese citizens panicked when the news was announced that the harvested fish from the *Lucky Dragon* were contaminated with radiation. Many also feared that Japan might be dragged into a nuclear war against the Soviet Union by associating with the United States, and thus opposed the US Security Pact.[51] With Japanese anti-American sentiment already high, the State Department was concerned that Adkins's Nagasaki maiden project might further anti-American sentiment overseas and even cause antinuclear protest in the United States. Having failed to prevent Tanimoto and Cousins's Hiroshima maiden project, the State Department moved more forthrightly against Adkins's Nagasaki maiden project in Alabama.

It would seem, however, that the State Department did not evaluate the potential impact of the Nagasaki maiden project accurately. Instead of worrying that the Japanese women maimed by America's atomic bombing of Nagasaki would be too visible and used by communists in their anti-American propaganda on the horrors of America's atomic aggression, the State Department could have approved of Adkins's Nagasaki project as an act of American benevolence to demonstrate American humanitarianism. After all, his project never attempted to criticize America's nuclear policy.

Moreover, the State Department misperceived the impact of the previous Hiroshima maiden project, which had actually contributed to favorable impressions of the United States among Japanese citizens. According to a US survey of Japanese public opinion in 1956, only 5 percent of Japanese had favorable impressions of the United States. But among them, "medical treatment of Hiroshima maidens" contributed a good deal to their favorable impressions. One respondent commented that "the U.S. is democratic and humanistic" and applauded "U.S. liberalism and respect for basic human rights."[52] Such opinions contrasted with Japanese views on the United States expressed in the survey of 1952, which had found that "most Japanese believe the United States thinks and acts only in material terms."[53]

Despite the US government's fears, communists did not mount any serious attacks on US policy because of the maiden projects. In fact, the voices of leftists were essentially drowned out by the tremendous enthusiasm among Japanese and Americans for the projects. Had Adkins's Nagasaki maiden project not ultimately been thwarted by the government, it would have improved the image of America's South.

Japan-Alabama Relations to the 2000s

From the 1950s to the early 1970s, Japan experienced tremendous economic growth. The country rose, phoenix-like, out of the ashes of the war to a country with a world-class economy. Japanese exports to the United States increased at a phenomenal pace during the 1950s and the 1960s. For example, while the Japanese auto industry produced a half million vehicles in 1960, its output quadrupled to 2.2 million vehicles in 1966, then increased another 50 percent by the 1970s.[54] By the mid-1970s, Japanese cars began to flood the US market, overwhelming US domestic production. The United States suffered an unfavorable trade balance with Japan; by 1964 it had sold to Japan $2.4 billion worth of goods and bought $2.9 billion worth of goods from Japan. In the economic boom years of the 1970s and 1980s, Japanese investments in America's visible landmarks such as Rockefeller Center in New York made Americans nervous that Japan was waging an economic war against them and that America would be bought by Japan.[55]

During the height of Japan's economic growth, the Alabama state government was eager to attract Japanese investment to the state, which has relatively cheap labor and land. The state opened the Alabama Development Office in Tokyo in 1980. In order to expand the state's economic and cultural ties with Japan, state government officials regularly participated in the annual meeting of the Japan-US Southeast Association, which was established in 1975 with the purpose of promoting trade and investment between Japan and southeastern states of the United States. As a result, Alabama has attracted such Japanese industries as Honda Manufacturing of Alabama, Sony Magnetic Products of America, Toyota Motor Manufacturing of Alabama, and Daikin America Inc. Japanese-affiliated companies had invested over $3 billion in Alabama and employed over 13,700 Alabamians by 2008. Alabama's exports to Japan in 2008 reached $732 million, making Japan its fifth largest export market.[56]

To develop friendship and understanding between the people of Japan and the United States, Alabama sponsored various cultural activities organized by nonprofit organizations and companies. In 1989, the Japan America Society of Alabama was established in Birmingham. A Japanese garden and tea house designed by Masaji Morai, a Japanese gardener, opened in the Birmingham Botanical Gardens in 1967, where every year the Japan America Society of Alabama (JASA) holds a Sakura (Cherry Blossom) festival. Daikin America Inc., a Decatur-based Japanese company, annually hosts a community party in celebration of the company's Japanese heritage. The annual Daikin festival features hot-air balloon rides and Japanese cultural displays. In the Birmingham area, those who are interested in learning about Japanese art can do so through the Bonsai Society, Sumie Society, and Ikebana Society. The Asian collection at the Birmingham Museum of Art also attracts Alabamians drawn to the beauty of Asian art.

Thus, Alabama's economic ties with Japan generated a wide range of cultural and educational programs on Japan and its people and have influenced Alabamians' daily lives. These cultural and educational programs gradually changed Alabamians' consciousness and views of Japanese. The images of the hated enemy, the wartime "Jap," and the "third race" in the Jim Crow era, were replaced with images of an economic powerhouse and, most recently, a fragile nation affected by frequent earthquakes and tsunamis.[57] The spirit of Minister Adkins, who tried to teach Alabamians about cultural diversity, racial equality, and respect for human rights through his aborted Nagasaki maiden project more than fifty years ago, lives on in the good will of both the private and government sectors in Alabama in the twenty-first century. His spirit continues to influence Alabamians' attitudes toward Japan today.

Notes

1. William Peter Fairney, *Satsuma Orange* (Auburn: Alabama Agricultural Experiment Station of Alabama Polytechnic Institute, 1911), 148–74.

2. The census shows that by 1930 there were five Japanese families living in Mobile, another five families in Birmingham, and one in both Tuscaloosa and Talladega. These records are available at select Family History Centers (FHC), http://www.familysearch.org/eng/library/fhc/frameset_fhc.asp.

3. Oi Kouji, *Louisiana Purchase Exposition, St. Louis in 1904: A Collection of Official Guidebooks and Miscellaneous Publications* (Tokyo: Eureka Press, 2009); Yoshida Mitsukuni, *Kaiteiban Bankoku Hakurankai* (Alhambra, CA, NHK Books, 1985), 24.

4. The museum at the Statue of Liberty in New York commemorated him as such. Ida B. Prine, *Kosaku Sawada: Nurseryman* (Federal Writer's Project, 1938), 573–77.

5. Leslie Bow, *Partly Colored: Asian Americans and Racial Anomaly in the Segregated South* (New York: NYU Press, 2010), 48.

6. Marvin L. Heaton, *The Historic Memories of Satsuma United Methodist Church* (Satsuma, AL: Satsuma United Methodist Church, 1969).

7. Jill K. Garrett, *A History of Florence* (Columbia TN: J K Garret, 1968), 71.

8. "Mobile, Orleans Cancel Carnivals," *Mobile Register*, December 13, 1941.

9. Greg Robinson, *By Order of the President: FDR and the Internment of Japanese Americans* (Cambridge: Harvard University Press, 2001).

10. "Suspicious Japs Can Be Reported," *Mobile Register*, December 9, 1941.

11. By the winter of 1940, no Japanese residents remained in Birmingham, for example. I checked the Birmingham city directories (which are similar to a telephone book) for 1940 to 1945 and did not find any of the previous Japanese residents's names listed. It appears that these families had left Birmingham prior to the outbreak of World War II. Some of their descendants later came back as Nisei or Sansei, however, after the war ended to live in the city again.

12. Jill K. Garrett, *History of Florence*, 71.

13. Faye Axford, *Limestone County during World War II* (Athens: Limestone County Historical Society, 1983), 14.

14. Garrett, *History of Florence*, p. 72.

15. "Speaking with the Pictures," *Life Magazine*, March 1, 1943, 12.

16. Allen Cronenberg, "Mobile and World War II," in *Mobile: New History of Alabama's First City*, ed. Michael Thomason (Tuscaloosa: University of Alabama Press, 2001), 233–34.

17. Ibid., 232–33.

18. "Sawadas of Alabama," *Pacific Citizen*, December 25, 1948.

19. "Happy Ending Seen for Kiyono Family of Alabama," *Pacific Citizen*, December 8, 1949. In 1952 the McCarran-Walter Immigration and Naturalization Act allowed Japanese and other Asians immigrants to become naturalized citizens.

20. The Alabama Encyclopedia site has more detailed information on Alabama's participation in the war, http://www.encyclopediaofalabama.org/face/Home.jsp.

21. Shirley Castelnuovo, *Soldiers of Conscience: Japanese American Resisters in WWII* (New York: Baison Books, 2011), 39. Memorandum for General White, "Reinstitution of Selective Service for Persons of Japanese Ancestry," May 4, 1943 (National Archives, RG 107, Box 22).

22. Castelnuovo, *Soldiers of Conscience*, 38–53.

23. Prof. David Kim has conducted extensive interviews with Japanese Americans about their experiences during WWII. Some of the transcripts are available at http://www-personal.umich.edu/~amnornes/david.html.

24. Castelnuovo, *Soldiers of Conscience*, 38–40.

25. Jeanne Wakatsuki Houston and James D. Houston, *Farewell to Manzanar: A True Story of Japanese American Experience during and after the World War II Internment* (New York: Random House, 1973), Wendy Ng, *Japanese American Internment during WWII: A History and Reference Guide* (Westport, CT: Greenwood Press, 2002).

26. Cronenberg, "Mobile and World War II," 241.

27. Frank Spangler editorial cartoons, 1939–45, Alabama Department of Archives and History. The date when this cartoon was drawn is not clear, as the original is not dated, but it was probably in 1941.

28. Ibid., the cartoon was drawn after 1942.

29. John Dower, *War without Mercy: Race and Power in the Pacific War* (New York: Pantheon, 1986).

30. George H. Gallup, *The Gallup Poll Public Opinion 1935–1971* (New York: Random House, 1972).

31. William Venice Tingle Papers, September 8, 1945, SPR, State of Alabama, Department of Archives and History.

32. Garrett, *History of Florence*, 74.

33. "Mixed Motions Follow Dramatic Surrender," *Mobile Register*, August 15, 1945.

34. *Montgomery Advertiser*, August 15, 1945.

35. Walter LaFeber, *Clash: U.S.-Japanese Relations throughout History* (New York: W. W. Norton, 1997), 249.

36. Julius Hardeman Papers, August 28, 1951, State of Alabama, Department of Archives and History, SPR, 487.

37. Andrew Gordon, *A Modern History of Japan: From Tokugawa to the Present* (Oxford: Oxford University Press, 2009), 364.

38. Rodney Barker, *The Hiroshima Maidens* (New York: Viking Penguin, 1985), 56–58.

39. Ibid., 93.

40. Michael J. Yavenditti, "Hiroshima Maidens and American Benevolence in the 1950s," *Mid-America* 64 (1982): 21–39.

41. My interview with Yao Chung and Yoko Suzuki on June 6, 2011.

42. Jason Morgan Ward, "No Jap Crow: Japanese Americans Encounter the World War II South," *Journal of Southern History* 73 (February 2007): 75–80.

43. My interview with Kay Takayama on February 9, 2011.

44. "Current Trends in Japanese Attitudes toward the U.S.," August 24, 1956, United States Information Agency, State Department file.

45. Carl A. Adkins, letter to Bishop G. Bromley Oxnam, July 9, 1955, State Department file, Rodney Barker, Collection, Peace Resource Center, Wilmington College, Ohio.

46. Letter from O. Bromley Oxnam to John Foster Dulles, July 10, 1955, State Department file, Rodney Barker, Collection.

47. Memorandum from Max Bishop to Walter Robertson, August 1, 1955, State Department File, Rodney Barker, Collection.

48. Letter from Walter Robertson to G. Bromley Oxnam, August 15, 1955, State Department File, Rodney Barker, Collection.

49. Memorandum of Conversation, September 22, 1955, State Department File, Rodney Barker, Collection.

50. Barker, *Hiroshima Maidens*, 82.

51. Michael Schaller, *Altered States: The United States and Japan since Occupation* (Oxford: Oxford University Press, 1997).

52. "Current Trends in Japanese Attitudes."

53. Saxon Bradford, "Psychological Factors in Japan," March 10, 1952, State Department File.

54. LaFeber, *Clash*, 327.

55. Gordon, *Modern History of Japan*, 399.

56. Consulate General of Japan, http://www.atlanta.us.emb-japan.go.jp/japanalabama.html.

57. Cities in Alabama, including Tuscaloosa and Birmingham, initiated various campaigns asking for donations to help their Japanese sister cities after massive disasters struck northeastern Japan on March 11, 2011.

Works Cited

Alabama Encyclopedia, http://www.encyclopediaofalabama.org/face/Home.jsp.

Axford, Faye. *Limestone County during World War II*. Athens: Limestone County Historical Society, 1983.

Barker, Rodney. *The Hiroshima Maidens*. New York: Viking Penguin, 1985.

———. Collection. Peace Resource Center, Wilmington College, Ohio.

Bow, Leslie. *Partly Colored: Asian Americans and Racial Anomaly in the Segregated South*. New York: New York University Press, 2010.

Bradford, Saxon. "Psychological Factors in Japan." March 10, 1952, State Department file, National Archives.

Castelnuovo, Shirley. *Soldiers of Conscience: Japanese American Resisters in WWII*. New York: Baison Books, 2011.

Consulate General of Japan. http://atlanta.us.emb-japan.go.jp/japanalabama.html.

Cronenberg, Allen. "Mobile and World War II." In *Mobile: New History of Alabama's First City*, Michael Thomason. Tuscaloosa: University of Alabama Press, 2001.

"Current Trends in Japanese Attitudes toward the U.S.," August 24, 1956. United States Information Agency, State Department file, National Archives.

Dower, John. *War without Mercy: Race and Power in the Pacific War*. New York: Pantheon, 1986.

Fairney, William Peter. *Satsuma Orange*. Auburn: Alabama Agricultural Experiment Station of Alabama Polytechnic Institute, 1911.

Family History Centers. http://www.familysearch.org/eng/library/fhc/frameset_fhc.asp.

Gallup, George H. *The Gallup Poll: Public Opinion, 1935–1971*. New York: Random House, 1972.

Garrett, Jill K. *A History of Florence*. Columbia, TN: J. K. Garrett, 1968.

Gordon, Andrew. *A Modern History of Japan: From Tokugawa to the Present*. Oxford: Oxford University Press, 2009.

Hardeman, Julius. Hardeman Papers, August 28, 1951. State of Alabama, Department of Archives and History.

Heaton, Marvin L. *The Historic Memories of Satsuma United Methodist Church*. Satsuma, AL: Satsuma United Methodist Church, 1969.

Houston, James D., and Jeanne Wakatsuki Houston. *Farewell to Manzanar: A True Story of Japanese American Experience during and after the World War II Internment*. New York: Random House, 1973.

Kim, David. Interviews with Japanese Americans. http://www-personal.umich.edu/~amnornes/david.html.

Kouji, Oi. *Louisiana Purchase Exposition, St. Louis in 1904: A Collection of Official Guidebooks and Miscellaneous Publications*. Tokyo: Eureka Press, 2009.

LaFeber, Walter. *Clash: U.S.-Japanese Relations throughout History*. New York: W. W. Norton, 1997.

Memorandum for General White. "Reinstitution of Selective Service for Persons of Japanese Ancestry," May 4, 1943. National Archives, RG 107, Box 22.

Mitsukuni, Yoshida. *Kaiteiban Bankoku Hakurankai*. Alhambra, CA: NHK Books, 1985.

Ng, Wendy. *Japanese American Internment during WWII*. Westport, CT: Greenwood Press, 2002.

Prine, Ida B. *Kosaku Sawada: Nurseryman*. Federal Writer's Project, 1938.

Robinson, Greg. *By Order of the President: FDR and the Internment of Japanese Americans*. Cambridge: Harvard University Press, 2001.

Schaller, Michael. *Altered States: The United States and Japan since Occupation*. Oxford: Oxford University Press, 1997.

Spangler, Frank. Editorial cartoons, 1939–1945. Alabama Department of Archives and History.

"Speaking with the Pictures." *Life Magazine*, March 1, 1943.

Tingle, William Venice. Papers, September 8, 1945. SPR, State of Alabama, Department of Archives and History.

Ward, Jason Morgan. "No Jap Crow: Japanese Americans Encounter the World War II South." *Journal of Southern History* 73 (February 2007): 75–80.

Yavenditti, Michael J. "Hiroshima Maidens and American Benevolence in the 1950s." *Mid-America* 64 (1982): 21–39.

3
Collective Aspirations of Japanese Americans in and beyond the WWII South

JOHN HOWARD

Perpetual Leave-Taking

Perhaps more hurtful than all the intimidation and fear, bigotry and violence, corruption and confinement, Japanese American incarceration was characterized by constant separation and partings. An immigrant generation that had embarked upon the biggest of journeys, to a new continent, found they had many more journeys yet to make. Some, understandably, grew weary. In 1945, however, many Nisei—described as "pathetically eager" to be American—called upon the shopworn maxims of American mobility. A new frontier! Westward, ho! Go west, young man! Westward the course of empire makes its way! California or bust! California here I come! (Right back where we started from.)[1]

In Michigan a train set out for California with Taro and Kame Dakuzaku aboard. The two had already been all over creation. Around the beginning of the century, Taro had left Okinawa to go to Hawaii, then San Francisco, and on to numerous towns and crossroad communities in the Central Valley. He had worked on plantations and railroads and in laundries before finally settling, he thought, in Florin, California, on a small farm. From Florin he and his wife, Kame—a former servant in the Okinawan royal palace, mother to six daughters and, at last, one son, now a soldier—were forced to move to Fresno, and then to a place called Jerome, in Arkansas. With rumors of Jerome's closing, they had been set "free" to relocate to Chicago. From there, they decided to join three of their daughters in Kalamazoo, Michigan. But the government's so-called resettlement program—which move in this series of involuntary displacements would, in truth, ever constitute *settlement*?—had not worked for them. So in June they decided to follow the lead of their Nisei children: to go back to Florin. A setback?[2]

Back in Arkansas, when Jerome closed, some of the fortunate ones were sent just up the road thirty miles to Rohwer. But with 5,700 to be transferred, there was not enough room. So some of the less fortunate ones were yet again compelled—yet again forced against their will—to go to other places, such as Heart Mountain, Wyoming, near the border with Montana. Back across the continent. "The reaction of the Jerome residents to the announcement was one of natural disappointment," an official conceded with dry understatement, "and of some bitterness that their cooperation in making it a clean and liveable center had gone for naught." Another administrator, Rachel Reese Sady, spoke in detail, with a bit more candor. "Complaints included accusations of splitting families," like the early days of eviction, "ignoring the second choices, insufficient weight given the needs of various [camps] for ministers"—again disadvantaging Buddhists—"inadequate explanation of the medical classifications, obvious clerical errors, [an] atmosphere of confusion and mystery in which the work was carried out, and dissatisfaction with the priority system set-up." The "priority system" was another War Relocation Authority (WRA) euphemism-code for what protestors rightly referred to as favoritism. Two groups were prioritized: those interested in working for major American corporations, as at the New Jersey vegetable farming and processing facility of Seabrook Farms—called "patriarchal and exploitative" by one scholar—and "soldiers' families, [who got their] preference regardless of choice or whereabouts of soldier." This "was considered by many to be uncalled-for 'flag-waving.' . . . Also, the interviews given by the Transfer Committee were severely criticized. Many got the feeling that they were only a formality, that individual cases actually had no chance at all, and that mistakes would not be corrected."[3]

Now that Rohwer too was closing and the Supreme Court's *Endo* case had reopened the West Coast to Japanese Americans, trains set out for California. Preparing to board on May 30, 1945, was *Rohwer Outpost* columnist and self-styled literary celebrity Bean Takeda. Trackside, Takeda shook hands, exchanged bows, and said his last good-byes. He felt "a small lump" in the back of his throat that made it "difficult to swallow." Reflecting on the conflicting emotions of that moment, on the difficulties of leaving this new home to return to a drastically transformed older home out west, Takeda described an experience that paralleled that of hundreds of other Rohwer residents: "When the time comes to leave the center, all sorts of things pass thru [*sic*] your mind. You think of the things you did and the things you didn't do. You think of the time wasted or the time well spent. . . . But mostly you think about the people you have met and the friends you have made. . . . You're going to miss these people. You're going to miss their companionship, their laughter, their encouragement, their intrinsic friendship. . . . For the moment, those friends and the fact that you're bidding them farewell are the most important things in the world." If Takeda articulated the sentiments of many Japanese Americans freed from concentration camps in seven states in 1945—the challenge to pick up stakes, sever old relationships, and start anew elsewhere—he also spoke to a pattern of events, a cycle of compulsory migrations, a perverse set of repetitions.[4]

The social and psychological effects of camp closing on over seventy-five thousand Japanese Americans remaining in WRA detention in 1945 frequently have been overlooked by historians. While many have focused on the decisions and difficulties of expulsion or attempted to re-create life inside the barbed-wire compounds, most writing about camp closing has probed economic hardships, tallying the intervening losses of income and private property, included only as an addendum to camp experiences. The stories told usually have been of the ones that got away, the Nisei. A significant number left the camps for university or outside employment in 1943 and 1944, and thus did not live through the process of camp shut downs and the traumas that summoned. They experienced it vicariously, through the stories of friends and family members. Because many aged seventeen to thirty-five signed up for the well-publicized resettlement program, the camps, as historian Roger Daniels notes, "increasingly held a higher proportion of older adults and small children, of Issei rather than Nisei," over the course of the war. In the same way that the second generation populates most narratives about Japanese American incarceration during World War II, resilient self-starters tend to predominate in accounts of the wars' end, as well as in upbeat histories of postwar Asian America, the march of the so-called "model minority," as coined in the 1960s. Issei and the relatively few Nisei still in camps in 1945 have been neglected. Further, some of the most destructive aspects of resettlement—in particular, the guiding principle of population dispersal—have been downplayed or implicitly validated.[5]

Bean Takeda and his Nisei colleagues at the office of the *Rohwer Outpost* promoted life after camp in narrow ways, as had their counterparts on the *Demon Tribune*. Their announcements, the WRA statements they reprinted, and the editorial comments they penned revealed a positivist, occasionally foolhardy optimism about postcamp and postwar possibilities. Starting over, for them, seemed much easier than many of their readers assumed—and for the first time, with original articles of a decidedly cynical cast, the Japanese-language section of the Rohwer paper, the *Jiho*, began to diverge sharply from the other pages of the *Outpost*, focusing repeatedly in 1945 on accounts of American prejudice on the outside. Issei mulled their options with great skepticism. Their misgivings circulated in stark contrast to Nisei trendsetters, who followed and even helped formulate the federal government policy of resettlement and dispersal.[6]

Trains departed camps in 1945 with Nikkei who were uncertain about the options, unsure of their direction. In a beautiful Japanese ritual, pregnant with meaning, passengers at windows each held the end of a long, colored strip of crepe paper, and at the other end, a well-wisher clung lightly. When wheels began to turn and the train pulled away, the streamers were pulled taut and slowly stretched, like so much elastic, supple and resilient, prolonging the connection, until at last they reached the breaking point. Individuals still in detention were left behind, standing at the tracks. People onboard were left to wonder about the way ahead. All were left holding the broken pieces.[7]

Of the songs that run through one's mind at such moments—the soundtrack to the movie of life—rousing tunes like "California Here I Come" surely gave way to more melancholy strains. "Ev'rytime we say goodbye, I die a little."

Normal American Communities

Orders came from the very top. President Franklin Roosevelt said that a key aim of the War Relocation Authority was to insure Japanese American "relocation into normal homes" after investigations and loyalty determinations. WRA director Dillon Myer dutifully reported the same to the House Un-American Activities Committee (HUAC) and the American Legion, emphasizing further a return "as quickly as possible to private employment." Both HUAC and the American Legion feared release, overstating the dangers to national security—there were none—and ignoring the dangers for Japanese Americans. Roosevelt differed with his secretary of the interior, Harold Ickes, who advocated immediate, large-scale movements out of the camps in 1944, given the increasing realization of incarceration' s unconstitutional basis and the utter lack of military necessity. Roosevelt insisted instead upon a gradual release program designed to scatter the internees.[8]

Worried about his own political career leading up to the race for an unprecedented fourth term, Roosevelt proposed that only "one or two families" be sent to "each county" off the West Coast. "Dissemination and distribution," he said, "constitute a great method of avoiding public outcry." Thus, as historian Greg Robinson concludes, FDR's "exclusive focus on placating West Coast public opinion and his order that the internees be 'disseminated' betray[ed] a cavalier disregard for the concerns of Japanese Americans, whom the President saw only as a problem, and to their right to choose where they lived."[9]

Whereas the *American Legion Magazine* fretted over the potential longevity of the camps, hysterically predicting they would become powerful Little Tokyos sending representatives and senators to Congress, mainstream daily newspapers such as the *New York Times* espoused a widespread view that a necessary resettlement program must avoid the grouping of large numbers of Japanese Americans into new ethnic enclaves. Some Japanese American leaders and journalists echoed the call. *Pacific Citizen* editor Larry Tajiri "spoke of the breaking up of the [prewar] Little Tokyos as a positive aspect" of expulsion and incarceration. Writing for *Common Ground*, Eddie Shimano was determined that they not be re-created, referring to life in camps, in the article's title, as a "Blueprint for a Slum." As WRA official John Baker wrote in camp publications, "The War Relocation Authority is definitely committed to the task of helping people in the relocation centers to resume normal lives in normal communities where they can be contented and secure." Once again, such Americanization implied Christianization, for an accompanying illustration of a normal American community depicted a small town with only one house of worship—with a cross atop the steeple.[10]

Though Roosevelt's "one or two families per county" plan was unworkable in detail, the guiding principle of dispersing Japanese Americans remained a cornerstone of resettlement policy. Camp newspapers toed the line. A striking feature of the *Rohwer Outpost* in 1944, for example, was the prevalence of job offers and relocation announcements from a wide geographical area, particularly the Midwest. A single issue on January 8 listed "outside employment" opportunities for factory work in Cleveland, for domestic workers in Saint Louis, a watchmaker in Omaha, and a short-order cook in South Haven, Michigan. A column on the same page told readers of successful relocations. George Yamauchi had gone to Davenport, Iowa; Alice Hatsumi Takahashi was in Ann Arbor, Michigan; Eugen Toshio Yoshida had started a new life in Cincinnati; and three more people had moved to Chicago. Within the next week, it said on the opposite page, relocation officer Laverne Madigan would be visiting Rohwer from New York to outline further options. The *Outpost*'s Bean Takeda was sent on a three-month tour of relocation destinations in the summer of 1944, reporting back regularly from Chicago, Cleveland, Atlantic City, Philadelphia, Washington, DC, and Bridgeton, New Jersey, home of Seabrook Farms. His positive references to the employment and housing conditions demonstrated the utility of his writings to WRA policy makers. Takeda's column, along with a permanent feature of the *Outpost*, the "Relocation Calendar," served two functions. On the one hand, they told the camp community who was moving and where, thereby aiding individuals and families considering a departure. On the other hand, they constantly reminded inmates that people were on the move, leaving camp, starting new lives in new parts of the country. By implication, they asked: Shouldn't you be doing likewise?[11]

WRA headquarters insisted that resettlement campaigning was the duty of all camp administrators and did not shirk from calling it "indoctrination." Teachers, in particular, were held to account. Adult schools inculcated skills foremost for "profitable relocation" during and after the war. As much as the traditional three R's, WRA high schools taught two others: "Relocation of families and of individuals where they will find community acceptance and suitable work [and] re-assimilation of Japanese Americans into the normal social and economic order of the nation." Social studies teachers played a crucial role: "Upon large wall maps of the United States constructed by students, cities and states to which many center residents have gone out have been marked; others to which they will be welcomed have been indicated." Additionally, well-meaning supporters outside the camps, such as Earl Finch, wrote letters of introduction and letters of recommendation, helping connect prisoners with potential employers."[12]

At Jerome, Virginia Tidball required her high school English students to write compositions on resettlement, and, unsurprisingly, the majority seemed to favor it, repeating words read in newspapers or heard in lectures. Nisei should find new homes outside, Akiko Higake wrote, and once there "should try to make a good impression [on] the public and not be conspicuous in any way." As Katsuto Nakano added, "We must avoid grouping together and practice assimilation.... The main part of gaining a favorable opinion is up to the evacuee." Hawaiians such as Clara Hasegawa felt differently. "I am just hoping that we will never be asked to leave this center until the war is over," she confided. "This relocating business is bound to separate us from all our friends." Hailing from Kauai, her father, a Buddhist minister interned in New Mexico, Michiko Odate worried about "racial discrimination," calling it "the worst problem that [a]ffects resettling." She also fretted that taking "employment near the eastern coast of this country" would leave people at war's end "quite far away from their former home." Teenagers understood the disadvantages for older inmates too. Higake noted that few Issei wanted to resettle. And "we can hardly blame them." After first coming "to this land with the dominant pioneering spirit of settling," why should they have to "face another [of] life's battles in the unknown regions?"[13]

As of mid-1944, the *Rohwer Outpost* prepared residents for the inevitable reopening of the West Coast while continuing to encourage resettlement elsewhere. Bean Takeda generally argued against thoughts of California. While acknowledging that a "certain number" should go back, he counseled caution, citing the vast movements of people into and around the state during the war, the subsequent housing shortage, and the likelihood that former friends there would be gone. Furthermore, news of vandalism and theft of property left behind on the West Coast, often in Buddhist temples, had circulated since the beginning of incarceration. Japanese Americans at Jerome and Rohwer feared that WRA "property officers may be consciously or unconsciously working with the Sons of the Golden West to make it possible that the former Japanese residents of California have no roots or ties to which to come back."[14]

With the lifting of the West Coast exclusion order, effective January 2, 1945, the *Rohwer Outpost* changed its tune. Bean Takeda began to consider a return to his native California himself. He urged his readers to "discredit any rumors you might hear about unpleasantness in our California hometowns." He also wrote that "there seems to be an organized move along the Pacific Coast to bluff evacuees into not going back. If we believe these wild rumors and are frightened into not returning, we are going to be the losers, economically and otherwise." In March 1945 Takeda praised a San Francisco resident for refusing to be intimidated by telephone threats: "That's the spirit we need to lick those bluffers." In April he tried to buoy hopes further, even as he admitted the very real dangers to Japanese Americans. "Of course, you'll say that it's easy enough for me, here in the camp, to utter such words of bravado. But I'm returning to California soon, and when I do, I shall expect to be treated roughly at first and perhaps even shot at."[15]

There were, in fact, innumerable incidents of violence against released Japanese Americans on the West Coast, as well as in every other section of the United States. Those in so-called mixed marriages were particularly visible—and vulnerable. Herbert Sasaki, a 442nd soldier who had sung tenor solos at the USO dances for Japanese Americans, wedded white Mississippian Arnice Dyer, and after a brief period in the Midwest, the couple set up permanent residence back in Dyer's hometown of Purvis, Mississippi, running her parents' chicken farm. Given the difficulties of interracial marriage in a state with a miscegenation law, Sasaki consistently avoided talking about the ceremony in the interviews he granted through the years. But in the *Los Angeles Times*'s obituary on Sasaki in 2005, it noted that, as a result of the marriage, the Ku Klux Klan had burned a cross in their front yard.[16]

For many Nisei women, resettlement first meant a new life near Camp Shelby, Mississippi. Moving out of the concentration camps, wives of soldiers had to find accommodations and often raise their children in the heart of the segregated South. Kazu Iijima and her husband, Tak, rented a room from a Protestant pastor and his wife in the town of Petal, where they were viewed, at best, as a novelty. "People would be driving," she recalls, "and they would stop in the middle of the street to stare at us." The Iijimas "used to have big arguments" with Reverend O'Neil "because he used to believe that the Negroes, as they called them, came from Adam's ribs so they were inferior people. And we used to play Paul Robeson records and Marian Anderson, . . . and he'd say that those were unusual people." Though white evangelicals might concoct any biblical excuse for African American subjugation, the Christian creation myth in fact held that women were formed from man's rib, and it served to justify *their* position of social inferiority. When the Iijimas moved out, Mrs. O'Neil sheepishly asked to borrow the Anderson and Robeson records to play for her women's group at the church.[17]

With severe housing shortages in Hattiesburg during the war years—such that some local opportunists rented out their chicken coops—Earl Finch stepped in to aid Japanese Americans in search of a home. Finch bought or rented area houses, which he then made available to couples such as the Taonos and Ishikawas. Given her college education and given the reluctance of some white public schools to accept Japanese Americans, Kay Ishikawa was advised to homeschool her children. But she insisted they needed the social interactions that only ordinary schooling could provide. So the Ishikawas then moved into another "Finch home" to be near a Catholic school that had accepted their son Robert. (The short-lived segregated public school for Japanese Americans in Hattiesburg apparently never enrolled more than five, and it closed after teacher Martha Suigi moved away.) Mary Nakahara lived in Finch homes in Hattiesburg, once she relocated there to help run the Aloha USO. Then, "Earl Finch sent me to Minnesota," she remembers, to manage an Aloha center near Camp Savage, home to the Military Intelligence Service. Nakahara assisted her mother and aunt in their move back to California from Rohwer. Then, with her new husband, soldier Bill Kochiyama, she resettled—yet again—in New York. There she worked at a Chock Full o' Nuts coffee shop and, enlightened by her wartime experiences, she embarked upon a new lifelong commitment to the struggles of working-class people of color.[18]

Whereas the USO dances at Shelby, Jerome, and Rohwer had marked an era of state-sanctioned courtship and intraethnic marriage-helping, in effect, to maintain racial segregation in the United States—the WRA resettlement program aimed to move Japanese American families into predominantly white normal American communities and thereby aid their social and racial ascent after the war. But these movements into segregated, often hostile, white neighborhoods and workplaces came at a cost.

The Suicide of Julia Dakuzaku

Eddie Shimano, the former editor of the Jerome newspaper, was so convinced of resettlement's urgency that he overstated the dire conditions in the camps, which he had left at the earliest opportunity. Writing for the magazine *Common Ground*, he insisted that resettlement needed to be done and "done fast if potentially valuable individuals are to be salvaged for the nation and for themselves. It is an uphill fight to maintain a balance, a perspective, and a faith in the nightmare of demoralization and despair that is a relocation center." Indeed, the expulsion and incarceration had had nightmarish consequences, but the camps themselves proved habitable and supportive environments for many—at least as compared to the world of prejudice and bigotry waiting just beyond the barbed-wire fence. Still, Shimano advocated "dispersal resettlement" and "the integration of the Japanese into American life . . . with surgical thoroughness and surgical disregard for sentiment."[19]

With leave clearance secured by their "yes-yes" status, Mary and Al Tsukamoto resettled in Kalamazoo, Michigan, with their only child, daughter Marielle, and other family members. There Mary's father Taro Dakuzaku, sister Julia Dakuzaku, and husband Al landed jobs at the Peter Pan Bakery. Gone were the mutual support and cultural collusiveness of their California hometown—and of the concentration camp. "Our life there [in Michigan] was one of seclusion," says Mary Tsukamoto, "and those who worked at outside jobs did so at night when their Japanese faces were not so visible; the rest of us stayed indoors as much as we could." After nearly three years of companionship in what had effectively become an ethnic enclave at Jerome and Rohwer, how disturbing and off-putting it must have been for Taro and Kame Dakuzaku—and for Issei from all the camps—to receive this sort of guidance from the Japanese American Citizens League (JACL): "To avoid attracting attention, Issei are advised not to speak Japanese on the streets and in other public places. They should not bow to each other because this makes them conspicuous." Thus, a chief sacrifice in resettlement was the forfeiting of personal dignity—to make oneself small, indeed invisible, in the public sphere.[20]

The bakery was a dangerous, depressing place, largely devoid of pleasure or of safety measures. "There were many opportunities to make mistakes, but the employee who made them did not last long." By now an elderly man, Taro Dakuzaku "had the tip of his finger cut off one night while he was feeding dough into a cutting machine." But he and other Japanese American laborers were afforded few protections and little compensation. He received $500 for his on-the-job injury and nothing more.[21]

Julia Dakuzaku was even more of a worry to her family members, because she *really* "wanted to live a normal life like other twenty-year-olds." She was an avid painter and dancer. Wherever possible, she gave amateur singing performances with the Dakuzaku Sisters. She didn't like the night shift, the tiring routine of working in the dark, sleeping during the daylight hours. She asked for reassignment and was granted it, temporarily. "When the customers saw her Japanese face on the line however, they became alarmed and began to boycott the bakery." Though the personnel officer attended the same First Methodist Church as the Tsukamotos and was counted among Mary's "very special friend[s]," he insisted that Dakuzaku return to the night shift. When she refused, "they had to fire her," according to Mary Tsukamoto. Tsukamoto "worried about her [sister] and her attitude. She was stubborn but also vulnerable to depression and despair." Dejected, Dakuzaku was turned down by numerous other employers: "Advertised job openings were not for her. Even when caring church members walked the streets with her to find daytime employment, Julia could not get a job." Mary arranged "several counseling sessions" for her sister with the Methodist minister. "In desperation," Julia finally found work with the WACs.[22]

Whereas Japanese American men were once classified as 4-C, enemy aliens ineligible for service, the mobilization of the 442nd had been a highly coordinated and widely publicized effort to redeem Japanese Americans through voluntary military duty. Soon Nisei men were drafted, including the Dakuzakus' only son, George, who was sent to England. And as we have seen, young women were encouraged to join the WACs. Many men and women resisted. So not only Mary Tsukamoto, but also the national JACL newspaper, *Pacific Citizen*, repeatedly described women's enlistment as the perfect means of reintegration into the body politic through service to the country. In her regular column, the pseudonymous Ann Nisei tried to overcome any misgivings on the part of potential inductees. Hardly Amazons, as some feared, Nisei WACs she encountered were "young, attractive and energetic," she wrote. They found army employment in a variety of occupations. They were not segregated from white women, and since "WAC requirements were specially lowered for Nisei women, you remember, to 100 lbs. and 59 inches in height," almost anyone could volunteer—provided they were citizens "of course." Newspapers gave significant coverage to Private Iris Watanabe, "the first Nisei evacuee to be inducted into the WACS." In what seemed a classic case of blaming the victim, however, Watanabe chided young women and men who, "by caging themselves [*sic*] in these relocation centers . . . don't give themselves a chance to succeed in life, just because of one rather unhappy and bitter experience." Nisei WACS also figured prominently in the broader campaign to "rehabilitate" the Japanese American minority and win over the white majority. Ayako Noguchi Nakamura, who resettled with her husband and over two thousand others at Seabrook Farms in New Jersey, went on a speaking tour as part of this campaign. She visited Christian aid organizations, social service agencies, and PTAs to trumpet the accomplishments of "Japanese Americans in the War Effort."[23]

Julia Dakuzaku had answered the waning wartime call of Uncle Sam and enlisted. But that too proved a crushing disappointment. The government, once again, proved it did not know what was best for her; it would not necessarily act in her best interests. She was stationed in a place called Pasco, Washington, far from friends, far from family. Shortly after Taro and Kame Dakuzaku returned by train to their farm in Florin, California, they received a telegram about their youngest, sixth-born daughter. Their hearts sank with the very first words, that hackneyed—utterly insufficient—expression of condolence: "We regret to inform you. . . ."[24]

The Tsukamotos too had returned to their hometown of Florin. Mary tried to act as simultaneous interpreter for her parents when a "tall, attractive, blonde lieutenant" arrived the next day with Julia's "flag draped pine box" and explained, for the first time, the cause of death: "She ended her life by her own choice." The suicide of Julia Dakuzaku would become a family secret. Some sisters were not told "until many, many years later" how she died. And some had great difficulty comprehending why she did it. But Mary eventually would come to describe her sister Julia, quite rightly, as "a victim [of] incarceration and war." Julia Dakuzaku died on September 9, 1945, exactly one month after the bombing of Nagasaki.[25]

Like Mary's parents, the Tsukamotos returned to farming but finally had to give up and pull up their grape vines in 1949. That same year Tsukamoto used her experience as a teacher in the camps to help secure a position with the by-now-desegregated Florin School, her alma mater. She would teach there until her retirement. And her autobiography, coauthored with Elizabeth Pinkerton in the 1980s, reflects what Pinkerton describes as Tsukamoto's "patriotic fervor that knows no rest." For Pinkerton, the Tsukamoto autobiography, entitled *We the People*, and the changes in the Florin schools before and after incarceration demonstrated, most forcefully, "why America is so great."[26]

Plantation versus Cooperative Colony

It did not have to end this way. Closing the camps was not a foregone conclusion—not for everyone. Although WRA officials again and again insisted that the concentration camps "by their very nature, can never be turned into normal communities," many people proposed just that. Through administrators' ruthless drives for efficient production and, more importantly, Japanese Americans' diligence in farming and service occupations that benefited their own, Jerome and Rohwer had been transformed into bustling towns that were, one after the other, difficult to abandon. Still, the WRA insisted that "life outside" was "infinitely preferable," and that as towns, the camps would "always have serious shortcomings." These shortcomings were taken as self-evident and were rarely articulated, as they bordered on falsehood: "As long as evacuees remain in relocation centers, their opportunities to lead a well-rounded and fully productive life will inevitably be more limited than in ordinary American towns and cities." In Rohwer in 1945, where almost five thousand people had chosen to remain in relative safety, within the heart of an ethnic support network, two alternative visions of the war's aftermath emerged. One represented a return to the old order; the other was a bold, more equitable plan. Naturally, the former, the American way, ruled the day. It could have been much different.[27]

By its own measures, the WRA's dispersal strategy succeeded. Of the 120,000 people who came into their custody—almost exclusively from California, Oregon, and Washington—nearly half left the camps to resettle in other sections of the country: a huge population redistribution. Though some of these, like the Dakuzakus and Tsukamotos, would again, shortly thereafter, relocate back to California, others by contrast found their old West Coast hometowns so changed as to necessitate the move east, as with Mary and Bill Kochiyama. With WRA regional offices in Denver, Little Rock, and San Francisco, with as many as fifty-eight special relocation offices from Salt Lake City to New York, and with publications such as *They're Friendly in New England*, administrators actively directed Japanese Americans toward particular jobs and communities. "The great social-engineering experiment of rounding up, penning, and strewing," as historian Richard Drinnon surmises, "had racist and totalitarian implications." "Through Myers executive agency the Roosevelt administration told citizens where they might live, what to do there for a living, how to dress, how to behave, how to talk and with whom to associate." Of course, officials with the WRA held a range of views and performed their tasks with mixed motivations. There was considerable sympathy for the inmates, a faith in assimilation, and the desire to make release from the camps acceptable to a wider public. The great majority wanted to resolve racial and ethnic conflict, and as we have seen, some even resigned their government posts in response to army and WRA excesses. But Dillon Myer and others seemed to be of one mind about the closing of the camps.[28]

Even the JACL had to acknowledge that some Japanese Americans would necessarily, understandably resist yet another risky forced relocation to a dangerous new place. At an "all-center conference" held in Salt Lake City in 1945 to discuss camp closing and resettlement, Rohwer delegates Chester Fujino, Shintaro Ito, and Lloyd Shingu stood by helplessly as the WRA rejected out of hand a JACL proposal that the government agency "stay in business indefinitely and be prepared to accept back into custody those of the evacuated people who could not, for reasons of age, infirmity, or demoralization, make some kind of successful readjustment to life outside the camps." In addition to these disparaging characterizations, there were affirming rationales for maintaining the camps as ongoing concerns. First, however, activists at Rohwer had to point out the flaws in one of the WRA's most touted "relocation opportunities."[29]

Plantations evoked mixed emotions for Japanese Americans in Arkansas. For most Hawaiians, plantations had been the first site of employment and livelihood in the United States, a source of fond family memories and pernicious workplace inequalities. Some had managed to work their way up and out of the fields, forming the core of a local service economy. Similarly, smaller-scale family farming had been a principal source of income on the West Coast, as it simultaneously gave rise to a host of related vocations and professions. During incarceration, large-scale collective agriculture, individual garden plots, and communal meal preparation demonstrated a continuing Japanese American affinity for food production. So WRA officials thought it only natural to promote outside employment on the Wilson Plantation: "One of the Best!"[30]

Located in the far northeast corner of Arkansas, near the Mississippi River, Wilson Plantation was a massive operation spread over sixty-three thousand acres—fifty-seven thousand of which were under cultivation, mostly in corn, alfalfa, and soybeans. Across five towns, ten thousand people lived in 2,200 houses. In addition to farming, residents worked in seventy-seven other trades, from lumber mills and granaries to an ice plant and box and crate factory, from a bank and medical clinic to filling stations and beauty parlors. Wilson officials marketed the plantation as a desirable postwar home for Japanese Americans. Carrying the WRA imprimatur, a January 1946 bulletin emphasized Arkansas's position as the leading strawberry producer in the United States, as well as the nation's number-three producer of rice. Also presumed relevant to Japanese Americans from California in particular, the plantation "is going to further diversify by entering into commercial truck crop farming." Ostensibly dedicated to truth in advertising—since readers of the bulletin could sign a form within and thereby enter into a binding contract—marketers cautioned that "there are no soft-cushion jobs. . . . Like all farming, no matter what section of the country, it is hard work. . . . But no one knows more about this than do Japanese American farmers."[31]

Of course, in the South plantation life carried all the connotations of exploitation and racial hierarchy that had made the section, as with the Pacific territories, immensely profitable for a small, avaricious planter elite. Further, it bore the specific legacy of slavery, a vicious economic system propped up by insidious social and cultural assertions of black inferiority. Despite occasional moments of alliance among people of color during World War II—as when Japanese Americans joined African Americans in the back of the bus or in confrontations with white bigots—Nisei and Issei throughout the war years fretted over modes of segregation and marginalization that cast them as similar to, as similarly positioned with, blacks on American racial scales. Wilson officials thus did not promise improved conditions for Japanese Americans along with African Americans; they vowed to effectively distinguish the former—indeed, segregate them—from the latter. That is, they agreed to let Japanese Americans participate in *some* white institutions and practices. "School buses are provided by The Plantation to carry all children to and from schools," the bulletin advised. "Your children will attend the white schools."[32]

Promotion threatened to degenerate into deception, with the hope that, if stated forcefully enough, any claim might be believed. "*EVACUEES HAVE NOTHING TO FEAR*," said J. H. Crain, general manager. "There is a general feeling of tolerance and fellowship toward Japanese Americans in this entire section of the country and they can depend on the Wilson Plantation to defend their rights and privileges as citizens and loyal aliens." As an example of this tolerance, "at the beginning of the 1945 fall term of school, one of the Japanese boys, now relocated on the Wilson Plantation, was elected vice-president of the Junior H.S. Class at Wilson, Arkansas." Further, Japanese American students were free to play on the white school's "football fields, tennis and basketball courts and"—in a crucial test of segregation in the Jim Crow South, with its outlandish theories of disease transmission—"swim in its pool." Of the many perks of life in Wilson, the bulletin boasted "rural mail service daily, except Sunday"; in more measured tones, it promised "adequate hospital services . . . in case of injury or severe illness"; and, in a clear case of a liability recast as an asset, it noted that "favorite Japanese foods and other choice needs and desires will be stocked in Plantation stores for your convenience and pleasure."[33]

Plantation stores were the crux of the problem—for so-called evacuees indeed had everything to fear in the economic organization of Wilson. It was, simply put, a classic postbellum scheme of tenant farming and sharecropping. Whereas under the briefly described "Plan No. 2," land could be rented for twelve dollars to eighteen dollars per acre, "providing you have your own farming equipment and finances to make your own crops"—out of reach for the great majority after incarceration—the elaborately detailed "Plan No. 1, for the family or bachelor with little or no money," was, in the end, the only option. Under it, the Wilson Plantation would "furnish as many acres of its rich alluvial soil to each family as its (the family's) workers can care for, advantageously"—that is, as judged by the overseers. "The Wilson Company will furnish all farming equipment," some to be logically shared with others, as well as "fertilizer, plants, seeds, housing and insecticides": "YOU will furnish only the labor." Proceeds from the harvest's sale would be split between sharecropper and owner, depending on the crop, at proportions from 50–50 up to 65–35. The critical paragraph 8 pointed out that "should you need financial assistance until proceeds of crops are in, the Wilson Plantation will advance you money. The same to be repaid at harvest time plus 6 percent interest per annum for the length of the loan." Thus did Wilson and all debt peonage schemes ensnare their laborers."[34]

Bragging that "no renter, sharecropper, or worker . . . was fired or lost his job on the Plantation during the depression period" was really beside the point. It was leaving the plantation that often became impossible. Located over forty miles from Memphis, residents were forced to buy basic consumer goods at the plantation store's inflated prices. In advance of harvest, they were forced to buy on credit, borrowing money at exorbitant rates. If the crop's yield—a "quick-cash" payment "at current market prices," dictated by the owners, the only game in town—did not cover expenses, as was all too common (and not just during agricultural depressions), then a cycle of debt resulted. The debts were compounded from one year to the next. Plantation housing—discretely sandwiched, in the contract, between potentially hazardous fertilizers and insecticides, all "furnished" by the owners—too often became jails. To leave would mean to run out on debts, an illegal act that would involve law enforcement officers, if not worse. To leave indebted, with nothing in the world but the clothes on your back, would mean to risk homelessness.[35]

As of early 1946, nearly one hundred Japanese Americans lived in Wilson. Others followed. Although the Arkansas legislature in 1943 had passed a racist, alien land law with astonishing majorities, only one dissenting vote each in the House and Senate, and though this law forbade sale or long-term lease of land to persons of Japanese descent, Wilson officials overlooked it. Though the measure, signed by Gov. Homer Adkins, had sparked outraged editorials from as far away as Detroit and statements of protest from as nearby as Clarksville, the plantation adopted a liberal interpretation, suggesting the statute was unconstitutional: "Arkansas' constitutional law . . . permits Japanese Aliens to buy and own their own land." Thus did they further hold out the hope—perhaps a false one—that instead of a downward cycle of debt, Japanese Americans would enjoy an upward spiral of good weather and thrifty savings, leading in some distant unforeseeable future to private property of their own.[36]

There was an alternative. Imagine it. Instead of individuals and families working for their own narrowly defined self-interest—and that of an all-powerful overlord—competing ruthlessly for the best land, their gain another family's loss, they might come together and toil on a large tract for the collective good, to be shared equally by all Japanese Americans. Imagine not an urban Little Tokyo but a rural Little Prefecture. Notions like this had circulated since the earliest days of the camps, especially in Arkansas.

"Cooperative group farming" was under study at Jerome and Rohwer, as well as Tule Lake, as early as the summer of 1943. "A conference of the Councilmen and Block Managers of Rohwer Center" met on October 28, 1943, and subsequently sent their findings directly to camp director Ray Johnston and WRA director Dillon Myer in Washington, DC. Instead of—or in addition to—"the WRA's dispersed resettlement aim," they asserted that "group relocation is the best solution, especially for prospective farmers." A group "need not be on a scale any larger than twenty to thirty families." But clustering was necessary, given that "the task of independent re-establishment of a large family amidst strangers and unknown territory is practically impossible to expect of these evacuees now." Though often remembered as a quiet camp with little if any outward signs of protest, Rohwer and its inmates' statement of dissent were taken very seriously, occasioning an eight-page response from Myer. While he circulated the proposal to all ten camp directors, conceding that it was "well thought up," he discouraged the leaders at Rohwer. "If by group relocation the Council means the purchase of a fairly large tract of land and the colonization of a considerable number of evacuees on this land, the WRA will have to answer that it actively discourages such plans." He argued that "fellow Americans"—presumably white—would mount "strong opposition." "Such special groups whether they are Japanese, Italian, Greek, Polish, or Turkish will meet with antagonism." One such special group had long lived in peace just up the road in Stuttgart, Arkansas. So Rohwer organizers were not to be deterred. By the time rumors swirled of camp closing, a sweeping new proposal of utopian design was put forward.[37]

Authored by a three-person "citizens committee"—Saburo Muraoka, C. Sumida, and T. Takasugi—the elaborate proposition for a cooperative colony was hard to rebut, given the precedent of the camps' successful cooperative stores. A colony would be on the scale, roughly, of the Wilson Plantation: up to one hundred thousand acres supporting and supported by up to fifteen thousand people. The key difference, of course, would be in the ownership and distribution of earnings. As the land would be cooperatively owned by all, there would be no overlord to reap excessive profits nor an impoverished underclass to generate them. All would be sustained with livable, middling incomes. Three of the existing camps, including Rohwer, along with their neighboring unutilized farmland, might be converted in this manner, especially given the improvements already undertaken. Land in Arkansas, once valued at six dollars per acre, had increased in value, with Japanese American industriousness, to ten times that amount, up to sixty dollars per acre. It made no sense to now abandon it; it would be unjust for the government to take it back and give it away. The committee proposed instead to pay for the land with a government loan, to be repaid over ten to thirty years. The combined loan for three colonies would amount to little more than the WRA annual budget, and it could provide indefinitely for up to half of the Japanese Americans remaining in the camps.[38]

It was brash but otherwise wholly un-American. Health care for all. Elder care for all. Farmland for all. Income for all. Profits for none. All excess income over expenses would remain with the cooperative, for the benefit of all. "Nonfarming residents will work . . . in industrial enterprises." Hospitals, retail and service establishments, even an "Old Folks Home," would be "operated under the co-operative system." Like the camps, all the activities of an ordinary town would be carried out, but with everyone assigned to the jobs that best suited them, without coercion. A meticulous budget followed. Every angle seemed to be coveted. It was a beautiful plan.[39]

The WRA balked. In the end, the government did give it all away. For a song, the Surplus War Property Administration sold the land to local farmers, at public auction, a mere five dollars to ten dollars per acre, a fraction of its value—as Japanese Americans were sent out into a hostile world, in small numbers, isolated, like the five families who followed Yokochi Nakagawa to a village east of Little Rock. Leaders of the cooperative movement exposed the government's rhetoric of pioneering as generational and ageist. Many of the Issei, they pointed out, were "well advanced in years and tired, [and] cannot be expected to have that dashing courage and undying pioneering spirit to open a new frontier alone. For them it must be security through unity." The cooperative colony, however, became one of history's forgotten alternatives.[40]

The extended period of incarceration and the growing familiarity and comfort with life in camp meant that, for most, the prospect of leaving was daunting. Roots had been laid down; bonds of friendship and community had been developed over nearly three years. The tar paper barracks had been personalized and made as homey as possible. Victory gardens and flowering vines were established and lovingly tended. Despite innumerable curbs to freedom in Arkansas, decamping would be a wrenching act, a time of heightened emotion, especially for these older, world-weary Issei. Kikuha Okamoto—formerly of Stockton—perfectly captured the feelings of ambivalence and uncertainty in a haiku written near the end of her tenure at Rohwer.

> Pulled out
> morning glory vines
> as day of departure nears[41]

Here, vines are endowed with dual symbolism. They represent, in one sense, the roots established while at Rohwer, the countless supportive links and connections created with other Japanese Americans there. However, vines also suggest an ensnaring, suffocating, restrictive phenomenon, perhaps the barbed-wire fence itself—and its limits to freedom of movement. The poem evidences a widely held, contradictory feeling among long-term inmates toward the prospect of camp closure and resettlement: a sense of joy at breaking free from the shackles of incarceration, tempered by a deep-seated pain at being forced, through another relocation, to sever the ties of camaraderie that had sustained them throughout the war years.

As it happened, Okamoto did not have to endure the complex, conflicted experience of leaving camp. Leaving behind her fifty-seven-year-old husband, Shiho, Kikuha Okamoto died of a heart attack in Arkansas on March 27, 1945, only months before the abandonment of Rohwer.[42]

Set in the year 2045, one century later, in Desha County, Arkansas, a short story from the *Rohwer Outpost* depicts a future for Japanese Americans in the state. Two figures emerge from a forest into a clearing where a row of broken-down shacks are visible. The two are "apparently human beings," one "a middle aged man, of Japanese descent," covered in hair, the other his fourteen-year-old son, who asks about the site. What, exactly, are they looking at? "That, my boy, is what remains of the Rohwer Relocation Center." His curiosity stirred, the boy asks more questions.

> "Where did all the people go, Pop?"
> "They scattered out, Son. Relocation they called it. Some went east, others went north to places like Chicago, and others returned to California."
> "Where is California, Pop?"
> "California, my son, is on the Pacific Coast. It used to be one of our great states, until it withdrew from the Union."
> "Why did it withdraw, Pop?"

"Because they wanted to keep it a white man's country, my son. Some of the people there didn't believe in liberty, equality, and democracy."

"Where did we come from, Pop?"

"My friend, we descended from the people who refused to leave the center here. They just stayed here, even after the center closed."

"Why did they refuse to leave, Pop?"

"For various reasons, son. Some were afraid to leave, others liked it here, and still others refused to leave on general principles."

"How many of us descendants are there here, Pop?"

"About 300 of us, Son, scattered throughout the woods. There may be more on the other side of the river. But here, son, let's be getting home. It's getting late, and mother probably has fried tree roots for us tonight."[43]

The author of this story, Rohwer journalist Bean Takeda, was something of an enigma. In his regular column for the *Outpost*, he vacillated between propagandizing for the War Relocation Authority and delivering blistering critiques of the American status quo—the circumstances that had led to the concentration camps. One week his column served as a vehicle for self-aggrandizement, the next it functioned as a thoughtful, sometimes poignant social commentary on camp life. Maybe he had made a frank trade-off with administrators, who closely monitored the paper: so many column inches of official policy in exchange for a few more individual musings. Such a trade-off would not have been uncommon for Japanese Americans under incarceration: the everyday substitutions, carefully modulated, of acquiescence to authority and resistance to injustice, the measuring of limits and opportunities, the necessary and the impossible.

Writing from the South, Takeda envisions a secession from the Union predicated upon race: that of a California given over completely to racial hatred and racial purity, with all nonwhites barred. The United States, it is implied, remains otherwise intact. And amazingly, by contrast with its former West Coast state, the United States remains associated—despite the historical traces in this very woodland clearing—with "liberty, equality, and democracy." An inventive writer who well-articulates rationales for staying, Takeda nonetheless cannot imagine a suitable existence for Japanese Americans in Arkansas, other than a primitive, rustic separatism characterized by ignorance—a lack of awareness of what goes on just on the other side of the river. Further, Takeda cannot imagine a world without gender inequality. Males, father and son, move about in the public sphere—even in this restricted rural one—debating its history, charting its future. Women remain at home, in the kitchen.

Some people in the camps could imagine much more. A world where both women and men could work in jobs outside the home. Jobs they enjoyed. A world where they earned the same income. A world in which racial categories no longer mattered. A world where all human needs were accounted for and—as best as was collectively possible—were met. A world where competitive individualism, self-centeredness, and greed were discarded in favor of cooperative endeavor and collaboration, with all benefits to be shared, equally. *That* kind of equality.

Imagine.

Notes

1. Michi Nishiura Weglyn, *Years of Infamy: The Untold Story of America's Concentration Camps*, updated ed. (Seattle: University of Washington Press, 1996), 43–45; *The Commonweal*, March 10, 1944.

2. Mary Tsukamoto and Elizabeth Pinkerton, *We the People: A Story of Internment in America* (Elk Grove, CA: Laguna, 1987), 270.

3. "The Closing of the Jerome Relocation Center," and Rachel Reese Sady, "War Relocation Authority, Community Analysis Section, July 14, 1944, Summary of Closing Procedures," both in part II, section 5, reel 138, War Relocation Authority Records (WRAR), Record Group 210, U.S. National Archives (NA), Washington DC; Mitziko Sawada, "After the Camps: Seabrook Farms, New Jersey, and the Resettlement of Japanese Americans, 1944–47," *Amerasia Journal* 13 (1986–87): 117.

4. *Rohwer Outpost*, June 2, 1945. Here and elsewhere in this chapter, I am indebted to the work of Andrew King, a former undergraduate at the University of York. His first-class research essay, drawn from archival materials I provided, is entitled "Ambivalence and Uncertainty: Responses to Camp Closing at the Rohwer Internment Centre," autumn term, 1999.

5. Roger Daniels, *Prisoners without Trial: Japanese Americans in World War II* (New York: Hill and Wang, 1993), 82.

6. For a systemic reading and periodic translations of the Japanese-language sections of both the *Denson Tribune* and *Rohwer Outpost*, I am grateful to Sahori Watanabe.

7. See, for example, series G, item H451, Still Picture Branch, WRAR, RG 210, NA.

8. Greg Robinson, *By Order of the President: FDR and the Internment of Japanese Americans* (Cambridge, MA: Harvard University Press, 2001), 218.

9. *Denson Tribune*, September 28, 1943; Lewis A. Sigler, "Solicitors Memorandum No. 15," July 10, 1943, series 1, folder 2, Jerome Relocation Center Collection (JRCC), University of Arkansas Libraries, Special Collections Division, Fayetteville, Arkansas (hereafter cited as UA); Dillon S. Myer, "The Relocation Program," box 1, folder 1, Robert A. Lefler Collection (LC), UA; Robinson, *By Order of the President*, 218–22.

10. *American Legion Magazine*, June 1943; *New York Times*, May 25, 1943; *Com-*

mon Ground, Summer 1943; all cited in "Bibliography on War Relocation Authority, Japanese, and Japanese Americans, October 1942–July 1943," series 1, folder 4, LC, UA; Robinson, *By Order of the President*, 236–37; *Denson Magnet*, April 1943, 3.

11. *Rohwer Outpost*, January 8, 1944.

12. Thomas James, *Exile Within: The Schooling of Japanese Americans, 1942–1945* (Cambridge, MA: Harvard University Press, 1987), 112–39; "Denson Schools Hand Book, Jerome Relocation Center," series 4, folder 1, Virginia Tidball Collection (TC), UA; Earl M. Finch, letter to H. Rex Lee, June 8, 1945, entry 16, box 489, folder 71.900H #2, WRAR, RG 210, NA; H. Rex Lee, letter to C. C. Holloway, entry 16, box 489. folder 71.900H #3, WRAR, RG 210, NA.

13. Akiko Higake, "Resettlement," n.d.; Katsuto Nakano, "Relocation," n.d.; Clara Hasegawa, "Relocation," August 12, 1943; Michiko Odate, "Resettlement," August 12, 1943; all in Tidball Student Essays, TC, UA.

14. *Rohwer Outpost*, September 27, 1944; Edgar Bernhard, letter to Ulys A. Lovell, December 31, 1943, series 1, folder 1, Ulys A. Lovell Collection, UA.

15. *Rohwer Outpost*, January 10, 20, March 3, April 7, 1945.

16. Herbert Sasaki, interview with author, Hattiesburg, MS, September 22, 1999; interview with Mark Santoki, n.p., n.d. (1999–2000); interview with Mississippi Oral History Program, October 23, 1998; *Los Angeles Times*, May 25, 2005.

17. Kazu Iijima, interview with Mark Santoki, n.p., February 2000. This story is also told in Glenn Omatsu, "Always a Rebel: An Interview with Kazu Iijima," *Amerasia Journal* 13 (1986–87): 95.

18. William T. Schmidt, "The Impact of the Camp Shelby Mobilization on Hattiesburg, Mississippi, 1940–1946" (PhD diss., University of Southern Mississippi, 1972), 100–101; Yuri Kochiyama, interview with Mark Santoki, Oakland, CA, 2 February 2000. On Kochiyama's later life and activism, see Diane C. Fujino, *Heartbeat of Struggle: The Revolutionary Life of Yuri Kochiyama* (Minneapolis: University of Minnesota Press, 2005), 110–311.

19. *Denson Tribune*, June 11, 1943.

20. Tsukamoto and Pinkerton, *We the People*, 174–75; *Rohwer Outpost*, January 13, 1945. In early 1943, a Joint Board consisting of US military and WRA officers issued a survey to Japanese American detainees entitled, "Application for Leave Clearance" that quickly became known as "the loyalty oath." Question 27 asked draft-age males if they would be willing "to serve in the armed forces of the United States." Question 28 asked detainees if they foreswear "any allegiance or obedience to the Japanese emperor." To many Japanese Americans, the "loyalty oath" was insulting because it questioned their loyalty to the only country most of them knew. Many Japanese Americans asked themselves why should they fight for the government that was imprisoning them and their families. How could they forswear allegiance to a foreign emperor to whom they had no allegiance? Those who answered "yes"

and "yes" to these questions were viewed by Japanese who answered "no" and "no" as collaborators with the government that was unjustly imprisoning them.

21. Tsukamoto and Pinkerton, *We the People*, 176–77.

22. Ibid., 178–79, 193, 275.

23. *Pacific Citizen*, February 19, 1944, March 3, 1945; Sawada, "After the Camps," 118; *Denson Tribune*, February 29, 1944.

24. Tsukamoto and Pinkerton, *We the People*, 191–93.

25. Ibid. For another example of suicide in the wake of incarceration, see *Pacific Citizen*, March 1, 1946.

26. Tsukamoto and Pinkerton, *We the People*, xi, 197, 202.

27. US War Relocation Authority, *The Relocation Program: A Guidebook for the Residents of Relocation Centers* (Washington, DC: Government Printing Office, 1943), 2, 4.

28. US War Relocation Authority, *The Evacuated People: A Quantitative Description* (Washington, DC: Government Printing Office, 1946), 8; US War Relocation Authority, *Administrative Highlights of the WRA Program* (Washington, DC: Government Printing Office, 1946), 6–7; US War Relocation Authority, *They're Friendly in New England: What New England Newspapers Say about Japanese Americans* (Washington, DC: Department of the Interior, n.d. [1944]); Richard Drinnon, *Keeper of Concentration Camps: Dillon S. Myer and American Racism* (Berkeley: University of California Press, 1987), 60.

29. *Rohwer Outpost*, January 31, February 14, 1945; Roger Daniels, *Concentration Camps: North American Japanese in the United States and Canada during World War II* (Malabar, FL: Robert E. Krieger, 1981), 167.

30. "WRA Bulletin: Relocation Opportunities," January 10, 1946, entry 16, box 489, folder 71.900H #3, WRAR, RG 210, NA.

31. Ibid.

32. Ibid. Gary Y. Okihiro, "Religion and Resistance in America's Concentration Camps," *Phylon* 45 (1984): 220, 229.

33. "WRA Bulletin: Relocation Opportunities." See Jeff Wiltse, *Contested Waters: A Social History of Swimming Pools in America* (Chapel Hill: University of North Carolina Press, 2007).

34. "WRA Bulletin: Relocation Opportunities."

35. Ibid. See Pete Daniel, *The Shadow of Slavery: Peonage in the South, 1901–1969* (1972; repr., Urbana: University of Illinois Press, 1990).

36. "WRA Bulletin: Relocation Opportunities." *Detroit Free Press*, February 16, 1943. On the protest statement by the Clarksville, Arkansas, branch of the American Association of University Women, see *Arkansas Gazette*, February 21, 1943.

37. *Denson Tribune*, September 24, 1943; D. S. Myer, memorandum to Project Directors, December 13, 1943, series 8, folder 3, LC, UA.

38. S. Muraoka, C. Sumida, and I. Takasugi. "Cooperative Colonization," August 1, 1944, part II, section 5, reel 145, Japanese American Evacuation and Resettlement Records (JAERR), University of California, Bancroft Library, Berkeley; "War Relocation Authority, Jerome Relocation Center, Report on Meeting in Project Director's Office, March 14, 1943," series 2, folder 3, US War Relocation Authority Jerome Relocation Center Records (USWRAJ), UA. A rival plan at Rohwer proposed three colonies on new lands in Colorado, Nebraska, and Texas. Jan Fielder Ziegler, *The Schooling of Japanese American Children at Relocation Centers during World War II: Miss Mabel Jamison and Her Teaching of Art at Rohwer, Arkansas* (Lewiston, NY: Edward Mellen, 2005), 190.

39. Muraoka et al., "Cooperative Colonization."

40. C. Calvin Smith, *War and Wartime Changes: The Transformation of Arkansas, 1940–1945* (Fayetteville: University of Arkansas Press, 1986), 74–75.

41. Violet Kazue de Cristoforo, ed., *May Sky, There Is Always Tomorrow: An Anthology of Japanese American Concentration Camp Kaiko Haiku* (Los Angeles: Sun and Moon Press, 1997), 145. See also Anna Hosticka Tamura, "Gardens below the Watchtower: Gardens and Meaning in World War II Japanese Incarceration Camps," *Landscape Journal* 23 (2004): 1–21.

42. De Cristoforo, *May Sky*, 95.

43. *Rohwer Outpost*, May 12, 1945.

Works Cited

Bernhard, Edgar. Letter to Ulys A. Lovell. December 31, 1943. Series 1, folder 1, Ulys A. Lovell Collection, University of Arkansas.

"Bibliography on War Relocation Authority, Japanese, and Japanese Americans, October 1942–July 1943." Series 1, folder 4, Robert A. Lefler Collection, University of Arkansas.

"The Closing of the Jerome Relocation Center." Part II, section 5, reel 138, War Relocation Authority Records, RG 210, National Archives.

Daniel, Pete. *The Shadow of Slavery: Peonage in the South, 1901–1969*. 1972. Reprint, Urbana: University of Illinois Press, 1990.

Daniels, Roger. *Concentration Camps: North America Japanese in the United States and Canada during World War II*. Malabar, FL: Robert E. Krieger, 1981.

———. *Prisoners without Trial: Japanese Americans in World War II*. New York: Hill and Wang, 1993.

De Cristoforo, Violet Kazue, ed., *May Sky, There Is Always Tomorrow: An Anthology of Japanese American Concentration Camp Kaiko Haiku*. Los Angeles: Sun and Moon Press, 1997.

"Denson Schools Hand Book, Jerome Relocation Center." Series 4, folder 1, Virginia Tidball Collection, University of Arkansas.

Drinnon, Richard. *Keeper of Concentration Camps: Dillon S. Myer and American Racism*. Berkeley: University of California Press, 1987.

Finch, Earl M. Letter to H. Rex Lee. June 8, 1945. Entry 16, box 489, folder 71, War Relocation Authority Records, RG 210, National Archives.

Fujino, Diane C. *Heartbeat of Struggle: The Revolutionary Life of Yuri Kochiyama*. Minneapolis: University of Minnesota Press, 2005.

Hasegawa, Clara. "Relocation." August 12, 1943, Tidball Student Essays, Tidball Collection, University of Arkansas.

Higake, Akiko. "Resettlement." N.d., Tidball Student Essays, Tidball Collection, University of Arkansas. James, Thomas. *Exile Within: The Schooling of Japanese Americans, 1942–1945*. Cambridge, MA: Harvard University Press, 1987.

Lee, H. Rex. Letter to C. C. Holloway. Entry 16, box 489, folder 71, War Relocation Authority Records, RG 210, National Archives.

Muraoka, S., C. Sumida, and I. Takasugi. "Cooperative Colonization." August 1, 1944. Part II, section 5, reel 145, Japanese American Evacuation and Resettlement Records, University of California, Bancroft Library, Berkeley.

Myer, Dillon S. Memorandum to Project Directors. December 13, 1943. Series 8, folder 3, Robert A. Lefler Collection, University of Arkansas.

———. "The Relocation Program." Box 1, folder 1, Robert A. Lefler Collection, University of Arkansas.

Nakano, Katsuto. "Relocation." N.d., Tidball Student Essays, Tidball Collection, University of Arkansas.

Odate, Michiko. "Resettlement." August 12, 1943, Tidball Student Essays, Tidball Collection, University of Arkansas.

Okihiro, Gary Y. "Religion and Resistance in America's Concentration Camps." *Phylon* 45 (1984): 220, 229.

Robinson, Greg. *By Order of the President: FDR and the Internment of Japanese Americans*. Cambridge, MA: Harvard University Press, 2001.

Sady, Rachel Reese. "War Relocation Authority, Community Analysis Section, July 14, 1944, Summary of Closing Procedures." Part II, section 5, reel 138, War Relocation Authority Records, RG 210, National Archives.

Sasaki, Herbert. Interview with Mississippi Oral History Program, University of Southern Mississippi, Hattiesburg, October 23, 1998.

Sawada, Mitziko. "After the Camps: Seabrook Farms, New Jersey, and the Resettlement of Japanese Americans, 1944–47." *Amerasia Journal* 13 (1986–87): 117.

Schmidt, William T. "The Impact of the Camp Shelby Mobilization on Hattiesburg, Mississippi, 1940–1946." PhD dissertation, University of Southern Mississippi, 1972.

Sigler, Lewis A. "Solicitors Memorandum No. 15." July 10, 1943. Series 1, folder 2, Jerome Relocation Center Collection, University of Arkansas Library, Special Collections Division, Fayetteville, Arkansas.

Smith, C. Calvin. *War and Wartime Changes: The Transformation of Arkansas, 1940–1945*. Fayetteville: University of Arkansas Press, 1986.

Tamura, Anna Hosticka. "Gardens below the Watchtower: Gardens and Meaning in World War II Japanese Incarceration Camps." *Landscape Journal* 23 (2004): 1–21.

Tsukamoto, Mary, and Elizabeth Pinkerton. *We the People: A Story of Internment in America*. Elk Grove, CA: Laguna, 1987.

US War Relocation Authority. *Administrative Highlights of the WRA Program*. Washington DC: Government Printing Office, 1946.

——. *The Evacuated People: A Quantitative Description*. Washington DC: Government Printing Office, 1946.

——. *The Relocation Program: A Guidebook for the Residents of Relocation Centers*. Washington, DC: Government Printing Office, 1943.

——. *They're Friendly in New England: What New England Newspapers Say about Japanese Americans*. Washington DC: Department of the Interior, n.d.

"War Relocation Authority, Jerome Relocation Center, Report on Meeting in Project Director's Office, March, 14, 1943." Series 2, folder, 3, US War Relocation Authority Jerome Relocation Center Records, University of Arkansas.

Weglyn, Michi Nishiura. *Years of Infamy: The Untold Story of America's Concentration Camps*. Seattle: University of Washington Press, 1996.

"WRA Bulletin: Relocation Opportunities." January 10, 1946. Entry 16, box 489, folder 71.900H #3, War Relocation Authority Records, RG 210, National Archives.

Ziegler, Fielder. *The Schooling of Japanese American Children at Relocation Centers during World War II: Miss Mabel Jamison and Her Teaching of Art at Rohwer, Arkansas*. Lewiston, NY: Edward Mellen, 2005.

4
Asian Immigration to Florida

Raymond A. Mohl

At the beginning of the twenty-first century, few states could challenge Florida's Sunbelt growth image and megastate status. Now the fourth largest state, following California, Texas, and New York, Florida had a dramatically rising demographic trajectory for most of the twentieth century. Indeed, between 1900 and 2000, the state's population growth rate never fell below 23.5 percent a decade; it was much higher than that during the boom years of the 1920s (52 percent), the 1950s (79 percent), and the 1970s (44 percent). Northern migration always provided a major source of Florida's population rise decade after decade, but after 1960, a substantial portion of the state's new population came as a consequence of immigration. According to the 1990 US census, the foreign-born, including several hundred thousand undocumented immigrants, comprised almost 13 percent of Florida's 12.9 million residents. Florida's foreign-born rose to 16.7 percent of total state population by 2000 and advanced still further to almost 19 percent of the state's 18.8 million residents in 2010. In recent decades, the growth rate of the immigrant population has matched or surpassed Florida's very high overall growth rate.[1]

The rapid rise of Florida's multicultural population generally has been attributed to the massive migrations of Cuban exiles to the Sunshine State since 1959. The heavy attention devoted to the outspoken and politically active Cuban exiles, who have mostly concentrated in south Florida, diverted journalistic and scholarly focus from the state's many other nationality groups and immigrant communities. In fact, however, as early as 1990 Florida's Cubans were outnumbered collectively by other Hispanic groups—Mexicans, Puerto Ricans, and Central/South Americans—all of whose numbers are now growing much more rapidly than the state's Cuban population. Many other immigrant newcomers also contributed to Florida's twentieth-century ethnic transformations. Several hundred thousand Haitians have made South Florida home in the past three decades. South Florida also has large concentrations of Nicaraguans, Jamaicans, Dominicans, Brazilians, French Canadians, and recently arrived Soviet Jews, as well as an aging cohort of East European Jewish retirees. Historically, Finns concentrated in Lake Worth, Palestinians in Jacksonville, Bahamians in Key West and Miami, Greeks in Tarpon Springs, Italians and Spaniards in Tampa. Over twenty thousand Maya Indians from Guatemala work as farm laborers and in nurseries and landscape jobs in the agricultural areas of southeast Florida. In the agricultural heart of rural central Florida, Mexicans of Aztec descent have come to dominate labor in the citrus and vegetable fields.[2]

Unknown to most observers, however, is that during the forty years after 1970, Asian newcomers emerged as the fastest-growing foreign-born or racial minority group in Florida. Of the 154,000 Asians who resided in Florida in 1990—triple the number in 1980—Filipinos, Chinese, and Asian Indians formed the largest groups, followed by Vietnamese, Koreans, Japanese, and Thais. By 2010, according to the US census, Florida's Asian population had surged to 455,000 (see table 4.1). When the census added Asians "in combination," that is multiracial people with some Asian heritage, the total number of Asians or part Asians in Florida totaled 571,244, representing an increase of 270 percent over twenty years. Filipinos, Indians, Vietnamese, and Chinese remained the largest Asian nationality groups, their numbers ranging between 40,700 and 62,300. The rising tide of Asians in Florida drives home the point that the Sunshine State has become—like California—a new multicultural cauldron, a state of great ethnic diversity and cultural change. The heavy concentration of attention on recent Cuban and Caribbean immigration has tended to mask other dramatic changes in Florida's demographic and cultural pattern. The diverse Asian immigration to Florida, especially after the immigration reform legislation of 1965, may in fact better reflect the migration trends and cultural patterns we might anticipate in future decades.[3]

Early Chinese Migration to Florida

The recent surge of Asian migrants and immigrants to Florida has some fascinating late nineteenth- and early twentieth-century precedents. In the post–Civil War era, southern state officials, business leaders, and large farming interests worried about the lack of an energetic and skilled labor force to move southern state economies forward. By the late nineteenth century, every southern state had established a bureau of immigration to attract workers from abroad and build the southern labor force. Thus, in Florida, state government, railroads, and big farmers promoted immigration as a major strategy for economic development. European immigrants, particularly Italians, gained special attention, since Florida was seen at the time as the "American Italy" because of its favor-

Table 4.1. Asian Population Increase in Florida, 1950–2010

Date	Number	% Increase
1950	1,142	—
1960	6,801	495.5
1970	21,772	220.1
1980	62,514	187.1
1990	154,302	146.8
2000	266,256	72.6
2010	454,821	70.8

Source: US Census, 1950–2010.

able climate, and Italian immigrants were perceived as experienced with citrus and vine culture. Similarly, Florida's growth advocates of the late nineteenth century singled out the importation of Chinese laborers as a solution for the perceived shortage of industrious agricultural laborers.[4]

Advocacy of Chinese immigration in post–Civil War Florida conformed to a wider pattern that prevailed in the South generally, as well as in the Pacific Coast region and in the British Caribbean. By the 1850s, for instance, British planters in British Guiana, Trinidad, Jamaica, Saint Lucia, and Barbados had responded to the end of slavery by importing Chinese immigrant contract laborers to work on sugar plantations. Such Spanish colonies as Cuba and Peru imported large numbers of Chinese indentured laborers as well, with as many as 125,000 Chinese workers brought to Cuba alone. The Chinese migration pattern extended to the United States following the Burlingame Treaty of 1868, which authorized the admission of Chinese immigrant laborers. The 1870 census recorded some sixty-three thousand Chinese people in the United States, a number that rose to over 105,000 by 1880. There was a high degree of "coming and going," however, as immigration historian Roger Daniels has pointed out. Perhaps as many as 300,000 Chinese immigrants arrived in America prior to passage of the Chinese Exclusion Act of 1882, although many ultimately returned to their homeland. Seeking better economic opportunities, most of the Chinese immigrants to the United States worked in the American west in California mines and agriculture and on the transcontinental railroads.[5]

Several thousand Chinese workers also filtered into agricultural and railroad work in the American South. Some came by way of Cuba, others from California or directly from China. During this period, a San Francisco labor contractor, Cornelius Koopmanschap, touted the advantages of Chinese labor at an 1869 southern commercial convention in Memphis. Koopmanschap later facilitated the importation of several hundred Chinese workers to Louisiana, Alabama, and

Georgia, primarily railroad workers on the Alabama and Chattanooga Railroad. This early labor migration occurred in the midst of a spirited post–Civil War debate about the appropriateness of imported Asian workers that took place in *Harper's Weekly* and *The Nation*, as well as in southern business journals such as *De Bow's Review*, *Southern Farmer*, and *Southern Cultivator*.[6]

Florida was still a raw, lightly settled, and mostly undeveloped state in the Reconstruction Era, with a population of about 140,000 in 1879, almost entirely distributed through the northern tier of the state stretching between Jacksonville and Pensacola. An emerging economy based on lumber, citrus, cotton plantations, phosphate mining, land drainage, and railroad construction all required a large work force of manual laborers. During this period, some white Floridians turned enthusiastically toward imported Chinese workers as a panacea for the state's labor needs, especially as African American mobility after the end of slavery left the plantations without a reliable labor supply. Reflecting the contemporary interest in Chinese immigration stirred by the Memphis commercial convention, the editor of the *Florida Times-Union* predicted in 1869 that "pig-tails, almond eyes, and chop-sticks will soon be common" in Florida. Editorial optimism failed to produce the expected wave of new immigrant workers, but interest in Chinese immigration persisted. A decade later George M. Barbour, author of an 1882 Florida guidebook, *Florida for Tourists, Invalids, and Settlers*, opined that Chinese immigrants could satisfy the demand for a stable labor supply in the postwar era. The Chinese as a people, Barbour wrote, were neat, quiet, thrifty, orderly, unobtrusive, and "in every way commendable." Although Florida had few Chinese residents at the time, Barbour expected that these Asian workers would soon be attracted to Florida: "Everywhere I found the people favoring Chinese immigration." Barbour noted especially "a general desire to replace the colored labor with Chinese labor." By the early twentieth century, a fairly extensive regional literature, particularly in the farm journal *Florida Agriculturist*, was still promoting Chinese immigration for plantation work and other labor needs. Black workers "were flocking to the cities," the journal's editor remarked in September 1904, and it was "practically impossible to get white immigrants to settle here [in Florida]." A year later, in October 1905, the *Florida Agriculturist* agreed "that the farmers of the country are justified in uniting in a demand that the Chinese exclusion law be repealed."[7]

For the most part, these optimistic assessments of the availability and usefulness of Chinese immigration were never fully transformed into reality in late nineteenth-century Florida. However, a small number of Chinese workers did come to Florida during these years, some by way of California, others by way of Cuba. They worked initially on plantations, in lumber and turpentine camps, and in railroad construction. The US census reported 108 Chinese residents of Florida in 1890 and 120 in 1900—almost certainly a considerable undercount, since it is unlikely that census takers would have encountered or recorded transient Chinese work gangs in rural areas. But the experiment with Chinese contract labor was plagued with difficulties. In one case in 1906, shortly after a Chinese work crew was contracted for labor at the Paradise Farms turpentine camp near Gainesville, the new workers went on strike in a dispute over hours, working conditions, and wages. By that time, many white Floridians had also become increasingly susceptible to the rising anti-immigration paranoia over the "yellow peril" that had begun to sweep the nation by the turn of the twentieth century. Nativism and racism soon terminated the contemporary discourse about the need for new immigrants of any background. Racial and religious differences, along with widely believed charges of immorality, gambling, and crime, raised concerns about the ability of the Chinese to assimilate to the American mainstream. The imposition of rigorous policies of racial segregation in the South by the 1890s created a dilemma for the nonwhite Chinese residents, as well as for white Floridians who sought to maintain the color line. Thus, by the beginning of the twentieth century, exclusionary policies had become the rule and the panacea of large-scale Chinese immigration had run its course in Florida.[8]

Despite the failure of ambitious plans for Chinese labor immigration, a permanent Chinese presence in Florida—albeit a very small presence—had been established by the early twentieth century. Chinese immigrants gradually filtered into Florida's major cities, where they established entrepreneurial niches in laundries, truck farming, small grocery stores, and eventually restaurants. Some left the work gangs for better economic opportunities in Jacksonville, Tampa, Pensacola, and later Miami; others migrated to Florida from northern Chinatowns in New York or Boston, and still others came from Cuba, which had daily steamship service to Tampa beginning in the 1890s. Chain migration over time supplemented and sustained these small urban communities of Chinese residents in Florida.[9]

The Chinese laundry tradition began in gold-rush-era San Francisco, where the disproportionate number of males created entrepreneurial opportunities in providing household and domestic service such as washing, ironing, cooking, cleaning, and other services. The laundry business required little capital or machinery, only the commitment to work hard and long. By the 1870s, according to Paul Siu's classic study *The Chinese Laundryman*, San Francisco had over five hundred Chinese laundries. As in California and elsewhere, Chinese immigrants in Florida found economic opportunity in the urban economy through small family-run laundries.[10] As early as 1889, for instance, Jacksonville had nine Chinese laundries. By the early twentieth century, Jacksonville's Chinese laundries numbered twenty-five, while Tampa had fifteen, Key West twelve, and Pensacola three.

In the early twentieth century Chinese Floridians discovered other economic niches as well. A few established truck farms near Jacksonville, Tampa, Miami, and elsewhere, growing mostly Chinese vegetables for restaurants and groceries in the northeastern states. Some of these Chinese truck farmers had originally farmed in the northeastern United States, supplying groceries and restaurants in the Chinatowns of New York, Boston, and Philadelphia. As early as 1907, for instance, a Chinese "agricultural colony" was established on the rural fringes of Jacksonville. By the 1940s, numerous small Chinese truck farmers persisted in the Jacksonville area; the 1940 census reported eighty-six Chinese farmers in the Jacksonville metropolitan region. Similarly, in the years prior to 1950, three Chinese families opened Chinese vegetable farms in the Sarasota/Bradenton area on Florida's west coast, initially to provide winter vegetables to the Chinese market in the Northeast. Later, as the number of Chinese restaurants grew in Florida, the market for Chinese farm produce was much closer.[11]

At least one Chinese immigrant, Lue Gim Gong, achieved success in Florida citrus. Departing for California from a South China village as a teenager in the late 1860s, Lue had been recruited in San Francisco in 1870 along with several dozen others as strikebreakers in a shoe factory in North Adams, Massachusetts, where he was befriended by relatives of Anson Burlingame, the American minister to China in the 1860s, who later negotiated the Burlingame Treaty with China on issues of trade and immigration. During winters, Lue traveled with the Burlingames to a citrus grove they owned in DeLand, Florida, and he later inherited the citrus property. Deeply interested in plant science, Lue experimented with new varieties of oranges, grapefruit, and tomatoes, developing freeze-resistant oranges and grapefruit and helping to establish Florida's emerging citrus industry. By the early twentieth century, Lue had become a horticulturist of some note, renowned as the "Chinese Burbank," a reference to the famous horticulturist Luther Burbank.[12]

Chinese immigrants in Florida also found an economic niche in small grocery stores, especially in black neighborhoods that were ignored by white retail merchants. Research on Chinese communities in Mississippi and Georgia has concluded that "the Chinese filled a strategic position between the white and black population by providing goods and services to blacks." The Chinese grocery store tradition also became common in Florida, where the Chinese served a "middleman" function in the black community. City directories reveal that by 1906 Jacksonville, Tampa, Miami, and Key West all had several Chinese groceries.[13]

The grocery store tradition in Florida took on new dimensions during the 1920s when two Chinese pioneers, Joe Wing and Joe Fred Gong, settled in Miami and opened a small grocery store in the city's African American community. The partners named Joe had both immigrated from China as teenagers to join their fathers who had already set up laundry businesses in America—one in Boston and one in Georgia. Both arrived in Miami in the mid-1920s intending to set up laundries in the midst of the South Florida real estate and economic boom. But laundry work in Miami was already dominated by earlier Chinese arrivals. Instead, the two Joes created an alternative economic niche for themselves in the grocery business in the black section of Miami. Joe's Market, as they called their store, had little competition from white merchants. Later, through chain migration, sons, uncles, nephews, and other kin arrived in Miami, almost all from a few villages in South China. New groceries, all called Joe's Market, were established for the newcomers, often using loans from Chinese trade or kinship organizations. By the mid-1960s, some thirty-eight separate Joe's Market groceries served Miami's black community. However, these Chinese groceries eventually suffered from rising crime and civil disturbances after the mid-1960s, as well as from price competition from large supermarket chains. Some stores were burned out in Miami's 1968 ghetto riot; others eventually were closed or sold to other merchants. Second- and third-generation family members abandoned the family business, went to college, began professional careers, and moved up the American economic and social ladder. Although the Chinese grocery store tradition has died out now in Miami, over some forty years the entrepreneurs of the first immigrant generation found an effective path to economic opportunity through these neighborhood institutions. For many decades, Joe's Market groceries also served an important mediating or "middleman" functions between black and white Miamians.[14]

The numbers of Chinese residents in early twentieth-century Florida remained relatively small. Indeed, there were only about 5,000 in the entire South in 1940 and a little over 10,000 in 1950. Florida had a disproportionately small number of the southern total; the US census reported 214 Chinese people in Florida in 1940 and 429 in 1950. The number of early Japanese immigrants was even smaller—about 1,000 in the southern states in 1940 and about 3,000 in 1950. In Florida, they numbered only 154 in 1940 and 238 in 1950. Yet, curiously, Florida was the site of an unusual Japanese agricultural colony, established in 1904 near present-day Boca Raton.[15]

Early Japanese Migration to Florida

Most turn-of-the-century Japanese immigrants to the United States came as contract laborers, working in Hawaii or in the Pacific West, although a few Japanese agricultural colonies had been established in Texas. Still other Japanese workers went in substantial numbers to Brazil and Peru as contract laborers on coffee, cotton, and sugar plantations. However, the Florida agricultural frontier seemed attractive to Kamosu Jo Sakai, an enterprising young man who had received a Western education in Japan and converted to Christianity. Many

Western-educated Japanese of the late nineteenth century, men like Sakai, experienced the rapid modernization of Japan and looked to the United States as a model of Western reform. As in Europe and China, many young and ambitious men sought better economic opportunities through emigration. For those reasons, Sakai came to the United States, initially to study business at New York University. In 1903 he arrived in Jacksonville with ambitious plans for a Japanese agricultural colony in Florida. Surprisingly, Jacksonville businessmen and even Florida's governor looked favorably upon the plan, apparently hoping thereby to stimulate Florida's agricultural development. Declining the offer from three North Florida counties of one thousand acres of free land, Sakai instead purchased land on credit in South Florida owned by the Model Land Company, the land-development arm of Henry Flagler's Florida East Coast Railway. Sakai returned to Japan in early 1904 to recruit colonists for the planned settlement. The ongoing Russo-Japanese War interfered with recruitment efforts, and problems with American immigration authorities created other delays, but ultimately about twenty Japanese settlers arrived in South Florida by the end of 1904. These were not typical Japanese immigrants with farming backgrounds, single men who came as temporary contract laborers. By contrast, most were well educated, some businessmen and college students, and many graduates of the Doshisha College in Kyoto. Jo Sakai was one of those graduates of this modernizing, Christian college that found its model for the ideal future in the United States.[16]

The new Japanese colony—called Yamato (the ancient name for Japan)—had initial difficulties. Sakai sought to build a settlement with families committed to a permanent future in Florida. Yet the first colonists were bachelor college students and businessmen, interested in Western culture, not the family pioneers Sakai hoped to recruit. The land chosen needed extensive, back-breaking clearing before any planting could begin. The summer heat and rains were discouraging. Sakai and his colleagues at first planned to cultivate rice, tea, and silk, but soil and climate conditions forced a switch to planting pineapples, along with tomatoes, beans, green peppers, squash, and eggplant. But by 1906, the Yamato Colony's fortunes took a turn for the better. Returns from the pineapple crop exceeded all expectations. The FEC Railway built a station near Yamato, permitting the Japanese farmers to ship their produce easily and quickly to northern markets. News of the colony's early success spread to Japan, encouraging others to join Sakai and the original settlers, although the newcomers were mostly farmers rather than college-educated Japanese with families. By 1908, over forty settlers resided at Yamato, and by the 1920s that number had risen to over sixty. A pineapple blight that struck in 1908, along with competition from Cuban pineapple growers, set the colony back temporarily. But Yamato's growers adapted to changing circumstances by planting more vegetables, which over time provided a lucrative income. By the 1920s, in the midst of the Florida real estate boom, several of the Japanese farmers also went into the real estate business or established landscaping firms. Although Jo Sakai died in 1923 and many settlers eventually returned to Japan, the Yamato colony quietly persisted with a few dozen settlers into the 1930s. During World War II, the FBI kept Yamato's Japanese residents under surveillance, although they were never interned as in the American West. Much of the Yamato land was confiscated by the federal government during the war for an Army Air Corps air training base. A few of the Japanese people remained in the Boca Raton area until the 1970s, but the old Yamato farmland has given way to modern subdivisions and commercial development, the Boca Raton Airport, and portions of the campus of Florida Atlantic University. However, one of the persisting Japanese settlers, George Sukaji Morikami, through his will, donated his land holdings to the nearby City of Delray Beach for a public park. Today, the popular Morikami Park and Museum, with its regular Asian festivals and other celebrations of Asian culture, serves as a reminder of the early Japanese presence in South Florida.[17]

Late Twentieth-Century Migration and Settlement Patterns

In the late nineteenth and early twentieth century Chinese and Japanese immigrations to Florida represent distinct and discrete episodes in US immigration history. Those early experiences—both in their origins and in their outcomes—seem distinctly different from the pattern of Asian immigration to Florida in the late twentieth century and after. This more recent Asian immigration to the Sunshine State stemmed primarily from three separate sources. First, US military involvement in Asia and the Pacific region generally brought diverse Asian newcomers to Florida: war brides or military spouses, military employees, and refugees. Second, and more importantly, federal immigration legislation in 1965 abolished the national origins quota system, which had heavily favored European immigrants. Under provisions of the new legislation, education, professional skills, and family reunification became the new standards for admission to the United States—a policy that over time dramatically shifted the base of American immigration from Europe to Latin America, the Caribbean, and especially Asia and the nations of the Pacific Rim. This shift in immigration policy led to a rapid rise in the nation's Asian population, from about 1.2 million in 1965 to 10.2 million in 2000 and 14.7 million in 2010. Finally, a secondary, internal migration of newcomers searching for better economic opportunities has been reflected in a rapid increase in the numbers of Asians in Florida, and in the Sunbelt states generally, since 1970. All three of these factors produced new immigrant streams to Florida after 1945.[18]

Census returns since 1960 have recorded the rising number of Asians in Florida, with the largest increases coming in the final decades of the twentieth century.

Table 4.2. Ten Most Numerous Asian Groups in Florida, 1970–2010*

Group	1970	1990	2010
Filipino	5,092	31,945	62,348
Asian Indian	—	31,457	58,359
Vietnamese	—	16,346	40,714
Chinese	3,133	30,737	40,691
Korean	—	12,404	19,705
Pakistani	—	2,800	11,468
Japanese	4,090	8,505	10,406
Thai	—	4,457	9,915
Iranian	—	—	8,371
Bangaladeshi	—	—	7,042

*Data provided for ten largest groups, as reflected in 2010 Census. Source: US Census, 1970, 1990, 2010.

In 1970, the total Asian population in Florida, including both foreign-born and native-born of foreign or mixed parentage, stood at 21,772. This number included 5,092 Filipinos, 4,090 Japanese, and 3,133 Chinese. By 1990, Florida's Asian foreign stock population soared over 600 percent to 154,302. Filipinos and Chinese remained among the top groups, now joined by Asian Indians. The advancing trend of Asian immigration to Florida continued over the following two decades, reaching 454,821 at the time of the 2010 US census. The number of Vietnamese rose rapidly during this period, while Filipinos, Asian Indians, and Chinese retained top ranking in Florida. Koreans, Pakistanis, Japanese, Thai, Iranians, and Bangladeshis filled out the remaining places among the ten largest Asian groups in Florida (see tables 4.1 and 4.2). Several trends stand out: Filipinos remained the largest Asian group throughout the entire period; the Japanese population, relatively large in the early postwar era, grew very slowly compared to other groups, while the Vietnamese group surged after 1970; and finally, after decades of post-1965 new immigration, the Asian population of Florida had become highly diversified by the early twenty-first century.

Since the 1960s, the new Asian immigrants have concentrated heavily in Florida's eight largest urban counties: Miami-Dade, Broward, Duval, Palm Beach, Orange, Hillsborough, Pinellas, and Seminole (see table 4.3). In 1990, just over two-thirds of Florida's Asians resided in those urban counties. By 2010, according to the US census, the percentage of Asians who lived in the large urban counties had risen to 75 percent. Big cities such as Miami, Jacksonville, Orlando, Tampa, Saint Petersburg, Fort Lauderdale, and West Palm Beach provided the

Table 4.3. Asians in Florida, by Urban County, 1970–2010*

County	1970	1980	1990	2000	2010
Broward	1,355	4,923	17,130	36,581	56,795
Orange	824	3,624	13,994	30,033	56,581
Hillsborough	1,040	3,876	11,379	21,947	42,076
Miami-Dade	5,379	14,069	26,307	31,753	37,669
Duval	2,555	6,107	12,940	21,137	35,901
Palm Beach	1,011	2,905	9,020	17,127	31,100
Pinellas	1,168	3,385	9,790	18,984	27,146
Seminole	120	1,463	4,843	9,115	15,692

*Data provided for eight urban counties with the largest Asian population, as reflected in the 2010 Census. Source: US Census, 1970–2010.

kind of economic opportunities, kinship communities, and cultural connections that attracted newcomers from the Pacific Rim and internal migrants relocating from other states.

Recent census reports, especially American Community Survey data for 2009, revealed notable variations in group settlement patterns. As early as the 1950s, for instance, Filipinos had begun to concentrate in Jacksonville and Pensacola, and in 2009 they remained by far the largest Asian group in the Jacksonville and Pensacola metropolitan areas. Chinese were the dominant Asian group in the Miami metropolitan area in the early postwar decades, but more recently they have been surpassed by Asian Indians. Asian Indians also dominate in the Orlando and Tampa metro areas. Surprisingly, Vietnamese have settled in far larger numbers in Orlando and Tampa than in Pensacola, where they have a more visible presence in the fishing and shrimping industry. And the Japanese, who were more dominant than the Chinese or Filipinos in many urban counties in the early postwar era, have not increased in numbers in any substantial way since 1960; in 2009, the Japanese barely appear among the largest six groups in metropolitan Florida (see table 4.4).[19]

Although the census statistics provide the best measure we have over time of the changing Asian immigration pattern, we must be sensitive to the possibility of substantial undercounts of Asians as well as of other immigrants to Florida in recent decades. A south Miami-Dade County farming community of several hundred Sikhs from India was somehow entirely missed by the 1990 census, as were several thousand Bangladeshis in Palm Beach County. In 1996, one Asian spokesperson in Miami claimed that the number of Asians in South Florida was as much as 50 percent higher than that reported in the 1990 census. Thus, cen-

Table 4.4. Top Asian Groups in Florida's Largest Metropolitan Areas, 2009

Miami Metro		Tampa Metro		Orlando Metro		Jacksonville	
Indian	40,584	Indian	21,458	Indian	23,313	Filipino	15,941
Chinese	25,777	Vietnamese	14,143	Vietnamese	12,400	Indian	6,986
Filipino	16,985	Filipino	12,298	Filipino	12,234	Chinese	4,032
Vietnamese	12,370	Chinese	8,392	Chinese	10,651	Vietnamese	3,596
Korean	5,882	Korean	4,657	Korean	3,732	Korean	2,610
Pakistani	5,013	Thai	2,355	Japanese	2,353	Cambodian	2,279

Source: US Census, American Community Survey, 2009.

sus statistics must be used carefully, but they nevertheless provide measureable evidence of demographic change over time.[20]

In retrospect, World War II set the United States on a new path in the Pacific Rim region, ultimately with major consequences for Asians already in the United States and for future Asian immigration. As ethnic historian Ronald Takaki has noted in his study *Strangers from a Different Shore* (1989), the war was "a crucial dividing line," as various Asian American groups were pulled "into a whirlpool of chaos and change." Japanese Americans were incarcerated in detention camps while Chinese, Filipinos, and Koreans provided strong support for the war effort. Subsequently, Congress repealed the Chinese exclusion law, opened immigration under the quota system for Filipinos, Chinese, Koreans, and Asian Indians, and permitted the naturalization of Asian immigrants. In California, where many Asians had settled, restrictions on alien land ownership were ended. The war and the subsequent occupation of Japan also brought American servicemen into contact with Asian populations for the first time since the turn-of-the-century conflict in the Philippines. Later wars in Korea and Vietnam had similar consequences.[21]

The new role of the United States in Asia and the long-term military presence in the region began to reshape postwar immigration patterns to the United States. Thousands of US servicemen brought home Asian spouses from Japan, China, Korea, and the Philippines. The War Brides Act of 1945 permitted alien wives (although not Japanese wives) to enter the United States outside the quota system. The McCarran-Walter Act of 1952 repealed the anti-Japanese Oriental Exclusion Act of 1924, thus facilitating the immigration of Japanese spouses of American military personnel. The numbers arriving were substantial. During the 1950s, for instance, about 46,000 Japanese citizens immigrated to the United States but over 39,000, or about 86 percent, of them were women, mostly military spouses. One study suggests that World War II war brides may have numbered as many as 100,000. Tens of thousands followed in the wake of subsequent wars in Korea and Vietnam. Over the entire period from 1947 to 1975, war brides and military spouses from Japan totaled 66,681, from Korea 28,205, from the Philippines 51,747, from Thailand 11,166, and from Vietnam 8,040.[22]

American military presence in the Pacific had other consequences, as well. Filipinos had begun working in the US Navy, mostly as mess stewards and attendants, after World War I. By 1930, over four thousand Filipinos were serving in the US Navy or on US merchant marine ships, while thousands of others were working in navy yards in the United States or as longshoremen in US ports. After World War II and the achievement of Philippine independence in 1945, the navy continued to recruit Filipinos for domestic work on ships and for shore duty at naval bases. By 1970, some fourteen thousand Filipinos were at work on US Navy ships and in American naval ports, including naval bases in Florida. In addition, a persisting American military presence in the Philippines until the 1990s, particularly Clark Air Base and Subic Bay Naval Base, led to a large number of military spouses over fifty years following World War II.[23]

Finally, the fallout from World War II and subsequent American involvement in Asian wars has produced new refugee communities in the United States. After the "fall" of China to Communist forces in 1949, up to 2,000 Chinese "refugees" were admitted to the United States annually; during the 1950s, about 32,500 Chinese legally entered the United States. The Vietnam War had much bigger consequences for American immigration, as large numbers of Vietnamese, Cambodians, Laotians, and Hmong entered the United States under a special refugee status. By 1985, for instance, some 634,000 Vietnamese refugees had settled in the United States along with 218,000 Laotians, 161,000 Cambodians, and over 60,000 Hmong. In a variety of ways, then, US military action in the Pacific region had long-term consequences for Asian immigration to the United States. Immigration historian David M. Reimers notes that "the presence of American troops in Asia during and after World War II, especially in Japan, China, and Korea, was a key factor in explaining South and East Asian immigration from 1945 to 1965."[24]

The national immigration patterns flowing from American military activities in the Pacific region were mirrored directly in Florida. With the exception of the Yamato Colony, the Japanese population in Florida had always been quite small. As late as 1950, there were only 238 Japanese residents in the entire state. During the 1950s, however, the state's Japanese population shot up more than sixfold to 1,591. Moreover, almost two-thirds of the Japanese immigrants in Florida were women, clearly suggesting the impact of arriving Japanese war brides and military spouses. The imbalance in the Japanese sex ratio continued over the next several decades. By 1980, some 70 percent of the 5,667 Japanese in Florida were women. The pattern was less common among Florida's Chinese and Filipinos in the postwar era since the sex ratio favored males in both cases by 1960, the first census in which the large number of military spouses from the 1950s would have been recorded.[25]

The military role of the United States in the Pacific had still other demographic implications for Florida. Two large US naval bases—in Jacksonville and in Pensacola—essentially served as way stations for Filipino immigrants to Florida. At least since 1960, Filipinos have been the largest single Asian group in the Sunshine State, although their dominance in relation to other groups began tapering off by the 1980s. By 2010, some sixty-two thousand Filipinos called Florida home, most of them concentrated in the state's four big metropolitan areas. In 1990, some 7,300 Filipinos had concentrated in Duval County, home of the US naval base in Jacksonville. Another 3,600 people from the Philippines had settled in the Pensacola metropolitan area, drawn by work at the US Naval Air Station there. Since that time, Filipinos have spread throughout the state, especially to three other big metropolitan areas—Miami, Tampa, and Orlando. By 2010, over 90 percent of Florida's Filipinos resided in the state's four large metros (see table 4.4). Many of the Filipino newcomers since 1970 have come as a consequence of the 1965 immigration reform, which permitted family reunification as well as entry of people with desirable skills, such as nurses, doctors, and engineers. In South Florida, for instance, the shortage of trained nurses in the early 1970s prompted Miami Beach's Mount Sinai Hospital to place job ads in the *Manila Times*. Within a decade, Mount Sinai employed almost two hundred Filipino nurses, many of whom lived nearby in dormitory-style residences subsidized by the hospital. Other Florida medical centers employed similar staffing strategies.[26]

The immigration of Asian wartime or postwar refugees provides still another explanation for the shifting composition of Florida's population in the second half of the twentieth century. The number of Chinese in Florida more than tripled during the 1950s to almost 1,600, some of whom were military spouses. It was the Vietnam War, however, that brought the greatest number of Asian war refugees to Florida. There were over seven thousand Vietnamese residents in Florida in 1980, and more than sixteen thousand in 1990, and almost forty-one thousand in 2010 (see table 4.2). In Miami, local churches and the regional office of the International Rescue Committee sponsored numerous Vietnamese refugees after the fall of Saigon in 1975. By the late 1970s, so many Vietnamese refugees crowded a section of Miami's Little Havana that for a time it was known as "Little Saigon." One large apartment complex reportedly housed as many as three hundred Vietnamese families. Over time, these refugees drifted away from this concentrated settlement, dispersing throughout the Miami metropolitan area. In the Florida Panhandle, Eglin Air Force Base served as a Vietnamese refugee center for almost two decades after the Vietnam War. Attracted by the climate and access to deep waters of the Gulf of Mexico, Vietnamese refugees, many of whom were fishermen and shrimpers, settled permanently in the nearby Gulf Coast cities of Pensacola and Panama City, numbering several thousand by 1990. However, even larger numbers of Vietnamese have settled in metropolitan Miami, Orlando, and Tampa (see table 4.4). Laotians, Cambodians, and Thais, as well as Amerasian children of Vietnam-era GIs, have also demonstrated a presence in Florida—mostly as a consequence of American military action in Southeast Asia in the 1960s and 1970s.[27]

New Asian immigration to Florida has other sources, as well. The Immigration Act of 1965 abolished the restrictive immigration legislation of the 1920s and tossed out the discriminatory quota system. Instead, the new immigration reform substituted family reunification and desired training, skills, and professions as new requisites for admission to the United States. Because of pressure from American labor unions, about 80 percent of new admissions initially stemmed from family reunification, while fewer than 20 percent of admissions went to those with employable skills. At the time of this new legislation, few political leaders or immigration reformers anticipated that the new immigration policy ultimately would open the gates to large numbers of Asian or Latin immigrants. But that is exactly what happened, as the family reunification preferences began to kick in during the 1970s and after.[28]

Once the "second-wave" Asian immigrants, who arrived in the postwar years or those who came singly after 1965, became citizens, they were eligible to bring close relatives to the United States. And once those newcomers became naturalized after five years or more, additional relatives became eligible for entry. The provision permitting entry of professionals and skilled technicians also had an impact. By 1980, more than nine thousand Filipino physicians and perhaps as many as fifty thousand Filipino nurses had come to the United States. In 1995 alone, over 5,300 Filipino nurses were admitted to the country under a special visa category. Similarly, Asian Indians made up one of the fastest growing new immigrant groups by the mid-1970s, when about twenty thousand were arriving each year; about 75 percent of the Asian Indians were engineers, scientists, professors, and other highly skilled technicians. Although not intended or anticipated, the Immigration Act of 1965 facilitated a dramatic expansion of Asian immigration by the 1970s.[29]

Since the Immigration Act of 1965, Florida's Asian population surged over the next four decades. In the large urban counties and metropolitan areas, the Asian population doubled and tripled or more during that forty-year period (see table 4.3). In the Orlando metropolitan area, for instance, the Asian population grew from under one thousand in 1970 to well over eighty-five thousand in 2010. In Alachua County, home of the University of Florida, the Asian population rose from under five hundred in 1970 to over thirteen thousand in 2010—much of this increase stemming from the arrival of Asian professors, students, and medical personnel at the university's medical school and large teaching hospital. Census counts from 1970 to 2010 reveal similar demographic growth profiles for the Asian population in virtually every one of Florida's large metropolitan areas.[30]

Many of Florida's new Asian residents arrived directly from their homeland. But clearly not all, or perhaps not even most, of the post-1965, second-wave Asian newcomers to Florida are direct immigrants to the Sunshine State. A large portion of the new immigrants are "secondary migrants"—those who have migrated internally within the United States in search of better business or professional opportunities or for some other reason. Florida is the fourth largest state, with an expanding population and a growing job market in service industries, tourism, technology, health care, and entrepreneurial businesses. The state has been on the receiving end of a massive internal Sunbelt migration since the end of World War II. It is not surprising that energetic and entrepreneurial Asian immigrants were attracted by the growth prospects of one of the largest Sunbelt states. Many of Florida's Vietnamese residents, for instance, came to Florida by way of California or Texas. Similarly, many Asian Indians first arrived in California, where, among other things, they often found an economic niche in the business of running small motels, especially franchise operations along major highways. Later, they spread out into other parts of the country, including Florida and the South. According to the Asian American Hotel Operators Association, by 1994 almost four hundred of Florida's hotels and motels were run by Indians. Thus, the tremendous magnetic attraction of the Sunbelt has affected both native-born Americans and newly arriving Asian Americans.[31]

Asian Life and Culture in Florida

Florida may be thought of as a center of Hispanic life and culture, but considerable Asian immigration since the 1970s has brought a diversity of new ethnic cultures to the Sunshine State. In Miami-Dade County, Hialeah may be 93 percent Hispanic, but as early as 1990 the city had become home to more than one thousand Asians, many of whom shopped at the Saigon Supermarket, ran small businesses and restaurants, and attended local Asian cultural events. In North Miami, some twenty-five Chinese businesses have clustered along several blocks of the city's main commercial thoroughfare. Miami Beach hosts several Filipino groceries serving the local community, especially Mount Sinai Hospital's nurses. Miami's Korean community supports several grocery stores and restaurants, as well as Baptist and Lutheran churches. Almost fifty-seven thousand Asians now reside in Broward County, some of them clustered in a Lauderdale Lakes neighborhood called "Little Asia," where Vietnamese and Chinese signs outnumber English on storefronts and strip shopping centers. In south Miami-Dade County, the Central City Grocery and the Trung My Supermarket, operated respectively by Chinese people from Hong Kong and Chinese people from Vietnam, serves a diverse Asian clientele, providing popular items such as herbal medicines, frozen fish cakes, roast duck take-out, and Chinese video rentals. Groceries, restaurants, video stores, beauty shops, insurance agents, and doctors' offices all provide a sense of ethnic and cultural identity. A biweekly Korean newspaper, the bilingual *Korean American Journal of Florida*, published in Miami since 1993 and with news bureaus in Jacksonville, Tampa, and Orlando, gets mailed to several thousand Korean households in Florida. In the 1990s, a Vietnamese paper, *Florida Viet Bao*, began publishing in Pembroke Pines. Chinese, Korean, and Japanese language schools serve immigrant children in Jacksonville, Coral Gables, Miami, Fort Lauderdale, Boca Raton, and Kissimmee. In Orlando, the Florida Vietnamese Buddhist Association operates the Long Van Temple for the city's growing Vietnamese community. In Jacksonville, an institutionally well-developed Filipino community supports a variety of cultural activities, including a popular Rizal Day parade.[32]

Chinese residents of Florida have created an especially vibrant ethnic cultural life in their new home. For instance, ten separate Chinese organizations in Miami sponsor an annual Chinese New Year Festival. The *Florida Chinese News*, published in Miami since 1986, has a staff of fifteen and a circulation of ten thousand. It competes with several other Chinese-language papers in South Florida, including the *United Chinese News of Florida*, *Asian Spectrum*, and the *Overseas Chinese News*. The latter paper, begun in 1990, has a weekly circulation of over ten thousand, mostly distributed free at Chinese restaurants and grocery stores, but large batches are shipped to Jacksonville, Tallahassee, Tampa, and Orlando; an additional three thousand copies are sent weekly to Atlanta to serve the Chinese community there. All of the Chinese papers combine local and Florida coverage with news from China, Hong Kong, and Taiwan. In Miami for a time in the 1990s Chinese people from Jamaica published their own monthly magazine, the *Dragon*, which offered both community news and discussion of cultural issues. One of the largest Asian groups in the three-county Miami metropolitan area, the South Florida Chinese have a wide institutional network, both to aid in adjustment to American society and to retain Chinese culture, especially across generations. As a spokesman for the Chinese School of Boca Raton noted, "we want the second generation to experience the Chinese culture and learn about our heritage."[33]

Among the Asian immigrants, no group had a faster growth rate since the 1970s than Asian Indians. In 1990, more than one-third, or about twelve thousand, of Florida's Asian Indians lived in metro Miami. Two decades later, the number of Asian Indians in the three South Florida counties had soared to over 40,600. Most of Florida's Asian Indians are professionals or small business proprietors who have found economic success in America. Many still cling to old country cultural ways. In the west Broward County community of Sunrise, for instance, a "Little India" has emerged centered on a shopping plaza with a variety of Indian shops and restaurants. In nearby Lauderhill, Indians, who came to the United States from Trinidad, run grocery stores providing traditional Indian foods and Indian movie rentals. In Hollywood, a refurbished downtown movie theater—now renamed the Bombay Hollywood Cinema—shows Indian films and attracts viewers from all over South Florida. The Indian Popular Culture Forum, a South Florida organization, promotes better economic and political ties between the United States and India. The Florida Hindu Parishad in Oakland Park provides religious services and cultural activities for over three hundred Hindu families. A Hindu temple in the Carrollwood suburb of Tampa provides a place of worship as well as a cultural center for almost four thousand Indians in the Tampa Bay region. Over ten thousand people in the Tampa region annually attend the India Festival of Gujarati Samaj. In Fort Lauderdale, several thousand people gather for the annual Festival of Holi sponsored by the local Florida Hindu Organization. In Boca Raton, the South Florida Association of Indians in America regularly celebrates India's Independence Day. *Desh-Videsh*, a monthly Asian Indian magazine established in 1993 in Coral Springs and with a national circulation of over fifty thousand, is widely distributed in Florida's urban areas. It serves as a "sounding board" for Florida's diverse community of Asian Indians, while also aiming "to help preserve the culture" in the United States. Two other newspapers, the weekly *East-West Times* from Orlando and the monthly *Khaas Baat* from Tampa, also help sustain the cohesiveness and continuity of Asian Indian communities in Florida.[34]

Muslims from South Asia are also represented in Florida's new cultural mix. The Florida Muslim Alliance, based in Orlando, the Islamic Association of Central Florida, and the Muslim Communities Association of South Florida have sponsored the establishment of mosques and religious centers throughout the state. Weekly newspapers published in Broward and Miami-Dade Counties—*Muslim Chronicle*, *Urdu Times*, and *Humwatan*—provide a cultural focus for Pakistanis in the Sunshine State. The Islamic School of South Dade and similar education centers elsewhere offer classes in the Muslim religion and Urdu, the language of Pakistan. Like other Asian immigrants, South Asian Muslims have concentrated in Florida's larger metropolitan areas—Miami, Orlando, Tampa, and Jacksonville. And like other groups, they have established cultural organizations and festivals in order to maintain homeland culture in the new land. One such organization, the Bangladesh Association of Florida, formed in 1991, promoted cultural activities aimed at retaining traditional ethnic identification in the United States. In typical fashion, this group sponsored the first Bengali Cultural Festival in Pompano Beach in celebration of the Bengali New Year. Florida Muslims have also worked hard to separate themselves and their organizations from radical fundamentalism and, by contrast, to establish their loyalty and commitment to the United States.[35]

As all these group activities suggest, Asian identity and culture in Florida have been maintained and nurtured through a myriad of Asian cultural organizations. When the Asian-American Federation of Florida, based in Broward County, published a *Community Directory* in 1992, some forty-six separate Asian organizations were listed as sponsors. These included the Asian-American Civic Alliance, the Association of Indians in South Florida, the Burmese-American Association of Florida, the Chinese Cultural Association, the Filipino Community Association of Florida, the Korean Association of Greater Miami, the Pakistan Cultural Society, the South Florida Formosa Association, the Thai-American Association of South Florida, the Florida Hindu Organization, the Malaysian Club, and the Foundation for Better Living of Laotians in Florida. The directory also listed hundreds of Asian restaurants, groceries, retail businesses, and professional services, conveying the impression of institutionally complete communities. These organizations and businesses in South Florida, and similar agencies in other parts of the state, provide a sense of group identity and cultural cohesion not unlike the ethnic organizations of European immigrants to the United States in the industrial era.[36]

Some scholarly studies, such as William Wei's *The Asian American Movement*, have suggested that a "pan-Asian" movement has emerged in the United States in recent decades. According to Wei, this Asian American movement focused on fighting racial discrimination through political activism—efforts that encouraged a distinct sense of Asian ethnic consciousness and solidarity. Some early efforts along these lines became evident in Florida during the 1980s and 1990s, although the idea of ethnic solidarity seemed more significant than political mobilization. Along these lines, during the 1980s a small newspaper aimed at the entire Asian American community, the *Florida Asian American*, was published in Fort Lauderdale. That paper eventually folded, but it was succeeded in 1990 by the monthly *International Asian-American*, also published in Fort Lauderdale and sponsored by the Asian-American Federation of Florida. The editor noted when the first issue was published that the paper would provide "a forum for the individual communities to read news about their own communities," while at the same time it would speak in "a united voice for all of the Asians—because alone each community is not very large." As one editorial put it, "it is time for Asians to assert their identity, their heritage and their rights to fullest participation and sharing in all responsibilities and duties in American society." Each issue of the *International Asian-American* had a separate page for the various Asian groups—"Pakistani News," "Indian News," "Vietnamese News," "Korean News," "Filipino News," and so on—both in English and in the language of the group.[37]

Other publications also emerged that appealed to the broader Asian community in South Florida. One such paper, the weekly *Asian Spectrum*, covered international, national, and local news of interest to Asians, mostly in English but with some pages in Chinese. The goal was, as the paper editorialized in February 1993, "building a bridge between cultures." Significantly, this paper challenged what it considered biased local media portrayals of gambling and criminal activity within the South Florida Asian American community. More importantly, it defended the Asian community against hate crimes and anti-Asian ethnic violence, such as the 1992 mass beating incident in Coral Springs, Florida, that resulted in the death of a young Vietnamese college student, Luyen Phan Nyugen. By the mid-1990s, however, both the *International Asian American* and *Asian Spectrum* had gone out of business, perhaps suggesting the weakness of the pan-Asian idea at a time when newcomers to the United States sought to establish their own separate identities as Chinese American or Korean Americans or Filipino Americans.[38]

Other efforts to provide Florida's Asian Americans with a sense of community or common cause can be found in the activities of the Asian-American Federation of Florida. This organization, founded in Hollywood in 1984, holds annual Asian art and film festivals in Dade and Broward Counties, sponsors many other cultural events, raises funds for Asian American scholarships, engages in political lobbying on behalf of Asian Americans, participates in cultural awareness programs in public schools, and generally represents the interests of the diverse Asian communities, especially in South Florida. The organization's 1996 Asian Arts Festival held in Homestead, according to one spokesperson from Thailand, presented "the opportunity to bring together all the different Asian communities and to educate the public—and the new generation of Asian Americans—about our cultures." In 1996, the Bangladesh Association of Florida held its annual Asian Cultural Festival in Delray Beach in an effort "to bring Asians from all countries together in one event." In Orlando, the Asian American Chamber of Commerce of Central Florida has been working to bring Asian business people together for expositions, business fairs, and banquets. Similarly, the successful 1992 legislative campaign of Korean American Mimi McAndrews not only made her the first Asian woman in the Florida legislature but also drew upon solidified Asian political support in her Palm Beach County district. McAndrews's supporters contended that she would speak for all Asians throughout the state of Florida. An attorney, McAndrews served only one term in the legislature but later helped to organize the Florida chapter of the Asian Pacific American Bar Association. In a variety of ways, then, the Asian American "movement" gained some traction in Florida, but some influences pulled in other directions.[39]

Some editors and organizations promoted an Asian American panethnic consciousness, but Asian nationality groups in Florida have been undergoing an internal consolidation of their own. This pattern is especially evident among Florida's Chinese residents, who have had to create their own group identity and solidarity. They have come not only from China, Taiwan, and Hong Kong but also from Vietnam, Thailand, Cuba, Jamaica, Panama, Suriname, Peru, Venezuela, Costa Rica, Honduras, and Mexico. These differences in background have often made it difficult to unite the Chinese, as do language differences among them. In Miami, according to one writer, "Chinese speak a mish-mash of languages, including Cantonese, Mandarin, Spanish and Hakka, spoken by Chinese in Jamaica," although many are multilingual. Like earlier European immigrant groups, who forged an ethnic or national identity only after arrival in the United States, they are in the process of developing a sense of their common heritage. There are no Chinatowns in Miami or other Florida cities, so the cultural diversity of ethnic religious life and culture among Asians in Florida may, to a certain extent organizations and newspapers mentioned earlier, serve to break down the barriers of language and background and bring the Chinese community together. A similar function has been served by the Organization of Chinese Americans, a national association founded in 1973, which currently has eighty chapters in the United States and many active members in Florida.[40]

Ethnic organizations have fostered group identity, but a wide range of religious affiliations has pulled in an opposite direction. For example, diverse Asian immigrant religious practice suggests a complicated process of adjustment and assimilation at work. Many Asian newcomers, such as those from the Philippines and Vietnam, come from cultures where Catholicism was institutionally strong. Others, such as the Korean and Chinese immigrants, traditionally have been influenced, even converted in large numbers, by missionaries from various Protestant Christian denominations. Not surprisingly, the Christian diversity of some Asian immigrants has been reflected in Florida. As early as the 1950s, for instance, a Chinese Sunday School was established by a downtown Baptist church in Miami. In 1955, the Chinese Baptist Church was formed as a "department" of the Flagler Street Baptist Church. In the early 1970s, Miami's Chinese Baptist Church became independent, eventually building its own place of worship in Sweetwater, west of Miami. In 1992, Kwong-Wah Lau, a Baptist preacher from Hong Kong, helped establish a second Chinese Baptist Mission in the Broward County city of Coral Springs. In the Tampa area, the Catholic Diocese of Saint Petersburg has missions to Koreans and Vietnamese, with Sunday masses in their own languages. The Archdiocese of Miami supports similar ministries for Korean, Vietnamese, and Asian Indian members. In Orlando, separate Korean congregations had been established by the mid-1990s, including Catholic, Baptist, Presbyterian, and Methodist churches. Pensacola has a Vietnamese Catholic parish and a Vietnamese Baptist Church. Seventh Day Adventist congregations serve Chinese residents of Jacksonville and Filipino and Vietnamese members in Orlando. These vast differences in religious beliefs and identification militates against group cohesion among Asian Americans in Florida.[41]

Two other trends suggest a possible weakening over time of Asian nationality communities. A large and growing proportion of Asian Americans have married outside the nationality group. The 2010 census reported 571,244 Asians in Florida, but 116,432 of them, or about 20 percent, were only partially Asian. Since the nineteenth century, the out-marriage pattern has characterized American immigrant families beginning with the second generation, and there is no reason to expect that pattern to diminish in the twenty-first century. Of course, the children of such marriages would be only half Asian, raising questions of ethnic consciousness and identity. In a recent article in *Commentary*, author Tamar Jacoby lays out the emerging pattern among Asian Americans. Well into the twentieth century, Jacoby writes, Asians were thought to be unassimilable, thus the prejudice, bigotry, and eventual exclusion they endured. More recent Asian immigrants and their children have adjusted or adapted to American ways, but most have held onto significant elements of their culture. Jacoby notes, "Not even the oldest and most acculturated Asian immigrants aspire to lose themselves or their heritage in a homogenized America." But the American-born children of Asian immigrants, the "transitional generation," seem "caught between their old world values and their evolving place in American society." As Jacoby suggests, the transforming power of American culture everywhere confronted cohesive ethnic communities with strong traditional values. The challenge for rising generations of Asian Americans is to pursue what immigration scholars Alejandro Portes and Ruben G. Rumbaut, authors of *Legacies: The Story of the Immigrant Second Generation*, have called "selective acculturation," adapting to the new culture but respecting their traditional heritage and retaining old-country values. In any case, in Florida and elsewhere, over time and across generations out-marriage, multicultural children, and teenage peer pressure might weaken the cohesiveness of Asian American families and communities.[42]

Conclusion

This essay has sought to demonstrate the long history of Asian immigration and internal migration to Florida, dating back to early Chinese and Japanese communities established around 1900. Since the mid-twentieth century, new Asian immigration and secondary internal migration has diversified the ethnic and racial base of Florida's rapidly growing population. Florida has "Latinized" dramatically since the Cuban Revolution in 1959, but the growing presence of an active and energetic Asian population in the Sunshine State, especially in the large metropolitan areas, has revealed Florida as an emerging multicultural state. Not all Floridians are happy or comfortable with the way Florida has been changing. In the 1990s, mirroring national trends, several anti-immigration groups supported petition drives for legislation to curb benefits to noncitizens. During that decade, organizations such as Floridians for Immigration Control and the Save Our State Committee found fertile ground. During the first decade of the twenty-first century, the "immigration wars" heated up again. Whatever the outcome of these debates over immigration policy, the Asian immigration of the past half century has contributed immutably to Florida's ethnic and racial diversity, as well as to the multiculturalism of future decades.

Notes

1. Raymond Arsenault and Gary R. Mormino, "From Dixie to Dreamland: Demographic and Cultural Change in Florida, 1880–1980," in *Shades of the Sunbelt: Essays on Ethnicity, Race, and the Urban South*, ed. Randall M. Miller and George E. Pozzetta (Westport, CT: Greenwood Press, 1988), 161–219; Raymond A. Mohl, "Florida's Changing Demography: Population Growth, Urbanization, and Latinization," *Environmental and Urban Issues* 17 (Winter 1990): 22–30; Leon F. Bouvier, William Leonard, and John L. Martin, *Shaping Florida: The Effects of Immigration, 1970–2020* (Center for Immigration Studies, December 1995), available at http://www.cis.org/articles/1995/florida.html; US Census Bureau, American Community Survey, 2009, www.census.gov/acs/www/.

2. Raymond A. Mohl and George E. Pozzetta, "From Migration to Multiculturalism: A History of Florida Immigration," in *The New History of Florida*, ed. Michael Gannon (Gainesville: University Press of Florida, 1995), 391–417; Raymond A. Mohl, "The Latinization of Florida," in *Florida's Heritage of Diversity: Essays in Honor of Samuel Proctor*, ed. Mark I. Greenberg, William Warren Rogers, and Canter Brown Jr. (Tallahassee: Sentry Press, 1997), 151–68; Raymond A. Mohl, "Ethnic Transformations in Late Twentieth-Century Florida," *Journal of American Ethnic History* 15 (Winter 1996): 60–78.

3. US Census Bureau, 1990, 2010 (www.census.gov), and American Community Survey, 2009; Jody A. Benjamin and Tanya Weinberg, "Asian Numbers Surge in Florida," Fort Lauderdale *Sun Sentinel*, May 24, 2001. Asians have also been the fastest growing group nationally since the 1970s. See Robert W. Gardner, Bryant Robey, and Peter Colin Smith, *Asian Americans: Growth, Change, and Diversity* (Washington, DC: Population Reference Bureau, 1985); William O'Hare and Judy Felt, "Asian Americans: America's Fastest Growing Minority Group," *Population Trends and Public Policy*, no. 19 (Washington, DC: Population Reference Bureau, 1991); Roger Daniels, "The Asian-American Experience: The View from the 1990s," in *Multiculturalism and the Canon of American Culture*, ed. Hans Bak (Amsterdam: VU University

Press, 1993), 131–45; David M. Reimers, "Asian Immigrants in the South," in *Globalization and the American South*, ed. James C. Cobb and William Stueck (Athens: University of Georgia Press, 2005), 100–134.

4. Walter L. Fleming, "Immigration to the Southern States," *Political Science Quarterly* 20 (June 1905): 276–97; George E. Pozzetta, "The Chinese Encounter with Florida, 1865–1920," *Chinese America: History and Perspectives* 2 (1989): 43–58; George E. Pozzetta, "Foreigners in Florida: A Study of Immigration Promotion, 1865–1910," *Florida Historical Quarterly* 53 (October 1974): 164–80. On Florida as the "American Italy," see Edward King, *The Great South* (Hartford, CT: American Publishing, 1879; reprint edition, Baton Rouge: Louisiana State University Press, 1972), 378.

5. Roger Daniels, *Coming to America: A History of Immigration and Ethnicity in American Life* (New York: HarperCollins, 1990), 239–50; Shih-shan Henry Tsai, *The Chinese Experience in America* (Bloomington: Indiana University Press, 1986), 1–32; Ronald Takaki, *A Different Mirror: A History of Multicultural America* (Boston: Little, Brown, 1993), 191–221; Gunther Barth, *Bitter Strength: A History of the Chinese in the United States, 1850–1870* (Cambridge: Harvard University Press, 1964), 187–97; Richard White, *Railroaded: The Transcontinentals and the Making of Modern America* (New York: Norton, 2011), 293–314. On the Burlingame Treaty of 1868, see Walter LaFeber, *The Cambridge History of American Foreign Relations: The American Search for Opportunity, 1845–1913* (Cambridge: Cambridge University Press, 1993), 18.

On Chinese indentured workers in the Caribbean, see Walton Look Lai, *Indentured Labor, Caribbean Sugar: Chinese and Indian Migrants to the British West Indies, 1838–1918* (Baltimore: Johns Hopkins University Press, 1993); P. C. Emmer, "Immigration into the Caribbean: The Introduction of Chinese and East Indian Indentured Laborers between 1839 and 1917," in *European Expansion and Migration: Essays on the Intercontinental Migration from Africa, Asia, and Europe*, ed. P. C. Emmer and M. Morner (New York: Berg, 1992), 254–276.

6. Stanford M. Lyman, ed. *Selected Writings of Henry Hughes* (Jackson: University of Mississippi Press, 1985), 24–25, 51–53; Lucy M. Cohen, "Entry of Chinese to the Lower South from 1865 to 1870: Policy Dilemmas," *Southern Studies* 17 (Spring 1978): 5–37; Lucy M. Cohen, "Early Arrivals," *Southern Exposure* 12 (July–August 1984): 24–30; Lucy M. Cohen, *Chinese in the Post–Civil War South: A People without a History* (Baton Rouge: Louisiana State University Press, 1984); Moon-Ho Jung, *Coolies and Cane: Rice, Labor, and Sugar in the Age of Emancipation* (Baltimore: Johns Hopkins University Press, 2008); Daniel Liestman, "Chinese Laborers in Reconstruction Alabama," *Alabama Heritage* (Spring 1988): 2–13. On the Memphis commercial convention of 1869, see Vicki Vaughn Johnson, *The Men and the Vision of the Southern Commercial Conventions, 1845–1871* (Columbia: University of Missouri Press, 1992), 193–220. For the controversy over Chinese workers, see "The Cooly Importation" *Harper's Weekly*, August 31, 1867, 546–47; "Coolies," *Harper's Weekly*, August 14, 1869, 514–15; E. L. Godkin, "The Chinese Invasion," *The Nation*, July 14, 1870, 20; "Coo-

lies As a Substitute for Negroes," *De Bow's Review*, August 1866, 215–17; William M. Burwell, "Science and the Mechanic Arts Against Coolies," *De Bow's Review*, July 1869, 557–71; "The Cooly-ite Controversy," *De Bow's Review*, August 1869, 709–24; George W. Gift, "The Labor Question—The Chinese," *Southern Farmer*, June 1869, 127–28.

For scholarly discussions of post–Civil War immigrant labor issues, see Andrew Gyory, *Closing the Gate: Race, Politics, and the Chinese Exclusion Act* (Chapel Hill: University of North Carolina Press, 1998); Najia Aarim-Heriot, *Chinese Immigrants, African Americans, and Racial Anxiety in the United States, 1848–82* (Urbana: University of Illinois Press, 2003), 103–39; and Isabella Black, "American Labor and Chinese Immigration," *Past and Present* 25 (July 1963): 59–76.

7. *Florida Times-Union*, September 16, 1869, quoted in Pozzetta, "The Chinese Encounter with Florida," 45; George M. Barbour, *Florida for Tourists, Invalids, and Settlers* (Jacksonville: Douglas Printing, 1882), 227; "Chinese Labor," *Florida Agriculturist* 31 (September 28, 1904): 616; "The Chinese and the Labor Problem," *Florida Agriculturist* 32 (October 18, 1905): 664. For similar articles promoting Chinese workers in Florida, see "Chinese Cheap Labor," *Florida Agriculturist* 1 (January 24, 1874): 30; "Chinese Cheap Labor," *Florida Agriculturist* 3 (March 9, 1881): 337; "Farm Laborers," *Florida Agriculturist* 31 (June 15, 1904): 376; "Would Chinese Labor Solve the Harvest Problem?" *Florida Agriculturist* 32 (October 18, 1905), 664–65.

8. Cohen, *Chinese in the Post–Civil War South*; Pozzetta, "The Chinese Encounter with Florida," 43–54; "Chinese in Paradise," *Florida Agriculturist* 33 (July 18, 1906): 457.

9. Josephine Shih Gordy, "Chinese in Southeast Florida, 1890–1992," master's thesis, Florida Atlantic University, 1994), 53–58; Pozzetta, "The Chinese Encounter with Florida," 50–53.

10. Paul C. P. Siu, *The Chinese Laundryman: A Study of Social Isolation* (New York: New York University Press, 1987), 47; Pozzetta, "The Chinese Encounter with Florida," 52–53.

11. Pozzetta, "The Chinese Encounter with Florida," 50–53; Kathleen Cohen, "Immigrant Jacksonville: A Profile of Immigrant Groups in Jacksonville, Florida, 1890–1920" (master's thesis, University of Florida, 1986), 91–100; Cindy H. Wong, "Chinese outside Chinatown: A Chinese Community in South Florida," *Chinese America: History and Perspectives* 4 (1991): 49–65.

12. Ruthanne Lum McCunn, "Lue Gim Gong: A Life Reclaimed," *Chinese America: History and Perspectives* 2 (1989): 117–135; Peter Kwong and Dusanka Miscevic, *Chinese America: The Untold Story of America's Oldest New Community* (New York: The New Press, 2005), 14; Gordy, "Chinese in Southeast Florida," 7–9; Gene M. Burnett, "Florida's Forgotten 'Chinese Burbank,'" in Burnett, *Florida's Past: People and Events that Shaped the State*, vol. 2 (Sarasota: Pineapple Press, 1988); Frederick Rudolph, "Chinamen in Yankeedom: Anti-Unionism in Massachusetts in 1870," *American Historical Review* 53 (October 1947): 1–29.

13. James W. Loewen, *The Mississippi Chinese: Between Black and White* (Cambridge, MA: Harvard University Press, 1971), 32–57; Cohen, "Immigrant Jacksonville," 94; Pozzetta, "The Chinese Encounter with Florida," 53; Gordy, "Chinese in Southeast Florida," 57–58. For an excellent study of the Chinese grocery store tradition in Mississippi, see Robert Seto Quan, *Lotus among the Magnolias: The Mississippi Chinese* (Jackson: University of Mississippi Press, 1982). On the "middleman" concept of Chinese grocers, see Edna Bonacich, "A Theory of Middleman Minorities," *American Sociological Review* 38 (October 1973): 583–94; Charles Choy Wong, "Black and Chinese Grocery Stores in Los Angeles' Black Ghetto," *Urban Life* 5 (January 1977): 439–64.

14. Gordy, "Chinese in Southeast Florida," 57–65; transcript of interview with Helen Chin, January 24, 1993 (interview conducted by Josephine Shih Gordy, copy in possession of author); transcript of interview with Gow Low, June 23, 1991 (interview conducted by Josephine Shih Gordy, copy in possession of author). See also Charles Whited, "The Wing Dynasty of Miami," *Miami Herald, Tropic Magazine*, December 10, 1967, 26–30.

15. Roger Daniels, "Asian Groups," in *Encyclopedia of Southern Culture*, ed. Charles Reagan Wilson and William Ferris (Chapel Hill: University of North Carolina Press, 1989), 418–21; US Census Bureau, *Sixteenth Census of the United States: 1940 Population*, vol. 2, *Characteristics of the Population*, part 2, *Florida-Iowa* (Washington, DC: US Government Printing Office, 1943), 16; US Census Bureau, *Census of Population: 1950*, vol. 2, *Characteristics of the Population*, part 10, *Florida* (Washington, DC: US Government Printing Office, 1952), 10–31.

16. Joanne M. Lloyd, "'Yankees of the Orient': Yamato and Japanese Immigration to America" (master's thesis, Florida Atlantic University, 1990), 57–75; George E. Pozzetta and Harry A. Kersey Jr., "Yamato Colony: A Japanese Presence in South Florida," *Tequesta: The Journal of the Historical Association of Southern Florida* 36 (1976): 66–77; George E. Pozzetta, "Foreign Colonies in South Florida, 1865–1910," *Tequesta: The Journal of the Historical Association of Southern Florida*, 34 (1974), 51–52; Jacqueline Ashton Waldeck, "Morikami: Immigrant to Icon," *Boca Raton News*, December 23, 1999.

On Westernizing influences in Japan that encouraged immigration to the United States, see Mitziko Sawada, *Tokyo Life, New York Dreams: Urban Japanese Visions of America, 1890–1924* (Berkeley: University Press of California, 1996).

17. Lloyd, "'Yankees of the Orient,'" 85–124; Pozzetta and Kersey, "Yamato Colony"; "Japanese at Yaniato, Fla., A Recent Settlement," in *Reports of the U.S. Commission on Immigration: Immigrants in Industries*, part 24: *Recent Immigrants in Agriculture* (Washington, DC: US Government Printing Office, 1911), 483–85; Linda Cicero, "The Sun Has Set on Palm Beach Japanese Colony," *Miami Herald*, February 22, 1981; Bob Knotts, "Japanese in Florida Were Victims of War Prejudice," Fort Lauderdale *Sun*

Sentinel, December 2, 1991; Larry Rosensweig, *Yamato, Florida: A Colony of Japanese Farmers in Florida* (Delray Beach, FL: Morikami Museum of Japanese Culture, n.d.); Stacie Orozco, "Celebrating Asia: The Culture and Food of the Orient on Display at the Morikami," *Boca Raton News*, October 11, 1998.

18. Reimers, "Asian Immigrants in the South," 100–134; US Census Bureau, *The Asian Population: 2000* (Washington, DC: US Department of Commerce, 2002); US Census Bureau, *Overview of Race and Hispanic Origin: 2010* (Washington, DC: US Department of Commerce, 2011), 4. On postwar immigration policy, see Ronald Takaki, *Strangers from a Different Shore: A History of Asian Americans* (Boston: Little, Brown, 1989), 406–71; David M. Reimers, *Still the Golden Door: The Third World Comes to America*, 2nd ed. (New York: Columbia University Press, 1992), 92–99; Bill Ong Hing, *Making and Remaking Asian America through Immigration Policy, 1850–1990* (Stanford: Stanford University Press, 1993); Mae M. Ngai, *Impossible Subjects: Illegal Aliens and the Making of Modern America* (Princeton, NJ: Princeton University Press, 2004), 227–70.

19. US Census Bureau, American Community Survey, 2009.

20. Fabriola Santiago, "'All Over Asia in One Weekend,'" *Miami Herald*, March 1, 1996.

21. Takaki, *Strangers from a Different Shore*, 357–405, quotation on p. 357.

22. Elfrieda Berthiaume Shukert and Barbara Smith Scibetta, *War Brides of World War II* (Novato, CA: Presidio Press, 1988), 185–218; Roger Daniels, *Asian America: Chinese and Japanese in the United States since 1850* (Seattle: University of Washington Press, 1988), 306–7; Reimers, *Still the Golden Door*, 21–26.

23. Bruno Lasker, *Filipino Immigration to Continental United States and to Hawaii* (Chicago: University of Chicago Press, 1931), 61–63; H. Brett Melendy, *Asians in America: Filipinos, Koreans, and East Indians* (Boston: Twayne Publishers, 1977), 83–84; Sucheng Chan, *Asian Americans: An Interpretive History* (New York: Twayne Publishers, 1991), 149; Daniels, *Coming to America*, 358–59.

24. Reimers, *Still the Golden Door*, 25; Daniels, *Asian America*, 306–7; Takaki, *Strangers from a Different Shore*, 461; Lawrence H. Fuchs, *The American Kaleidoscope: Race, Ethnicity, and the Civic Culture* (Hanover, NH: Wesleyan University Press, 1991), 353.

25. US Census Bureau, 1960, 1970, 1980 (www.census.gov); Marion F. Houston, Roger G. Kramer, and Joan Mackin Barrett, "Female Predominance in Immigration to the United States since 1930: A First Look," *International Migration Review* 18 (Winter 1984): 908–63; Bok-Lim C. Kim, "Asian Wives of U.S. Servicemen: Women in Shadows," *Amerasia Journal* 4, no. 1 (1977): 91–115.

26. US Census Bureau, 1960, 1980 (www.census.gov), and American Community Survey, 2009; "Philippines' 'Brain Drain' Brings Nurse," *Miami Herald*, November 14, 1982; Jacksonville *Florida Times-Union*, February 28, 1986, September 10, 1990; Yen

Le Espiritu, "Filipino Navy Stewards and Filipina Health Care Professionals: Immigration, Work and Family Relations," *Asian and Pacific Migration Journal* 11, no. 1 (2002): 47–66.

27. US Census Bureau, 1960, 1980, 1990, 2010 (www.census.gov); Daniels, *Asian America*, 306; "Vietnamese Find Home in Little Havana," *Miami Herald*, November 14, 1982; Patty Billington, "A New Home in Panhandle: Region Lures Vietnamese," *Miami Herald*, December 1, 1991; Paul D. Starr, "Troubled Waters: Vietnamese Fisherfolk on America's Gulf Coast," *International Migration Review* 15 (Spring–Summer 1981), 226–38.

By the mid-1990s, some two thousand Amerasian children had settled in Florida under the 1987 Amerasian Homecoming Act.

See Fort Lauderdale *Sun Sentinel*, April 3, 1994; Jacksonville *Florida Times-Union*, April 30, 2000.

28. Reimers, *Still the Golden Door*, 61–91; Reed Ueda, *Postwar Immigrant America: A Social History* (Boston: Bedford Books, 1994), 64–68.

29. Takaki, *Strangers from a Different Shore*, 419–71; Reimers, *Still the Golden Door*, 91–122; Gary R. Hess, "The Forgotten Asian Americans: The East Indian Community in the United States," *Pacific Historical Review* 43 (November 1974), 576–77, 595–96; Roger Daniels, *History of Indian Immigration to the United States: An Interpretive Essay* (New York: Asia Society, 1989); Marcia Mogelonsky, "Asian-Indian Americans," *American Demographics* 17 (August 1995): 32–39; Philip J. Leonhard and Parmatma Saran, "The Indian Immigrant in America: A Demographic Profile," in *The New Ethnics: Asian Indians in the United States*, ed. Parmatma Saran and Edwin Eames (New York: Praeger, 1980), 136–62.

30. US Census Bureau, 1970, 2010 (www.census.gov).

31. Elliott Barkan, "New Origins, New Homeland, New Region: American Immigration and the Emergence of the Sunbelt, 1955–1985," in *Searching for the Sunbelt: Historical Perspectives on a Region*, ed. Raymond A. Mohl (Knoxville: University of Tennessee Press, 1990), 124–48; June Marie Nogle, "Immigrants on the Move: How Internal Migration Increases the Concentration of the Foreign-born," Center for Migration Studies report, February 1996, available at http://www.cis.org; Haya El Nasser, "New Face of the South: Recent Asian Influx Taking Region by Storm," *USA Today*, June 2, 1998. For Asian Indians as hoteliers in Florida, see "Equal Opportunity," *Florida Trend* 37 (May 1994), 61–63. For evidence of extensive economic entrepreneurialism among Asians in Florida, see US Census Bureau, *1987 Economic Censuses. Survey of Minority-Owned Business Enterprises: Asian Americans, American Indians, and Other Minorities* (Washington, DC: US Government Printing Office, 1991), especially tables 5, 6, and 7. See also Ueda, *Postwar Immigrant America*, 64–67, 91–92.

32. *Miami Herald*, November 14, 1982, January 1, 1991, April 21, 1991, April 6, 1993, September 13, 1993; *Sun Sentinel*, January 5, 1993, December 19, 1993, June 13,

1996; *Florida Times-Union*, June 24, 1989, June 7, 1992; Rebecca Novak, "North Miami's Orient," *Asian Spectrum*, March 7, 1993; Blanche Mesa, "Asian Shops Serve a Growing Market in Dade," *Miami Herald Neighbors*, May 30, 1991.

33. *Miami Herald*, February 5, 1990, July 31, 1991, February 10, 1995; *Sun Sentinel*, December 19, 1993; Jordan Bressler, "Profit Isn't Chinese Paper's Goal," *Hollywood Hometown Herald*, November 27, 1994; Gordy, "Chinese in Southeast Florida," 118–126; Gary Tie-Shue, "The Chinese Jamaican Experience: Adjustment and Advancement," *Dragon*, 10 (May–June 1994): 8, 10; (July–September 1994): 8.

34. *Miami Herald*, June 24, 1991, March 2, 1994, March 30, 1994, April 13, 1994, May 23, 1994, October 1, 1994, July 19, 1995, October 28, 1995; *Sun Sentinel*, August 16, 1993, November 11, 2004; Orlando *East-West Times*, December 1, 2010; Clarissa J. Walker, "Hitting Home: Asian Publications Go Beyond Mainstream Media," *Sun Sentinel*, June 13, 1996; Indu Hathiramani, "Preserving Our Heritage," *Desh-Videsh* 3 (October 1997): 25–27; Katyayani Jhaveri, "Embracing Indian Culture in the US," *Desh-Videsh* 18 (August 21, 2011): 54–55.

35. *Miami Herald*, February 7, 1993, May 16, 1993, September 13, 1993, March 14, 1994, May 20, 1994, April 13, 1995; *Palm Beach Post*, February 11, 1994, December 20, 1998; James D. Davis, "Islam in South Florida," *Sun Sentinel*, February 15, 1977; Jeffrey Kleinman, "Bangladeshi Group Spreads a Tradition," *Miami Herald*, October 13, 1991; Andrea Elliott, "Reject Jihad, Local Muslim Leader Says," *Miami Herald*, October 13, 2001.

36. Florence Allbaugh, ed. *Asian American Federation Community Directory* (Davie, FL: Asian-American Federation of Florida, 1992), 32–38.

37. William Wei, *The Asian American Movement* (Philadelphia: Temple University Press, 1993); Yen Le Espiritu, *Asian American Panethnicity: Bridging Institutions and Identities* (Philadelphia: Temple University Press, 1992); *Miami Herald*, February 5, 1990; *International Asian American* (March 1990), 2.

38. *Asian Spectrum*, February 7, 1993, February 14, 1993; *Miami Herald*, September 14, 1992; Allbaugh, *Asian American Federation Community Directory*, 16–19; Michael McLeod, "Death of an American Dream: The Inside Story of the Life and Murder of Lu Nyugen," *Sunshine: The Magazine of South Florida*, December 13, 1994, 6–15.

39. Asian-American Federation of Florida, *The Fourth Annual Asian Arts Festival, 1994* (Fort Lauderdale: Asian-American Federation of Florida, 1994); Allbaugh, *Asian American Federation Community Directory*, 10–15; *Miami Herald*, February 25, 1992, September 24, 1994, March 1, 1996, March 3, 1997; *Sun Sentinel*, March 24, 1996; *Orlando Sentinel*, March 27, 1996; Elisa Lee, "She's the First Asian Woman in the Florida Legislature," *Asian Week* 15 (March 11, 1994): 1, 14. See also Wendy Page, "Striving for Asian Political Influence," *Asian Spectrum*, June 27, 1993.

40. *Miami Herald*, May 28, 1991, July 29, 1995, October 31, 1996; Gordy, "Chinese in Southeast Florida," 72–101; *Chinese in the Americas Project* (Miami: Miami-Dade Community College, 1994), brochure; Organization of Chinese Americans,

17th Annual National Convention Program (Washington, DC: Organization of Chinese Americans, 1995), Nicole White and Jerry Berrios, "Multiethnic Mix Includes Chinese Roots," *Miami Herald,* February 12, 2006.

41. Gordy, "Chinese in Southeast Florida," 65–72; Rev. Leonard J. M. Plazewski (Corpus Christi Catholic Church, Temple Terrace, Florida), letter to author, February 26, 1996; David Briggs, "Abandoning Old Ways for New: Southeast Asian Refugees Turn to Christianity," *Miami Herald*, August 11, 1996; Patty Pensa, "Vietnamese Keeping Faith, Culture in Florida Parish," *Birmingham News*, October 31, 2003.

42. US Census Bureau, 2010 (www.census.gov); Tamar Jacoby, "In Asian America," *Commentary* 110 (July–August 2000): 21–28, quotations on pp. 27–28; Alejandro Portes and Ruben G. Rumbaut, *Legacies: The Story of the Immigrant Second Generation* (Berkeley: University of California Press and Russell Sage Foundation, 2001).

Works Cited

Aarim-Heriot, Najia. *Chinese Immigrants, African Americans, and Racial Anxiety in the United States, 1848–82*. Urbana: University of Illinois Press, 2003.

Allbaugh, Florence, ed. *Asian American Federation Community Directory*. Davie, FL: Asian-American Federation of Florida, 1992.

Arsenault, Raymond, and Gary R. Mormino. "From Dixie to Dreamland: Demographic and Cultural Change in Florida, 1880–1980." In *Shades of the Sunbelt: Essays on Ethnicity, Race, and the Urban South*, edited by Randall M. Miller and George E. Pozzetta. Westport, CT: Greenwood Press, 1988.

Asian-American Federation of Florida, *The Fourth Annual Asian Arts Festival, 1994*. Fort Lauderdale: Asian-American Federation of Florida, 1994.

Barbour, George. *Florida for Tourists, Invalids, and Settlers*. Jacksonville: Douglas Printing, 1882.

Barkan, Elliott. "New Origins, New Homeland, New Region: American Immigration and the Emergence of the Sunbelt, 1955–1985." In *Searching for the Sunbelt: Historical Perspectives on a Region*, edited by Raymond A. Mohl. Knoxville: University of Tennessee Press, 1990.

Barth, Gunther. *Bitter Strength: A History of the Chinese in the United States, 1850–1870*. Cambridge, MA: Harvard University Press, 1964.

Black, Isabella. "American Labor and Chinese Immigration." *Past and Present* 25 (July 1963): 59–76.

Bonacich, Edna. "A Theory of Middleman Minorities." *American Sociological Review* 38 (October 1973): 583–94.

Bouvier, Leon F., William Leonard, and John L. Martin. *Shaping Florida: The Effects of Immigration, 1970–2020*. Center for Immigration Studies, December 1995, http://www.cis.org/articles/1995/florida.html.

Burnett, Gene M. "Florida's Forgotten 'Chinese Burbank.'" In *Florida's Past: People and Events that Shaped the State*. Vol. 2. Sarasota: Pineapple Press, 1988.

Burwell, William M. "Science and the Mechanic Arts against Coolies." *De Bow's Review* (July 1869): 557–71.

Chan, Sucheng. *Asian Americans: An Interpretive History*. New York: Twayne Publishers, 1991.

"The Chinese and the Labor Problem." *Florida Agriculturalist* 32 (October 18, 1905).

"Chinese Cheap Labor." *Florida Agriculturalist* 1 (January 24, 1874): 30.

"Chinese Cheap Labor." *Florida Agriculturalist* 3 (March 9, 1881): 337.

"Chinese in Paradise." *Florida Agriculturalist* 33 (July 18, 1906): 457.

Chinese in the Americas Project. Miami: Miami-Dade Community College, 1994, brochure.

"Chinese Labor." *Florida Agriculturalist* 31 (September 28, 1904): 616.

Cohen, Kathleen. "Immigrant Jacksonville: A Profile of Immigrant Groups in Jacksonville, Florida, 1890–1920." Master's thesis, University of Florida, 1987.

Cohen, Lucy M. *Chinese in the Post–Civil War South: A People without a History*. Baton Rouge: Louisiana State University Press, 1984.

———. "Early Arrivals." *Southern Exposure* 12 (July–August 1984): 24–30.

———."Entry of Chinese to the Lower South from 1865 to 1870: Policy Dilemmas." *Southern Studies* 17 (Spring 1978): 5–37.

"Coolies." *Harper's Weekly*, August 14, 1869, 514–15.

"Coolies as a Substitute for Negroes." *De Bow's Review*, August 1866, 215–17.

"The Cooly Importation." *Harper's Weekly*, August 31, 1867.

"The Cooly-ite Controversy." *De Bow's Review*, August 1869.

Daniels, Roger. *Asian America: Chinese and Japanese in the United States since 1850*. Seattle: University of Washington Press, 1988.

———. "The Asian-American Experience: The View from the 1990s." In *Multiculturalism and the Canon of American Culture*, edited by Hans Bak. Amsterdam: VU University Press, 1993.

———. "Asian Groups." In *Encyclopedia of Southern Culture*, edited by Charles Reagan Wilson and William Ferris. Chapel Hill: University of North Carolina Press, 1989.

———. *Coming to America: A History of Immigration and Ethnicity in American Life*. New York: Harper Collins, 1990.

———. *History of Indian Immigration to the United States: An Interpretive Essay*. New York: Asia Society, 1989.

Emmer, P. C. "Immigration into the Caribbean: The Introduction of Chinese and East Indian Indentured Laborers between 1839 and 1917." In *European Expansion and Migration: Essays on the Intercontinental Migration from Africa, Asia, and Europe*, edited by P. Emmer and M. Morner. New York: Berg, 1992.

Espiritu, Yen Le. *Asian American Panethnicity: Bridging Institutions and Identities*. Philadelphia: Temple University Press, 1992.

———. "Filipino Navy Stewards and Filipina Health Care Professionals: Immigration, Work and Family Relations." *Asian and Pacific Migration Journal* 11, no. 1 (2002): 47–66.

"Farm Laborers." *Florida Agriculturalist* 31 (June 15, 1904).

Fleming, Walter L. "Immigration to the Southern States." *Political Science Quarterly* 20 (June 1905).

Fuchs, Lawrence H. *The American Kaleidoscope: Race, Ethnicity, and the Civic Culture*. Hanover, NH: Wesleyan University Press, 1991.

Gardner, Robert W., Bryant Robey, and Peter Colin Smith. *Asian Americans: Growth, Change, and Diversity*. Washington, DC: Population Reference Bureau, 1985.

Gift, George W. "The Labor Question—The Chinese." *Southern Farmer* (June 1869).

Godkin, E.L. "The Chinese Invasion." *The Nation*, July 14, 1870.

Gordy, Josephine Shih. "Chinese in Southeast Florida, 1890–1992." Master's thesis, Florida Atlantic University, 1994.

Gyory, Andrew. *Closing the Gate: Race, Politics, and the Chinese Exclusion Act*. Chapel Hill: University of North Carolina Press, 1998.

Hathiramani, Indu. "Preserving Our Heritage." *Desh-Videsh* 3 (October 1997).

Hess, Gary R. "The Forgotten Asian Americans: The East Indian Community in the United States." *Pacific Historical Review* 43 (November 1974).

Hing, Bill Ong. *Making and Remaking Asian America through Immigration Policy, 1850–1990*. Stanford: Stanford University Press, 1993.

Houston, Marion F., Roger G. Kramer, and Joan Mackin Barrett. "Female Predominance in Immigration to the United States since 1930: A First Look." *International Migration Review* 18 (Winter 1984).

Jacoby, Tamar. "In Asian America." *Commentary* 110 (July–August 2000).

"Japanese at Yaniato, Fla., A Recent Settlement" In *Reports of the US Commission on Immigration: Immigrants in Industries*. Part 24: *Recent Immigrants in Agriculture*. Washington, DC: US Government Printing Office, 1911.

Jhaveri, Katyayani. "Embracing Indian Culture in the U.S." *Desh-Videsh* 18 (August 21, 2011).

Johnson, Vicki Vaughn. *The Men and the Vision of the Southern Commercial Conventions, 1845–1871*. Columbia: University of Missouri Press, 1992.

Jung, Moon-Ho. *Coolies and Cane: Rice, Labor, and Sugar in the Age of Emancipation*. Baltimore: Johns Hopkins University Press, 2008.

Kim, Bok-Lim. "Asian Wives of U.S. Servicemen: Women in Shadows." *Amerasia Journal* 4, no. 1 (1977).

King, Edward. *The Great South*. 1879. Reprint, Baton Rouge: Louisiana State University Press, 1972.

Kwong, Peter, and Dusanka Miscevic. *Chinese America: The Untold Story of America's Oldest New Community*. New York: New Press, 2005.

LaFeber, Walter. *The Cambridge History of American Foreign Relations: The American Search for Opportunity, 1845–1913*. Cambridge: Cambridge University Press, 1993.

Lai, Walton Look. *Indentured Labor, Caribbean Sugar: Chinese and Indian Migrants to the British West Indies, 1838–1918*. Baltimore: Johns Hopkins University Press, 1993.

Lasker, Bruno. *Filipino Immigration to Continental United States and to Hawaii*. Chicago: University of Chicago Press, 1931.

Lee, Elisa. "She's the First Asian Woman in the Florida Legislature." *Asian Week* 15 (March 11, 1994).

Leonhard, Philip J., and Parmatma Saran. "The Indian Immigrant in America: A Demographic Profile." In *The New Ethnics: Asian Indians in the United States*, edited by Parmatma Saran and Edwin Eames. New York: Praeger, 1980.

Liestman, Daniel. "Chinese Laborers in Reconstruction Alabama," *Alabama Heritage* (Spring 1988).

Lloyd, Joanne M. "Yankees of the Orient: Yamato and Japanese Immigration to America." Master's thesis, Florida Atlantic University, 1990.

Loewen, James W. *The Mississippi Chinese: Between Black and White*. Cambridge, MA: Harvard University Press, 1971.

Lyman, Stanford M., ed. *Selected Writings of Henry Hughes*. Jackson: University of Mississippi Press, 1985.

McCunn, Ruthanne Lum. "Lue Gim Gong: A Life Reclaimed." *Chinese America: History and Perspectives* 2 (1989).

McLeod, Michael. "Death of an American Dream: The Inside Story of the Life and Murder of Lu Nyugen." *Sunshine: The Magazine of South Florida* (December 13, 1994).

Melendy, H. Brett. *Asians in America: Filipinos, Koreans, and East Indians*. Boston: Twayne Publishers, 1977.

Mogelonsky, Marcia. "Asian-Indian Americans." *American Demographics* 17 (August 1995).

Mohl, Raymond A. "Ethnic Transformations in Late Twentieth-Century Florida." *Journal of American Ethnic History* 15 (Winter 1996).

———. "Florida's Changing Demography: Population Growth, Urbanization, and Latinization." *Environmental and Urban Issues* 17 (Winter 1990).

———. "The Latinization of Florida." In *Florida's Heritage of Diversity: Essays in Honor of Samuel Proctor*, edited by Mark I. Grenberg, William Warren Rogers, and Canter Brown Jr. Tallahassee: Sentry Press, 1997.

Mohl, Raymond, and George E. Pozzetta. "From Migration to Multiculturalism: A History of Florida Immigration." In *The New History of Florida*, edited by Michael Gannon. Gainesville: University Press of Florida, 1995.

Ngai, Mae M. *Impossible Subjects: Illegal Aliens and the Making of Modern America*. Princeton, NJ: Princeton University Press, 2004.

Nogle, June Marie. "Immigrants on the Move: How Internal Migration Increases the Concentration of the Foreign-born." Center for Migration Studies report, February 1996, available at http://www.cis.org.

O'Hare, William, and Judy Felt. "Asian Americans: America's Fastest Growing Minority Group." *Population Trends and Public Policy*, no. 19. Washington DC: Population Reference Bureau, 1991.

Organization of Chinese Americans. *17th Annual National Convention Program*. Washington, DC: Organization of Chinese Americans, 1995.

Portes Alejandro, and Ruben G. Rumbaut. *Legacies: The Story of the Immigrant Second Generation*. Berkeley: University of California Press and Russell Sage Foundation, 2001.

Pozzetta, George E. "The Chinese Encounter with Florida, 1865–1920." *Chinese America: History and Perspectives* 2 (1989).

———. "Foreign Colonies in South Florida, 1865–1910." *Tequesta: The Journal of the Historical Association of Southern Florida* 34 (1974).

———. "Foreigners in Florida: A Study of Immigration Promotion, 1865–1910." *Florida Historical Quarterly* 53 (October 1974).

Pozzetta, George E., and Harry A. Kersey Jr. "Yamato Colony: A Japanese Presence in South Florida." *Tequesta: The Journal of the Historical Association of Southern Florida* 36 (1976).

Quan, Robert Seto. *Lotus among the Magnolias: The Mississippi Chinese*. Jackson: University of Mississippi Press, 1982.

Reimers, David M. "Asian Immigrants in the South." In *Globalization and the American South*, edited by James C. Cobb and William Stueck. Athens: University of Georgia Press, 2005.

———. *Still the Golden Door: The Third World Comes to America*. 2nd ed. New York: Columbia University Press, 1992.

Rosensweig, Larry. *Yamato, Florida: A Colony of Japanese Farmers in Florida*. Delray Beach, FL: Morikami Museum of Japanese Culture, n.d.

Rudolph, Frederick. "Chinamen in Yankeedom: Anti-Unionism in Massachusetts in 1870." *American Historical Review* 53 (October 1947).

Sawada, Mitziko. *Tokyo Life, New York Dreams: Urban Japanese Visions of America, 1890–1924*. Berkeley: University Press of California, 1996.

Shukert, Elfrieda Berthiaume, and Barbara Smith Scibetta. *War Brides of World War II*. Novato, CA: Presidio Press, 1988.

Siu, Paul C. P. *The Chinese Laundryman: A Study of Social Isolation*. New York: New York University Press, 1987.

Starr, Paul D. "Troubled Waters: Vietnamese Fisherfolk on America's Gulf Coast." *International Migration Review* 15 (Spring–Summer 1981).

Takaki, Ronald. *A Different Mirror: A History of Multicultural America*. New York: Norton, 2011.

———. *Strangers from a Different Shore: A History of Asian Americans*. Boston: Little, Brown, 1989.

Tsai, Shih-shan Henry. *The Chinese Experience in America*. Bloomington: Indiana University Press, 1986.

Ueda, Reed. *Postwar Immigrant America: A Social History*. Boston: Bedford Books, 1994.

US Census Bureau. American Community Survey, 2009, www.census.gov/acs/www/.
——. *The Asian Population: 2000*. Washington DC: US Department of Commerce, 2002.
——. The Asian Population: 2010. Washington DC; US Department of Commerce, 2011.
——. *Census of the Population: 1950*. Vol. 2, *Characteristics of the Population*, Part 10, *Florida* Washington DC: US Government Printing Office, 1952.
——. *1987 Economic Censuses. Survey of Minority-Owned Business Enterprises: Asian Americans, American Indians, and Other Minorities* (Washington, DC: US Government Printing Office, 1991.
——. *Overview of Race and Hispanic Origin: 2010*. Washington DC: US Department of Commerce, 2011.
——. *Sixteenth Census of the United States: 1940 Population*. Vol. 2, *Characteristics of the Population*. Part 2, *Florida-Iowa*. Washington DC: US Government Printing Office, 1943.
Wei, William, *The Asian American Movement*. Philadelphia: Temple University Press, 1993.
White, Richard. *Railroaded: The Transcontinentals and the Making of Modern America*. New York: W. W. Norton, 2011.
Wong, Charles Choy. "Black and Chinese Grocery Stores in Los Angeles' Black Ghetto." *Urban Life* 5 (January 1977).
Wong, Cindy H. "Chinese outside Chinatown: A Chinese Community in South Florida." *Chinese America: History and Perspectives* 4 (1991).
"Would Chinese Labor Solve the Harvest Problem?" *Florida Agriculturalist* 32 (October 18, 1905).

5
Chinese in Florida

History, Struggles, and Contributions to the Sunshine State

Wenxian Zhang

As the southernmost state in the United States of America, Florida is famous for its sunshine beaches and tourist attractions. Though it is believed that Native Americans settled in the Florida peninsula for thousands of years, the written history of the state did not begin until 1513 when Juan Ponce de Leon allegedly sighted the Florida coast and landed in Saint Augustine. There was no record of a Chinese population by the time Florida attained statehood in 1845. It was only after gold was discovered in California in 1848 that the Chinese began to arrive in the United States in large numbers, most of whom settled on the West Coast. Chinese people first came to Florida in the years after the Civil War, concentrated mainly in railroad construction, laundry, restaurant, and grocery business. Their population grew very slowly until after World War II, when the discriminatory immigration policies were finally lifted. The openings of Walt Disney World and other tourist attractions, the end of the Vietnam War, and the more recent addition of the Florida Splendid China cultural theme park have all brought new waves of Chinese immigrants to the Sunshine State.

During the early years, Chinese immigrants tended to be small business proprietors, working in low-wage and low-skilled jobs in the labor-intensive service sector. In addition, small-scale Chinese truck farms and experiments with Asian crops have contributed to the growth of agriculture. In recent decades, thousands of ethnic Chinese from mainland China, Taiwan, Hong Kong, and other places around the world have settled in the Sunshine State. Many of them are well educated, engaging in all ranges of professional work that are different from those early immigrants. According to the most recent census data, more than seventy-two thousand Chinese currently live in Florida.[1] About half of them are in the greater Miami and Fort Lauderdale region, and the rest are scattered around in the greater Orlando, Tampa, and Jacksonville metropolitan areas and other parts of Florida.

As Florida evolves over the years, Chinese Americans have been making contributions to the growth of the fourth largest state in the nation. Some of the notable examples include: Lue Gim Gong, a horticulturist who settled in DeLand, Florida in the late nineteenth century and was awarded in 1911 the Wilder Silver Medal for developing a strain of frost-resistant oranges; Edmond J. Gong, a Miami native and Harvard graduate, who is the first Chinese and Asian American to serve in the Florida House of Representatives and the Senate during the 1960s to 1970s and later became an assistant US attorney for the Southern District of Florida; and Nelson Ying, a first-generation Chinese American, US-trained nuclear physicist, successful entrepreneur, and a well-respected philanthropist and community leader in Central Florida.

In both the United States and Florida, Chinese have remained as one of the largest ethnic minority groups from Asia. As they congregate in major metropolitan areas seeking economic opportunities, kinship, and cultural connections, they have been playing an increasingly visible role in the state's economic, social, and political affairs. In recent years, Chinese Americans have formed various social groups to promote not only business interests but also language learning and cultural preservation in Florida and contributed significantly to the state's ethnic and cultural diversity. This chapter will trace the experience of Chinese in Florida from early immigration to the opening of the Splendid China Florida theme park, review their struggles of assimilation and efforts in preserving ethnic identities, and examine Chinese Americans' contributions to the Sunshine State's economy and cultural development for more than one hundred years.

Early Settlement

The history of Chinese immigration to Florida began in the mid- to late nineteenth century. Immediately after the Civil War the state was struggling with the dire need to rebuild the new South.[2] With the smallest population among all southern states, Florida had vast areas of uninhabited land and an almost nonexistent industrial base. During the mid- to late nineteenth century, the state economy was based chiefly on lumber, citrus, cotton plantation, phosphate mining, land drainage, and railroad construction, all requiring a growing labor force.[3] Therefore many Floridians believed the quickest and most practical strategy for economic development was to attract a large number of industrious immigrants. Such a position was embraced by not only the state, county, and local government officials but also railroad companies, farm groups, real estate firms, wealthy landowners, industrialists, and mine operators. Prior to 1900, open calls for immigration were issued to welcome all types and nationalities, among them Chinese citizens were noted especially. As early as 1866, the *St. Augustine Examiner* urged the state to consider the wholesale importation of "coolies" as laborers for

Florida's cotton fields.[4] Three years later, a proposal was drafted at the Chinese labor convention in Memphis that urged southerners to cooperate in efforts to import laborers of the "Mongolian race" from both California and Cuba at one hundred dollars per head with wages of eight to twelve dollars per month.[5]

Underneath the naive fervor for Chinese immigrants was white Floridians' discontent with the black population. Many ethnic stereotypes common at the time believed that without the coercive power of the slave system, newly freed black men were neither efficient nor dependable workers. They were "unreliable, lazy and unproductive," only suited for raising cotton, unable to use farm machinery effectively and not possessing the abilities for intensive farming.[6] In contrast, Chinese workers were thought to be "in every way commendable" and far superior to black people.[7] They were more industrious, thrifty, and docile and far more desirable as field hands, possessing special talents for working the soil and with expertise in orchard tending, vine cultivation, and gardening. Therefore the quickest solution to Florida's labor problems was the wholesale importation of Chinese coolies to work the South's mines, to till its fields, to pick its cotton, and to man its machinery in factories.[8] *Florida Agriculturist* issued repeated calls for the annulment of the Chinese Exclusion Act of 1882 so that large-scale employment of Chinese laborers would be possible.[9]

However, despite the high expectations, the proposed Chinese settlement in Florida never materialized. As both the Democrats and Republicans fought for control of the state, the Chinese question quickly became entangled in the Reconstruction-era politics.[10] While the recruitment of Chinese workers was favored by Democrats, Republicans charged that Chinese immigration was not free or voluntary and was actually "a specious pretext for the revival of slavery."[11] Furthermore, importation of Chinese workers would only serve the interests of large landowners and developers and leave the ordinary people more vulnerable to exploitation. By the early 1900s, the state's economy went through serious depressions. With the labor market filled with a large number of unemployed people, calls for immigration were finally muted, and a Florida-for-Floridians sentiment was on the rise. Chinese people quickly came under attack for their heathen religion and their alleged immorality and criminality. In the end, Chinese labor never became a significant factor in Florida, even though for a few decades newspapers frequently speculated and politicians charged back and forth about the issue.

Nevertheless, quite a few Chinese immigrants did make their way to Florida, some by way of California, New York, or Boston, others from Cuba. From the 1840s to the early 1870s, Chinese indentured laborers and smuggled Chinese citizens from British colonies were brought to Cuba, where they worked on railroads, in agriculture, cigarette-making, and as peddlers and domestics. Spanish officials, like their counterparts in the United States, in an effort to seek an alternative to African slave labor in Cuba, imported 125,000 Chinese laborers between 1850 and the closing of the "coolie" trade by the United States in 1874.[12] It is within this framework that Cuba became the front door for Chinese immigrants into Florida and the rest of the southern states. In addition, some Chinese laborers made their way into Florida from the Tennessee and Alabama gateway, as three thousand Chinese "coolies" were recruited from California to build the Alabama Great Southern Railway with some finding their way into Florida soon afterward.[13] Even after the Chinese Exclusion Act, which blocked entrance of Chinese laborers to the United States, went into effect, they were still permitted to enter the port of San Francisco en route to Cuba via railway to Tampa. It was reported that in 1917, over 3,107 Chinese immigrants passed through the port of Tampa on their way to Cuba.[14] Accordingly, the smuggling of illegal immigrants was occasionally reported in the local media, as was the case in 1920, when thirteen Chinese immigrants were caught and repatriated.[15]

Initially working in railroad construction, on plantations, and in lumber and turpentine camps, some Chinese workers left the work gangs for better economic opportunities in Jacksonville, Tampa, Pensacola, and later Miami and even Key West. They were able to carve out a successful niche in the state's economic structure, as demonstrated by the thriving Joe's Markets in Miami's black neighborhoods. In addition to laundry businesses in Florida, they also ran several small truck farms in the Jacksonville area growing winter vegetables for the Chinese markets in the North. However, most of the early Chinese business ventures were a temporary and small-scale phenomenon, as noted by Pozzetta, their development hindered by the lack of a sizable ethnic clientele and by an economic system that pushed Chinese residents into a restricted set of marginal occupations.[16]

Laundry Business in Tampa

During the early years of Chinese immigration to Florida, as in most other parts of the country, laundries accounted for the overwhelming majority of Chinese business ventures, with restaurants and groceries trailing behind. Since the laundry business required little capital or machinery, only the commitment to work long and hard, from the late 1880s every major city in Florida had one or more Chinese laundries. Jacksonville counted seven Chinese laundries in 1886, and by 1917 that number increased to 25. Two Chinese males were recorded as running a laundry business in West Palm Beach, according to the 1900 US census, and ten other Chinese laundrymen were also noted in Key West, Florida.[17] However, it was in Tampa that a large number of Chinese laundries thrived in the late nineteenth century. According to the *Tampa Tribune*, the city had 48 Chinese laundries in 1895, employing 197 washing maids, most of them African Americans.[18]

Because of its port and proximity to Cuba, a group of Chinese people settled in Tampa in the late nineteenth century. In 1886, the city's first Chinese restaurant opened across the street from the Ybor factory. Called El Chino Pajarito or the Little Chinese Bird, the owner passionately backed the efforts of Cuba's rebels, going as far as giving knives to patriots to kill Spaniards. According to the historical marker erected in 1962, "Cuban exiles in the 1890s met to plot for independence at a restaurant operated on this site by the patriot Antonio Menendez, a Chinese from Cuba."[19] Initially, the Tampa business community quietly accepted the Chinese immigrants as long as they did not compete with the commercial and financial development of the city. The small Chinese community in Tampa had about sixty people from 1895 to 1900. Most were licensed as businessmen, operating laundries as bona fide merchants, and a few were in the trade business importing Chinese novelties, herbs, and other things. Arriving in the Florida frontier, those new immigrants faced tremendous challenges including legislative measures imposed directly against them. When the Chinese laundrymen were in direct competition with a local steam laundry operated by Mr. J. Mac Towne, a popular and respected citizen, he was influential in having local ordinances changed that restricted his Chinese competitors.[20] In 1899, the Chinese laundry operators petitioned Tampa City Council for a reduction of their occupation license to ten dollars from twenty-five dollars, which was as much as a merchant with twenty thousand dollars in stock. The petition was denied on the grounds that the Chinese operators sent their money away and were not desirable citizens after all.[21]

Following the national trend, eventually the hostility toward foreign immigrants peaked in Florida by 1892, ten years after the Chinese Exclusion Act went into effect, based on the charges that the Chinese immigrants were trouble makers, immoral, had heathen religious beliefs, and held onto their old customs and traditions. The Florida Agricultural Commissioner urged a closing of the doors to any new classes of undesirable immigrants who might be unable to survive in an agricultural-capitalist economy for fear they would become a burden to the state rather than an asset.[22] Among several regulations implemented, one law required that all Chinese laborers in the United States must file with the Internal Revenue Service in the district in which they resided, photograph themselves, and obtain certificates of residence that must be exhibited whenever called for by an agent of the government. The penalty for failure to have such certificates was deportation to the country from which the defendant came. In 1898, nine Chinese citizens were detained for this violation, despite the fact that some of them had lived in Tampa for more than ten years.[23]

Throughout the nation local restriction laws were passed to control the Chinese population and their activities. They were prohibited from testifying in the courtroom against any white person and from taking the bar exam in order to practice law.[24] In 1904, Harry Wing's laundry at 307 Polk Street in Tampa was robbed of $306 cash and the case remained unsolved.[25] In the following year, Hop Lung Li of Port Tampa was the sole witness against Robert Green, charged with entering a building with intent to commit a crime. However, the local court hearing the case made fun of his language difficulties, much to the amusement of the court and to the humiliation of Li.[26]

Despite the racial segregation and antimiscegenation legislation imposed in the Deep South, there were occasional reports of interracial marriages between white people and other ethnicities. According to the 1900 US census, Frances Crumpler, who was born in China in 1862, married Herbert Crumpler in 1892, who was originally from England. The couple lived in Hillsborough County, Florida, and had two children together.[27] Chester Chin Wing, who operated a Chinese restaurant located at 1005 East Scott Street in Tampa, married an American woman in 1903 and had a daughter two years later. However, he ran into trouble with the US Immigration, went to jail, and lost his restaurant business. His wife and daughter soon left him and his wife adopted her mother's maiden name to avoid any repercussion.[28] On June 17, 1913, it was reported that Charlie Chow, a Chinese immigrant who married an African American woman with two children, was arrested for operating an opium den in Tampa.[29] In addition, according to the 1920 US census, both Patricia Diago and Rosa Garcia were cigar workers in Tampa, both were born to a Chinese mother and a Cuban father, and Florentino Gonzales, who played baseball with the Tampa Grays as a star pitcher in 1899, was also born to a Cuban father and a Chinese mother.[30]

However, because of the antimiscegenation laws and the impact of the Chinese Exclusion Act on new immigration, most Chinese laborers were forced to live celibate and lonely lives. Since so many avenues of relaxation were unavailable to the average Chinese person living in Tampa, some indulged in a passion of gambling that was no less or greater than the passion for gambling by other elements of the Tampa community. Nevertheless, they were targeted and a few were arrested as a result. Corruption came along with the crackdown. In 1906, a Tampa deputy was detained for extorting money from the Chinese gamblers of Ybor City in return for his protection.[31] On August 14, 1917, the *Tampa Times* noted that Charley P. Lee, a Chinese laundryman and restaurant operator, was arrested for living with a white woman.[32]

Because of the discriminative measures in place that restricted the flow of new immigrants, Chinese manual laundries in Tampa could not sustain their business and compete with steam laundries. By the early 1920s, there were only nine laundries owned by Chinese residents in the city, including Wah Sing's laundry store located in downtown, where curious tourists gathered to stare at him.[33]

Chinese Grocery Stores in Miami

While the small Chinese community in Tampa declined steadily over the years, Southeast Florida saw a boom of Chinese grocery stores in the fast-growing Miami area. Around the turn of the twentieth century, a few Chinese residents of Miami engaged in the laundry business. However, they could not compete with services provided by black workers and other immigrant workers. When Henry Flagler extended the railroad to Miami and developed the city as a resort for tourists, many Bahamian women were employed as maids, cooks, and washing ladies in the city's new hotels and restaurants, and most wealthy white settlers also had their own black servants for daily household work.[34]

By the 1920s, Florida experienced a period of land boom, and that is the time when Joe Wing and Joe Fred Gong migrated to the state and launched the Chinese grocery store tradition in Miami. Joe Wing, who came to the United States in 1909 at age seventeen, first learned the laundry business at his father's store in Boston. He worked in Chinese restaurants in New York and Chicago and then ran a grocery store in Mississippi before relocating to Florida. Meanwhile, in 1914, Joe Fred Gong also emigrated from China as a teenager to join his father's laundry store in Georgia. He then tried his luck in Miami but struggled in the laundry business in the mid-1920s. That is the time he befriended Joe Wing and seized a new business opportunity in the fast-growing region of the state. Due to the racial segregation in the South at that time, black people were not allowed to shop in white-owned stores, so the two Joes decided to open a grocery store located at NW Third Avenue and Tenth Street in Overtown, a black neighborhood where there was little competition.[35] Called Joe's Market, the store was actually named after their Chinese last name Zhou (Chou or Chow), a common surname in China. Because of the confusion in the United States over the East Asian custom of having the family name first, the two partners had begun using Joe as their first names and adopted new family names. They believed the pronunciation not only was close to their original Chinese family name, but also blended nicely with American culture.

The cofounders soon went separate ways and each opened a new grocery store in Miami. Through family kinship connections, Gong began to open and sell grocery stores to newly arrived relatives. He even arranged loan payments through Chinese trade organizations for those who could not afford to purchase an established store. Before long, Joe's Markets began to pop up, and by 1967 there were thirty-eight independently owned and operated markets in and around Miami.[36] Although the grocery business was hard work with long hours and a low profit margin, it offered new immigrants an opportunity to make an honest living and sustained the growth of the Chinese community in South Florida.

Following Chinese tradition, Gong went back to China and married a woman picked out by his mother. His wife joined him in 1929 and together they had five children in Miami. Each of the Joe's Markets was truly a family business. The father and mother ran the store, and the kids were expected to help as soon as they were old enough. The children worked in the family grocery stores, which stayed open seven days a week from early morning to late evening, averaging fourteen hours each day. They stocked shelves, marked goods, and checked out groceries. That left little time for vacation or outings, and when the family did go out together, it was usually to visit other Chinese-speaking friends and relatives.[37] "There was always something to do," as noted by Eddie Gong, Joe Fred Gong's son, "sweep the floor or clean out the meat compartment or divide sugar or rice into one-pound bags."[38]

Initially, the relationship between Chinese store owners and their African American customers was polite and cordial, according to research done by Gordy, as grocers often extended credit to those whom they knew well, and with few exceptions, most debts were eventually repaid.[39] However, as many of the first generation of Chinese immigrants approached retirement age, they began to face increasing competition from modern supermarket chains. More significantly, when the civil unrest unfolded in the 1960s, the neighborhood began to deteriorate and crime rose sharply. After the assassination of Dr. Martin Luther King Jr., out of the sheer frustration with prolonged and widespread discrimination in the country, civil disturbances reached their peak in 1968. During the racial riots, Miami neighborhoods where Chinese stores operated experienced a series of looting and shooting. Almost every store was robbed, some were burned down, two Chinese grocers were killed, and half a dozen were shot or beaten.[40] After the riots and the crime wave that swept through the neighborhood, only a few stores survived in the early 1970s; and by 1986 only one store remained open.

Cultural Identity and Integration

Most immigrants coming to America sought new opportunities and better lives. However, the early Chinese settlers in the United States were not regarded as true immigrants but as "sojourners." Since the late nineteenth century, because of the Chinese Exclusion Act and other discriminative measures implemented, it was almost impossible for Chinese immigrants to become naturalized citizens. Traveling from a long distance and isolated by a different language, skin color, and clothes, they relied on their own culture and customs to adjust to life in the new continent. A big part of Chinese tradition is ancestor worship. Strongly influenced by Confucian philosophy, many believe that one should always return to the motherland at the end of one's life, no matter how far one must travel. This is also the case for those settled in Tampa, who often dreamed of their homeland

and desired to return home for a visit. When Bean Kee, a Chinese laundryman, who maintained the traditional Chinese dress and hair, died in Tampa in August 1895, his body was embalmed and sent to China for burial. The funeral expenses and transportation to China cost $400. Two Chinese men accompanied the body as far as San Francisco, where it was transferred to a steamer destined to China.[41] Around that time, a ticket from Tampa to Hong Kong cost $118.50.[42]

The language barrier was definitely an obstacle that prevented some Chinese immigrants from adapting to and joining the mainstream culture. Early Chinese immigrants had a strong belief in hard work, but many of them had difficulty in effectively communicating and interacting with local Americans, as the economic system of the time had pushed them into marginal occupations of laundry, grocery, and restaurant businesses that required long working hours. They generally labored more than ten or twelve hours a day, six or seven days a week, with their business operations defining their world: work, social activities, and cultural life.[43] Since early Chinese immigration to Florida was a small-scale phenomenon, there was no Chinatown like San Francisco or New York that they could rely on for support. Nevertheless, some of the Chinese settlers did attempt to integrate into mainstream American society. A practical way was through religious affiliations, and it is through Sunday schools that many Chinese immigrants began to learn the language and interact with local Americans. The traditional Chinese belief system is a mixture of Buddhism, Taoism, and Confucianism, but it is not a well-organized religion compared with that in the West. Since Christianity was already known to the Chinese people through various foreign missionaries who went to China to preach, it was only natural for some of the immigrants to attend religious services in America. In the early reports in Florida, a willingness to accommodate the Chinese residents into local communities through religious affiliation is noted. Lue Gim Gong was baptized in 1876 at a Chinese Sunday school in North Adams, Massachusetts, and was already a devoted Christian before his migration to Florida ten years later.[44] As early as 1890, *Tampa Journal* indicated an interest in the mission work by the Chinese community.[45] The Chinese Mission School continued to flourish and by 1898 its program was held every Sunday at the First Baptist Church of Tampa.

Although many believed that Chinese Americans lacked civic commitment, Quong (Kuang) Wah's name appeared on the voter registration list for 1888 in Tampa. Born in China in 1860, he immigrated to the United States in the 1880s, and along with his cousin Sam Wah, opened a Chinese laundry at 413 Polk Street. The advertisement on a board near the entrance to his store—twenty cents for pants, thirteen cents for shirts with collars, ten cents for shirts or sheets, five cents for neckties, and four cents for socks—offered a glimpse of the Tampa economy in 1889. [46] In a municipal election, Quong Wah declared his candidacy for the city council. Poll returns indicate that he received one vote, apparently that of his own. Dubbed as the "Plumed Knight" or "Knight of the Washboard" by local Tampa newspaper, Quong Wah continued to pay his business occupation tax to operate a restaurant, and he continued to pay his poll tax as a registered voter in district 6.[47] Besides him, other Chinese registered voters in Tampa in 1890 included Lee Yik, Sam Sing, Lun Sing, and Wah Sing.[48]

While adapting to life in the new world, Chinese immigrants also received generous assistance from local communities. It was through the goodwill of Fanny Burlingame that Lue Gim Gong was able to learn English and later inherited the Burlingame's family citrus grove in DeLand, Florida, when she passed away in 1903. According to Dominic L. Koo (Koo Sce-yi), a Chinese American judge in Dade County from 1973 to 1981, "one case of discrimination [against the Chinese] is overshadowed by ten cases of concern and kindness by the American people."[49]

Perhaps because of their quiet and cordial nature, many Chinese immigrants got along well with their new countrymen. As noted by Samuel Lee, an ordained deacon of the Chinese Baptist Church and associate professor of mechanical engineering at the University of Miami, "The Chinese culture teaches us not to fight, but to bear with the person. So if you treat me badly, I'll do my best to show you that I am due respect. And if I can't do it in my generation, I'll do it in the next one."[50]

However, when facing injustice, not everyone was willing to quietly "swallow the bitterness" and move on. Lue Gim Gong had to fight for his compensation, and some Chinese immigrants also learned to use legal tools to defend their rights. In 1906, after Hubert D. King, president of Tampa City Council, alleged in a statement to the city council that the California Chinese Restaurant of Tampa was an opium joint, owner Wing Eng filed a lawsuit against King seeking $5,000 in damage compensation.[51] Little did he know that only a few decades later, a grandson of a laundryman would become the "boy president" of the United States, and the first American of Chinese descent to hold public office in Florida.[52] The Joe's Markets of Miami left a legacy of a younger generation of Chinese immigrants who were well-educated and successful, partly as a result of their parents' hard work. Eddie Gong, who served in Florida's House of Representatives from 1963 to 1966 and the state senate from 1967 to 1973, is a lawyer, and two of his sisters are doctors. Gong, along with Dominic Koo, blazed trails as Asian American elected officials in Florida.[53]

During the early years, because of their small numbers, kinship and community organizations were an important aspect of Chinese family life and their support system. For those who were far away from home, especially during times of hardships and racial violence, these networks provided the ties that helped immigrants cope with the transition and survive in the new world. Notable among the early groups was the On Leong Association, started by George

Eng, who came to Miami in 1925 via San Francisco and New York.[54] Then there were the Chinese American Benevolent Association of Miami, founded by Joe Kwan, and the On Leong Chinese Merchants Association, organized by those who came to Florida from Cuba. All shared goals of promoting business and support, preserving Chinese traditions and cultural heritage, enhancing Chinese American interests, providing social services for the aged and needy, and sponsoring youth and educational programs.[55]

Perhaps the history of the Chinese Floridians in the twentieth century is best represented in Miami. While the small Chinese community in Tampa declined, Miami grew to become the largest metropolitan area in Florida, and along the way the Chinese population also began to rise. In 1955, from an initial twenty families, the Chinese Department of the Flagler Street Baptist Church was established. In 1968, Rev. Kwong-Wah Lau, a Hong Kong native, became Florida's first ordained Chinese pastor.[56] The church's membership soon grew to more than two hundred, with two services provided on each Sunday, and sermons delivered in both Mandarin and English.[57] By that time, scattered throughout Dade County, Chinese Americans were fragmented into three general groups: a diminishing number of grocers who traditionally operated markets in the black districts; restaurant owners who served Chinese food; and an increasing number of the professionals who entered medicine, law, teaching, and other fields. South Florida has truly become a multicultural society. Within the Chinese community, besides Protestants, there are also Buddhists, Catholics, and even Jewish Chinese in the greater Miami region.

After the federal immigration reform of 1965 that eliminated the previous discriminatory legislations and favored skills, training, and family reunification, the Chinese population in Florida began to increase sharply. Although not as visible or cohesive as other ethnic groups, they still maintain their cultural identity and are occasionally praised as a "model minority" by mainstream media. According to the Miami Police Department in 1972, there were no Chinese juvenile delinquents nor any Chinese adults in jail.[58] Nowadays, the Chinese and Chinese American population in Florida is a proud, highly educated, hard-working, and prosperous group who have melded into the mainstream of American society. They have no need to band together in cramped enclaves where little English is spoken, as their ancestors did in other cities a century ago; and unlike their forebears, they are not making their fortunes and returning to China to retire. They are staying, to make their homes here.[59]

Florida Splendid China

Florida is known for its sunshine and tourist attractions. Since the 1970s, the openings of Walt Disney World, Universal Studios, and Sea World have brought new large waves of immigrants to central Florida. Frank and Josephine Chen, who immigrated to the United States in 1968, built their fortune through real estate development. During a 1986 trip to central Florida, they bought a barren strip of 560 acres located off US Highway 192, just west of Disney World. After visiting the original Splendid China in Shenzhen, they began to consider a similar attraction in Florida. Through negotiation with China Travel Service, the largest tourism firm in mainland China, a partnership was formed with a total investment that eventually reached over $100 million. Under the agreement, the Chens provided the land and management services, while China Travel Service supplied the building materials, the architects, and the personnel.[60]

Constructing the attraction proved to be a unique experience that exposed Americans to the Chinese work ethic and introduced Chinese workers to American culture. Some 120 Chinese artists were recruited to come to the United States to work on the exhibits. To fulfill the requirement of both governments, each had to file immigration documents. No women were included, and most men were masters in their artistic fields, including calligraphy, painting, stone carving, bonsai sculpting, and pottery. Every Chinese province was represented in the meticulously designed Florida attraction. Leading exhibits included the Great Wall, comprising 6.5 million one-by-two-inch bricks, one-sixteenth the original size; and a full-size reproduction of a street scene in Suzhou, a city known as the Venice of the East. Much of the construction and tens of thousands of figurines were built on a scale of 1:15—everything was handcrafted, carefully detailed, and sculpted by Chinese artists. Reporters visiting the construction site were frequently astounded by the craftsmanship and the marvelous attention to detail that was given to the tiny structures. The workmanship was so exacting and the colors so enticing that one easily became absorbed in the work.

After a couple years of painstaking construction, on Saturday, December 18, 1993, hundreds of public officials, local dignitaries, and special guests attended the grand opening ceremony of Florida Splendid China. Former US president Richard Nixon, Florida governor Lawton Chiles, Nobel laureates C. N. Yang, T. D. Lee, and C. C. Ting, former secretary of state Alexander Haig, US representatives John Mica and Bill McCollum, and Orlando mayor Glenda Hood served on the Honorary Opening Day Committee. Governor Chiles proclaimed December 18 "Splendid China Day." Chinese president Jiang Zemin, former president Yang Shangkun, Premier Li Peng, and Chinese ambassador Li Daoyu sent their congratulatory remarks. Vice Premier and Foreign Minister Qian Qichen and three other Chinese officials attended the ceremony. President Jiang's invitation, "Let the world learn about China" was chosen as the park's mission statement. Qian Weichang, vice chairman of the Chinese Political Consultative Conference, commented on the occasion: "Chinese culture does not only belong to the Chinese people, it is the common wealth of people of the world. An opening China needs to know more about the rest of the world, and the world needs to know more about China as well. The Splendid China Theme Park, reflecting the characteristics of Chinese culture and ideology, can serve as a window of Chinese history and culture."[61]

On the following day, when Florida Splendid China officially opened for business, more than three thousand tourists flocked to the new attraction.[62] Initially, the park was well received by the general public and praised by newspapers across the country. The *Chicago Sun Times* commented: "There are no rides and no glitz, but there is a marvelous immersion in Chinese culture and history, including performances by 165 of China's top entertainers."[63] The *Houston Chronicle* noted: "Strictly from a visitor's standpoint, Splendid China is a remarkable achievement. . . . Attention to detail is mind-boggling. . . . Throughout its 76 acres, the facility is awash with color and beauty."[64] The *New Orleans Times Picayune* called the attraction an "exquisite, monumental work."[65] The *Tampa Tribune* enthused, "Walking among even miniature replicas of Chinese landmarks, one begins to feel a figure in a Chinese painting—a tiny part of an expansive space, a pinpoint in a timeline 5,000 years long."[66] The *Miami Herald* remarked: "From an artistic point of view, much of Splendid China is so good it really doesn't belong here. There are no rides, no light shows, no water slides, no monsters, and no trips to outer space at this park. You're supposed to walk through it quietly and admire it. Set against all the other thundering tourist attractions of Central Florida, Splendid China shines like a small jeweled Fabergé Easter egg in the middle of Jurassic Park."[67]

Altogether, the park planned to employ between three hundred and four hundred people. Half would be Chinese entertainers, tour guides, chefs, and artisans. In the end, the attraction brought 550 jobs to the local economy, 250 of which were part-time. Four hundred jobs were held by central Floridians and 150 were Chinese entertainers and crafts specialists. Once construction began in December 1991, nearly two thousand local contractors, surveyors, landscape architects, electricians, and rock sculptors were hired to work on the project, with half of the $100 million investment spent on labor. By the first year of operation, Florida Splendid China had become a top taxpayer in Osceola County.[68] The opening of Florida Splendid China not only attracted new immigrants to the region but also promoted the friendship between Florida and China and fostered a better understanding by mainstream Americans about Chinese civilization. The attraction sponsored many events such as a lunar new year celebration, moon festival, kite festival, martial arts competitions, the reunion of former US diplomats to China, and the gathering of American families with adopted Chinese children. The park also made efforts to enhance its appeal for students, youth groups, conventioneers, and senior citizens with advertisements promoting "a relaxed cultural experience" and "Splendid China Learning Adventures" and sent performance groups to other parts of the country to promote Chinese culture and the Florida attraction.[69]

Although the park greatly raised public awareness about Chinese history and cultures, it was a complete disaster in economic terms. The fundamental error of Florida Splendid China was that its design was not based on a careful study of American tastes. The park leadership failed to apprehend the tourism culture in the highly competitive Florida market, where vacationing Americans would choose thrills over cultural enlightenment. As one of the region's many second-tier attractions, its passive experience of a walk-through outdoor museum park had limited appeal to central Florida tourists. Focusing on the details of workmanship during the construction, they lost sight of what it would take to get Americans into the attraction. Day-to-day operations also suffered from poor management. Frequent changes of top leadership made it impossible for the attraction to develop successful long-term strategies, and its public relations campaigns were poorly sustained and largely ineffective.

On December 31, 2003, after ten years of operation, Florida Splendid China dimmed its lights and faded away. Optimistically conceived yet poorly researched, well-executed but improperly managed, it never flourished in the competitive central Florida market. Political controversies and demonstrations also plagued the park during its ten-year history, and it finally fell victim to the region's struggling tourism business following the 2001 terrorist attacks.

Although the project represented one of the most disastrous overseas investments ever made by a Chinese company, it is an important chapter in Chinese and Chinese American history in Florida in the late twentieth century.

Notable Chinese Americans in Florida

As representatives of the first and second generations of Chinese residents of Florida and the new wave of immigrants after World War II, three Chinese Americans are featured here to highlight their role and contributions to the development of the Sunshine State.

Lue Gim Gong (ca. 1858–1925) was a Chinese American horticulturist who made notable contributions to the growth of Florida's citrus industry. Born in Taishan, Guangdong Province, Lue left China at age twelve and immigrated to the United States with help from his uncle. He first worked in a shoe factory in San Francisco, but he soon went with a group of Chinese workers to another shoe factory in Massachusetts, where he learned English at a Chinese Sunday school, became a Christian, and joined the Baptist Church. He met Fanny Burlingame, cousin of Anson Burlingame and a volunteer teacher who greatly influenced Lue's life. Intrigued by Lue's fresh intelligence, she invited Lue to live in her house as an "adopted" son. Lue spent much time working in Burlingame's large garden and conservatory filled with exotic plants. He was familiar with plants since he had worked in the orange groves in his hometown, where his mother taught him how to cross-pollinate blossoms and graft stock. When the Burlingame family purchased an orange grove in Florida, Lue joined them in DeLand in 1886. The following year he became an American citizen and cast his first vote in a general election. The severe freezes in the 1890s greatly motivated him to work on developing a strain of orange that would resist frost. He crossed the Florida Harts Late orange with a variety from the Mediterranean region, and the result was a sweet, juicy fruit that could endure severe weather. Named the Lue Gim Gong orange, it was described as probably "the hardiest of all sweet orange varieties now commonly cultivated in America. It is a noteworthy fruit because of the length of time the fruit may be held on the tree."[70] For his achievement in horticulture, Lue was awarded a Silver Wilder Medal by the American Pomological Society in 1911, then the highest national agricultural award and the first time it was given to a citrus grower, and a road was also named by Ransom Olds in Pinellas County to honor Lue.[71] Even though Lue was called the "wizard of citrus growers" and the "Chinese Burbank of Florida," fame did not bring him fortune. As his name spread, thousands of visitors came to his grove and he would give away free samples of his fruit and plants, and he was often cheated by his distributors who refused to pay for materials purchased.[72] Three years before his death, his mortgage became overdue and public donations were raised to save his property. It took seventy-five years to finally honor Lue, when a memorial garden was dedicated on October 15, 1999.

Edmond Joseph Gong (1930–) is the son of Joe Fred Gong, one of the cofounders of Joe's Market, and a classic example of the new generation of Chinese Americans. Eddie Gong was born in Miami in 1930. As the only boy in the household, his parents had great hope for him. Like any other first generation of Chinese immigrants, Joe Gong toiled and saved for his children's education and a brighter future. Although he did not have the chance to receive higher education, he worked hard to provide such opportunities for his children and did not expect them to run a laundry or grocery store when growing up. Eventually, all of the Gongs's five children graduated from college and became successful professionals. Of Eddie's four sisters, two became doctors—one a pediatrician, the other a radiologist, and two of his nephews are attorneys.[73] Growing up in Miami, Eddie and his sisters had to help out with their father's grocery business, and there was no Chinese language school for the siblings to learn their native language properly. Unlike his father, however, Eddie was eager and ready to assimilate into the mainstream American life. When he was a high school junior in Miami, Eddie Gong demonstrated his leadership skills and was named the president of the Boys Forum of National Government in Washington, DC, which was sponsored by the American Legion to give youth an opportunity to observe the functions of the federal government. On August 5, 1947, Eddie Gong along with 102 other teenagers visited the White House and was warmly received by Pres. Harry S. Truman. Five years later, Gong graduated from Harvard University cum laude and attended Harvard Law School and University of Miami afterward. As a second-generation Chinese American, he quickly discarded the traditional way of thinking of his parents and fully embraced American individualism and culture. In 1955, he published an article endorsing interracial marriage in *American Magazine*.[74] Titled "I Want to Marry an American Girl," the essay stood in sharp contrast to the antimiscegenation debacle of his grandfather's and father's generations a few decades earlier. Gong was the first person of Chinese descent and the first Asian American elected to the Florida State Legislature, serving in the House of Representatives from 1963 to 1967 and the State Senate from 1967 to 1973. He later became an assistant US attorney for the Southern District of Florida and a public policy consultant.

Nelson Ying (1942–), a nuclear physicist, entrepreneur, philanthropist, and community leader in central Florida, is a representative of the new wave of Chinese students and professionals who arrived after the end of World War II. In 1955, Ying came to New York from Shanghai along with his parents, with only $600 in their pockets. After receiving his BS degree from the Polytechnic University in 1964, Ying continued his graduate studies at Adelphi University, earning a master's and a PhD in physics. First working as a NASA trainee and a captain in the US Army Corps of Engineers, Ying later became a professor of physics at the University of Central Florida and then president and chief executive officer of the China Group and of Quantum Nucleonics. Through these undertakings and with vision and determination, Ying became a very successful entrepreneur in Florida. Like many other Chinese Americans, he has a strong belief in education and has personally benefited from the advanced knowledge learned in the United States. Seeing it as a way to inspire the science leaders of tomorrow, he created and sponsors the Dr. Nelson Ying Science Competition through the Orlando Science Center, where he serves on the Board of Trustees. The contest not only awards scholarships to aspiring students but also honors the referring science teachers and the school principals. As a trustee of the University of Central Florida Foundation, he financed the Barbara Ying International Center to commemorate his late wife and to improve the quality of student life on campus. In addition, Ying is a director of the Eastern States Buddhist Temple and a corporate council member of the Economic Development Commission of Mid-Florida and contributed to the construction of the new headquarters building for the Heart of Florida United Way, the Patricia Ying Central Florida Distribution Center located in Orlando.

Contributions

The advancement of Chinese residents in Florida is closely tied with the development of the local communities. Since their arrival in the late nineteenth century, Chinese immigrants and Chinese Americans have made notable contributions to the growth of the Sunshine State's economy. First brought to Saint Augustine by Spanish settlers in 1565, citrus has become a very significant factor of the state economy and in the lives of millions of Floridians. Not only can its origins be traced back to Asia, Chinese Americans also made direct contributions to the growth of Florida's citrus industry, as demonstrated by Lue Gim Gong a century ago. In addition, early Chinese immigrants also brought with them new varieties of vegetables, crops, and flowers. Since the first half of the twentieth century, Florida has become a production base of Asian vegetables for restaurant and grocery businesses in the North.

Besides their direct role in the state economy, there are also records of Chinese Americans serving in the US armed forces. Frank A. Chinn was a naturalized Chinese American and a private in Company 188, US Regiment, during the Spanish-American War. He died on February 27, 1900, at Tampa, Florida.[75] Four decades later when the United States geared up for World War II, Gow Low, son of Joe Wing, cofounder of Joe's Market in Miami, was drafted by the air force to serve in 1941. He had hoped to study and become an aircraft engine mechanic but was rejected for being underweight. Returned to his grocery business, years later he would send his own son to become an air force lieutenant and a dermatologist.[76]

In recent years, Chinese Americans along with other immigrants have become a driving force in urban development. A good example is the Mandarin Plaza in Orlando. Financed by a group of Chinese American investors, it has become a miniature melting pot of ethnic diversity. Besides the anchoring Chinese grocery store, the plaza also houses Vietnamese, Korean, Filipino, Thai, and Japanese businesses including restaurants, salons, gift stores, and other retailers. Located on West Colonia Drive between Kirkman Road and Pine Hills Road, the former Westside Crossing Plaza is in an area where the region's Asian population has exploded in recent years. By retrofitting the mostly vacant strip center, the shopping mall has contributed to the economic revitalization of the area.[77]

As noted above, the opening of the Florida Splendid China in the 1990s brought hundreds of jobs to central Florida, and contributed millions of dollars to the state economy. Though it is regarded as a complete disaster in business terms, the theme park helped raise the awareness of Chinese culture and promoted the state's tourism. By the time of its closing, Florida already exported over $649 million to China, ranking the country among the top ten destinations for the state's products. With China's entry to the World Trade Organization, business ties between the two markets have grown even further. According to the statistics of the Florida-China Chamber of Commerce, Miami's trade with China reached $3.9 billion in 2009.[78] Nowadays, greater China has become the largest non-Latin trading partner of Florida, and Orlando and Miami are tied for third, behind New York and Los Angeles, as the most popular US destination for overseas tourists. After the relaxation of visa restrictions by the US government, local tourism leaders also expect to see an increase in Chinese tourists in the coming years.

In addition to those who arrived directly from greater China, many Chinese residents of Florida today are secondary migrants who came to the Sunshine State in search of better business opportunities. Attracted by the benign climate and the thriving economy, many Asian Americans began to migrate to the Sunshine State in the twentieth century. Notable among the Chinese newcomers are well-educated and highly skilled professionals. Many of them first studied at graduate schools in the United States and then worked as professors and research scientists at the leading institutions across the state. A significant number of people also work as computer programmers, electronic engineers, and chemists at various large corporations in Florida. The state's hospitals also experienced an increase of Chinese American medical specialists. They also are active in international trade, wholesale and retail, construction and real estate, tax, accounting, financial service, and other areas of business. Because of the state's booming economy and the continual growth in population, many of them have become independent and successful business owners, managing restaurants, grocery stores, gift shops, and other businesses. Altogether, they have been making noteworthy contributions to the state economic development over the years.

Not only have Chinese Americans recently grown into an underlying force in the state economy, more significantly they have contributed to Florida's ethnic and racial diversity. In addition to Chinese evangelical or Baptist churches across the state, there are also various Buddhist temples. For many Floridians, Chinese products and services have become an aspect of their daily lives. In the 1990s in the Orlando area alone, the number of Chinese restaurants has increased from about eighty to more than two hundred. From those business clusters Asian cultures begin to take root, where people may see African American lion dancers and Italian American Kung Fu masters join Chinese Americans in their traditional dresses celebrating the lunar new year, dragon boat racing, and moon festival each year.

For decades, Chinese Americans have formed various social groups to promote not only business interests but also language learning and cultural preservation in Florida. As one of the largest Asian American groups in the state, the Chinese residents of Florida are a very diverse and dynamic community. They have come not only from mainland China, Hong Kong, Taiwan, and other parts of the United States but also from Cuba, Vietnam, Mexico, Jamaica, Panama, Peru, and Brazil. Those diverse groups of people are bonded together through different community organizations to forge their common cultural identity. Currently, there are numerous Chinese-related cultural and nonprofit organizations active in Florida, including: the Organization of Chinese Americans, Florida-China Association, United Chinese Association of Florida, Chinese American Scholars Association of Florida, Chinese American Association of Central Florida, Chinese Association of Science, Education and Culture of South Florida, Chinese American Association of Tampa Bay, Coral Springs Chinese Cultural Association, Jacksonville Chinese Association, Orlando Chinese Professional Association, and the Suncoast Association of Chinese Americans, to name a few. Some regional and some statewide in scope, all are dedicated to the promotion of cultural awareness, the integration of Chinese Americans, and the enhancement of educational, business, economic, and broad friendship ties between Florida and China.

Chinese Americans have made solid contributions to the cultural diversity in Florida. To raise their profile and promote the cultural awareness, they have cosponsored the Asian Heritage Month celebration and cultural parades, organized community service events, established web presence, published papers and newsletters, financed minority scholarships, and supported weekend language schools. Moreover, Chinese Americans have begun to be much more vocal and politically active, inviting candidates to address issues of community concerns before election time and sponsoring census drives and voter registrations. Their publications not only contain useful information on trade and travel, community, scholarships, job listings, matchmaking, immigration and healthcare but also serve as voices of Chinese Americans in Florida. Some organizations have also built their own cultural centers with schools and small libraries. Nowadays from Miami to Jacksonville, every major city in Florida has a number of Chinese schools for children to learn the language, and there are Chinese and Chinese American Students Associations at all large universities across the state. Among the recent efforts, a notable example is the annual Chinese New Year Festival, cosponsored by the Florida Chapter of the Organization of Chinese Americans, the Chinese Activity Center, the Chinese American Benevolent Association, the Chinese Baptist Church of Miami, the Miami Chinese Language School, the Chinese Women's Club, the National Chinese Welfare Council of Miami, and the World Kwong Tung Community Association. Attended by thousands each year, the festival features Chinese folk dances, dragon and lion dancing, Peking opera, and Chinese music among others. Additionally, in July 2007, Xiaozhen You was crowned in Miami as the first Miss Florida Asia. The pageant's mission is to help Asian American women increase their cultural awareness and nurture them to be future leaders.

According to the 2010 US census report, there are more than seventy-two thousand people of Chinese heritage currently residing in Florida.[79] Although still less than 1 percent of the state's total population, it represents an impressive increase of 56 percent since 2010. Looking forward, it is reasonable to assume that the Chinese American population will continue to grow in Florida and they will continue to make important contributions to the history and culture of the Sunshine State in the foreseeable future.

Notes

1. US Census Bureau, "Profile of General Population and Housing Characteristics: 2010 Demographic Profile Data-Florida," http://factfinder2.census.gov/faces/nav/jsf/pages/searchresults.xhtml.

2. George Pozzetta, "Chinese Encounter with Florida: 1865–1920," *Chinese America: History and Perspectives* 2 (1989): 43.

3. Raymond A. Mohl, "Asian Immigration to Florida," *Florida Historical Quarterly* 74, 3 (1996): 264.

4. "Coolie Labor for Cotton," *St. Augustine Examiner*, November 24, 1866, 1.

5. Roger Daniels, "Asian Groups," in *Encyclopedia of Southern Culture*, ed. Charles R. Wilson and William Ferris, (Chapel Hill: University of North Carolina Press, 1989), 418–21.

6. George Pozzetta, "Foreigners in Florida: A Study of Immigration Promotion, 1865–1910," *Florida Historical Quarterly* 53 (October 1974): 166.

7. George M. Barbour, *Florida for Tourists, Invalids, and Settlers* (Jacksonville: Douglas Printing, 1882), 227.

8. Pozzetta, "Foreigners in Florida," 171.

9. *Florida Agriculturist*, July 20, 1904, August 23, 1904, September 28, 1904, November 1, 1904.

10. Pozzetta, "Chinese Encounter with Florida," 47.

11. *Tallahassee Sentinel*, July 24, 1869.

12. Gary R. Mormino and George E. Pozzetta, *The Immigrant World of Ybor City* (Urbana, IL: University of Illinois Press, 1987), 72.

13. Burke Davis, *The Southern Railway: Road of Innovators* (Chapel Hill: University of North Carolina Press, 1985), 184–85.

14. *St. Petersburg Times*, August 11, 1917.

15. "Thirteen Chinks Chased on Way: Bemoan Sad Fate as They Watch over Rail at Fading Country That Refuses Welcome," *Tampa Morning Tribune*, June, 1920.

16. Pozzetta, "Chinese Encounter with Florida," 54.

17. US Census Bureau, Twelfth Census of the United States, 1900, Dade County, Lake Worth Precinct 2, West Palm Beach, 240 (A522); and Monroe County, Key West.

18. *Tampa Tribune*, August 25, 1895.

19. "El Chino-Pajarito Restaurant", Historical Marker Database, http://www.hmdb.org/marker.asp?marker=15295.

20. Julius Gordon, *The Chinese Colony in Hillsborough County, Florida* (Tampa, FL: privately published, 1999), 18.

21. Ibid, 27–28.

22. Ibid, 5.

23. *Tampa Weekly Tribune*, March 31, 1898; *Tampa Tribune*, April 15, 1898, April 20, April 25, 1898.

24. Gordon, *Chinese Colony*, 7.

25. *Tampa Weekly Tribune*, July 14, 1904.

26. *Tampa Weekly Tribune*, February 5, 1905.

27. US Census Bureau, Twelfth Census of the United States, 1900, 29th Precinct, Hillsborough County, Florida, 154:80.

28. Gordon, *Chinese Colony*, 22.

29. *Tampa Times*, June 17, 1913.

30. Gordon, *Chinese Colony*, 47–48.

31. *Tampa Weekly Tribune*, September 21, 1906.

32. *Tampa Times*, August 14, 1917.

33. *Tampa Daily Tribune*, May 18, 1923.

34. Josephine S. Gordy, "Chinese in Southeast Florida, 1900–1992" (master's thesis, Florida Atlantic University, 1994), 58.

35. Sam Jacobs, "Markets Kept Overtown Stocked," in *Mostly Sunny Days: A Miami Herald Salute to South Florida's Heritage*, edited by Bob Kearney (Miami: Miami Herald Publishing, 1986), 129.

36. Gordy, *Chinese in Southeast Florida*, 61–63.

37. Molly Sinclair, "Chinese Found Success in Miami," *Miami Herald*, March 7, 1972, 1D.

38. Sam Jacobs, "Markets Kept Overtown Stocked: For Almost 40 Years, Joe's Markets Provided Groceries in Black Neighborhoods and a Good Living for the Families that Owned the Stores," *Miami Herald*, January 27, 1986.

39. Gordy, *Chinese in Southeast Florida*, 59–61.

40. "Chinese in Dade Watch and Hope," *Miami Herald*, February 24, 1972; Sinclair, "Chinese Found Success," 1D.

41. Gordon, *Chinese Colony*, 21.

42. *Tampa Weekly Tribune*, October 7, 1897.

43. Cindy Wong, "Chinese outside Chinatown: A Chinese Community in South Florida," *Chinese America: History and Perspectives* (1991): 49–66.

44. Ruthanne McCunn, "Lue Gim Gong: A Life Reclaimed." *Chinese America: History and Perspectives* 2 (1989): 119.

45. *Tampa Journal*, January 2, 1890.

46. *Tampa Journal*, February 14, 1889; August 24, 1889.

47. *Tampa Weekly Tribune*, May 26, 1904; June 6, 1907; June 27, 1907; July 4, 1907.

48. Voter Registration Rolls, City of Tampa, 1888–1890.

49. Pat Gurosky, "They're in Mainstream Don't Need Chinatown," *Miami News*, February 24, 1972, 2D.

50. Molly Sinclair, "Language Is Chinese: Accent Is American," *Miami Herald*, March 9, 1972.

51. *Tampa Weekly Tribune*, September 18, 1906; December 6, 1906; December 27, 1906; July 18, 1907; September 5, 1907.

52. Nicknamed the "boy president of the USA", Gong was elected the president of the Boys Forum of National Government in Washington, DC, in 1947. For additional information, see Eddie Gong, "I Want to Marry an American Girl," in *Chinese American Voices: From the Gold Rush to the Present*, ed. Judy Yung, Gordon H. Chang, and Him M. Lai (Berkeley, CA: University of California Press, 2006), 240–46.

53. Erin Chan, "Increased Visibility for Asians," *Miami Herald*, May 13, 2002, 1B.

54. Jack Oswald, "Miami's Chinese Fete Eng," *Miami News*, July 13, 1958, 12A.

55. Gary Gibbs, "Founder of Joe's Markets Buried: Chinese Center Was Joe Kwan's Dream," *Miami News*, January 6, 1977.

56. "Bamboo Curtain Won't Open for Church, Says Minister," *Miami Herald*, April 1, 1972.

57. Mary Ann Giordano, "Chinese-English Service Bridges Far East, West," *Miami Herald*, May 2, 1977.

58. Molly Sinclair, "Ancient Traditions in a Modern World," *Miami Herald*, March 5, 1972.

59. Gurosky, "They're in Mainstream," 1D.

60. Wenxian Zhang, "A Splendid Idea Turned Sour in Florida: The Rise and Fall of Florida Splendid China," *Florida Historical Quarterly* 84, 3 (Winter 2006): 411–42.

61. Djun Ming, "Splendid China Takes Root in US," Xinhua News Agency, December 18, 1993.

62. Annie Tin, "The Public Gets to See the Splendor: Florida Splendid China Opened to the Paying Public Sunday and Drew More Than 3,000 Visitors, Surpassing Expectations," *Orlando Sentinel*, December 20, 1993, A1.

63. Joan Dunlop, "Splendid China: No Glitz, but Marvelous Miniatures." *Chicago Sun Times*, April 3, 1994, Travel 3.

64. Harry Shattuck, "Splendid Florida: Splendid China Is State's Latest Offering," *Houston Chronicle*, May 15, 1994, Travel 1.

65. Millie Ball, "Florida's China Is Splendid," *Times Picayune*, April 16, 1995, Travel 3.

66. Cindy Rupert, "Park Recreates Splendid China Landmarks," *Tampa Tribune*, July 31, 194, Travel 4.

67. Michael Browning, "A Splendid China Setting Florida's Newest Theme Park a Small and Elegant World," *Miami Herald*, December 19, 1993, 1A.

68. Annie Tin, "New Park Is Splendid for Tax Rolls: Osceola Looks East–to China–for Some of the Goodies Walt Disney World Brought to Orange," *Orlando Sentinel*, December 17, 1993, D1.

69. George Diaz, "Theme Park Has Splendid Karate Competition," *Orlando Sentinel*, November 14, 1994, D13; Adrian McCoy, "Splendid New Year," *Pittsburgh Post Gazette*, January 19, 2001, Arts & Entertainment, 29.

70. Harold Hume, *The Cultivation of Citrus Fruits* (New York: Macmillan, 1926).

71. Ann Liebermann, "Ransom Eli Olds and the American Dream," in *Reflections of Oldsmar*, ed. Jerry Beverland (Oldsmar, FL: On Demand Printing, 2009).

72. McCunn, "Lue Gim Gong," 117–35.

73. Gordy, *Chinese in Southeast Florida*, 61–62.

74. Gong, "I Want to Marry an American Girl,": 15–17, 82–85.

75. Gordon, *Chinese Colony in Hillsborough County*, 21.

76. Gordy, *Chinese in Southeast Florida*, 61–62.

77. Sarah Hale, "Asian-themed Shops, Restaurants to Create Chinatown in Orlando, Florida," *Orlando Sentinel*, March 1, 2003, 1.

78. Florida-China Chamber of Commerce, http://floridachina.org/default.aspx.

79. US Census Bureau, "Profile of General Population and Housing Characteristics: 2010 Demographic Profile Data-Florida," http://factfinder2.census.gov/faces/nav/jsf/pages/searchresults.xhtml.

Works Cited

Barbour, George M. *Florida for Tourists, Invalids, and Settlers*. Jacksonville: Douglas Printing, 1882.

Daniels, Roger. "Asian Groups." In *Encyclopedia of Southern Culture*, edited by Charles R. Wilson and William Ferris. Chapel Hill: University of North Carolina Press, 1989.

Davis, Burke. *The Southern Railway: Road of Innovators*. Chapel Hill: University of North Carolina Press, 1985.

"El Chino-Pajarito Restaurant." Historical Marker Database, http://www.hmdb.org/marker.asp?marker=15295.

Florida Agriculturist. Vol. 29, no. 29 (July 20, 1904).

———. Vol. 31, no. 34 (August 24, 1904).

———. Vol. 31, no. 39 (September 28, 1904).

———. Vol. 31, no. 44 (November 2, 1904).

Florida-China Chamber of Commerce. http://floridachina.org/default.aspx.

Gong, Eddie. "I Want to Marry an American Girl." *American Magazine* 160, no. 3 (September 1955).

———. "I Want to Marry an American Girl." In *Chinese American Voices: From the*

Gold Rush to the Present, edited by Judy Yung, Gordon H. Chang, and Him M. Lai. Berkeley: University of California Press, 2006.

Gordon, Julius. *The Chinese Colony in Hillsborough County, Florida*. Tampa, FL: privately published, 1999.

Gordy, Josephine S. "Chinese in Southeast Florida, 1900–1992." Master's thesis, Florida Atlantic University, 1994.

Hume, Harold. *The Cultivation of Citrus Fruits*. New York: Macmillan, 1926.

Jacobs, Sam. "Markets Kept Overtown Stocked." In *Mostly Sunny Days: A Miami Herald Solute to South Florida's Heritage*, edited by Bob Kearney. Miami: Herald Publishing, 1986.

Liebermann, Ann. "Ransom Eli Olds and the American Dream." In *Reflections of Oldsmar*, edited by Jerry Beverland. Oldsmar, FL: On Demand Printing, 2009.

McCunn, Ruthanne. "Lue Gim Gong: A Life Reclaimed." *Chinese America: History and Perspectives* 2 (1989).

Ming, Djun. "Splendid China Takes Root in US." Xinhua News Agency, December 18, 1993.

Mohl, Raymond A. "Asian Immigration to Florida." *Florida Historical Quarterly* 74, no. 3 (1996).

Mormino, Gary R., and George E. Pozzetta. *The Immigrant World of Ybor City*. Urbana, IL: University of Illinois Press, 1987.

Pozzetta, George. "The Chinese Encounter with Florida: 1865–1920." *Chinese America: History and Perspectives* 2 (1989).

———. "Foreigners in Florida: A Study of Immigration Promotion, 1865–1910." *Florida Historical Quarterly* 53 (October 1974).

US Census Bureau. "Profile of General Population and Housing Characteristics: 2010 Demographic Profile Data-Florida." http://factfinder2.census.gov/faces/nav/jsf/pages/searchresults.xhtml.

———. Twelfth Census of the United States, 1900, Dade County, Lake Worth Precinct 2, West Palm Beach, 240 (A522); and Monroe County, Key West. Washington DC: Bureau of the Census, 1978.

———. Twelfth Census of the United States, 1900, 29th Precinct, Hillsborough County, Florida. Washington, DC: Bureau of the Census, 1978.

Voter Registration Rolls. City of Tampa. 1888–90. Tampa Tribune, Florida History and Genealogy Library of Tampa-Hillsborough County Library.

Wong, Cindy. "Chinese outside Chinatown: A Chinese Community in South Florida." *Chinese America: History and Perspectives*, 1991.

Zhang, Wenxian. "A Splendid Idea Turned Sour in Florida: The Rise and Fall of Florida Splendid China." *Florida Historical Quarterly* 84, no. 3 (2006).

6
"Chinese for the South"

Mississippi Delta Chinese Migration Chains

John Jung

Early Chinese immigrants from the mid-nineteenth century until the late 1960s came primarily from Guangdong Province in southeastern China. They settled predominantly in the western and Rocky Mountain states, where many lived in or near communities with a sizeable Chinese population. However, as early as the 1860s, a few of these immigrants found their way to the midsection of the country, including the southern states, where they lived in social and cultural isolation.

The Delta Chinese settled over a large area, covering roughly one hundred miles from just below Memphis in the north to just above Vicksburg in the south and extending roughly twenty to thirty miles from the Mississippi River on the west toward the eastern foothills. When the Arkansas side of the Delta is included, it extends another ten miles or so to the west from the river. The Delta Chinese formed a unique community in many respects. Virtually all operated small, family-run grocery stores located mainly in black neighborhoods. This fact required them to disperse across the region to avoid saturation of grocery stores. Consequently, they were relatively isolated and had limited social contact with other Chinese people as compared to those living in or near Chinatowns.

Why and how did the first Chinese immigrants come to the Delta? A brief 1880 news article, with the headline "Chinese for the South," provides one popular explanation. It reported that a Mississippi planter stated that, "in view of the negro exodus from the South, and the disturbed condition of things in California," planters in his region were seeking Chinese laborers." The author concludes, "Probably some Chinamen will be set to work in Southern Mississippi in a few weeks."[1] A similar news article indicated that Chinese laborers would come to New Orleans from where they would be transported to regions south of Memphis.[2]

Labor contractors sought Chinese immigrant men as cheap labor for the

Figure 6.1. "What shall we do with John Chinaman?" Artist unknown, *Frank Leslie's Illustrated Newspaper*, September 25, 1869 (Library of Congress)

Delta cotton fields to replace slave laborers freed by emancipation. The Chinese Six Companies, a benevolent association in San Francisco, responded to inquiries from the South about the availability of Chinese coolie labor by insisting that Chinese laborers would not likely leave California for the lower compensation they would receive in the Delta.[3]

Some recruiters did have some initial success. Census records for Mississippi in 1870 listed seventeen Chinese farm laborers in Bolivar County who came from Hong Kong. The 1880 census showed about the same number but in different locations. In Arkansas over fifty of the seventy-three Chinese residents listed in 1870 for Arkansas County were farm laborers, but in the 1880 census there were none, although there were a small number in other parts of the state. Census records in both states for 1900 or later, however, listed no Chinese farm laborers. This finding suggests that their stay in the Delta was too brief for many Chinese farm workers to have later become merchants as some have assumed.[4]

This conclusion is not surprising. As there were virtually no Chinese women in the region, and mixed marriages were strongly opposed by Chinese people as well by the white population, these single men would have been unable to marry and start families. In addition, men recruited to work as laborers would likely be strangers to one another and have no kinship bonds to make them stay together in the Delta. For any that did remain, it is doubtful, given their low wages, that they would have raised enough capital to open some of the grocery stores that were to become the economic future for the Delta Chinese community.

Another conjecture is that the earliest Chinese immigrants in the Delta may have included men who worked on rail construction in neighboring states like Texas around the 1870s. When those jobs ended, they may have sought work in the Delta.[5] This conjecture is consistent with anecdotal evidence from descendants of two laid-off workers on the Southern Pacific Railroad, Wong On and Wong Dai.[6] The belief was that they traveled up the Mississippi River headed for Cairo, Illinois, with a few other Chinese workers from Louisiana. However, they settled instead in Mississippi towns along the river in Bolivar and Washington Counties during the late 1870s to pick cotton in the Delta. Working as independent tenant farmers rather than as sharecroppers, they raised enough capital over several years to quit farming and start selling groceries from a small one-room shack at Stoneville.

However, there is no firm evidence that many Chinese laborers from Texas came to the Delta or whether any stayed long enough to become grocers. They were more likely to have found other work in places like Houston, San Antonio, and New Orleans, which were much closer to where their previous work ended than in the more distant Delta, where they did not have firm prospects for work.[7] Another conjecture is that some left sugar plantations in Cuba and came to Louisiana and eventually came to the Delta in search of work.[8]

Whereas there is only speculation about the origins of the first Chinese people in the Delta, documentation does exist about those who came to the region later. The present chapter will focus on how social networks of pioneer Chinese immigrants in the Delta led others to migrate to the region.[9] Detailed accounts from oral histories and interviews with a small sample provides a picture of how Chinese residents already in the Delta assisted relatives to join them. Those with successful grocery stores spread the news to relatives in other parts of the country. They urged and aided relatives to come and help run their grocery stores.

The lure of better economic opportunities was certainly important, but another factor for moving to the Delta was the increasing dangers of staying in the west. By the 1870s many Chinese in the Pacific Coast and Rocky Mountain regions faced virulent anti-Chinese sentiments that eventually led to a law in 1882 excluding admission of Chinese laborers into the United States.[10] In western regions of the country, violence and threats to physical safety in many communities forced Chinese people to flee for their lives.[11] By moving to regions where they would be few in number such as the Delta, they hoped they might be a smaller threat to the local population and incur less hostility and violence than that inflicted on them in places like the West Coast.

However, even if they were safer in the Delta, they still had to find a way to earn a decent living. In the 1870s farm labor was the only work widely available for Chinese workers in the Delta. After trying tenant farming, they found it was not to their liking. Moreover, white planters soon discovered that it was less costly to recruit black sharecroppers who would also be easier for them to take advantage of.[12]

Unlike in other parts of the country where many Chinese workers managed to eke out a living from hand laundries, there was a noticeable absence of Chinese laundries in the Delta. Census listings for the Delta in 1910 showed only one Chinese laundry in Greenville, but no Chinese laundries could be found in the Delta for later years. On the edge of the Delta in Vicksburg, five Chinese laundrymen were listed in the 1900 census, but only one in 1920.[13] In the small rural communities of the Delta, getting food to eat was a higher priority for farm laborers than having clean clothes to wear for working in the fields.

Fortunately for the Chinese workers, their arrival to the Delta was at an opportune time. During the last decades of the nineteenth century, some white-owned cotton plantations closed their commissaries, which had been the only source of groceries and work supplies for their black workforce. Moreover, black people with income from work unrelated to farming were not dependent on expensive commissaries for food and supplies. This situation provided an economic opportunity for the Chinese residents to establish their financial independence as merchants by opening grocery stores that primarily served the black population.

White-owned grocery stores in the main business sections of towns did not rely on black customers for success nor did they treat them as well as they did white customers. This racial bias against black people worked in favor of the Chinese grocers in creating a customer base for them.[14] Furthermore, Chinese located their stores in black neighborhoods, making them more conveniently accessible to their customers. Chinese grocers generally lived in the back of their stores, making it possible for them to open early and close late. Finally, and more importantly, they established a more informal and cordial relationship with black cotton field workers and were willing to extend credit to the end of the month for reliable customers, a consideration that was unheard of from white grocers.[15]

Delta Chinese grocers recruited relatives living in other parts of the country as well as from China. Due to the series of Chinese Exclusion Acts starting in 1882, some of these relatives, who came to be known as "paper sons," had to obtain false identity documents to circumvent these laws to gain entry to the United States. Recruitment of kin already in other parts of the United States or still in Guangdong villages was an ongoing collective endeavor over years, if not decades. Unlike the short-term time commitment of contract farm workers, kin tended to come and stay in the Delta for years, if not for entire lifetimes. Recruiting kin to the Delta not only served to build the economic growth of their stores but also generated the growth of the Chinese population through marriages and the ensuing development of families. Over time, they built strong family bonds that often extended across many small towns in the region.

Aggregate Data: Census Records

According to census records,[16] there were only 18 Chinese residents of Mississippi in 1870, with an increase to 129 in 1880. On the Arkansas side of the river, the 1870 census showed 106 Chinese, and 134 in 1880.[17] No data is available for the 1890 census, which was destroyed in a fire. In the 1900 census, there were 198 Chinese residents of Mississippi, mostly in Washington, Coahoma, and Bolivar Counties, with only one or two in a few other counties in or near the Delta. The number of the Chinese population generally increased for Mississippi to 206 in 1910 and to 254 in 1920. On the Arkansas side, there were 57 in 1900, a drop to 46 in 1910, but an increase to 73 in 1920, mostly in small Delta towns in the counties of Chicot, Jefferson, Desha, and Phillips. Virtually all of the Chinese residents were male until the 1920 census, when there were 246 males and 8 females counted in Mississippi. In 1920, the number born in China, 211, was between four to five times greater than those born elsewhere, 43.

Although there was generally a net increase in the number of Chinese residents over the period from 1900 to 1920, upon closer examination a surprising finding was that the counties in Arkansas and Mississippi with the highest number of Chinese residents showed a virtual complete turnover of the Chinese population between consecutive decades, with only one person being listed as living in the same county for two consecutive census periods.[18]

Part of the turnover can be attributed to older members dying, but this can only account for a small reduction. The majority must have moved out of the Delta, as only two men could be found living in the same town or even in other towns in the state across two consecutive decennial census periods. They moved to other states, perhaps for family reasons or economic opportunities, and some may have returned to China. Nonetheless, there was a net increase in numbers for all but one comparison of census figures over two consecutive decades. The gain reflected the number of new Chinese people moving to the Delta, some from China and some born in other states, as well as the children born in the Delta.

The totals generally increased slightly in most counties from 1900 to 1920, with the exception of Washington County, which showed a large decline from sixty to twenty-eight, whereas Bolivar County grew from twenty-six to sixty, and Sunflower County had an even larger increase from eight to forty-three over the same period. For Arkansas counties, Chicot went from two to nine, Desha from one to eleven, Crittenden from zero to five, Lee from zero to four, and Mississippi from one to five. On the other hand, Jefferson County had a drop from ten to three.

How Chinese People Got to the South

The growth in the total number of Chinese residents in the Delta and the information from census records on their occupations and residence is compatible with the view that they found economic opportunity in the Delta, which was denied to them in other regions. However, knowing "why" they went to the Delta sheds no light on the process of "how" their move took place.

Immigration case files contain information about where immigrants came from, their age and gender, when and where they entered the United States but rarely record their intended destination. The testimony found in transcripts of interrogations is misleading in the many cases involving "paper sons," where the applicant has assumed the identity of another person eligible for admission, because it reflects memorized facts that do not pertain to the applicant but to his alleged identity.

Census records provide counts of the number of Chinese immigrants that reside in a given city and state in the year when the census was taken, categorized on variables such as age, gender, marital status, and occupation. Invariably, census data are undercounts because they do not include persons who are not at home or who are hiding when census takers come to their residences.

Immigration files and census records are static sources of information about Chinese immigrant populations. They cannot provide answers to important questions about the dynamic processes that lead immigrants to move, sometimes more than once, to different destinations is largely unknown because such information was either not recorded or was difficult to obtain from immigrants. Tracking is also difficult because names of immigrants were often false or "paper names" and it was not unusual for some to have multiple names. In addition, immigration officers, unfamiliar with the Chinese name order, which is the reverse of Western name order, often confused Chinese surnames with their given names. Misspellings of Chinese names were also common because they are so different from Western names.

Evidence from oral histories, written accounts, and interviews can be more informative about the temporal and spatial nature of migration. They can also reveal the networks of family and friends that facilitated movement. Such data can provide a more detailed look that encompasses many years, unlike the census data that is recorded only once every ten years.

Knowledge about these processes is of particular value for understanding how Chinese immigrants, who initially settled on either coast prior to moving toward the midsections of the country, came to be in the Delta. To what extent did this migration involve direct moves to the Delta as opposed to journeys with intermediate destinations? In what other places did some immigrants live before coming to the Delta? And, to what extent was there out-migration? What factors led some Chinese residents to leave the Delta to resettle in other regions?

Oral histories, interviews, and personal documents allow a greater depth of understanding how Chinese residents of the Delta came to be there. However, these sources are also fallible due to forgetting, inaccurate recall, and deliberate distortions. As subjective evidence, testimony from different sources may yield conflicting accounts. Accordingly, one must be careful in weighing evidence.

The Chinese people of the Mississippi Delta have always been a small population in absolute size, not reaching its peak of about 1,200 until the 1960 census, but it was still substantial enough to afford enough cases for studying early migration networks. Inasmuch as they were a close-knit group, often involving several generations of relatives living nearby, any migration patterns that are identified can often be corroborated by testimony from family members.[19]

Case Histories of Chain Migration

Several case histories will be presented to illustrate the complex interconnections among relatives that were essential to their successful migration to the Delta from many parts of the United States and Canada. The specific places they came from and how they made their way to the Delta differed among individuals, but all of their journeys required committed networks of family members to play vital roles in helping newcomers find their way to the Delta and eventually to succeed in operating a grocery store. This process of "serial migration" involved Chinese people already in the Delta recruiting relatives to join them there from other regions as well as from China.[20] The remigration often involved several intermediate steps, rather than a single move, to reach a Delta destination.

From Cuba Sugar Plantations to New York to the Delta

Hong Chuck Kun, born in 1906 in Gu Jiang village in Sun Wei County, Guangdong, first went to Cuba at the tender age of twelve to work, growing and peddling fruits and vegetables for a decade to earn money to send home. When the sugar market weakened with the depression of the 1930s, he tried delivering sugar to New York but eventually settled in New York for a while before joining his uncle Sit Gon in the grocery business in Saint Louis. From there he moved to the Delta where his cousin in Greenville, Sit Chan Wah, owned a successful grocery store, Mee Jon. In 1932, Hong, with financial assistance from Sit Chan Wah, opened his own store in Greenville, Fok Chung Co. There he met and married Mamie, a daughter of Willie Wy, the oldest presumed son of the earlier mentioned Chinese pioneer in the Delta, Wong Dai, in 1935.[21]

From A Laundry in New England to Greenville

Joe Kay Chek, a schoolteacher in the village of Wang Sek, Kaiping County, in the Pearl River Delta of Guangdong, China, had four sons, Joe Nam, Joe Yuke, Joe King, Joe Guay, and a daughter, Nue Yuen. When Kay Chek died at age fifty-seven, the family of six was in dire straits as Joe Nam was only eighteen, Joe Yuke thirteen, Joe King seven, Nue Yuen four, and Joe Guay only two years old. At this time, a devastating flood savaged the village. Their meager home was destroyed and they lost everything they had. They survived only through the generosity of a good family friend, Gin Got, a pioneer laborer for the transcontinental railroad. After he retired and returned to the village, he became a good friend of Kay Chek and provided his family with temporary housing and farming tools.[22]

Gin Got arranged financial backing for Joe Yuke to come to America when he was seventeen, with the help of one of Joe Yuke's cousins, Doy Sel (Joe Ying). Joe Yuke found railroad work in Montana initially. Eventually he settled in Sacramento, California, where he worked as a cook in a noted establishment called the Sutter Club and held the position of secretary in the Bing Kung Association, one of the Chinese family associations.

Joe Yuke's move to America paved the way for the three other sons of Kay Chek to come later. They all, at one time or another, found employment working on railroad construction. When the railroad work tapered off, they had to seek other lines of work. Joe Nam operated laundries in New York and later in Holyoke, Massachusetts, with Joe King. Remittances of the overseas brothers enabled the family back in the village to survive. The youngest son, Joe Guay, left Hong Kong at age twenty-five in 1902 by ship to Vancouver, BC, and then traveled by train to Montreal. After staying there for over a week, a party of ten men that included himself and his alleged or "paper" brother, Joe Yook Fong, got on a train. After a short ride, they traveled in two wagons for several hours to a frame house where a man called the inspector met them. After another short train ride they reached the border town of Ogdensburg, New York. They proceeded to cross over into the United States but were immediately apprehended and imprisoned at the nearby town of Canton along with about twenty to thirty other Chinese men. A month later, Joe Guay and Joe Yook Fong had a court hearing, and Joe Nam testified on Joe Guay's behalf. He claimed that Joe Guay was born in San Jose, California and that when Joe Guay was six years old the family went to China, and he was now returning to the United States. On the basis of this testimony, Joe Guay was adjudged to be a US citizen and allowed to remain in the country.

Upon his release a month later, he and his alleged brother took the train to New York, where Joe Nam met them. A week later, he went to work at the family laundry in Holyoke, Massachusetts, which his three older brothers ran with Joe Hen Fuie, a nephew or cousin. Around 1912 they learned that a person

Figure 6.2. Joe Gow Nue grocery store at the foot of Washington Street, Greenville, MS (Library of Congress)

from their village, Joe Gow Nue, was ready to retire from his grocery business in Greenville, Mississippi.[23] Joe Nam and Joe King journeyed south to look over the situation. Finding it favorable and seeing it as an opportunity to get out of the laundry business, which was very labor-intensive, they bought the grocery store, retaining its original name, Joe Gow Nue Company. They left the laundry business operation in Holyoke to Joe Guay. It was not until the early 1920s that Joe Guay also quit the laundry business to join his brothers in Greenville to operate the Joe Gow Nue grocery.

The Joe Gow Nue grocery was one of the first Chinese grocery stores to operate in the Delta, opening around 1910. It occupied a prominent location right next to the levee at the foot of Washington Street, the main street in Greenville. The photograph, which was probably taken in the 1920s, shows that benches were placed in front of the store where customers could congregate and socialize.

Probably the largest Chinese merchant store in the Delta, the Joe Gow Nue Grocery store functioned like a community center or association hall for Chinese people throughout the region. It provided temporary housing for newcomers, assisted in immigration matters, and helped with remittances to China. It sold imported food and nonfood items such as chopsticks, tea pots, and beaded sandals from China as well as fresh Chinese vegetables such as bok choy, long beans, gai lan, and fu gua grown in the garden next to the store. The store occupied an extremely large building, 161 feet long and 32 feet wide, providing a large warehouse for storage of freight carloads of staples such as sugar, hay, and mule feed as well as containing five rooms that served as temporary lodging for newcomers to the region.[24]

As the business grew, the men invited their brother Joe Yuke in Sacramento, California, to join them. He came to look the situation over but decided to return to Sacramento. Around 1924, Joe Nam and Joe King retired and returned to China. Joe King was not of retirement age but was pressured by his brothers to retire because of his increasing involvement with Arlee, a mixed-race daughter of Wong On, a grocery store owner in nearby Stoneville. He was one of the earliest Chinese to settle in Mississippi and had married a black woman, Emma Clay. Arlee, being bilingual, was a valued employee at the Joe Gow Nue store and she continued to work for the new owners of the store.[25]

When his older brothers departed, Joe Guay needed new partners to operate the Greenville store. He decided to bring in two sons of his cousin Hen Fuie, Joe Duck-fue from Canada and Joe Duck-kong, who was already operating a grocery store in Morgan City, Mississippi.

Over the ensuing years the partners brought over many relatives, friends, and younger members of the family from China. In the 1920s Joe Guay was instrumental in bringing Tuk-yip Chow, an adopted grandson of (Joe) Doy Sel, to the Delta. Tuk-yip's son, James K. Chow, came to the Delta in the late 1920s and had a grocery in Shelby. Joe Guay also purchased papers in the late 1920s to bring over Joe Nam's two grandsons, J. G. Sing and Yick Joe, although papers for the latter indicated that he was Joe Guay's third son. Joe Guay also brought his younger son, Joe Ting, to Greenville from China to help with the store in 1927.

Joe Duck-fue's oldest son, James N. Chow, came in 1926 and his other sons, Lucky, Woodrow, and Jimmie, came in the early 1940s. Joe Duck-kong's son, Jim-tong, and his cousin Duck Chu came in the late 1940s. Although each of them eventually had their own grocery stores, they all had first lived and served their apprenticeship in the Joe Gow Nue store or in a second store, Joe Gow Nue No. 2, that opened in 1935. When Joe Guay, the last of the original brothers who developed the store died in 1945, the partnership dissolved. In 1947 the remaining partners decided to divide their properties. Joe Ting assumed control of the Washington Street store, while Joe Duck-fue with help of James Ngo Chow managed the Nelson Street store.

Joe Wah-Young, the eldest son of Joe Guay, had been working as a civil engineer in China but decided it best to return with his wife and children to the United States when Mao Zedong and the Chinese Communists in 1949 forced the Nationalist government of Chiang Kai-Shek to flee to Taiwan. Although he held a civil engineering degree from the prestigious Massachusetts Institute of Technology, he noticed the success of Delta Chinese in the grocery business that enabled them to send their children to college. Following their example, Joe Wah-Young entered the grocery business first with a store in Tchula and moved to Greenville to run one there in 1960.[26]

From a North Dakota Restaurant to the Delta

Sometime in the 1870s, Wong Mon Oak left China and immigrated to Portland, Oregon, where he operated an herb store in the old Chinatown that fronted his opium smuggling. In 1879 he brought over his older brother's son, Wong Bing Choong, who later opened his own herb store. Around 1897 Bing Choong brought over his ten-year-old brother, Jew Wong, who first went to Canada and then crossed illegally into the United States. Jew attended school for four years and then worked in Bing Choong's herb store.[27]

In 1911 Jew Wong went to China to get married. A son, Henry, was born in 1912. After returning to the United States in 1914, he ventured forth to look for work and traveled to Utah, New Mexico, and other states. He ended up in Fargo, North Dakota, in 1915, where he found work at the Chicago Café. He eventually became its owner. In 1920, he brought his wife and son over from China to help him with the restaurant. Their four daughters, Mae, Amy, Madeleine, and Jean, were all born in Fargo.

Jew was instrumental in getting two younger brothers, Ben and Gilbert, to enter the restaurant business in Fargo. Ben may have worked at the Chicago Café, but he operated a restaurant in Fergus Falls, Minnesota. When a group of Chinese people decided to open the Fargo Café, Jew got Gilbert, who as a student had previously worked at Bing Choong's herb store in Portland before coming to Fargo, to join the partnership.

In 1927 Jew took his wife, son, and four US-born daughters back to his village in China. A second son, Paul, was born there in 1928. After attending school for a while in the village, Henry went to school in Canton (Guangzhou). When he was old enough for college, his father wanted him to return to Fargo where he enrolled at North Dakota Agricultural College (later North Dakota State University). While attending college, Henry was also a partner with his uncle Ben in operating the American Café in Fargo.

Jew Wong contracted tuberculosis, and by 1934, he realized that he did not have much longer to live. He decided it was imperative for him to bring the second son, Paul, who was then six, to Fargo, where he lived with his brother, Henry, and attended school for five years. But with the restaurant business continually declining during the Great Depression, Henry decided to search for other ways to earn a living. He journeyed to the Mississippi Delta in 1939 with his brother to look for opportunities because their oldest sister, Mae, had married a Delta grocer in Shelby, James K. Chow.

After a short time in the Delta, Henry decided he did not want to be involved with it and was ready to go back to Fargo. However, around that time, another of his sisters, Amy, married Danny Yee from Detroit in 1940 through a match arranged in China. They wanted to open a grocery store in the Delta. James K. Chow located a grocery store for Henry and Danny in Leland that had been closed by creditors. The brothers-in-law operated it together for a few years until Danny left to join the military service. Then Danny's father moved from Detroit to help work in the store, but he and Henry had conflicts. Consequently, Henry left for the San Francisco region where he attended Stanford University, earning a bachelor's degree in chemistry. Henry then went back to Guangzhou to open a soap factory, but inflation was so bad he had to return to the Delta to operate a grocery store in Hollandale for almost a decade. He later sold this store to his younger sister Jean and her husband, Tony Mah, and then returned to North Dakota State University to obtain a master's degree in chemistry. In 1961 he started work in the defense industry in Burbank, California.

From Guangdong to Boyle, Shaw, and Cleveland

Several kinsmen, Jew Doy Lin, Jew Dock Kee, and Joe T. Im, from Gor Doi village in the Hen Gong region in Guangdong, China, immigrated to Mississippi to form a partnership, Joe Brothers in the early 1920s.[28] Whether any of them lived and worked in other parts of the country or in other occupations before they came to the Delta is unclear as none of their children could provide such information.[29] Joe Brothers operated several grocery stores in Cleveland, Boyle, and Shaw, located north of Greenville. As their retail and wholesale grocery business prospered, these village cousins sought other relatives to help them with the expanding business.

Jew Guey Moon, born in Hoiping about 1889, came to the United States in or around 1908, arriving in San Francisco with purchased identity papers that belonged to a ten-year-old son of Jew Moy, a partner in the Quong Hong Sing Co. located in Merced, California. He first worked on farms and ranches in the area around Sacramento, California, and then in the sawmills around Lodi. He later found employment as a cook on the Tonopah and Tidewater Railroad in northern California and Nevada. About 1911, he purchased a partnership for $1,000 in the Sun On Chong Co. in Sacramento, California, as did a village kinsman, Jew Hen Lett. By the mid-1920s, however, Jew Hen Lett left to join his father in his grocery business in Boyle.

Jew Guey Moon returned to China in 1920 to be married in an arranged match. Guey returned to work in the United States, and around 1926 he joined the Joe Brothers in the Delta. Every few years he would make return visits to his wife and family. After his wife died in 1934 during the birth of their third child, he returned to the village and remarried the next year in an arranged match to Wong Shee. She managed to come to the United States in 1939 just ahead of the outbreak of World War II with their daughter, Lillie, and her half-sister, Sue King. Joe Sing, Guey's nephew, accompanied them using papers Guey purchased that alleged he was Guey's son.

The Joe Brothers store served poorer customers, white and black. Another store operating under the name Modern Stores catered mainly to white customers who were more affluent. Located in the main business section of Cleveland, with attractive window displays of merchandise, it was a clean and tidy store that could compete with the best of the white-owned stores.

In the early 1930s, major changes occurred with Joe Brothers partnership. Jew Doy Lin and Jew Dock Kee, two older members, returned to China. Jew Doy Lin gave his share of the business to his sons, J. H. Lett and Sung Fun Joe, and Jew Dock Kee gave his share to his sons, S. C. Chow and Tang Jack Chow. Another senior partner, Joe T. Im, sold his share to John S. Wong and moved to New York where he entered the import-export business.

After the end of World War II, Joe Brothers' partners were finally able to bring their wives and children from China to join them in the Delta, which led them to operate their own stores to provide for their own families. Jew Moon Guey took over the store in Boyle, Ralph Jue opened a store in Pace, and Tang Jack Chow, Ernest Seto Joe, and Joe Wong Sr. each had other stores in Cleveland. As older partners retired and returned to China or moved to work in other parts of the country, Joe Brothers dissolved.

From Laundries in the Midwest to the Delta

George Quong Yee came illegally from Canada but successfully claimed to have been born in San Jose, California, after city records were destroyed in the 1906 San Francisco earthquake and fire. He operated a laundry in Detroit, Michigan, and had four sons born in China who grew up in the Detroit laundry.[30] The oldest son, Danny, as noted earlier, married Amy Wong, originally from Fargo, North Dakota. They operated a grocery store in Leland not far from one in Shelby run by her sister Mae and her husband, James K. Chow. Two other sons, Kin and Harry, came later to the Delta in the 1940s where each operated grocery stores in Greenville. A fourth son, Bill, had a successful grocery store in nearby Leland.[31]

Tuck Chon (George Seu), born in Canton, China, in 1912, came to the United States at age thirteen to join his older brother, Shui Tuck Hi, and work in his laundry in Chicago for nine years from 1925–34. Upon learning of a better economic opportunity from relatives in the grocery business in the Delta in 1929, his brother went to investigate, leaving George with a cousin to run the laundry. George did not move to the Delta until 1934, when he joined two older brothers and an uncle who had two grocery stores in Greenville, one in a black and one in a white neighborhood. In 1940, George returned to China for an arranged marriage, returning with his bride in 1941 to operate the Min Sang grocery store, which he operated for over seventy years in Greenville.[32]

From Laundries in the Northeast to the Delta

Yet and Yuen Shee Gong came in 1912 to New York and Boston before moving to New Orleans to open a grocery, Gong Company. They sent their son, Sing Gong, back to China in 1922 to marry. After returning, Sing Gong moved to Duncan where he opened the Sing Gong store in 1934.[33]

Joe T. Ling's great-grandfather and grandfather immigrated to Boston in the late 1890s where they had a laundry, but in 1920 his grandfather moved to the Delta to open a grocery store in Glendora. The same year he brought his son, Joe T. Ling, age fifteen, over from China to help in the store. In 1926 he was sent back the village to marry. After returning, he moved to Sunflower to open a store. Unfortunately, business was not good, so after one year he moved to Duncan in 1930 where he had a grocery store across from the Sing Gong store for almost a decade until he moved to Cleveland, where in 1941 he built a new two-story building to house another grocery store with living quarters above it.[34]

From Laundries and Restaurants in the Midwest and North to the Arkansas Delta

The route from Guangdong to the Arkansas side of the Mississippi River to run grocery stores for members of three families, Chu, Wong, and Low, was rather circuitous.[35] The Chu family came from laundries in Michigan and Illinois prior to entering the grocery business in rural Arkansas. The Wong family was involved with restaurant operations in Minnesota before starting a grocery store business in Arkansas. The Low family operated both laundries and restaurants in different northern cities before entering the grocery business in Duncan, Mississippi, and indirectly on the Arkansas side of the Delta when Gow Sek Low married Eva, the daughter of a Round Pond grocery man. Over time, the lives of these three families, all operating grocery stores in Arkansas, became closely intertwined as several marriages occurred among their children. Chu Kwok Kin came alone to the United States in the late 1890s, leaving his wife in the village. His attempt to gain entry failed and he became a contract worker on a Mexican railroad. In 1903 Chu gained legal entry into the United States and he began to work in laundries in the Midwest.

Chu had been away from the village for almost ten years before his wife heard from him again. Finally he was able to return to the village in 1915. He returned to the United States with his wife, crossing Canada and entering the United States at New York. In 1918, he purchased a laundry in Traverse City, Michigan, but then moved the next year to open another one in Havana, Illinois. During the Depression, business was so bad that he sent his family back to China to live with relatives for a few years but not before he arranged a match for his oldest daughter, Emma, to marry Yit Fong, the son of Jook Wan, a family friend from their village who operated a grocery store in Round Pond, Arkansas, and later one in Hughes.

Around 1934, Chu Kwok planned a trip to China to join his family and decided to visit Emma and Yit before he departed. They persuaded him to stay in Arkansas and establish a grocery store in Crawfordville with a nephew. Chu Kwok soon found better grocery opportunities in Biscoe, and later in Marvell, but needed his two oldest sons, Foon and Ching, to return from China to help.

Concerned about the impending war with Japan, he decided it was time to bring the rest of the family back to the United States. However, his wife had no visa and the decision was made to send the two youngest children, Eva and Don, back to the United States by themselves. Finally, at the last moment, a visa was obtained, and the oldest son, Ching, returned to the village to escort his mother back. While he was there, he was introduced to Nellie Wong as a prospective wife. They married in 1940 just before they came back to the United States. They went to Round Pond, Arkansas, to run a grocery store (described in more detail in the section below on the Wong family). Later, Nellie's younger sister, Anna, married Gordon Chou, son of a Chinese family who had immigrated from Hoiping to Pine Bluff, Arkansas, where they operated a grocery.

Chu's two other sons, Foon and Don, each married a sister from a Seid family from Portland, Oregon. In 1940, Foon Chu married Lily Seid and they settled in Forrest City, Arkansas, where they operated a hardware and jewelry store. A decade later, in 1951, Foon's younger brother Don married Lily's younger sister, Annie. They came to the Delta and operated a grocery in Madison, Arkansas, between 1950 and 1960 before moving to Forrest City, Arkansas, where Don worked as a jeweler and did watch repairs. The Seid sisters' older brother, Bing, operated a grocery in Crawfordville for many years before moving to Memphis.

The Wong Family

The father, Lim Sing Wong, of the aforementioned Nellie Wong had first immigrated to the United States alone in 1901, leaving his betrothed behind in the village in Guangdong. In his early twenties, he entered the United States at Seattle and worked on vegetable farms in the region before contracting to work briefly in Alaska on a sea-going salmon cannery. He did not find this work to his liking, so he worked as a cook in the Pacific Northwest with an uncle. After working several years, he managed to save enough to return to China to marry Mah Bo-Nui. Soon he came back to the United States and around 1914 he and his uncle ran a restaurant in Durango, Colorado, that served copper mine workers. After World War I ended, copper mining declined so they left the region. Wong returned to China to be with his wife and two sons, King-Man and Jimmie, but around 1921, he brought his wife and youngest son to the United States and opened a restaurant in Faribault, Minnesota.

After a few years, the Wongs, with their three sons, moved to North Dakota to operate a restaurant in Minot located on the Great Northern and Soo Railroad route. When the Depression hit, business was so poor that in 1931 they decided to return to China. Those were the circumstances when Nellie entered the earlier-described marriage match to Chu Ching Quong from Arkansas. The newlyweds left for the United States on one of the last ships to leave Hong Kong before the war, bringing along her younger brother Henry and sister Anna. They went to Round Pond, Arkansas, where Chu Ching's father operated a grocery store. Nellie and her husband operated a general store in Round Pond for forty-one years. Life in Arkansas was an isolated existence for them as the few Chinese in the area were still miles away.

The Low Family

Gow Sek Low's father came over from China around 1900 to Boston, where he first worked in a laundry before having a succession of jobs as a waiter in restaurants in New York, Detroit, and Chicago. A friend with a grocery store in Duncan, Mississippi, asked Gow's father to come help him there. Soon after, in 1926 he left for Miami to help a friend run a laundry but instead started his own grocery store, Joe's Markets. He was so successful that he was able to expand, eventually having thirty-eight branch stores in Miami and other areas in Florida.

Gow Sek Low married Eva Quong, Emma's younger sister, who, as mentioned earlier, was married to Yit Fong, owner of an Arkansas grocery in Round Pond and friend of Chu Kwok Kin. Thus, three Chinese families coming from diverse backgrounds of restaurants in Minnesota and laundries in Michigan and Boston, through marriages among their children, came to operate Delta grocery stores.

Conclusions

Oral histories, written records, and interviews of some of their descendants provided details of how some Delta Chinese grocers came to be in the Delta. Strong familial bonds among relatives enabled family members from all over the country to be reunited, even though in some instances the process may have taken years, if not decades. Objective data such as official census records would not have been adequate for the discovery of these stories of immigration, migration, and remigration, which were often intricate, among the Delta Chinese.

The first Chinese immigrants to come to the Delta were all male, either single or married men who left their wives and children behind in China. The married men generally made return visits every few years to Guangdong villages to reunite with their wives, children, and other relatives. Although restricted by legal and strong cultural prohibitions, an indeterminate number of Chinese immigrants married, or had common-law relationships, with non-Chinese women, typically black, that produced some mixed-race children. The larger Chinese community strongly disapproved of such relationships, which they realized would further weaken the standing of Chinese residents with the white community.

Single men, after working in the Delta and saving money for several years, commonly returned to Guangdong for marriages arranged by their parents, as was commonly the practice, to total strangers in most instances. After several months, the men came back to the Delta alone to resume work and send money back to support their wives and eventual children. In addition, by the 1920s after more people of Chinese descent were born in the United States, some Delta Chinese men found American-born wives, as young as fifteen or sixteen, either through Western courtship methods or by traditional matches arranged by parents.

Before coming to the Delta, many Chinese immigrants worked in other regions, not only in the United States but also in other countries, including Canada and Cuba, rather than coming directly to the Delta, as was the case of early contract farm laborers. They worked in many different occupations, including railroad construction, fishing, manufacturing, laundry, and restaurant work before they migrated to the Delta where, as early as 1880, some found that the grocery business provided an economic opportunity for them. By 1910, virtually all Chinese people in the Delta were operating small grocery stores and living in the back of the buildings. Their stores were typically located in black neighborhoods, which was convenient for their primary customers.

Unlike in other parts of the country where a large percentage of Chinese people were classified as laborers, the Chinese residents of the Delta were almost exclusively grocers until well past the middle of the past century. According to the Chinese Exclusion Act of 1882, laborers were not permitted to bring over their families from China, whereas merchants, a category that included grocers, could. By the end of the 1920s, more Chinese grocers began to bring their wives and children from Guangdong to the Delta to help with work in their stores. In some cases, the move was done in stages, in part because of the expense, and other considerations such as the usefulness in moving entire families at the same time. Thus, the oldest son, sometimes as young as ten years of age, would be the

Figure 6.3. Family dinner inside the Mee Joe Grocery Store, Greenville, MS (Rachel Sit Wong)

sole member to come first because he could immediately work in his father's store, whereas very young children would be an expense without any contribution to the workload. Other men started families in the Delta with their American-born Chinese wives from many parts of the country. Consequently, during the 1920s the Delta Chinese community drastically changed from a bachelor society to one populated with families.[36]

For different reasons some Chinese people eventually left the Delta. Some moved to escape the racial prejudice toward them, a condition that varied considerably in different towns. Others sought more lucrative business opportunities elsewhere if they were unsuccessful in the grocery business. Still others left for personal reasons such as finding communities where their children could attend better schools than those available to them in the segregated Delta, while others had a desire to reunite with relatives working in other parts of the country.

These examples illustrate how and why early Chinese immigrants came to the Delta and demonstrate the critical role played by family networks in their migration to this region from all over the country. Sharing information, financial resources, business operations, and housing was common. Without the assistance and collaboration from their networks, it would have been very difficult for an individual Chinese immigrant to succeed in a new business. Their common ties to Chinese traditions, values, and culture enabled them to build strong ties across the broad expanse of the Delta. As they increased in number, and established families, they created a "community" that spread over many miles and in many small towns. Through the work contribution of all family members in running their stores, these pioneers succeeded with their grocery businesses and made valuable contributions to their communities throughout the Delta. Their children and grandchildren, in large number, benefited from these stores, which financed their higher education that prepared them for careers in many professions and white-collar occupations.[37]

Few, if any, of the children who grew up working side by side with their parents and siblings in the stores continued in the family grocery stores. Instead, due to the better career opportunities for them outside of the Delta, most of them moved to metropolitan areas such as Houston, the San Francisco Bay area, and southern California. Upon retirement, many of their parents also left the Delta to live near or with their children.

As a consequence, few of the earlier Delta Chinese grocers, from the 1920s to the middle of the past century, and their descendants can still be found in the Delta today. This unique Chinese "community of grocers," which made significant contributions to the towns where they once thrived, has virtually vanished from the Delta. In its place, however, new immigrants from other regions of China and other countries have come seeking their economic opportunities with family-run grocery stores in the Delta.

Notes

1. "Chinese for the South." *New York Times*, March 8, 1880, 1.

2. "Chinese Laborers for the South." *Natchez (Ms.) Democrat*, July 22, 1879. 2. A decade earlier at the Chinese Labor Convention in Memphis, a labor contractor, Cornelius Koopmanshaap, made the same point and argued for bringing coolies from Hong Kong rather than California. "Chinese Labor," *New York Times*, July 14, 1869.

3. "Chinese Labor for the South: Reply of the 'Six Companies' of San Francisco," *New York Times*, April 28, 1879.

4. John Thornell, "Struggle for Identity in the Most Southern Place on Earth: The Chinese in the Mississippi Delta," *Chinese America: History and Perspectives* (2004): 63–69.

5. "The Chinese. The First Installment for Texas—How They Looked and Acted—What They Require," from *Saint Louis Dispatch*, December 30. *New York Times*, January 3, 1870, 3.

6. Robert Seto Quan, *Lotus among the Magnolias: The Mississippi Chinese* (Jackson: University Press of Mississippi, 1982), 7–9.

7. However, most Chinese rail workers in Texas probably stayed and found other work in the region. Mel Brown, *Chinese Heart of Texas: The San Antonio Commu-*

nity, 1875–1975 (Austin, TX: Morgan Printing, 2005), 19. Irwin A. Tang, "The Chinese Texan Experiment," in *Asian Texans: Our Histories and Our Lives*, edited by Irwin A. Tang, (Austin, TX: It Works, 2007), 38.

8. Lucy M. Cohen, *Chinese in the Post-Civil War South: A People without A History*. (Baton Rouge: Louisiana State University, 1984). Moon-Ho Jung, *Coolies and Cane: Race, Labor, and Sugar in the Age of Emancipation* (Baltimore: Johns Hopkins University Press, 2006).

9. Important issues such as the Chinese experiences in adapting to a predominantly black and white society with strong racial segregation, the nature of the grocery store operations, the role of Christianity and the church, family life, and education of children are beyond the scope of this paper.

10.Chinese Exclusion Act, An Act to Inaugurate Certain Treaty Stipulations Relating to Chinese, Forty-Seventh Congress, 1882, sess. 1, chap. 126; 22 stat. 58.

11. Jean Pflazer, *Driven Out: The Forgotten War against Chinese Americans* (New York: Random House, 2007).

12. James W. Loewen, *The Mississippi Chinese: Between Black and White* (Prospect Heights, IL: Waveland Press, 1988), 26.

13. Joshua Lee, "A Tale of Two Charlie's: The Story of Charley Wah, Charley Lee Soo, and Interracial Relationship in Mississippi and Washington, D.C." (Master's thesis, University of California, Irvine, 2005).

14. Loewen, *Mississippi Chinese*, 33–34.

15. Ibid. p. 33. Chinese immigrants, even though they lacked proficiency in English, managed to succeed in operating small grocery stores. For example, one remedy for poor language skills was to display goods so that customers could point to what they wanted. Another procedure was to save the last "copy" of any product so that they could reorder it by showing it to their supplier.

16. HeritageQuest Online, which tabulates frequencies by race and birthplace, is broken down by county, city, and state in addition to images of the raw data census sheets, http://persi.heritagequestonline.com/hqoweb/library/do/persi.

17. The 1880 count was probably wrong because the code C, for "Colored," was probably miscounted as Chinese as most of the people coded as C had Arkansas birthplaces, which would not have true of any of the Chinese residents counted.

18. Such high turnover during this period was not unique for Delta Chinese. A spot check of Italians showed no overlap between the twenty-one Italians in 1910 and twenty-two in 1920 in Greenville or between the nine Italians in 1910 and thirty in 1920 in Clarksdale. Such high mobility was not examined for other regions of the country, but it might have been widespread for a developing country.

19. The Chinese resident of the Delta are not a representative sample of Chinese immigrants in the United States but is better suited for identifying details of secondary migration than for those in regions with very few or very many Chinese people.

20. Susan Ossman, "Studies in Serial Migration," *International Migration* 42 (2004): 111–21.

21. Personal communication from Carolyn Hong Chan, daughter of Hong Chuck Kun and Mamie Wy, to John Jung, November 27, 2015.

22. Helen Wong. "Through My Eyes: A Family History," unpublished, 2007.

23. According to Joe Ting, his great uncle, Joe Gow Nue, arrived in Mississippi in 1883 after working on the Southern Pacific railroad line that ended in New Orleans, where he and others took a barge headed for Cairo, Illinois, but they landed instead at Hollandale, Mississippi, and eventually went to Greenville, where he bought the Joe Gow Nue store. Quan, *Lotus among the Magnolias*, 9–10.

24. Paul Wong, "A Letter from Paul Wong," in Ted Shepherd, *The Chinese of Greenville, Mississippi* (Greenville, MS: Burford Brothers Printing), 73–75.

25. When J. S. Hen married Arlee, some disapproval arose among other Chinese because mixed-race marriages were prohibited in the South and provoked white criticism toward the Chinese population.

26. Wong, "Through My Eyes," 2007.

27. Paul Wong emails to author, March 5, 2008, November 16, 2011, March 29, 2011, April 27, 2011, April 29, 2011, May 28, 2011, June 6, 2011, June 28, 2011.

28. Bobby Joe Moon, emails to Author. July 5, 2007, July 23, 2007, July 27, 2007, July 30, 2007, September 17, 2007, October 1, 2007, December 31, 2007, and January 4, 2008.

29. Such gaps in knowledge of family history are not unusual because many immigrants did not disclose sensitive information such as immigration experiences to their American-born children.

30.Paul Wong email to author, June 6, 2011.

31. Helen Hong, "The Yee's," in Ted Shepherd, *The Chinese of Greenville, Mississippi.*, 92–94.

32. Frieda Seu Quon. "Growing Up Chinese in Greenville, Mississippi," in Ted Shepherd, *The Chinese of Greenville, Mississippi*, 80–81.

33. Rosie Gong Gee, "The Gongs of Duncan, Mississippi," in *Reflections on the Chinese Mission School, Cleveland, Mississippi*, ed. Paul Wong and Doris Ling Lee (Cleveland, MS: Delta State University Press, 2011), 35–37.

34. Jimmie Ling Joe, "The Lings," in *Reflections on the Chinese Mission School, Cleveland, Mississippi*, ed. Paul Wong and Doris Ling Lee (Cleveland, MS: Delta State University Press, 2011), 47–48.

35. Henry Wong email to author, March, 24, 2007, and letter to author, April 11, 2007.

36. This change had major consequences for the Delta Chinese community. Although the Mississippi Constitution passed in 1890 reserved white schools for those of the Caucasian race, this situation did not pose a major concern for the Chinese population until the 1920s simply because there were virtually no Chinese children

previously. In 1924 when Gong Lum's daughters were denied admission to white schools, he filed a lawsuit on their behalf that eventually reached the US Supreme Court, which in a landmark decision upheld the Mississippi Supreme Court ruling that blocked Chinese children access to white schools. US Supreme Court, *Gong Lum et al. v. Rice et al. No. 29*, submitted October 12, 1927, 275 US 78. Over the next decade the Baptist Church helped educate Chinese children by working with the community to establish Chinese Mission Schools in Greenville and Cleveland. This outreach was providential for churches as it proved to be highly effective in attracting Chinese people to Christianity. John Jung, "Gong Lum v. Rice 1927: Mississippi School Segregation and the Delta Chinese," *Chinese American Forum* 26, no. 3 (2011): 20–24.

37. John Jung, *Chopsticks in the Land of Cotton: Lives of Mississippi Delta Chinese Grocers*, (Cypress, CA: Yin and Yang Press, 2008).

Works Cited

Brown, Mel. *Chinese Heart of Texas: The San Antonio Community, 1875–1975*. Austin, TX: Morgan Printing, 2005.

Cohen, Lucy M. *Chinese in the Post–Civil War South: A People without a History*. Baton Rouge: Louisiana State University, 1984.

Gee, Rosie Gong. "The Gongs of Duncan, Mississippi." In *Reflections on the Chinese Mission School, Cleveland, Mississippi*, edited by Paul Wong and Doris Ling Lee. Cleveland, MS: Delta State University Press, 2011.

HeritageQuest Online. http://persi.heritagequestonline.com/hqoweb/library/do/persi.

Hong, Helen. "The Yee's." *The Chinese of Greenville, Mississippi*. By Ted Shepherd. Greenville, MS: Burford Brothers Printing, 1999.

Joe, Jimmie Ling. "The Lings." In *Reflections on the Chinese Mission School, Cleveland, Mississippi*, edited by Paul Wong and Doris Ling Lee. Cleveland, MS: Delta State University Press, 2011.

Jung, John. *Chopsticks in the Land of Cotton: Lives of Mississippi Delta Chinese Grocers*. Cypress, CA: Yin and Yang Press, 2008.

———. "Gong Lum v. Rice 1927: Mississippi School Segregation and the Delta Chinese." *Chinese American Forum* 26, no. 3 (January 2011).

Jung, Moon-Ho. *Coolies and Cane: Race, Labor, and Sugar in the Age of Emancipation*. Baltimore: Johns Hopkins University Press, 2006.

Lee, Joshua. "A Tale of Two Charlie's: The Story of Charley Wah, Charley Lee Soo, and Interracial Relationship in Mississippi and Washington, D.C." Master's thesis, University of California, Irvine, 2005.

Loewen, James W. *The Mississippi Chinese: Between Black and White*. Prospect Heights, IL: Waveland Press, 1988.

Ossman, Susan. "Studies in Serial Migration." *International Migration* 42 (2004).

Pflazer, Jean. *Driven Out: The Forgotten War against Chinese Americans*. New York: Random House, 2007.

Quan, Robert Seto. *Lotus among the Magnolias: The Mississippi Chinese*. Jackson: University Press of Mississippi, 1982.

Quon, Frieda Seu. "Growing Up Chinese in Greenville, Mississippi." In *The Chinese of Greenville, Mississippi*. By Ted Shepherd. Greenville, MS: Burford Brothers Printing, 1999.

Tang, Irwin A. "The Chinese Texan Experiment." In *Asian Texans: Our Histories and Our Lives*, edited by Irwin A. Tang Austin, TX: It Works, 2007.

Thornell, John. "Struggle for Identity in the Most Southern Place on Earth: The Chinese in the Mississippi Delta." *Chinese America: History and Perspectives*. 2004.

US Congress. Chinese Exclusion Act. An Act to Inaugurate Certain Treaty Stipulations Relating to Chinese. Forty-Seventh Congress, 1882.

US Supreme Court. *Gong Lum et al. v. Rice et al. No. 29*. October 12, 1927, 275 US 78.

Wong, Helen. "Through My Eyes: A Family History." Unpublished, 2007.

Wong, Paul. "A Letter from Paul Wong." In *The Chinese of Greenville, Mississippi*. By Ted Shepherd. Greenville, MS: Burford Brothers Printing, 1999.

7
Second-Generation Chinese Americans from Atlanta, Augusta, and Savannah, Georgia

Overcoming "Otherness"

DANIEL BRONSTEIN

Introduction

Second-generation Chinese Americans from Georgia, born roughly between 1910 and 1950, grappled with the larger national tension between being forever foreign or embracing the attributes of honorary whiteness during the 1950s and 1960s. The conflict was complicated by their residing in a state rigidly segregated based on racial differences between *white* and *black*. The small Chinese presence prevented the creation of Chinatowns and the legal recognition of where they and the few other Asians stood in the *biracial* hierarchy of Georgia. Southerners of European and African heritage also had deep historical roots in Georgia, while the Chinese immigrants were relative newcomers whose culture and "complexion" were peculiar to them. Since they could not gain legal acceptance as a "third" race, they embraced many of the values of *white* southerners, who increasingly treated them as "honorary whites" rather than as "perpetual foreigners" after 1940.[1] They moved to the white side of the racial divide by attending social institutions off limits to African Americans like white churches and white schools. Gradually, they found employment in white companies and even married local European Americans. By the late 1960s, the perception of "honorary white" had by and large replaced the "perpetual foreigner" image in Georgia.

Intact Families and the Family Business

The years between 1850 and 1920 are commonly referred to as the period of the "split household" in Chinese American history, with men living apart from their wives and extended family in China. Chinese communities in Augusta, Savannah, and Atlanta followed this paradigm with the men sharing living quarters with male relatives, friends, or living alone. Successful business operators visited

China to see family rather than sending for wives and young children to join them. After 1920, a new family structure emerged and coexisted with the older "split household" paradigm. Some Chinese American families became "small producer" households with wives joining husbands in the United States and their US-born children serving as a source of cheap labor for the "mom-and-pop" family business.[2] Augusta and Savannah had more of these "small producer" households during the 1920s and 1930s while Atlanta, with few exceptions, retained its "split household" family community until the mid-1960s. These family businesses provided steady income for families and eventually a surplus for retirement and putting children through higher education. The business acumen of these families improved their status in the eyes of local whites, who viewed them as "hard-working" people and different from local African Americans.

Augusta after 1920 had the largest US-born population of the three cities during the Exclusion Era. This city afforded Chinese immigrants the unique opportunity to operate American-style grocery stores in black areas for almost a century between 1875 and 1970. European immigrants usually functioned as merchants in southern black neighborhoods, but in Augusta few European immigrants became merchants in black areas.[3] Chinese merchants operated almost half of the stores in black neighborhoods by the 1920s. The number of African American grocery stores continued to decrease as China-born and US-born Chinese established more stores.[4] Financial success in the retail grocery businesses was not the only reason for why Augusta became one of the largest cities of settlement for first-wave Chinese immigrants in the South. Grocers in Augusta, who were considered "merchants" by the Chinese Exclusion Law, used this category to bring their families from China to the United States.[5] The arrival of families enabled a noticeable US-born population to take hold in the 1920s. Before that time, no two-parent Chinese families with children were enumerated in the 1900 federal census for Richmond County; the four US-born males enumerated in the 1910 federal census were California-born adults making a living as laundry operators. By 1920, four Chinese immigrants had set up households with wives and children.[6] A decade later, approximately ten married couples and forty-five children lived in the back of their grocery store–residences in Augusta. The Augusta- born generation continued to increase through the 1930s and 1940s with the birth of more children to these families and the arrival of other intact families to the city. The family sizes ranged from two to nineteen children born roughly between 1915 and 1945.[7] By the end of the Second World War, written documents and personal recollections put the number of children—both born in the United States and China—at about eighty-six.[8]

The US-born Chinese American population in Savannah remained smaller than Augusta's for most of the Exclusion Period because of the fewer number of intact families. As a seaport, Savannah had historically been attractive to immigrants throughout the eighteenth and nineteenth centuries. This included Germans and Irish settlers who went into the retail grocery business in black and immigrant areas before the first Chinese settlers arrived in the early 1880s. Chinese immigrants wanting to become merchants in Savannah had to sell merchandise that appealed to white consumers such as Asian specialty products. Local demand supported only enough business for one store of this type. Instead, almost all Chinese residents operated hand laundries until the 1920s.[9] Chinese laundrymen typically had more trouble having families join them in the United States because of the meager income most earned and the Chinese Exclusion Law ban on "laborers" from entering the United States. A laundry operator was included in the "labor" category.[10] No families with children lived in the city in 1900, and only one with children resided in Savannah a decade later.[11] By the early 1920s, three households lived in the city with their ten children. The 1930 federal census, the last one to be released for public viewing with the population census schedules, counted twenty US-born people of Chinese heritage living in the city. During the 1930s, some Chinese families successfully established retail grocery stores in racially mixed areas of Savannah.[12] The US-born population surpassed the China-born population sometime during the 1930s with approximately thirty to thirty-five second-generation Chinese Americans residing in Savannah.[13] This total held until the late 1940s.

Atlanta's Chinese population differed significantly from its aforementioned neighbors during the Chinese Exclusion Period. Unlike Augusta and Savannah, the majority of Chinese immigrants living in Atlanta operated hand laundries, which primarily served white clientele from the 1880s until the 1960s.[14] African American neighborhoods already had a large number of both African American and Jewish immigrant grocers, so the Chinese could not establish the same type of retail grocery stores found in Augusta.[15] The heyday for the Chinese-operated hand laundries in Atlanta was during the first two decades of the twentieth century after which competition from steam laundries and the harsh Chinese Exclusion Laws began to take their toll on Atlanta's Chinese population because most of the laundrymen remained single or separated from their families in China. Consequently, few intact Chinese families and school-age children lived in Atlanta. One Chinese immigrant couple and their two children were counted in the 1900 census, but the family either moved or was somehow missed in 1910.[16] California-born laundry operators constituted all the US-born males in 1910 and 1920. Only two families lived in the city by the time of the 1930 census; two others arrived in the mid-1930s.[17] Surviving records and recollections from children indicate that Atlanta's Chinese community had perhaps fifteen US-born children living in the city by the outbreak of the Second World War.[18]

Most of the children in these three cities were born and raised in the back of their parent's grocery store, laundry, or restaurant. A 1928 INS inspector's report describes the living and working conditions of Augusta retail grocer S. Y. Loo, his wife Do Shee, and their three children, Wah Chow, Chow Lin, and Mon Hong: "The place of business of Loo Yet Sing is at 1301 Twiggs Street, Augusta, Georgia and is in a one-story frame building of approximately 25 x 60 feet dimensions. Living quarters in the rear of the building were occupied by Loo Yet Sing and his family. In the store part of the building there was a large stock of staple and fancy goods, including fresh meats, which I estimate to be worth at least $1800.00."[19] The Loos went on to raise seventeen surviving children. A few grocers lived in two-story structures so the family could live above the store. This business-residence pattern remained typical with intact families because it served a double function. Parents invested most of their money in the business, which they hoped to pass on, usually to their oldest male child or used any savings to send offspring to college or a professional school so he/she had the option to pursue another career. Living in African American neighborhoods shielded families from having to buy or rent houses in white areas where they may not be welcomed or would be barred completely. Despite residing in black areas, the economic success of Chinese American families brought respect from white elites, who increasingly saw them as being distinct from their African Americans customers.

Everyone who lived at home contributed some of their time to running the family business. Sons and daughters of grocery store operators recalled helping their parents as clerks and as delivery boys and girls when they were not in school or pursuing leisure activities.[20] The older children, especially, had little leisure time because of the long hours needed to help parents with the business and look after younger siblings. One daughter of a restaurant proprietor in Savannah remembered working as a cashier, waitress, and cook.[21] The son of a laundry operator and his siblings assisted in the washing, folding, and packaging of clothes on Sundays.[22] The Wongs and their nine children worked many hours in their family grocery store in Savannah trying to earn enough money to survive.[23] Most of the families in the cities eventually ran two stores with the children assisting their parents in both operations. The Rufo and Lum families had this arrangement for their Augusta stores.[24]

Older children took on additional duties as translators for their immigrant parents and other Chinese immigrants who had difficulties communicating in English. Woo Wing Jin, who went by the American name Eugene Woo after he came to the United States in 1919, helped his immigrant parents and the other grocers overcome the language barrier by helping them communicate with the non-Chinese wholesale grocers and immigration officials.[25] Ruby Lum Wong, the oldest of eleven Lum children, and her older female siblings assisted their parents, who did not speak any English upon their arrival in Augusta after leaving San Francisco in 1927. Although the father had been born in San Francisco, he worked as a shoemaker in Chinatown's ethnic economy and did not need to learn much English.[26]

After 1910, the composition of the Chinese American populations in Atlanta, Augusta, and Savannah represented two coexisting familial models. In Augusta and Savannah, the Chinese American community became more homogenous and family oriented. Both parents were of Chinese descent. Atlanta, however, had few intact families in its Chinese community. The family structure in Savannah and Augusta gradually moved most family businesses into "small producer" units while the majority of Chinese businesses in Atlanta continued as "split households" until the men passed away or returned home. For those parents with children living in Georgia, families shared the responsibility of working in the laundry, restaurant, and grocery, which reduced the need for paid laborers and enabled the businesses to be open for a wide variety of hours. Furthermore, for some Chinese Americans, it served as valuable training for future careers when they came of age and took over the family enterprise or set up their own businesses. Finally, despite continued business dealings with African Americans, economic prosperity was one factor that helped Chinese Americans gain greater respect from local whites who saw them as astute business people.

Chinese American Families and the Christian Churches

The establishment of Chinese American families in Georgia nurtured a close spiritual and social relationship between themselves and the larger white Christian churches in Augusta, Savannah, and to a much lesser degree in Atlanta. Beginning in the 1910s, parents and children attended Sunday schools and became members of church congregations instead of founding their own independent religious institutions like in the larger Chinatowns or like African Americans had done in these cities. The conversion to Christianity by Chinese parents and the immersion of children in this faith brought greater acceptance of the local Chinese Americans as "honorary whites" by white elites who usually attended these same churches. Embracing Christianity created a sense of greater belonging in the South, where, with the exception of a few Jewish families, most professed to belonging to some denomination of the Christian faith. It inculcated a strong Christian identity in many of the second-generation children that was often indistinguishable from local whites.

The close relationship between Chinese residents and local white churches in Augusta and Savannah began before the settlement of families. Individual white missionaries with southern roots and southern-based churches had set up missions in China since the nineteenth century. With the coming of Chinese people to Georgia and other parts of the South, churches sought to convert them with the hope that they would spread the Christian gospel upon their return to

China. Augusta's First Baptist Church opened a Chinese Sunday School in 1885 with this purpose in mind. Two women, A. Smith Irvine and Isabella Jordan, organized the school and remained intimately involved with its activities for decades. Although neither woman had been active in the Christian missionary movement in China, two friends of Jordan, William Stokes and his wife, had been missionaries in China and, no doubt, influenced her interest.[27]

Savannah's Independent Presbyterian Church opened its first Chinese Sunday school in 1897 with seven Chinese in attendance. Church minister James Y. Fair organized the school with the help of Robert Jung Chan, the city's most well-known Chinese resident. According to Chan's daughter, he arrived in Savannah on the day that this church was destroyed in a fire in 1889. Chan began going to services before the establishment of the school. Chan recalled its early years in a 1939 interview: "Have many Chinese men here then, no women. Every Sunday we used to go to Bible class, sing, learn scripture, learn praying." Chan encouraged others to attend the school and join the church, including one of his clansman, Jung Home Kigue, who also became a lifelong member.[28]

The arrival of Chinese women and children from other parts of the United States and China in the 1920s enhanced the close relationship between the Sunday schools and the Chinese American communities in Augusta and Savannah. The schools were convenient venues for learning not just about Christianity but also about the language and customs of the United States.[29] One older Chinese male recalled in a 1970s interview that some women invited him to attend services after he came over from China in 1909.[30]

In Augusta, most families became members of the First Baptist Church's congregation, which supplied Chinese immigrants with many of the tools that they needed to survive in the United States. This congenial relationship is depicted in surviving photographs from the 1920s. The majority of Chinese American children from Augusta had some childhood connection with the Baptist Church. Some Chinese members also became teachers and leaders of the Sunday school. In 1943, the church ordained its first Chinese American deacon, Paul Jue, who had been an active member in the church since he had come to Augusta from San Francisco during the early 1920s. This welcoming environment created by Augusta's First Baptist Church also happened in the Mississippi Delta, where the Baptist missions assisted the newly arrived Chinese families and established a Sunday school and church for them in Cleveland, Mississippi.[31]

Some of Savannah's white churches also permitted Chinese men and their families to become full members of their congregations. Wives and children of Robert Jung Chan and Jung Home Kigue joined the Independent Presbyterian Church. Woo Lat and his family joined the Bona Bella Presbyterian Church. Woo's family had resided in Augusta and attended services at First Baptist.[32] It is not known why he did not continue his relationship with a Baptist church in

Savannah. As in Augusta, the Chinese American community converted to Christianity and became noticeably involved in church activities.

Local white churches in Atlanta, however, did not have the same enduring relationship with Chinese residents. Obituaries of Chinese residents in Atlanta usually did not mention the descendant's membership in a local church. An exception was an obituary for Jung Wing, who was reported to have converted to Christianity at Atlanta's Second Baptist Church.[33] One son of a laundry operator recalled that local churches did take an interest in persuading him and his family to join, but that there was never one church that attracted the Chinese immigrants like in Augusta and Savannah.

The close ties between local white churches and Chinese American communities in Augusta and Savannah continued when the US-born generation reached adulthood. In Savannah, Archie Chan and Geraldine Chan Sieg stayed with the Independent Presbyterian Church until their deaths in 1986 and 2005, respectively.[34] Phillip Wong became superintendent of the Sunday school of Augusta's First Baptist Church between 1970 and his death in 1991. Ray Rufo was ordained a deacon of the church in 1977.[35] Besides being a place of prayer, the church served as a social magnet for Chinese Americans to meet one another from different parts of the United States. Betty Joe met her future husband Harry Eng, who was originally from Los Angeles, through Augusta's First Baptist Church. He had been stationed at Fort Gordon near Augusta. They married and moved to Los Angeles, where they remained active in the local Baptist church.[36]

The Chinese-operated Sunday schools in Atlanta, Augusta, and Savannah helped nurture a close relationship between the sponsoring white churches and Chinese who regularly attended them. Local missionaries saw their efforts of teaching Christianity to immigrants as part of the greater missionary movement in China. Unlike African Americans who formed their own churches because of Jim Crow laws, the Chinese in Georgia were not "racially" excluded from local white-run churches. Not having to create distinctive religious organizations, people of Chinese descent adapted to white southern Christianity and embraced their "honorary white" status. Throughout the late nineteenth and early twentieth centuries, the support of the local white churches helped Chinese Americans acquire more of the privileges of whiteness and gain access to "white only" facilities throughout the state.

Educating a Growing Chinese American Population during Jim Crow

Chinese American parents in Georgia, like other immigrant parents, desired that their children find success through education as well as prepare for the possibility of moving back to China. Prejudice experienced by people of Chinese descent in the United States combined with a desire to help China modernize (and later to fight the Japanese during the 1930s and 1940s) pushed many parents to think of ultimately returning home. Furthermore, in most cities with large Chinese American populations, children were segregated and had substandard educational opportunities. Georgia's isolation from major Chinese population centers and its Jim Crow segregation threatened to make it harder for children to learn about their Chinese heritage and integrate themselves into the biracial society. Augusta, unlike Savannah and Atlanta, had a larger Chinese population, which prompted the establishment of two Chinese schools simultaneously where children learned about their heritage. Acceptance of children of Chinese descent in white educational facilities in Georgia after the 1920s was an important privilege of "whiteness." Ultimately, it helped them become "honorary whites" and establish favorable conditions for settling in the state.

Public education began to take shape in Georgia during the early 1870s following the return to power of a white-dominated Democratic Party in the state legislature. The state education system that emerged rigidly segregated children based upon their racial background with children of African heritage being forced to attend separate "colored" educational facilities.[37] In California, European Americans reacted similarly and wanted nonwhite children to go to schools apart from whites. Chinese Americans living in San Francisco were forced to enroll in the city's public "Oriental School" from the 1880s until the 1920s.[38] However, unlike California, Georgia's biracial schooling system did not stipulate whether the children of Chinese heritage had to attend a particular school. Local city education boards made their own decisions about Chinese American enrollments.

Savannah's education officials initially barred Chinese American children from attending white schools, basing its decision on a strict interpretation of the Georgia educational statute that had established separate educational facilities for "white" and "colored" children.[39] Geraldine Chan, the daughter of Savannah's leading Chinese citizen, Robert Jung Chan, recalled that she was not able to go to white public schools until she was in her teens in the mid-1920s. Because of this, her parents decided that she should receive her education through private instructors.[40] For reasons unknown, the school board reversed its original decision sometime in the 1920s, and the few school-age children of Chinese ancestry were able to enroll in Savannah's white public schools.[41] It is not clear, however, why this change occurred, especially during a decade when anxieties about racial mixing were at its height. Perhaps, the reversal was due to the improving racial status of the Chinese in the eyes of local white elites. Almost forty Chinese Americans born or raised between 1920 and 1940 attended the city's all white schools.[42]

In Augusta Chinese American children also attended white public schools from the 1920s onward. Little is known about the education of school-age children prior to the second decade of the twentieth century, or if there was an initial ban on Chinese American attendance at white schools. William Joe, his younger sister Frances, and other children of Chinese ancestry born in the 1910s and early 1920s attended Central Elementary School. After John S. Davidson Elementary School opened in 1934, most Chinese American children went there.[43] High school was not coed, so Chinese females went to Tubman High School; males went to Richmond Academy High School.[44] The exact number of Chinese Americans attending schools in Augusta is not known, but a conservative estimate for the early 1930s would be between thirty to thirty-five students. Regardless, these students attracted enough attention for the state government to take up the issue of whether or not children of Asian descent belonged in white public schools.

The state legislature dealt with school segregation and children of Chinese ancestry during its 1931 legislative session. In July, the Richmond County delegation introduced a bill to the house to cut off funds to white public schools that had Chinese American students.[45] The legislation also stated that the presence of children of Asian descent in white schools violated Georgia's constitution.[46] Chinese American parents took action by going to Atlanta to induce legislators to vote against the bill. Legislators and school officials investigated the situation and concluded by the end of the month that the bill should be rejected.[47] This decision contrasted with Mississippi's segregation law regarding Chinese American children, which was upheld in the state supreme court in the case *Gong Lum v. Rice* in 1924–25 and then by the US Supreme Court in 1927.[48]

The Chinese American population of school-age children in Atlanta was considerably smaller than Augusta's and Savannah's during the same period. It did not rise above more than ten to fifteen children at any time before the 1960s. Only two intact families lived in the city during the 1920s, and it is not known if these children attended white public schools.[49] The children of the Cheung family all attended white public schools during the 1930s, 1940s, and 1950s. The Jew and Chew families also sent their children to similar schools.[50] No local opposition movement to the Chinese American presence in Atlanta's white public schools has been found.

Chinese Americans were also never barred from attending white public colleges and universities in Georgia. The Jim Crow system that barred and later resisted African American enrollment in state-operated white postsecondary educational institutions was not applied to people of Chinese ancestry. Collegiate attendance rates were low for those born before the mid-1920s because most young men took over family businesses or started their own ventures after completing high school. From this same period, Chinese American women married, became homemakers, and unofficial partners in their spouse's business. Albert

Joe of Augusta was exceptional for the time because he studied engineering at the Georgia Institute of Technology (Georgia Tech) from 1942 to 1946. He went on to use this degree as an engineer in a private firm in New York City.[51]

Almost every Chinese American male born after 1928 in Atlanta and Augusta received a college degree. Although collegiate attendance among Chinese American males from Savannah increased, they remained lower because most young men took over a family business.[52] Collegiate and graduate school attendance rates were particularly high for Chinese American males from Augusta. The four sons of the Rufo family and the six sons of the younger Joe family exemplified the trend of higher education and career advancement. Three of the Rufos and three of the Joes attended the University of Georgia in Athens (UGA). The remainder went to Augusta College or Georgia Southern College in Statesboro. After graduating from college, seven Joe and Rufo children went on to receive one and sometimes two professional degrees, with health care being the overwhelming specialization. Nine were able to make a living in their chosen fields.[53] The exception was the oldest Joe son who served in the US Air Force in the Korean War (1950–53) and decided to remain in the service as a career until his premature death in 1973.[54]

In general, Chinese American women faced greater obstacles in attaining the same postsecondary educational levels as their male counterparts because their parents usually allocated money for sons to go on to college and not for their daughters.[55] Chinese immigrant parents in Georgia, however, felt differently and gave many of their daughters the chance to go to college. Collegiate attendance was lowest for females born in Augusta before 1928. The one exception was the medical career of Dr. Margaret Wong, who studied medicine at the Medical College of Georgia in Augusta between 1942 and 1946 and practiced in Maryland.[56] Collegiate opportunities improved for Chinese American women born after 1928, and most received baccalaureate degrees. For example, Evelyn Woo graduated from the University of Georgia's nursing program in 1951.[57] She encountered no difficulty finding employment as a nurse, first in Augusta and later in Atlanta. Two of her younger sisters also received health care degrees from UGA.[58]

The majority of Chinese Americans in these cities received their undergraduate degrees in Georgia instead of going to states with big Chinese American populations. A smaller number went out of state because of choice or because the University of Georgia system did not have the postsecondary specializations. William G. Joe graduated from the Citadel in 1937 and Wing L. Jung from the US Military Academy in 1939.[59] Both wanted to be officers in the US Army and eventually retired as colonels. Unlike the experiences of African Americans, the enrollment of the majority of Chinese Americans in Georgia schools of higher learning illustrates that they were not forced by racial intolerance to go outside the state to find opportunities.

Although arguably all Chinese immigrant parents in Georgia were concerned about their children's ability of maintaining connections with their homeland, only Augusta's community set up Chinese language schools in the late 1920s.[60] The Chinese American communities in Savannah and Atlanta were not able to set up Chinese schools, most likely because of the small number of school-age children each city had at any one time. Augusta's Chinese School (中華學校), which opened periodically between 1928 and 1961, was similar to other schools sponsored by the Chinese Consolidated Benevolent Association (CCBA) throughout the United States.[61] Approximately ten to fifteen children of various ages attended the school in its heyday. Classes met in the evenings after regular school and dinner, with instruction in the Guangzhou dialect. The curriculum consisted of reading, writing, recitation, and calculating with an abacus. The death of its longest-serving teacher, C. H. Lam (more on him below), in 1961 brought disorganization to the school, and it closed shortly thereafter.[62]

The Woos of Augusta, one of the largest clans in the city, were able to set up a separate school for their children around the same time the CCBA opened its school. The On Ding Chinese School (安定學校) was comparable in student enrollment size, curriculum, and meeting times as the CCBA's Chinese school. Its teachers, however, spoke a country dialect from Kwong On Village and neighboring villages in the Kaiping District, which was several miles inland from Hong Kong and Guangzhou. The school closed its doors in the mid-1950s because of dwindling enrollment.[63]

Chinese language schools in the United States were frequently plagued by not having full-time teachers. Typically, individuals from the community taught in these schools as well as working several jobs.[64] Augusta's schools were fortunate in that they had the same dedicated educators for most of their existence. Woo Leong Tong served as the teacher at the Woo family school from 1928 until his death in early 1943. The school was without a teacher until 1946 when Dr. K. K. Hu taught there until its closure. The CCBA had two teachers during its history. The name of its first teacher was Lum, whose background and later career are unknown. The CCBA's second teacher starting in 1937 was Professor C. H. Lam, a graduate of Beijing University and an educator at several universities in China. He had come to the United States in 1922 to help organize and serve as a principal of a Chinese school in San Francisco. Teaching was not a full-time occupation, and Lam divided his time between teaching, administrative duties of the CCBA, and running his family's grocery store with his sons. Despite his many commitments, he remained devoted to his teaching until his death.[65] Woo and Hu of the On Ding School were also part-time educators, with the former operating a grocery and the latter studying to become a physician at the University of Georgia's School of Medicine during the late 1940s.[66]

Students who had attended both schools recalled the good intentions of the teachers and expressed regret that they had not taken their Chinese schooling more seriously. Some retained the ability to write their name and perhaps simple sentences in Chinese. One lingering problem for students in all Chinese language schools was allocating time for studying the Chinese curriculum while keeping up with their primary schooling.[67] Raymond Rufo, who went to the CCBA's school during the 1940s, recalled that it was hard balancing the work of both schools and added that there were no opportunities to practice Chinese other than with his parents and other immigrants.[68] Evelyn Woo, a student at the Woo family school during the 1930s and 1940s, reminisced that she used the school more as a social outlet to meet with friends than as a venue for serious learning.[69]

Beginning in the 1920s, Chinese Americans began attending white public schools in Georgia despite the state's biracial schooling system. White southerners vehemently resisted formal integration well into the 1960s, they permitted children of Chinese descent to enroll in them without vigorous protests from white families. White teachers and peers appear to have accepted their presence, although to what extent is unknown. The tolerance illustrated in Georgia proves that not all southern states had a universal response as to which schools children of Chinese heritage had to attend. It also served to "whiten" the Chinese children in the eyes of local whites and pave the way for more permanent settlement of families in the state. Higher education ultimately provided an outlet for most second-generation Chinese Americans to go into different careers.

To sum up, during the 1920s, two Chinese language schools opened in Augusta to cater to the sizable Chinese American community in hopes of helping the children maintain their connection to their parents' homeland; no Chinese schools were founded in Savannah and Atlanta. Ultimately, these schools would be for most Chinese American children their only link with their cultural heritage outside what their parents and relatives taught them. Children from Augusta retained a stronger sense of their Chinese heritage because of the Chinese school, but this in no way undermined their integration into the social fabric of Augusta.

The Second World War and the Three Communities

K. Scott Wong's *American First: Chinese Americans and the Second World War*, the only published in-depth study on Chinese American involvement in the Second World War, successfully concludes that the war improved social mobility and gave that generation a new confidence in themselves as Americans.

Furthermore, the war years provided Chinese Americans the opportunity to dismantle or challenge social, political, and economic barriers that had marginalized people of Chinese descent for decades.[70] Chinese Americans held fund-raising rallies that contributed money to the Chinese war effort and, later, the Allied war effort. Men and women from different parts of the country also served in the armed forces and worked in defense industries.[71] Georgia's Chinese Americans are also representative of this trend with men going into the service as well and women assisting in home front activities.[72] While serving in integrated units was typical for most Chinese Americans, in Georgia this arrangement moved them closer to being "white" by association as in the case of attending white schools.

Japanese territorial aggression on the Chinese mainland in the 1930s generated widespread sympathy among non-Chinese throughout the United States that translated into more positive attitudes about Chinese Americans.[73] For example, the "Bowl of Rice Movement," which was a nationwide campaign between 1938 and 1941 to raise money for China's war refugees, held parades in major US cities and was supported by Chinese and non-Chinese Americans.[74] Georgia's major communities also participated in the effort to support China. Augusta's CCBA hosted a fund-raiser in November 1939, which included dinner and a Chinese film.[75] Ultimately, Augusta's Chinese Americans raised about $28,000 during the war to support China and the United States.[76] No fund-raising figures have survived for Atlanta and Savannah, but there were probably smaller charity drives in these cities.

Following the US declaration of war in December 1941, Chinese Americans living in the United States joined the American armed forces and defense industries. K. Scott Wong estimates that twelve thousand to fifteen thousand Chinese Americans or 20 percent of the adult Chinese male population wore uniforms between 1942 and 1946.[77] Most Chinese Americans ended up serving in divisions with European Americans, despite the armed forces being officially segregated until 1947.[78] One notable exception was the Fourteenth Air Service Division (FASD). Its units began training in 1943 and went to China in late 1944 and early 1945. Tom P. Wong, one of the founders of Atlanta's postwar Chinese restaurant Ding Ho, served in the FASD's 555th Air Service Squadron from its inception.[79] Wong also appears to be the only Chinese American in Atlanta to have gone into the armed forces because the city's Chinese American community consisted primarily of older laundrymen and restaurant operators or children too young to serve.[80]

The Chinese American communities in Savannah and Augusta had more men of eligible age for military service because of the establishment of intact families in the 1920s and 1930s. Approximately eight men from Savannah and twenty from Augusta were inducted into the armed forces.[81] Not all the men were drafted or volunteered for the war. Wing Fook Jung of Savannah and William Joe of Augusta served in the Second World War as part of their careers in the US Army. Joe was with the 101st Airborne Division in Europe.[82] Jung's military service record, which fortunately survived the fire at the National Personnel Records Center in 1973, states that he was posted in the Asian Pacific theater as an infantry unit commander and later a battalion executive officer between December 1941 and March 1943. He then returned to the United States for military schooling at Fort Benning, Georgia. In February 1945, Major Jung was assigned to the India-Burma theater as the headquarters commandant at the Chungking (Chongqing) Station Command in China.[83]

George Joe of Augusta, who entered the army in 1942, recalled that he was the only person of Asian descent attached to his fighter outfit in Great Britain where he worked as a radio mechanic.[84] George Jue and Wing G. Jung (not the career army officer) of Savannah remembered similar situations in their units while in the Pacific Theater.[85]

Integrated units forced men of different backgrounds to work together for their survival in hostile territory. Individual and societal prejudice against people of Chinese descent was lessened as a result of this military policy; unfortunately, this was not the case for Japanese Americans and African Americans. Conversely, Chinese Americans fighting in Asia had to face the possibility that they would be the victims of friendly fire because they "looked like the enemy."[86]

Many Chinese Americans saw combat and some were taken prisoner or killed in battle.[87] Wah Chow (Charles) Loo of Augusta received basic engineering instruction and specialized training from the army before being sent to Europe in late 1944. While participating in the Rome-Arno campaign with the 337th Infantry as a rifleman in early 1945, he was captured and became a German POW for the last few months of the war.[88] Charles Dick enthusiastically joined up shortly after the outbreak of war and became a fighter pilot in Europe with the army air force. Sadly, he became one of the few men of Chinese descent in Georgia not to return from the war after he was reported missing in action in 1943.[89]

Comparing home front experiences for Chinese Americans in Atlanta, Augusta, and Savannah has been difficult because of the paucity of written sources and people to interview. In Atlanta, a newspaper article from 1944 reported that Atlanta laundryman Chew Quan Lung was an active member in United China Relief, a membership corporation coordinating the fund-raising activities of eight Chinese relief organizations. Founded and headquartered in New York State in 1941, branches of the Chinese Relief Association operated in all three cities and other major cities raising money to send to needy people in China.[90] Moreover, branches of the Chinese Relief Association operated in all three cities raising money. The names of local Chinese and non-Chinese who were involved in these local operations, however, have been lost.[91]

The absence of young men created a labor shortage for Chinese families throughout the United States. Chinese American women in Savannah and Augusta took on greater responsibilities in family businesses as a result of this. Catherine Woo Jue helped her parents run the family business in Savannah when her older brother Harold entered the army.[92] While Bot Wong was in the army air force between 1943 and 1946, Mamie Wong Lee assisted her widowed mother, Ching Shee, with operating the grocery store in Augusta.[93]

Chinese American women also found employment opportunities in the US civil defense industry and to a lesser degree in the armed forces.[94] Jean Dick Joe went to California, where she worked at the Sacramento Air Depot in its woodshop for about a year.[95] Chinese American participation in the Allied war effort gave this generation greater confidence in its social interaction with European Americans and helped move many away from the restricted ethnic enclaves that had confined their parents and grandparents. These changes were less pronounced in Atlanta, Augusta, and Savannah with most of the men and women already living in non-Chinese neighborhoods and socializing with African Americans and European Americans. Despite the new opportunities that arose during mobilization, most war veterans returned home and took over the family business; their sisters, who had assumed many of the responsibilities of their brothers during the war, became unofficial partners in their future husbands' businesses. Still, it remained an important episode in the lives of these men and women. Tommy Wong, who served in the US Marines in the Pacific, recalled it as "one of the most rich and rewarding experiences of my life."[96] Finally, it improved the image of Chinese Americans in the perceptions of local whites who shared the same experience of fighting "with them" in the Second World War.

Finding Employment during Segregation

Prior to the Second World War, Chinese Americans rarely found employment outside their community. Even with educational credentials and the ability to speak English without an accent, non-Chinese firms usually rejected Chinese American applicants because they did not look "white." This perception of all people of Chinese descent as permanent outsiders threatened to forever keep them confined to the same jobs as their parents.[97] In many cases, parents tried to persuade their children to "return" to China where they could use their professional degrees and training. World War II and the ensuing Cold War, however, created alternative employment opportunities for Chinese American men and some women in the armed forces, defense industries, and health care professions.[98] By the 1960s, European Americans touted their success as a "model minority" vis-à-vis other non-Asian minorities and viewed them increasingly as "honorary whites."[99] This evolving designation impacted Georgia's Chinese Americans who had the additional dynamic of living in a state with legally sanctioned racial discrimination. Because they possessed advanced college degrees and had already gained some privileges of "whiteness," they slowly moved into occupations normally reserved only for whites in Georgia by the mid-1950s.

Second-generation Chinese Americans from Augusta, Savannah, and Atlanta did not grapple with the decision of going to live in China like Chinese Americans in cities with much larger Chinese American communities, such as San Francisco, Los Angeles, and Seattle. As they reached adulthood in the 1930s and 1940s, the door to living in China closed with Japan's invasion and later the establishment of the People's Republic of China in late 1949.[100] As they had during Japan's occupation, Augusta's Chinese American leaders continued to support the Nationalist government in exile on Taiwan.[101] Community leaders in Savannah and Atlanta probably held similar views about the regime change and backed the anti-Communist government in Taiwan.

With the door of going to mainland China closed, many Chinese Americans remained in Georgia and went into the same self-employed businesses as the immigrant generation. Before the late 1960s, the retail grocery store business remained profitable for Chinese American families in Augusta. Most first-born males and a few of their younger brothers followed their parents into this occupation. These men, usually World War II veterans, started their own grocery stores or took over their parents' stores. Recently discharged US Army veterans Thomas Wong, Bot Lee Wong, Alexander Loo, Charles Loo, William G. Joe, and Frank Lum bought grocery stores in black neighborhoods.[102] Joe went back on active duty in the US Army in 1951 after the commencement of the Korean War and stayed in the service until his retirement as a colonel in 1967.[103] George Tom, also a veteran, assumed most of the duties in his parents' store and eventually ran all of its operations by the early 1950s.[104] A few other younger sons also became independent grocers. William G. Joe's younger brothers, George and Harry, were grocers as were Charles and Robert Wong, the younger siblings of Thomas Wong.[105] The entry of the second generation into this occupation brought the number of Chinese American–owned stores in black areas to fifty-four in 1952; African Americans had only three.[106]

The smaller Chinese American male population in Savannah usually operated grocery stores and later convenience stores. Raymond Jue and Harvey Woo, the oldest sons of Woo Lat and Sam Lee Jue, became independent grocers by the mid-1930s. Their younger brothers also opened their own grocery stores following their military service in World War II.[107] The most successful family business to counter the challenge of supermarket chains by the 1970s was a convenience store chain established by Woo Lat around 1952 and run by his sons and in-laws.[108]

Unlike their supermarket competitors, convenience stores concentrated on attracting customers during the morning and evening hours while supermarkets kept limited daytime hours.[109] Known as Seven Eleven Minit, it grew to five stores by the time of Woo's death in 1964. Woo's grandchildren continued to operate the stores until the end of the twentieth century.[110]

Although de jure segregation existed in Georgia until the 1960s, Chinese American men from all three cities began finding employment outside of the laundry, restaurant, and grocery store careers of parents and older brothers after World War II. Tommy Wong, for example, worked as a federal postal worker in Savannah from the late 1940s until the 1970s.[111] Others went into occupations requiring advanced college degrees and professional training. While attending the dental school at Emory University in the 1950s, Raymond Rufo was asked by an older Chinese American friend how he was going to make a living as a dentist in Augusta since his practice could not survive with only Chinese American patients. Rufo received his DDS in 1957 and opened his first practice in Augusta with a European American colleague.[112] He went on to have a long career in dentistry with most of his patients being non-Chinese. Ralph Wong of Augusta began his pharmacy career in 1960 at Lake View Pharmacy, Inc., one of the main pharmacies in the city that also filled prescriptions after regular business hours. Wong went on to establish Brynwood Pharmacy in 1970 with his wife, Mae, who was also a career pharmacist originally from Richmond, Virginia.[113] Other Chinese Americans went into pharmacology during the 1960s, which the *Augusta Herald* reported in Augusta in 1967.[114] In Atlanta, laundry operator Shiu Dun Jew's sons became an architect and a pharmacist. Their older brother, who immigrated to Atlanta later in life in the early 1960s, was the only one to take over a laundry from a relative in the post-1965 era. Unlike his brothers, he had limited English-speaking skills and lacked the US education credentials.[115] William L. Wong, son of Atlanta laundryman Jim A. Wong, was a construction engineer with Lockheed Martin in Atlanta.[116]

Chinese American women in the United States not only had to contend with anti-Chinese prejudice but also sexual bias that limited them to housework and a few occupations generally opened to all women. The majority of Chinese American women in Georgia who were born before 1930 became homemakers and unofficial partners in their spouse's businesses. As with the first generation, taking care of the family and working in the store often overlapped since most families continued to live in the back or above their store-residences until the 1960s.[117]

Ruby Lum Wong raised three children and worked with her husband, K. F. Wong and son Phillip with managing the K. F. Wong Grocery in Augusta for over sixty years.[118] Ruby's youngest sister, Lorraine, supported her then husband, grocer Harry Joe, with his business and raised four children.[119] May Wong Lee and her husband, Joe Fang, operated Lee's Corner Market in Savannah.[120] Catherine Woo Jue helped with the family store in Savannah.[121]

There were, however, exceptions. The most notable women were Gerald Chan Sieg of Savannah and Dr. Margaret Wong of Augusta. Sieg's prolific career as a writer and poet spanned almost a century. Sieg, the daughter of Robert Chan, won her first poetry prize in 1927 with "The Sad Lady," while still in high school. A poem, "The Chinese Laundryman," describes the loneliness of Savannah's Chinese laundry operators. She wrote two books about her family history, *The Christmas Box* (the title inspired by her father who ordered a box from China every year for his family and friends) and *We Six* (the number of Chan children).[122] One of her least-known works was an interview with her parents for the Federal Writer's Project in 1938.[123]

Titled "Laundryman," it was set in the family's Willie Chin Laundry and the family apartment. The interview provides a rare account about a laundry operator and his family residing in the United States. Newspapers and journals also published her writings. Besides writing, she earned a living primarily as a fashion and advertising director of one of Savannah's most prominent department stores.[124]

Becoming a medical doctor was not possible for women until the 1960s, except for the career of Dr. Margaret Wong. Her parents, grocer Wong Wing Hee and Jam Lin, encouraged her to go into medicine, a profession that even very few Chinese American men were able to pursue.[125] She attended the Medical College of Georgia to be a doctor of medicine in the early 1940s. Dr. Wong began practicing in Maryland in the late 1940s for that state's board of health and spent most of her career there.[126]

Beginning in the early 1950s, an increasing number of Chinese American women in Georgia established careers as nurses and secretaries. Nationally, women of Chinese heritage became independent wage earners outside the ethnic economy of Chinatowns and family businesses.[127] Frances, Elizabeth, and Pauline Joe of Augusta all had secretarial positions. The first two worked for a short time in the New York City metro area and later returned to Augusta. Pauline remembered upon her graduation from the Junior College of Augusta in 1947 that she could either be a secretary or, perhaps, a teacher. She began doing clerical duties at Fort Gordon in 1949, a major US Army installation that was very active in the emerging Cold War.[128]

Evelyn Woo Loo of Augusta, the oldest daughter of Eugene and Alice Woo, worked on the nursing staff of Talmadge Memorial Hospital from the early 1950s until 1962 when she moved with her husband to Atlanta where she continued her nursing at Grady Memorial Hospital.[129]

Three daughters of the Loo family also became nurses in Augusta.[130] Rosa Wong Joe of Atlanta and Kathy Liu Rufo of Savannah became registered nurses in the late 1950s. The latter also taught at the Medical College of Georgia in Augusta through the 1960s.[131]

Other Chinese American men and women from Augusta, Atlanta, and Savannah left Georgia for western and northern states where they could find higher paying positions. Four sons and three daughters of the Loo family moved from the state.[132] Only two of the eight Rufo children stayed in Georgia.[133] California, in particular, had a budding postwar economy in which the private and public sectors gradually lowered occupational barriers against people of Chinese descent. Anna Joe of Augusta settled in San Diego, California, as a clinical lab researcher.[134] Her three sisters also moved permanently to California or lived there for their working careers.[135] Arthur Lum left Augusta in 1950 to join the US Air Force for four years and later worked as a clerk in one of Sacramento's large Chinese American supermarkets called the Bel Air Market.[136] Stephen Liu, son of Henry and Mary Jung Liu of Savannah, moved to Long Beach, California, following his graduation from Georgia Tech for a career as an aeronautical engineer.[137] Charlie Wong, the older brother of Tommy, was an employee for United Airlines in Denver, Colorado.[138] One daughter and one son of the Cheung family of Atlanta worked in a federal office in Washington, DC, and the other as an engineer in Buffalo, New York, respectively.[139]

Atlanta's growth as the leading commercial and population center in Georgia during the 1950s and 1960s increased employment opportunities for Chinese Americans from Augusta who began settling there in the 1950s. Local business leaders and politicians touted Atlanta as the "city too busy to hate" because the city's process of desegregation allegedly lacked the violence found in other southern cities.[140] Chinese Americans had initially been attracted to Atlanta because of its postsecondary schools like the Georgia Institute of Technology. Students began enrolling at universities in the city during the 1940s, and their numbers increased as more Chinese Americans wanted degrees in the engineering and pharmaceutical fields. A few decided to settle in Atlanta starting in the early 1950s. Robert "Bobby" Woo graduated from Georgia Tech with a degree in ceramic engineering in 1959. After a few years in the army and furthering his education at the University of Georgia, he settled permanently in Atlanta, working as a computer programmer for Southern Railway in the late 1960s.[141] Others made Atlanta their home because of federal jobs or because they wanted a fresh start in private business. Robert Joe worked for the Federal Aviation Administration beginning in the late 1950s.[142] Charles Loo relocated to the city, where he opened several coin laundromats.[143] At least three other Chinese Americans from Augusta decided that Atlanta afforded them better prospects.

In short, the post–World War II period brought significant occupational and economic achievements for second- and third-generation Chinese Americans. Unlike their parents, who were usually self-employed because of limited educational skills and job discrimination, an increasing number found employment in the private and public sectors in Georgia and other US states. West Coast states, such as California, afforded Chinese Americans from Georgia and other southern states the opportunity to escape the lingering restrictions of Jim Crow. Chinese Americans from Atlanta usually stayed in the city because of its growing economy and smoother process of desegregation. Certainly long-standing racial prejudice continued to blind some employers, but more and more Chinese American men seeped through the cracks. Chinese American women not only had to contend with racial bigotry but also potential sexual bias that kept most helping in the family business or doing secretarial work until the 1950s. A higher percentage of women had their own careers and incomes that were not tied to the family businesses after the 1960s. The ability of Chinese American men and women to find employment in all-white institutions or to establish practices catering to white customers demonstrates their emerging status as "honorary whites" in still segregated Georgia.

Matrimony for Chinese Americans in the Biracial South

China-born Chinese males encountered two primary legal obstacles when trying to establish intact families inside the United States. US immigration laws discouraged and prevented many from bringing wives and children to the United States. Furthermore, most US states had antimiscegenation laws specifically banning marriages between people of Asian and European heritage.[144] These impediments were deliberately designed to keep people of Asian descent as "perpetual foreigners" in the United States. When US-born Chinese Americans reached marital age during the 1930s and 1940s, an increasing number of them selected Chinese American spouses who lived in the United State instead of going on wife-seeking trips to their ancestral villages as their fathers had done. Among this generation rates of marriage to people of European descent were low because of possible rejection from family and antimiscegenation laws. Beginning in the late 1940s, however, these statutes began to be overturned in most US states except in the South, which held out until 1967.[145]

The second generation from Augusta, Savannah, and Atlanta followed these two patterns of not going to China for matrimony and preferring to wed spouses of Chinese heritage. The cost and distance compelled families to make arrangements for eligible partners to court and wed Chinese Americans from major Chinatowns on the West Coast and cities and towns with smaller Chinese American populations. Intermarriage was an option few tried because of Georgia's rigid racial segregation that included an antimiscegenation statute. This began to change in the late 1950s, despite the law, with people of Chinese descent being treated as "whites" in the biracial hierarchy in the state.

Prior to the 1910s, Chinese communities consisted mostly of single or married men who did not have their wives and younger children with them. A small number entered into relationships with non-Chinese women, but for the most part Chinese Americans in Georgia had the same unbalanced gender ratios found in other parts of the United States.[146] Around 1900, the more prosperous grocers and a few laundrymen sent for family to join them, which was one factor in the decline of out-marriages in Augusta, Savannah, and Atlanta until the 1950s.

Even if parents accepted the decision of their children to marry outside the Chinese American community, antimiscegenation statutes in several US states, particularly on the West Coast, explicitly banned clerks from issuing marriage certificates to Chinese American–European American couples. The state legislature of Georgia voted unanimously in 1925 to rewrite its "race law" to prevent a "white person" from marrying a spouse with any "ascertainable trace of either Negro, African, West Indian, Asiatic Indian, Mongolian, Japanese, or Chinese blood in their veins." It became law in 1927 and discouraged any further out-marriage among Chinese Americans in Georgia.[147]

Antimiscegenation laws hindered but did not stop out-marriage because not all states had such laws, or they banned only certain "races" from marrying people of European descent. South Carolina's antimiscegenation law never included specific references to Asians and was never revised to include them. Instead, the statute, as it existed between 1879 and 1967, stated that "it shall be unlawful for any white man to intermarry with any woman of either the Indian or negro races, or any mulatto, mestizoe [*sic*] or half breed, or for any white woman to marry any person other than a white man."[148] Therefore, Chinese Americans circumvented Georgia's harsh antimiscegenation law by crossing the border into South Carolina to wed partners of European heritage.

South Carolina's vague antimiscegenation statute was particularly important for the pioneer Chinese American families in Savannah that had to either find suitable partners of Chinese heritage elsewhere or out-marry with the local population. Most of the children married European Americans from Savannah or from neighboring counties. Geraldine Chan wedded Edward A. Sieg in South Carolina in 1927. Sieg, who had lived in Mexico and Cuba before coming to Savannah, was a prolific nonfiction writer, Spanish translator, and operator of a secret service detective agency. It was a loving match that lasted until Sieg's death in 1969.[149]

Her older brother Archie married Eunice Shaw in December 1930. They lived in Savannah for the rest of their lives and raised their three children and cared for the aging Robert and Cecilia Chan. The coming of more Chinese American families and a few unmarried China-born men to Savannah during the 1930s increased marriage within the Chinese American community. Mary Jung, daughter of Charles Fore Jung, married Henry Liu in 1935. Liu, who immigrated to the United States in 1909, ran a restaurant in Savannah for several decades. The couple resided briefly in New York City where his oldest daughter was born.[150] Besides this marriage, at least two other Savannah-born women married China-born men who made Savannah or nearby Tybee Island their home. Two Woo daughters, Dorothy and Catherine, both married two sons of the Jue family of Savannah, Raymond and George, while their younger sister Lily married George Wong of Savannah.[151] Only a few wedded Chinese Americans from other states. These spouses usually came from families in southern states. Tommy Wong's spouse, Lora Lee, was born and raised in Miami, Florida. His younger sister, Florence, wedded Miami restaurant operator Dewey Wong.[152] Two sons of Woo Lat married Chinese Americans from Mississippi and Arkansas.[153]

While Savannah's early Chinese American children began marrying European Americans and China-born males, Augusta's first Chinese American children to reach marital age in the early 1930s were overwhelmingly women. Most of the sons were not of marital age at that time and US military service during the Second World War delayed their marriages until the late 1940s except for Hon Woo who married a Chinese American from Cleveland, Ohio, in 1940.[154]

Because parents ordinarily did not send daughters to China to find spouses, US-born women usually found husbands among Chinese Americans. Chinese American women from Augusta wedded Chinese Americans from major Chinese population centers on the West Coast. Four daughters of the Lum family, for example, married partners from California. Mabel Lum wedded Jack Ng, who operated a noodle factory in San Francisco's Chinatown, in October 1935.[155] The two had been childhood friends while the Lums lived in San Francisco. Her younger sister Helen had an arranged marriage to Cecil Lew, who had an import/export business in Santa Barbara, California. The Lews had sent photographs of their son to the Lums who agreed to let their daughter marry him. They never met prior to their marriage in Augusta in December 1939.[156] Networking was important given Augusta's isolation from the larger Chinatowns and the rigid biracial system that punished interracial marriage. While some of the early marriages came about through family connections, the Second World War and the Cold War brought some Chinese American servicemen to nearby Camp (later Fort) Gordon. Mildred Lum and Betty Joe met their future California-born spouses while they were stationed at the military installation in the 1940s and 1950s.[157]

Beginning in the late 1940s, Chinese American males from Augusta began selecting spouses from other states with smaller Chinese populations in the Midwest and Northeast rather than looking only to the major Chinatowns on the West Coast. William Tom met his future wife in Cincinnati, Ohio, while passing through the city after his honorable discharge from the army in 1946. His younger brother, George, wedded her younger sister, Ida Yee. George Joe's spouse, Jean Dick, was from Ashland, Kentucky, where her family ran a restaurant. She met him while living with her older sister Soonta. The Dicks, who were really Woos, had built close marital ties with a Jue family in Augusta. Soonta married Augusta grocer Paul Jue, while her cousin Mary wedded Paul's older brother, Henry.[158] Family connections were even more essential for finding suitable spouses of Chinese ancestry in cities and towns without large Chinese American populations because of the absence of other places of socialization for young adults.[159]

The continued rise of Augusta's Chinese American population allowed some marriages to occur within the community from the late 1940s onward. Charles Loo, who ran a local grocery store, wedded Evelyn Woo, who worked as a nurse at one of Augusta's major hospitals, in 1961. They then moved to Atlanta where he ran three coin laundromats and she continued her nursing practice there.[160] Scott Loo, Charles's younger brother, wedded Dorothy Woo. Both had lengthy careers as pharmacists in Augusta.[161] In addition to these unions, at least three other marriages occurred between Chinese Americans who had been born and raised in Augusta during the 1930s and 1940s.

Chinese American children from Atlanta first attained marital age only in the 1950s. Prior to that decade, Chinese American families in Atlanta had not developed close social and familial contacts with the Chinese American communities in Augusta and Savannah. Such ties had already existed between Savannah and Augusta since the late 1920s. Most of the children wedded spouses of Chinese heritage from different parts of the United States or European Americans because the local Chinese American population was very small.[162] Harry Cheung and his younger brother married women from a Chinese American family in 1954.[163] Atlanta's postwar growth enticed some Chinese Americans from Augusta and Savannah to settle there during the 1950s and 1960s. In 1957, Herbert Joe of Augusta married Rosa Wong of Atlanta while attending Georgia Tech. Joe later ran a convenience store in Augusta with one of his older brothers between 1964 and 1970. Wong was a nurse on staff of major hospitals in Augusta and Atlanta.[164] Her older brother married a daughter of Tybee Island's wealthy business entrepreneur T. S. Chu.[165] Wong's younger sister Ruth married a European American from New York City in 1970.[166]

Matrimony between Chinese Americans and European Americans began to slowly increase in Augusta during the late 1950s and 1960s as it did in other parts of the United States. Out-marriage did not become an option in Augusta until local Chinese Americans began being perceived as "honorary whites" through their shared experience of going to white schools, white churches, and having white friends. Even with growing social ties, however, Jim Crow still frowned on any sort of mixed unions so the marriages were conducted quietly without mention in the local newspapers. The state of Georgia still had its antimiscegenation statute, so couples went to North Augusta, South Carolina, or Aiken, South Carolina. A double wedding ceremony joined two couples in 1952.[167] During the next decade, at least four other such marriages occurred in these towns between Chinese Americans and European Americans. One South Carolina attorney general told an *Augusta Chronicle* reporter in 1967 that "we always had to make decisions about what races could intermarry and which couldn't. . . . We've ruled, for instance, that a Filipino is a Caucasian."[168] This precedent was obviously applied to Chinese Americans as well.

For the most part, Asian American/European American marriages went unnoticed in print, and the law was not enforced with the same vigor as preventing African American and European American unions. The enforcement of Georgia's antimiscegenation statute only briefly became an issue in June 1954 in Columbus, Georgia, when a judge issued a marriage certificate to a US soldier stationed at Fort Benning and his Japanese immigrant wife. Although the marriage did not involve a person from the three cities of study, it does show what Chinese Americans could potentially encounter if they tried to marry in Georgia. Matrimony between US soldiers and Japanese and Korean women was a common phenomenon starting in the 1950s following the establishment of military bases in both countries after the Second World War.[169] According to newspapers in Savannah, Atlanta, and Augusta, the couple moved to Philadelphia after his discharge from the army. The press also reported that Georgia's attorney general investigated the legality of the marriage once it was brought to his attention. He concluded that the marriage was clearly in violation of Georgia's antimiscegenation law, which was a felony punishable by imprisonment for two years; however, legal authorities took no action, most likely because the couple had left Georgia. Interestingly, when defending the issuance of the certificate, the judge who married the couple said: "She looked white. I knew she wasn't a negro." Moreover, Columbus's newspaper, *Muskogee County Ordinary* further explained: "There wasn't anything thought about a person of the Asiatic race. If she had been a person of African descent, we wouldn't have issued the license."[170] Clearly, local and state officials were more focused on potential nuptials between European Americans and African Americans. Nevertheless, the statute remained a state law until the US Supreme Court unanimously ruled that all antimiscegenation laws were unconstitutional in *Loving vs. Virginia* (1967).[171] Ethnocentrism usually prevented Chinese Americans from selecting spouses who were of other Asian ancestries. Anti-Japanese feeling, for example, became so widespread in Chinese American communities throughout the 1930s and 1940s that most of them supported the roundup and placement of Japanese Americans on the West Coast into internment camps. Individual attitudes softened in the postwar years as they slowly overcame Old World animosities and found unity through their shared experiences of being from Asia. Out-marriage rates between Chinese Americans and other Asian Americans increased in the 1960s and beyond. Mia Tuan has noticed this marital pattern among third-generation Chinese Americans and Japanese Americans.[172] A few Chinese Americans from Augusta and Savannah who moved to states with higher Asian American populations wedded Japanese Americans. Steven Liu and Howard Woo of Savannah married Japanese Americans after settling in California. Both had moved out to California to assume engineering positions.[173] Emily Woo, the youngest daughter of Eugene and Alice Woo, met her future husband, Roy Takeuchi, while working as a dietitian in San Francisco. They settled in Stockton, California.[174]

Before 1965, few people of Chinese ancestry lived in Georgia. Jim Crow segregation and pressure within the Chinese communities in these cities hindered Chinese Americans from marrying African Americans and European Americans. Traveling to China on wife-seeking trips became more difficult with the Sino-Japanese War (1937–45) and the foundation of the People's Republic of China in 1949. Chinese Americans first found spouses from cities on the West Coast like San Francisco and Los Angeles. Later, they also met and married Chinese Americans from cities in Georgia and areas with smaller Chinese populations like Cincinnati, Ohio, or Drew, Mississippi. Out-marriage with European Americans became more acceptable to community members and some local whites during the 1950s, although couples had to go out of state to South Carolina for marriage certificates until Georgia's anti-miscegenation law was overturned in 1967. The ability of Chinese Americans to select spouses of European heritage was the final barrier to fall because of the South's aversion to "race mixing" and evidence of their growing status as "honorary whites" in the still rigidly segregated racial hierarchy.

Conclusion

People of Asian descent in the United States grappled with two major conflicting stereotypes imposed on them by European Americans—the "perpetual foreigner" and the "honorary white."[175] People of Chinese descent in Georgia, who were born or came to the state as children between 1910 and 1950, dealt with both images along with the added dynamic of residing in a *biracial* state designed for people of European and African descent. Besides being racially segregated, Georgians and other southerners of European and African heritage had formed strong regional identities shaped largely by evangelical Christianity, slavery, and the Civil War that remained undiluted because the state retained much of its bucolic infrastructure and attracted few postbellum immigrants during the "second wave" of European immigration. Such racial and historical consciousness in Georgia had the potential to heighten the "perpetual foreigner" stereotype for people of Chinese descent. Georgia's second generation overcame this image by assuming many of the attributes of white southerners and with it the privileges of "whiteness" that they accumulated over several decades. They also, however, retained aspects of their Chinese heritage that did not undermine this budding perception of being near white.

Chinese American families in Georgia usually embraced white southern evangelical Christianity by actively participating in the activities of Chinese Sunday schools and later joining the major white congregations. They did not establish their own churches nor belong to African American churches unless they married into the African American community. The bonds between Chinese Americans and white churches in Savannah and Augusta became stronger than in Atlanta because the latter had fewer Chinese American families in residence. Adopting the dominant religion of the region, Christianity, did much to erase the boundary between being foreigner and citizen in these cities. Christianity became an important component of their identity in childhood and later in adulthood.

Most second-generation Chinese Americans in these cities received their secular educations in white public schools and learned about their Chinese heritage through parents and community organizations. Children of Chinese heritage had to initially find a place within Georgia's biracial public schooling system, which segregated "white" from "colored" children. Their enrollment in schools with European Americans went unquestioned after 1931, and most later went on to attend state-run white colleges for the duration of de jure segregation. Augusta's Chinese community, unlike Savannah's and Atlanta's, had greater wealth and a larger youthful population that prompted the establishment of two Chinese language schools run by community groups where the children received basic instruction in local dialects. Going to "white" educational institutions helped Chinese American children form closer social relationships with whites, thus helping them overcome their "outsider" status and also avoid the stigma of being perceived as "black." Children in all three cities retained a sense of their "Chineseness" through parents, but Augusta's Chinese Americans had a stronger knowledge of their written language and cultural traditions because of the Chinese language schools.

Greater integration occurred during the 1940s and 1950s as Chinese Americans in Georgia became viewed as "honorary whites," while still retaining aspects of their cultural heritage that did not hinder their acceptance by southern whites. Evidence of this emerging status can be seen in changing employment and spousal selections among the second-generation. Chinese American men born in the late 1920s tended to go into the same blue collar occupations as their parents while their younger male siblings pursued advanced college degrees and training for mostly white collar careers as health care professionals. Women born between 1915 and 1930 usually became unofficial partners in the family business or had independent careers in clerical and secretarial positions with the federal government and white businesses. Their younger sisters had more education and went into similar careers as their brothers of the same age. These changes occurred while de jure segregation continued to hinder African Americans well into the 1960s.

Second-generation Chinese Americans from Georgia generally married spouses of Chinese heritage, but they also acquired greater freedom to select spouses with other cultural backgrounds. Their Chinese American partners came from established Chinatowns on the West and East Coasts and later included closer cities or towns in the Midwest and South. Chinese Americans with ties to Arkansas, Mississippi, and Florida and other cities in Georgia were strong candidates for matrimony with one another because they had similar experiences of being "Chinese" and "southern." Gradually, however, Chinese Americans in Georgia began traversing the long-held Jim Crow obsession of preventing "race-mixing" by marrying local whites they met through their social and professional relationships. The state still had its anti-miscegenation law, which banned matrimony between "whites" and nonwhites," so couples went to South Carolina to circumvent the statute. Being able to marry European Americans was arguably the final privilege of "whiteness" extended to people of Chinese descent in Georgia.

Chinese Americans in Georgia, unlike Chinese Americans in other parts of the United States, had to abide by Jim Crow's rigid racial codes, separating white from black, or be considered "permanent outsiders" to the region. Their initial status gradually mutated from "otherness" during the 1910s and 1920s to acceptance as "honorary whites" by the mid-1960s.

Notes

1. The most seminal work that has influenced historians writing about the Chinese people in the South is James Loewen's *The Mississippi Chinese: Between Black and White* (1971; repr., Prospect Heights, IL: Waveland, 1988), which examines Chinese immigrant communities in the Mississippi Delta as a "third race" in a biracial region. Loewen argues that Chinese immigrants were treated as "black" citizens by the local white population in Mississippi for several decades after their arrival. In my chapter, I do not wish to argue that the Chinese residents in the three cities I study were initially seen as "black" by the local population. I prefer to use the term "perpetual foreigner" for two reasons. The first reason is that the Chinese people them-

selves never saw themselves as "black." Furthermore, the few surviving records from the 1880s through the 1920s are not clear where they stood in the biracial structure of these cities.

The Mississippi Chinese and their descendants continue to fascinate scholars. Two of the more recent works are John Jung's *Chopsticks in the Land of Cotton: Lives of Mississippi Delta Chinese Grocers* (Cypress, CA: Yin and Yang Press, 2008) and Leslie Bow's *Partly Colored: Asian Americans and Racial Anomaly in the Segregated South* (New York: New York University Press, 2010).

2. Evelyn Nakano Glenn, "Split Household: Small Producer and Dual Wage Earner: An Analysis of Chinese Family Strategies," *Journal of Marriage and Family* 45 (No. 1): 37–39.

3. Howard Rabinowitz, *Race Relations in the Urban South* (New York: Oxford University Press, 1978), 112–13.

4. Several articles have been published about Chinese immigrants and their descendants in Augusta. See Eileen Law and Sally Ken, "A Study of the Chinese Community," *Richmond County History* 5, no. 2 (Summer 1973): 23–41; Catherine Brown and Thomas Ganschow, "The Augusta, Georgia, Chinese: 1865–1980," in *Georgia's East Asian Connection, 1733–1983*, ed. Jonathan Goldstein (Carrolton, GA: West Georgia College, 1983), 27–37; Ganschow, "The Chinese in Augusta, GA: A Historical Sketch," *Richmond County History* 19, no. 4 (Winter 1987): 8–21. One third-generation Chinese American resident of Augusta wrote an unpublished paper, "The Chinese Community of Augusta: Between Light and Shadows" in the early 1980s.

5. See chapters 2 and 3 of my dissertation, "The Formation and Development of Chinese Communities in Atlanta, Augusta, and Savannah, Georgia: From Sojourners to Settlers, 1880–1965 (PhD diss., Georgia State University, 2008), for more information on local occupations and the impact of segregation and the Chinese Exclusion Act on the three Chinese communities.

Erika Lee's *At America's Gates: Chinese Immigration during the Exclusion Era, 1882–1943* (Chapel Hill: University of North Carolina Press, 2003) and "Defying Exclusion: Chinese Immigrants and Their Strategies during the Exclusion Era," in Sucheng Chan, ed., *Chinese American Transnationalism* (Philadelphia: Temple University Press, 2006) provide good analysis of the class categories used by the Chinese. Although she found that using the "native born" category was preferable because it was harder for immigration officials to prove fraudulent, the Chinese in Augusta overwhelmingly used the merchant category because of their success in the retail grocery store business. A careful search of port entries through San Francisco shows twelve sons and seven wives entering as dependents of merchants residing or claiming to reside in Augusta between 1903 and 1943 (*Lists of Chinese Applying for Admission to the United States through the Port of San Francisco, 1903–1947* [National Archives Microfilm Publication M1476, 27 rolls]).

6. US Census Bureau, 1920 Federal Census: Augusta Ward 4, Richmond, Georgia; Roll: T625_276; Page: 4B; Enumeration District: 88; Ibid, Augusta Ward 3, Richmond, Georgia; Roll: T625_276; Page: 7A; Enumeration District: 80; Ibid, Augusta Ward 2, Richmond, Georgia; Roll: T625_276; Page: 10A; Enumeration District: 75; 1920; Ibid, Augusta Ward 4, Richmond, Georgia; Roll: T625_276; Page: 19A; Enumeration District: 89; Ken and Law, "A Study of the Chinese Community," 37.

7. Infant mortality rates of children born to these families were low in the 1920s as only two death certificates for infants have been found. (Georgia Health Department, Office of Vital Records, Standard Certificate of Death, Richmond 4330 [February 8, 1927]; Richmond 22602 [August 14, 1927]). A few children were born before and after this date span. The year 1945 is chosen as the end date because a third generation of Augusta-born offspring came into being shortly after the Second World War.

8. Naturalization petitions including the names of children have been one of the main primary sources in reconstructing family sizes in Augusta. Obituaries have also been useful primary sources for family statistics. Oral history fills in some of the blanks.

9. See George B. Pruden Jr.'s article "History of the Chinese in Savannah, Georgia," in *Georgia's East Asian Connection, 1733–1983*, ed. Jonathan Goldstein (Carrollton, GA: West Georgia College Press, 1983). Gerald Chan Sieg, a Chinese American from Savannah, wrote about the history of that community in "Georgia's Chinese Pioneers," *Atlanta Journal Constitution*, March 7, 1965.

10. Records of the Immigration and Naturalization Service, Series A, Subject Correspondence Files, pt. 1: Asian Immigration and Exclusion, 1898–1941, reel 1, page 42; Bronstein, "Formation and Development of Chinese Communities" 70.

11. US Census Bureau, 1900: Savannah, Chatham, Georgia; Roll: T623 186, page: 10A, Enumeration District: 59; ibid, 1910: Militia District 2, Chatham, Georgia; Roll: T624_177; page: 5A, Enumeration District: 49.

12. Bronstein, "Formation and Development of Chinese Communities," 38–42. Chinese merchants in Savannah did not send for spouses using the merchant wife category. Immigration records show that they sent for wives while living in other cities of the United States. (*Lists of Chinese Applying for Admission to the United States through the Port of San Francisco, 1903–1947* (National Archives Microfilm Publication M1476, 27 rolls).

13. Pruden, "History of the Chinese in Savannah, Georgia," 20. As with Augusta, naturalization petitions have been one of the main primary sources in reconstructing family sizes in Savannah. Obituaries have also been useful primary sources for family statistics. Oral history fills in some of the blanks.

14. Jianli Zhao, *Strangers in the City: The Atlanta Chinese, Their Community, and Stories of Their Lives* (New York: Routledge, 2002), 21–67. Although the book focuses more on the post-1965 immigrants, the author includes an interview of a Chinese

American family with roots in Augusta. Zhao mentions that she found it difficult finding older pre-1965 Chinese Americans from Atlanta to interview. This is further evidence of the small size of the US-born Chinese population from Atlanta.

15. For more general treatments of immigration in Atlanta, see Ann Mebane, "Immigrant Patterns in Atlanta, 1880 and 1896" (master's thesis, Emory University, 1967), and Richard Hopkins, "Occupational and Geographic Mobility in Atlanta, 1870–1896," *Journal of Southern History* 34, no. 2 (1968): 200–213. Steve Hertzberg's *Strangers within the Gate City: The Jews of Atlanta, 1845–1915* (Philadelphia: Jewish Publication Society of America, 1978) is a well-written community study of Atlanta's Jewish population.

16. US Census Bureau, 1900 Federal Census: Atlanta Ward 3, Fulton, Georgia, roll: T623 199, page: 20B, Enumeration District 59. A search for this family in the states of California, New York, and Massachusetts has been unsuccessful.

17. US Census Bureau, 1930 Federal Census, Atlanta, Fulton, Georgia; Roll: 361; page: 15A, Enumeration District 53. Immigration records show that a few of Atlanta's Chinese laundry operators used the category "native-born" to send for "paper sons" rather than actual family members. This was a common practice among the Chinese "first-wave" immigrants.

Many books have been written about the methods Chinese immigrants used to come to the United States and how the US federal government tried to stop fraudulent entry. See Erika Lee's *At America's Gates* and Estelle Lau's *Paper Families: Identity, Immigration Administration, and Chinese Exclusion* (Durham: Duke University Press, 2006). John Jung, a Chinese American from Macon, Georgia, wrote about how his parents and other male relatives came over as paper sons to several southern cities including Atlanta. See *Southern Fried Rice: Life in a Chinese Laundry in the Deep South* (N.p.: Yin and Yang Press, 2005).

18. Naturalization Petitions, Northern District of Georgia, Atlanta Division, box 15, vol. 58, no. 6490, and box 14, vol. 54, no. 6070. One Chinese American herbalist lived with his China-born wife and US-born children in Atlanta between 1914 and 1932. Their infant daughter died and is buried in the old Chinese section of Atlanta's Greenwood Cemetery. Standard Certificate of Death for Apple Young, Fulton 9279 (1926 April 24), Death Certificates, RG 26–5–95, Georgia Archives. It is not known where this family moved after leaving Atlanta.

19. Chief Patrol Inspector John H. Scott in Tallahassee, Florida, to the District Director in Jacksonville, Florida, May 28, 1928, Box 2692, Folder 28187/5–9 Loo Yet Sing, RG 85, Chinese Exclusion, NA-SF.

20. City directories for Augusta and Savannah from the 1930s, 1940s, 1950s, and 1960s frequently list the children as clerks or helpers in the grocery store.

21. Kathy (Liu) Rufo, interview by author, tape recording, Augusta, Georgia, August 30, 2005.

22. Harry Cheung, letter to the author, June 12, 2005.

23. Tommy Wong, letter to the author, October 7, 2005.

24. Raymond Rufo, interview by author, tape recording, Augusta, Georgia, August 30, 2005; Walter Lum, letter to the author, February 12, 2006.

25. Evelyn (Woo) Loo, interview by author, tape recording, Augusta, Georgia; August 2, 2005; Ellen Dong, interview by author, tape recording, Augusta, Georgia, August 9, 2005; James Woo, interview by author, tape recording, Augusta, Georgia, August 15, 2005.

26. Interrogation transcripts of Lum Yuen, April 30, 1910, Box 525, Folder 10481/10157 Lum Yuen, RG 85, Chinese Exclusion, NA-SF; Walter Lum, interview by author, tape recording, Augusta, Georgia, January 17, 2007; Lorraine (Lum) O'Quinn, interview by author, tape recording, Augusta, Georgia, January 17, 2007.

27. Eda Stertz, *A Celestial Pilgrimage* (Augusta. GA: First Baptist Church of Augusta Georgia, 1985), 3; *A Brief History of the First Baptist Church Augusta, Georgia, 1817–1945* (Augusta, GA: Walton Printing, n.d.), 21; Isabella Jordan, *A Century of Service: First Baptist Church, Augusta* (Augusta, GA: n.p., 1921), 43. These women could not be located in the population census schedules for 1900, 1910, and 1920.

28. Lowery Axley, *Holding Aloft the Torch: A History of the Independent Presbyterian Church of Savannah, Georgia* (Savannah, GA: n.p., 1958), 45; "Oldest Chinese Community Member Dies," *Savannah Morning News*, June 11, 1953; "Funeral Rites Today for Robert Chan," *Savannah Evening Press*, June 11, 1953; Gerald Chan Sieg, "Georgia's Chinese Pioneers," *Atlanta Journal-Constitution*, March 6, 1965, pp. 18, 20, 22; "Pioneer Chinese Settler Dies at Age of 82," *Savannah Morning News*, March 1, 1957. No other records of the activities of the Sunday school have survived.

29. Paul Siu, *The Chinese Laundryman: A Study in Social Isolation*, ed. John Kuo Wei Tchen (New York: NewYork University Press, 1987), 272–279. Siu wrote about the relationship between the Chicago Sunday schools and laundrymen without nuclear families in these pages.

30. Sally Ken, "The Chinese Community of Augusta, Georgia, from 1873–1971," *Richmond County History* 4 (1972): 29.

31. Loewen, *Mississippi Chinese*, 84–85; Sieglinde Lim de Sanchez, "Crafting a Delta Chinese Community: Education and Acculturation in Twentieth Century Mission Schools," *History of Education Quarterly* 43, no. 1 (Spring 2003): 84–86.

32. Obituary of Lat Woo, *Savannah Morning News*, October 14, 1964; *A Celestial Pilgrimage*, 5.

33. "Jung Wing, 90, Pioneer, Dies," *Atlanta Constitution*, January 29, 1944.

34. Obituary of Archie C. Chan, *Savannah Morning News*, May 14, 1988; Polly P. Stramm, "Native Savannahian Remembered as a Pioneer, *Savannah Morning News*, July 1, 2005, http://old.savannahnow.com/stories/070205/3137182.shtml (accessed on February 18, 2008).

35. Stertz, *A Celestial Pilgrimage*, 7; Law and Ken, "A Study of the Chinese Community," 29–30.

36. Stertz, *A Celestial Pilgrimage*, 7; Betty Joe Eng, letter to author, May 19, 2007.

37. For more information about Georgia's education system, consult *A History of Public Education in Georgia, 1734–1976*, ed. Oscar H. Joiner, James C. Bonner, H. S. Sheahouse, T. E. Smith, introduction by Claude Purcell (Columbia, SC: R. B. Bryan, 1979).

38. Children of Chinese descent began going to other non-Chinese public schools in the city after that time. Victor Low, *The Unimpressible Race: A Century Education Struggle by the Chinese in San Francisco* (San Francisco: East West, 1982).

39. Pruden, "History of the Chinese in Savannah, Georgia," 17.

40. Ibid, 21. This family, considered by most to be the first intact Chinese family in the state, had to deal with the educational rules of the state and county. The exact date and reason of the reversal is not known.

41. The exact date of when the school board changed its policy is not known because no written records, such as minutes of the meetings, have been located for this study.

42. Catherine Woo Jue, letter to author, August 5, 2006; Tommy Wong, letter to author, August 5, 2006.

43. Gary Tom, email to author, October 13, 2005; Toni Loo Timmons, letter to author, February 25, 2007.

44. *The Rainbow* (Augusta, GA: Junior College of Augusta and Academy of Richmond County, various years). Most editions for this yearbook are available, except for the gap during the Second World War.

45. "Measure Provides Board to Replace Four Commissions," *Augusta Chronicle*, July 3, 1931. The bill also targeted schools that had children of Japanese descent.

46. "Primary Grades Called Important," July 11, 1931; "Harmony Urged on Education Board," *Augusta Chronicle*, July 12, 1931.

47. Law and Ken, "A Study of the Chinese Community," 34.

48. Loewen, *Mississippi Chinese*, 66–68; John Thornell, "Struggle for Identity in the Most Southern Place on Earth: The Chinese in the Mississippi Delta," in *Chinese America History and Perspectives* (San Francisco: Chinese Historical Society of America, 2003), 67–68; Sanchez, "Crafting a Delta Chinese Community," 78–81.

49. *Atlanta City Directories* (New Haven, CT: Research Publications, 1920–30).

50. Harry Cheung, letter to author, June 12, 2005; William Lau, interview by author, tape recording, Atlanta, Georgia, November 5, 2005; Henry Jew, interview by author, tape recording, Atlanta, Georgia, November 5, 2005; Alys Chew Yeh, letter to author, April 28, 2008.

51. Pauline Joe Holleran, interview by author, tape recording, Evans, Georgia, January 31, 2007.

52. Catherine Woo Jue, letter to author, August 5, 2007; Kathy Liu Rufo, letter to author, January 31, 2007; *Blue Print* (Atlanta: Georgia Institute of Technology, various years).

53. Raymond Rufo, letter to author, January 31, 2007; John Joe, letter to author, January 29, 2007; *The Pandora* (Athens, GA: Franklin Printing House, various years).

54. Obituary of David Joe Jr., *Atlanta Constitution*, January 3, 1973.

55. Judy Yung, *Unbound Feet: A Social History of Chinese Women in San Francisco* (Berkeley: University of California Press, 1995), 130–31; Huping Ling, *Surviving on the Gold Mountain: A History of Chinese American Women and Their* Lives (Albany: State University of New York Press, 1998), 97–98.

56. Dr. Margaret Wong, interview by author, tape recording, Augusta, Georgia, August 17, 2005.

57. Evelyn Woo Loo, interview by author, tape recording, Augusta, Georgia, August 2, 2005. For more information about Chinese Americans in nursing and medicine, see pages 142 and 143 of Yung's *Unbound Feet*.

58. Ellen Woo Dong, interview by author, tape recording, Augusta, Georgia, August 9, 2005; Emily Woo Takeuchi, letter to author, August 12, 2007.

59. George Joe, interview by author, tape recording, North Augusta, South Carolina, June 8, 2004. William Joe also graduated from the two-year Junior College of Augusta in 1934.

60. Him Mark Lai, "Chinese Schools in America before the Second World War," in *Becoming Chinese American: A History of Communities and Institutions* (New York: Altamira Press, 2004), 276–77.

61. *Ruzhou Chen, ed., 1946 Handbook of Chinese in America, (New York: People's Foreign Relations Association of China, 1946), 519.*

62. Law and Ken. "A Study of the Chinese Community," 35; Molly Wong Lew, letter to author, September 21, 2005.

63. *1946 Handbook of Chinese in America, 519*; Ellen Dong, interview by author, tape recording, Augusta, Georgia, August 9, 2005.

64. Lai, "Chinese Schools in America," 297.

65. Mary Carter-Winter, "Chinese School Is 75 Years Old," June 19, 1960; "Death Takes Prof. Lam, Educator," *Augusta Chronicle*, October 22, 1961.

66. "Two Young Chinese Physicians at Medical College," *Augusta Chronicle*, October 14, 1947.

67. Lai, "Chinese Schools in America," 297; Mia Tuan, *Forever Foreigners or Honorary Whites?: The Asian Ethnic Experience Today* (New Brunswick: Rutgers University Press, 1998), 107–8.

68. Raymond Rufo, interview by author, tape recording, Augusta, Georgia, August 30, 2005.

69. Evelyn Woo Loo, interview by author, tape recording, Augusta, Georgia, August 2, 2005.

70. K. Scott Wong, *Americans First: Chinese Americans and the Second World War* (Cambridge, MA: Harvard University Press, 2005), 209.

71. Ibid, 58.

72. There was at least one World War I Chinese American veteran who lived most of his life in Atlanta. The obituary of Jim Wong recalled his military service (obituary of Jim Wong, *Atlanta Constitution*, August 14, 1945).

73. Adam McKeown, *Chinese Migrant Networks and Cultural Change: Peru, Chicago, Hawaii, 1900–1936* (Chicago: University of Chicago Press, 2001), 86–92. McKeown refers to the 1930s and 1940s as an important period of "diasporic nationalism" in which the Chinese Nationalist government worked hard to enlist the support of overseas Chinese by fostering nationalistic sentiment abroad so these Chinese would assist China in its war against Japan.

74. For more information on the "Bowl of Rice Parties," consult Yong Chen's *Chinese San Francisco, 1850–1943: A Trans-Pacific Community* (Stanford, CA: Stanford University Press, 2000), 241–48 and Judy Yung's *Unbound Feet*, 239–40.

75. "Meeting Called on China Relief," *Augusta Chronicle*, October 11, 1939; "General Committee for Rice Bowl Party," *Augusta Chronicle*, October 18, 1939; "Chinese Women Leaders in Rice Bowl Party," October 23, 1939. Seeto Woo, Chi H. Lam, Foon Wong, Sam Lee, T. K Lau, Paul Jue, J. P. Wong, and Joy Young were chosen as the male members of the Rice Bowl planning committee. Ruby Lum Wong (Mrs. Wong Foo), Soonta Dick Jue (Mrs. P. K. Jue), Francis Joe, and Margaret Jue Lau (Mrs. T. K. Lau) were the female members.

76. Law and Ken, "A Study of the Chinese Community," 35.

77. Wong, *Americans First*, 58.

78. Ibid, 70.

79. National Archives and Records Administration, NA Form 13164, Tom P. Wong; Obituary of Tom P. Wong, *Atlanta Constitution*, May 10, 1993. His obituary informs the reader about his military stint almost forty year earlier. For more information about the 555th Air Service Squadron, see Wong's *Americans First*, pages 162–92.

80. Estimating the number of Chinese American men who were eligible for service has been difficult because federal population census schedules for 1940 have not been released for public viewing. Harry Cheung, letter to author, June 12, 2005.

81. The numbers for the three cities only include Chinese American males who resided most of their lives in the United States. The focus of this chapter is on the US-born and reared generation. Law and Ken, "A Study of the Chinese Community," 35.

82. National Archives and Records Administration, NA Form 13164, William Joe; Obituary of William Joe, *Augusta Chronicle*, February 26, 1999.

83. National Archives and Records Administration, NA Form 13164, Wing F. Jung; Lee Jung Jr., returned questionnaire, January 30, 2006.

84. George Joe, interview by author, tape recording, Augusta, Georgia, June 8, 2004.

85. George Jue, letter to the author, October 12, 2005; Wing G. Jung, telephone interview, October 22, 2006.

86. Wong, *Americans First*, 153.

87. The US Armed Forces spent time and money training some Chinese Americans for specialized positions. Theodore Jue of Savannah became a sonar operator on the USS *Joseph P. Campbell* from late 1943 until early 1946. According to K. S. Wong, Chinese Americans could only enlist in the US Navy as mess stewards or cabin boys until 1942 (National Personnel Records Center, Military Personnel Records, NA Form 13164, Theodore Jue; Wong, *Americans First*, 60).

88. National Personnel Records Center, Military Personnel Records, NA Form 13164, Wah C. Loo.

89. Jean Joe, interview by author, tape recording, Augusta, Georgia, June 8, 2004; Law and Ken, "A Study of the Chinese Community," 35.

90. New York Public Library, Finding Aid for United China Relief records, 1928–1947 http://www.nypl.org/research/manuscripts/mss/msschina.xml (accessed June 25, 2011); Princeton University Library, Mudd Manuscript Library, http://diglib.princeton.edu/ead/eadGetDoc.xq?id=/ead/mudd/publicpolicy/MC135.EAD.xml (accessed June 25, 2011). In 1946, the organization became known as United Service to China. The Finding Aid records from the New York Public Library show that one or two folders in a box contain some material about fundraising in Georgia in 1946.

91. *1946 Handbook of Chinese in America*, 519.

92. Catherine (Woo) Jue, letter to the author, October 3, 2005.

93. Peggy Wong, interview by author, February 13, 2007.

94. Yung, *Unbound Feet*, 252–77.

95. Jean (Dick) Joe, interview by author, tape recording, Augusta, Georgia, June 8, 2004.

96. Tommy Wong, letter to author, October 27, 2005, in the author's possession. Chinese Americans from these communities also were drafted into the Korean War Conflict. No book has been written about Chinese Americans and the Korean War Conflict. Not enough information has been uncovered to include a paragraph about it. I have found military records of two deceased men (one from Savannah and one from Augusta) and collected some basic oral history from one veteran. One question to consider is how Chinese American Korean War veterans felt about participating in the war after the Chinese mainland entered hostilities?

97. Gloria Chun, *Of Orphans and Warriors: Inventing Chinese-American Culture and Identity* (New Brunswick, NJ: Rutgers University Press, 2000), 17–18, 26–28.

98. Yen Le Espritu, "Changing Lives: World War II and the Post War Years," in *Asian American Studies: A Reader*, ed. Jean Yu-wen Shen Wu and Min Song (New Brunswick, NJ: Rutgers University Press, 2000), 149–51.

99. See Tuan, *Forever Foreigners or Honorary Whites?*, 30–37; for more analysis of the "model minority myth," see Frank Wu, *Yellow: Race in America beyond Black and White* (New York: Basic Books, 2002), 39–77.

100. Chun, *Of Orphans and Warriors*, 69–82.

101. Law and Ken, "A Study of the Chinese Community," 36.

102. Peggy Wong, conversation with author, Augusta, Georgia, February 25, 2007; Alexander Loo, telephone interview with author, March 1, 2007; Evelyn Woo Loo, letter to author, June 26, 2007; Frank Lum, letter to author, June 10, 2007.

103. National Archives and Records Administration, NA Form 13164, William Joe.

104. Ida Yee Tom, telephone interview with author, January 13, 2006.

105. George Joe, interview by author, tape recording, North Augusta, South Carolina, December 10, 2005; Lorraine Lum O' Quinn, interview by author, tape recording, Augusta, Georgia, January 17, 2007.

106. *Augusta City Directories*, 1945–65. The city directory stopped including racial designations after 1952.

107. Catherine Woo Jue, letter to author, August 5, 2006; *Savannah City Directories*, 1947–65.

108. *Savannah City Directories*, 1951–65; Catherine Woo Jue, letter to author, April 26, 2007.

109. James Mayo, *The American Grocery Store: The Business Evolution of an Architectural Space* (West Port, CT: Greenwood Press, 1993), 205–6.

110. *Savannah City Directories*, 1965–95.

111. Tommy Wong, letter to author, August 5, 2006; *Savannah City Directories*, 1951–65.

112. Raymond Rufo, interview by author, tape recording, Augusta, Georgia, August 30, 2005.

113. Ralph Wong, interview by author, tape recording, Augusta, Georgia, June 6, 2004; James Woo, interview by author, tape recording, Augusta, Georgia, August 15, 2005; *Augusta City Directories*, 1960–70.

114. "Chinese Live It Quietly," *Augusta Herald*, March 26, 1967.

115. William Lau and Henry Jew, interview by author, tape recording, Atlanta, Georgia, November 5, 2005.

116. Obituary of William L. Wong, *Savannah Morning News*, February 20, 2004.

117. Alice Yun Chai, "Adaptive Strategies of Recent Korean Immigrant Women in Hawaii," in *Beyond the Public/ Domestic Dichotomy: Contemporary Perspectives on Women's Lives*, ed. Janet Sharistanan, (New York: Greenwood Press, 1987), 87.

118. *Augusta City Directories*, 1930–91; "Tragedy at a Family Store," *Augusta Chronicle*, February 20, 1991.

119. Lorraine Lum O' Quinn, interview by author, tape recording, Augusta, Georgia, January 17, 2007.

120. Obituary of May Lee Wong, *Savannah Morning News*, November 17, 2005. The obituary has switched her maiden and married names.

121. Catherine Woo Jue, letter to author, April 26, 2007.

122. Pruden, "History of the Chinese in Savannah," 21; Nannelle Chan, letter to author, 15 October 2006.

123. *Laundryman*, Georgia Writers Project, Federal Writers Project (No place of publication: Works Progress Administration, 1939), 1–24.

124. Polly P. Stramm, "Native Savannahian Remembered as a Pioneer, *Savannah Morning News*, July 1, 2005, http://old.savannahnow.com/stories/070205/3137182.shtml, accessed December 23, 2007; Jerry Sieg Dillon, letter to author, May 20, 2007.

125. Yung, *Unbound Feet*, 142.

126. Dr. Margaret Wong, interview by author, tape recording, Augusta, Georgia, August 17, 2005.

127. Ling, *Surviving on the Gold Mountain*, 119–23.

128. *Augusta City Directories*, 1940–65; Obituary of Elizabeth Joe, *Augusta Chronicle*, January 30, 1987; Obituary of Frances Joe Hom, *Augusta Chronicle*, September 25, 2000; Pauline Joe Holleran, interview by author, tape recording, Evans, Georgia, January 31, 2007.

129. Evelyn Woo Loo, interview by author, tape recording, Augusta, Georgia, August 2, 2005.

130. Tina Loo Tom, email to author, June 30, 2007; Gee Guen Joe, letter to author, November 10, 2007.

131. Rosa Wong Joe, letter to author, October 1, 2007; Kathy Liu Rufo, interview by author, tape recording, Augusta, Georgia, August 30, 2005.

132. Tina Loo Tom, email to author, June 29, 2007.

133. Ray Rufo, letter to author, January 31, 2007.

134. Anna Joe, interview by author, tape recording, Augusta, Georgia, February 25, 2007.

135. John Joe, letter to author, January 29, 2007.

136. Arthur Lum, letters to author, June 10, 2007 and July 14, 2007. For more about the history of Sacramento's lucrative Chinese American supermarkets, see Alfred Yee *Shopping at Giant Foods: Chinese Supermarkets in Northern California* (Seattle: University of Washington Press, 2003).

137. Kathy Liu Rufo, letter to author, January 31, 2007.

138. Tommy Wong, telephone conversation with author, March 18, 2007.

139. John Jung, email to author, November 25, 2006.

140. The veracity of the "city too busy to hate" mantra has remained argumentative especially for several civil rights activists who remember otherwise. For treatment of Atlanta's race relations after 1900, see Ronald H. Bayor, *Race and the Shaping of Twentieth-Century Atlanta* (Chapel Hill: University of North Carolina Press, 1996).

141. Margaret Shannon, "Atlanta's Bobby Woo: 200 Millionth American," *Atlanta Journal-Constitution*, December 31, 1967.

142. Robert Joe, letter to author, November 10, 2007.

143. Paige Tom, email to author, December 6, 2006.

144. Hrishi Karthikeyan and Gabriel J. Chin, "Preserving Racial Identity: Population Patterns and the Application of Anti-Miscegenation Statutes to Asian Americans, 1910–1950," *Asian Law Journal* 9 (2002): 14–19.

145. See Rachel F. Moran, *Interracial Intimacy: The Regulation of Race and Romance* (Chicago: University of Chicago Press, 2001), and Charles F. Robinson II. *Dangerous Liaisons: Sex and Love in the Segregated South* (Fayetteville: University of Arkansas Press, 2003).

146. Loewen, *Mississippi Chinese*, 60–64; John Kuo Wei Tchen, *New York before Chinatown: Orientalism and the Shaping of American Culture, 1776–1882* (Baltimore, MD: Johns Hopkins University Press, 1999), 159–63; Mary Ting Lui, *The Chinatown Trunk Mystery: Murder, Miscegenation, and Other Dangerous Encounters in Turn-of-the-Century New York City* (Princeton, NJ: Princeton University Press, 2005), 143–74.

147. House Bill No. 460, July 13, 1925, Bills and Resolutions, Georgia State Legislature, RG 37-1-1, Box 247, Georgia Archives, Georgia Legislative Documents, 157, http://galfe2.gsu.edu/cgi bin/homepage.cgi (accessed on December 23, 2007); Peter Wallenstein, *Tell the Court I Love My Wife: Race, Marriage, and the Law* (New York: Palgrave MacMillan, 2002), 136–37; Peggy Pascoe, *What Comes Naturally: Miscegenation Law and the Making of Race in America* (Oxford: Oxford University Press, 2009), 140–50.

148. Official Opinion No. 719, Attorney General Daniel McLeod to South Carolina Probate Judges, September 15, 1961, Attorney General Opinions, Box 131, South Carolina Department of Archives and History.

149. Obituary of Edward A. Sieg, *Savannah Evening News*, February 17, 1969; Nannelle Chan, letter to author, October 15, 2006, and January 2, 2007.

150. Kathy Liu Rufo, interview by author, tape recording, Augusta, Georgia, August 30, 2005.

151. Gary Tom, email to author, February 12, 2007.

152. Tommy Wong, letter to author, August 5, 2006; Tommy Wong, telephone conversation with author, March 18, 2007.

153. Gary Tom, email to author, February 12, 2007.

154. Naturalization Petitions, Southern District of Georgia, Augusta Division, Box 2, No. 932, National Archives and Records Administration.

155. "Childhood Romance Culminates in Marriage of Chinese Couple," *Augusta Chronicle*, October 18, 1935; Walter Lum, interview by author, tape recording, Augusta, Georgia, January 17, 2007; *1946 Chinese Business Directory*, 483.

156. "Chinese Couple United in Marriage Here," *Augusta Chronicle*, December 4, 1939; Walter Lum, interview by author, tape recording, Augusta, Georgia, January 17, 2007; Walter Lum, telephone conversation with author, December 12, 2007.

157. Mildred Lum Loo, letter to author, June 10, 2007; Betty Joe Eng, letter to author, May 19, 2007.

158. Jean Dick Joe, Interview by author, tape recording, North Augusta, South Carolina, June 8, 2005; Mary Woo Jue, letter to author, June 10, 2005.

159. The War Brides Act (1946) had little bearing on the Chinese American families in Augusta and Savannah. The legislation enabled the wives of Chinese American veterans to immigrate outside the paltry quota of 105 allocated for Chinese nationals following the repeal of the Chinese Exclusion Act in 1943. Most of Georgia's Chinese American veterans found partners in the United States. Only army veteran Thomas Wong, eldest son of one of the oldest Chinese American families in the Augusta, wedded Sheun Yee Ng in Hong Kong in 1949 (Naturalization Petitions, Southern District of Georgia, Augusta Division, box 4, no. 1771).

160. Paige Loo Tom, email to author, February 23, 2007.

161. Tina Loo Tom, email to author, June 18, 2007.

162. Alys Chew Yeh, letter to author, April 28, 2008. Three of the five Chew children married European Americans after leaving Georgia.

163. John Jung, email to author, November 25, 2007, March 24, 2008.

164. Herbert Joe, letter to author, October 1, 2007; Rosa Wong Joe, letter to author, October 1, 2007.

165. Obituary of William L. Wong, *Savannah Morning News*, February 20, 2004.

166. Ruth Wong Arnow, letter to author, October 1, 2007.

167. Names have been purposely omitted.

168. "Race Laws 'Knocked off books'—McLeod," *Augusta Chronicle*, June 13, 1967. What McLeod said was true. The attorney general for South Carolina had to make several rulings as to whether certain "races" could marry in the state. Some of these decisions dealt with US soldiers who wanted to bring Japanese and Korean wives to South Carolina (Attorney General T. C. Callison to an army major, 22 June 1954, Attorney General Opinions, Box 131; Attorney General Daniel McLeod to A. Ray Hinnant, Judge of Probate Richland County, 9 September 1959, Attorney General Opinions, Box 131, both in Office of the Attorney General Law Library, Columbia, SC).

169. For more information about US soldiers marrying Japanese and Korean women and their resulting offspring, see Paul Spickard's *Mixed Blood: Intermarriage and Ethnic Identity* (Madison, WI: University of Wisconsin Press, 1989). Ji-Yeon Yuh's. *Beyond the Shadow of Camptown: Korean Military Brides in America* (New York: New York University Press, 2002) discusses the experiences of Korean women who married US servicemen.

170. "Jap Marriage Ban Questioned in Columbus," *Atlanta Journal*, June 13, 1954; "State May Prosecute Ex-GI for Taking Japanese Bride in Violation of Race Laws," *Augusta Chronicle*, June 13, 1954; "Georgia Law against Mixed Marriages Is Ques-

tioned by Muscogee Ordinary," *Savannah Morning News*, June 13, 1954; "State Miscegenation Violation Here," *Muskogee County Ordinary*, June 11, 1954. This marital controversy occurred at a time when the American Civil Liberties and the Japanese American Citizens League were searching for an Asian-Caucasian couple, particularly a Caucasian soldier and Japanese woman, to challenge an antimiscegenation law in a southern state. See Pascoe, *What Comes Naturally*, 232–34.

171. The newspapers in Augusta and Savannah reported many of the marriages of Chinese Americans in Augusta and Savannah. Chinese Americans who out-married did not have marriage notices printed in the local press because they did not wish to cause potential controversy. The first Chinese American–European wedding did not appear in the *Augusta Chronicle* until 1969 and went without interference from state officials. This contrasted with the first post-Loving marital attempt in Georgia by a white US soldier at Fort Benning who wanted to marry an African American woman in May 1971. The local judge refused to issue the certificate. It took an order by a federal judge to override the local judge's refusal ("Racial Law Faces Test," *Atlanta Constitution*, May 21, 1972; "Suit Lifts Georgia's Mixed Marriage Ban," May 22, 1971; "Mixed Marriage Laws Are Killed," February 11, 1972; Wallerstein, *Tell the Court I Love My Wife*), 236.

172. Tuan, *Forever Foreigners or Honorary Whites?*, 118–19.

173. Kathy Liu Rufo, letter to author, January 31, 2007; Gary Tom, email to author, February 12, 2007.

174. Emily Woo Takeuchi, letter to author, August 12, 2007.

175. Tuan, *Forever Foreigners or Honorary Whites?*, 152–67.

Works Cited

Atlanta City Directories. New Haven, CT: Research Publications, 1920–91.

Augusta City Directories. New Haven, CT: Research Publications, 1940–65.

Axley, Lowery. *Holding Aloft the Torch: A History of the Independent Presbyterian Church of Savannah, Georgia*. Savannah, GA: n.p., 1958.

Blue Print. Yearbook. Atlanta: Georgia Institute of Technology, various years.

A Brief History of the First Baptist Church of Augusta, Georgia, 1817–1945. Augusta, GA: Walton Printing, n.d.

Bronstein, Daniel. "The Formation and Development of Chinese Communities in Atlanta, Augusta, and Savannah, Georgia: From Sojourners to Settlers, 1880 1965." PhD dissertation, Georgia State University, 2008.

Chai, Alice Yun. "Adaptive Strategies of Recent Korean Immigrant Women in Hawaii." In *Beyond the Public/Domestic Dichotomy: Contemporary Perspectives on Women's Lives*, edited by Janet Sharistanan. New York: Greenwood Press, 1987.

Chief Patrol Inspector John H. Scott in Tallahassee, Florida, to the District Director in Jacksonville, Florida. May 28, 1928. Box 2692, Folder 28187/5–9 Loo Yet Sing, RG 85, Chinese Exclusion, National Archives, San Francisco.

Chen, Ruzhou, ed. *1946 Handbook of Chinese in America*. New York: People's Foreign Relations Associations of China, 1946.

"Chun, Gloria. *Of Orphans and Warriors: Inventing Chinese-American Culture and Identity*. New Brunswick, NJ: Rutgers University Press, 2000.

Espritu, Yen Le. "Changing Lives: World War II and the Post War Years." In *Asian American Studies: A Reader*, edited by Jean Yu-wen Shen Wu and Min Song. New Brunswick, NJ: Rutgers University Press, 2000.

Glenn, Evelyn Nakano. "Split Household: Small Producer and Dual Wage Earner: An Analysis of Chinese Family Strategies." *Journal of Marriage and Family* 45, no. 1.

House Bill No. 460. July 13, 1925. Bills and Resolutions, Georgia State Legislature. RG 37–1–1, box 247, Georgia Legislative Documents. Georgia Archives. http://galfe2.gsu.edu/cgibin/homepage.cgi. Accessed on December 23, 2007.

Interrogation transcripts of Lum Yuen. April 30, 1910. Box 525, folder 10481/10157, Lum Yuen, RG 85, Chinese Exclusion. National Archives, San Francisco.

Jordan, Isabella. *A Century of Service: First Baptist Church, Augusta*. Augusta, GA: n.p., 1921.

Karthikeyan, Hrishi, and Gabriel J. Chin. "Preserving Racial Identity: Population Patterns and the Application of Anti-Miscegenation Statutes to Asian Americans, 1910–1950." *Asian Law Journal* 9 (2002).

Ken, Sally. "The Chinese Community of Augusta, Georgia From 1873–1971." *Richmond County History* 4 (1972).

Lai, Him Mark. "Chinese Schools in America before the Second World War." In *Becoming Chinese American: A History of Communities and Institutions*. New York: Altamira Press, 2004.

Laundryman. Georgia Writers Project, Federal Writers Project (N.p.: Works Progress Administration, 1939).

Law, Eileen, and Sally Ken. "A Study of the Chinese Community." *Richmond County History* 5, no. 2. (Summer 1973).

Lee, Erika. *At America's Gates: Chinese Immigration during the Exclusion Era, 1882–1943*. Chapel Hill: University of North Carolina Press, 2003.

———. "Defying Exclusion: Chinese Immigrants and Their Strategies during the Exclusion Era." In *Chinese American Transnationalism*, edited by Sucheng Chan. Philadelphia: Temple University Press, 2006.

Ling, Huping. *Surviving on the Gold Mountain: A History of Chinese American Women and Their Lives*. Albany: State University of New York Press, 1998.

Lists of Chinese Applying for Admission to the United States through the Port of San Francisco, 1903–1947. Microfilm publication M1476, 27 rolls. National Archives.

Loewen, James. *The Mississippi Chinese: Between Black and White*. Cambridge: Cambridge University Press, 1971.

Lui, Mary Ting. *The Chinatown Trunk Mystery: Murder, Miscegenation, and Other Dangerous Encounters in Turn-of-the-Century New York City*. Princeton, NJ: Princeton University Press, 2005.

Mayo, James, *The American Grocery Store: The Business Evolution of an Architectural Space*. West Port, CT: Greenwood Press, 1993.

McKeown, Adam. *Chinese Migrant Networks and Cultural Change: Peru, Chicago, Hawaii, 1900–1936*. Chicago: University of Chicago Press, 2011.

National Archives and Records Administration. NA Form 13164. Tom P. Wong.

———. NA Form 13164. William Joe.

———. NA Form 13164. Wing F. Jung and Lee Jung Jr. Returned questionnaire. January 30, 2006.

National Personnel Records Center. Military Personnel Records. NA Form 13164. Theodore Jue.

———. Military Personnel Records. NA Form 13164. Wah C. Loo.

Naturalization Petitions. Northern District of Georgia, Atlanta Division. Box 15, vol. 58, no. 6490, and box 14, vol. 54, no. 6070.

———. Southern District of Georgia, Augusta Division. Box 2, no. 932, and box 4, no. 1771. National Archives and Records Administration, Atlanta, Georgia.

New York Public Library. Finding Aid for United China Relief Records, 1928–1947. http://:www.nypl.org/research/manuscripts/mss/msschina.xml.

Office of the Attorney General Law Library, Columbia, SC. Attorney General Opinions, Box 131.

Official Opinion No. 719. Attorney General Daniel McLeod to South Carolina Probate Judges. September 15, 1961. Attorney General Opinions, Box 131. South Carolina Department of Archives and History.

Pandora, The. Yearbook of University of Georgia. Athens, GA: Franklin Printing House.

Pascoe, Peggy. *What Comes Naturally: Miscegenation Law and the Making of Race in America*. Oxford: Oxford University Press, 2009.

Princeton University Library. Mudd Manuscript Library. http://diglib.princeton.edu/ead/eadGetDoc.xq?id=/ead/mudd/publicpolicy/MC135.EAD.xml.

Pruden, George B., Jr. "History of the Chinese in Savannah, Georgia." In *Georgia's East Asian Connection, 1733–1983*, edited by Jonathan Goldstein. Carrollton, GA: West Georgia College Press, 1983.

Rabinowitz, Howard. *Race Relations in the Urban South*. New York: Oxford University Press, 1978.

The Rainbow. Yearbook. Augusta, GA: Junior College of Augusta and Academy of Richmond County.

Records of the Immigration and Naturalization Service, Series A. Subject Correspondence Files, pt. 1: Asian Immigration and Exclusion, 1898–1941.

Sanchez, Sieglinde Lim de. "Crafting a Delta Chinese Community: Education and

Acculturation in Twentieth Century Mission Schools." *History of Education Quarterly* 43, no. 1 (Spring 2003).

Savannah City Directories. New Haven, CT: Research Publications, 1947–95.

Siu, Paul. *The Chinese Laundryman: A Study in Social Isolation*. Edited by John Kuo Wei Tchen. New York: New York University Press, 1987.

Stertz, Eda. A Celestial Pilgrimage. Augusta, GA: First Baptist Church of Augusta, Georgia, 1985.

Tchen, John Kuo Wei. *New York before Chinatown: Orientalism and the Shaping of American Culture, 1776–1882*. Baltimore, MD: Johns Hopkins University Press, 1999.

Thornell, John. "Struggle for Identity in the Most Southern Place on Earth: The Chinese in the Mississippi Delta." In *Chinese America History and Perspectives*. San Francisco: Chinese Historical Society of America, 2003.

Tuan, Mia. *Forever Foreigners or Honorary Whites?: The Asian Ethnic Experience Today*. New Brunswick, NJ: Rutgers University Press, 1998.

US Census Bureau. 1900 Federal Census: Atlanta, Fulton, Georgia. Roll: T623_199. Enumeration District 59. National Archives.

———. *1900 Federal Census: Savannah, Chatham, Georgia*. Roll: T623_186. Enumeration District 59. National Archives.

———. *1910 Federal Census: Militia District 2, Chatham, Georgia*. Roll: T624_177. Enumeration District 49. National Archives.

———. *1920 Federal Census: Augusta Ward 2, Richmond, Georgia*. Roll: T625_276. Enumeration District 75. National Archives.

———. *1920 Federal Census: Augusta Ward 3, Richmond Georgia*. Roll: T625_276. Enumeration District 80. National Archives.

———. *1920 Federal Census: Augusta Ward 4, Richmond Georgia*. Roll: T625_276. Enumeration District 88. National Archives.

———.Roll: T625_276. Enumeration District 89. National Archives.

———. *1930 Federal Census: Atlanta, Fulton, Georgia*. Roll: 361. Enumeration District 53. National Archives.

Wallenstein, Peter. *Tell the Court I Love My Wife: Race, Marriage, and the Law*. New York: Palgrave MacMillan, 2002.

Wong, K. Scott. *Americans First: Chinese Americans and the Second World War*. Cambridge, MA: Harvard University Press, 2005.

Yung, Judy. *Unbound Feet: A Social History of Chinese Women in San Francisco*. Berkeley: University of California Press, 1995.

Zhao, Jianli. *Strangers in the City: The Atlanta Chinese, Their Community, and Stories of Their Lives*. New York: Routledge, 2002.

8
Immigrant Dreams and Second-Generation Realities

Indian Americans Negotiating Marriage, Culture, and Identity in North Carolina

Vincent H. Melomo

Introduction: Being Indian and Southern

> If I'm in an Indian setting I'll say I'm Bengali. Or, if I'm talking to somebody who I feel is a little bit more wordly I'll say I'm Indian. . . . I mean I think for myself it's the fact that I'm an Indian American. I think probably that captures most of it. . . . I also, you know . . . there's a part of me that even has a Southern identity also. Which is also, you know kind of weird [laughing].
>
> —Neel

Either born or raised in the South, second-generation Indian Americans[1] speak with a southern accent, love their college sports, are active in local civic life, and generally would like to someday raise their families in the South. However, at the same time, they are also in varieties of ways maintaining ties to India and participating in a transnational, diasporic culture that changes and challenges existing constructions of southern identity and culture. Some second-generation Indians are finding spouses in India, some are working for or creating businesses and nonprofits with operations in India, and most are at least visiting India on occasion and listening to the music and watching the movies that are produced there. All are in some fashion taking part in the Indian American communities, institutions, and culture that now populate the southern landscape. As significantly, rather than being an isolated ethnic enclave with little intimate social contact with other southerners, through friendships and marriages they are forming attachments to other non-Indian southerners who are also now taking part in these global flows themselves. This chapter seeks to explore this complexity of experience of second-generation Indian Americans in North Carolina by focusing on the issue of marriage.[2]

Marriage is the site where constructions of Indian and American identities, values, and cultural models most directly conflict, and marriage is thus a key point of struggle in the lives of young people raised as both Indians and Americans. This chapter will address why marriage is such an important issue for Indian Americans and discuss how the second generation is negotiating the marriage process as it becomes a more central issue in their lives. In doing so, I will focus the discussion on the issue of arranged marriages, and the boundaries of marriage. I will discuss some of the ways in which second-generation Indian Americans are getting married, and consider some of the various choices they are making about marriage, considering how these choices are tied to their intersecting identities. Throughout this discussion we will see that the key issue second-generation Indian Americans struggle with is how to ensure that their own desires are satisfied while at the same time their parents' interests are satisfied; they struggle with how to live out a more American romantic model and still in some way marry the right person according to an Indian model of marriage.[3]

Hall writes that we see in the New World "the beginning of diaspora, of diversity, of hybridity and difference."[4] In the United States, and in the American South in particular, local contexts have been affected by global interactions since the first Europeans came to these shores and continue to be so in new ways with new immigrants from other shores.[5] In the stories of second-generation Indian Americans in the South we see new forms of diaspora, hybridity, and diversity emerging. In exploring the context of Indian Americans in North Carolina we can see how local and global histories intersect and shape their experiences, as well as shape a new history of the South.

From the Global to the Local: Placing Indian Americans in the Context of the South

Nearing the close of the twenty-first century, the world became increasingly characterized by movements of people and culture, complicating existing notions of national, ethnic, and cultural identity.[6] In this late modern age, global forces intersect with local contexts, shaping personal lives in newly complex ways.[7] This global condition forced anthropologists and other students of society and culture to examine more closely how people reproduce and reshape cultures and identities in new contexts.[8] In the United States, this increased complexity of identity and culture was largely the result of dramatic changes made to immigration policy in 1965. Since then, there has been a tremendous increase in the size and diversity of America's foreign born, particularly from Latin America and Asia. These immigrant communities have impacted all areas of the United States, but they have had a particularly striking presence in the

American South, a region largely bypassed by earlier waves of immigration, and a region whose history, culture, and identity has been dominated by discourses of "black" and "white" people. Beginning in the 1990s, the children of these new immigrants began coming of age. Growing up, this second generation was often placed in the difficult position of having to mediate their parents' culture and a more dominant American culture(s), while also confronting the contradictions of both. How the children of recent immigrants negotiate these dilemmas, and create new cultures and identities in the process has only begun to be explored.[9] Furthermore, the research that has been conducted on this second generation has paid little attention to their experiences in the American South.

While the growth in the size of the Latino population in the United States has received the bulk of attention in academic and popular discussions of a changing American and southern society and culture, the growth in size and influence of the Asian population has been no less significant.[10] Among Asian Americans throughout the United States, and in the South in particular, Indian Americans have been one of the largest and fastest growing groups. As has occurred throughout the South, the Indian American population in North Carolina has grown dramatically, from nearly ten thousand in 1990 to over fifty-seven thousand by 2010.[11] In North Carolina, Indian Americans have made up the largest Asian community for decades. While the population is concentrated in the state's metropolitan areas, Indian Americans are found across the landscape in smaller cities and towns. The Indian Americans of North Carolina are a mostly suburbanized, middle-class, geographically dispersed population. As such, they are much like other Indian Americans across the country because they live outside of the major centers of South Asian immigration and community found in New York, New Jersey, and California.[12]

Whereas economic troubles and anti-immigrant sentiments limited immigration to the South in the late nineteenth and early twentieth century, the development of a "New South" lured immigrants toward the end of the twentieth century.[13] During this time, North Carolina became an attractive destination for new settlers from within the United States and abroad, drawn to the economic opportunity, the low cost of living, and generally good quality of life. The increasing flows of Indian immigrants since the 1970s have coincided with and contributed to the economic development and overall growth of the "New South." The more technology-based, service-oriented, post-Fordist economy of the growing cities of the South was particularly attractive for the well-educated professionals who were coming from India at the time.[14] The location of many large and small public and private universities in the research area also made it an attractive destination for Indian Americans looking for opportunities in higher education for themselves and their children. As populations increased and the southern economy grew, a variety of other business opportunities became available for Indian Americans. Most notably, drawing upon the support of caste and kin networks, Indian Americans invested in the hotel sector but also operated gas stations and small retail stores, bringing them into many of North Carolina's smaller towns. Some doctors emigrating from India during this time were also drawn to rural North Carolina, particularly since native-born doctors were increasingly abandoning such areas in search of the higher wages specialists drew in larger cities.

This economic development in the American South has followed popular movements for civil rights and official policies of racial integration.[15] Since the 1960s, some southern states, and North Carolina in particular, have tried to shed images of racial intolerance in an attempt to encourage economic development. However, despite the changes brought by the civil rights era, racial prejudice is still common, institutionalized discrimination is still apparent, and segregation is inscribed on the landscape. Although the southern landscape and a southern identity are typically imagined as rural, the New South is characterized more by suburban sprawl. In the South, as well as throughout much of the United States, this growth has occurred along lines of class and race. The inner city and rural poor, and particularly poor African Americans, have been largely excluded from the benefits of the newer developments. A de facto apartheid has occurred leaving relatively rich white belts around poorer, mostly black, urban centers.[16] These realities shape where Indian Americans live and with whom their children grow up and also shape their experiences of and relationships to American culture. As a result of their class position, as Indian Americans moved into the South they typically moved into mostly white, middle- to upper-middle class neighborhoods in the suburban fringe.[17]

In North Carolina, there are few Native Americans, even fewer Asians, and until recently, few Latinos—historically, there has been a "white"/European American majority and a large "black"/African American minority.[18] Neither "black" nor "white," and importantly, mostly non-Christian, Indian immigrants stand outside the major southern categories of difference. Their children thus grow up as part of a relatively small minority group with limited opportunities for community and connection with others like them, particularly outside of metropolitan areas. Unless attending a magnet school in an urban area, most second-generation Indian Americans recall being the only, or one of a handful of, Indian Americans in their classes or schools.

Some Indian Americans I spoke with shared painful memories of discrimination during their elementary and secondary school years. Their stories focused on the unsettling nature of being publicly recognized as "different." They told of being called "brown," being asked "what are you?," or being confused with the other category of America's "Indians" (that is Native Americans) and being asked "what tribe are you from?" Due to their own experiences with prejudice and difference growing up in the South, the second generation is in some ways more likely to see themselves as people of color and identify with African Americans. However, largely because of their class position, second-generation Indian Americans grow up more familiar with, and are thus typically more comfortable with, white southern culture.

The indeterminate racial positioning of Indians in North Carolina is perhaps best shown through the story of one young woman I spoke with, Sumi, who grew up in a small town in the eastern part of North Carolina. Hers was the only Indian family in the area for a while, until her aunt moved in down the road, and she mostly associated with white European Americans throughout high school. She said that in her high school, each club nominates two people for homecoming queen—one who was "white" and the other "black." Sumi was nominated for the position, but the school did not know how to classify her as a nominee. She was told that she would have to choose whether she wanted to be the "white" or "black" candidate. Feeling terribly uncomfortable about having to claim either identity, particularly at the exclusion of the other, in the end she ended up declining to participate at all.

The first generation of Indian Americans is a very diverse group, including regional, linguistic, class, caste, and religious differences. In coming to the United States, these multiple and complex Indian identities intersect with American ones concerning race, class, and region. The class and race identities of Indian Americans in the South shape the experiences of the immigrant group and their children in important ways. Most significantly, they shape whom the children grow up with and thus shape their attitudes about whom they desire and may someday want to marry. It is at the intersection of all these complex identities that the second generation struggles to carve out their place in a southern landscape. The struggles of second-generation Indian Americans derive from their complex location in two ways: one, in dealing with pressures from their parents, who are interested in reproducing their culture in a new context; and two, in dealing with the pressures and desire to be included in a society that may also exclude them. By understanding these aspects of their experience we can better understand the struggles of the second generation concerning the issue of marriage.

The Immigrant's Dream and the Second Generation

To begin to understand the experiences of second-generation Indian Americans, both young women and men, it is important to understand how they are caught up in and come to embody their parents' immigrant dreams. Their parents' immigrant dreams are of two closely interrelated parts, one part more "material" and one part more "moral." The dreams are a product of their parents' own experiences of immigration, of their hopes and ambitions, and losses and regrets. By being in the United States, many immigrant parents feel that they have made compromises. These compromises are based on a similar one constructed in India, one that is common in modernity, which the immigrants reproduce in the United States. Although Indian immigrants may have a greater degree of financial success and material wealth, and the greater status that follows, they also fear that there are things they may lose along the way. What they fear they may lose is something perceived as moral, familial, or spiritual—things they feel are tied to Indian culture and not American.

The two aspects of the parents' immigrant dreams, the material and the moral, intersect and come together at the point of marriage. Although these two aspects are intimately related, they can also be considered separately. The more "moral" dimension of the parent's immigrant dreams relates to the reproduction of family values and gender roles; and the more "material" dimension of the parent's dreams relates to the reproduction of class position through their children's educational and career choices.

In order to stave off the feelings of loss that may come from immigration, many immigrant parents, from India and elsewhere, struggle to achieve what has been called "accommodation without assimilation"—they struggle to become fully integrated in the society without being fully assimilated.[19] That is, they may try to compartmentalize their American work and their Indian home lives, happily accommodating themselves to the dominant society, while struggling against being fully assimilated by resisting the adoption of some dominant American values. Through their family relations, social networks, ethnic organizations, and religious centers, as well as frequent visits to India if possible, immigrant Indians have struggled to negotiate this compromise and maintain a sense of "being Indian" on a new landscape. Like most immigrants, they seek to enjoy some of the material benefits and satisfactions of American society, while otherwise trying to hold onto aspects of their culture and values. These often include essentialized ideas about family, marriage, gender, and religion, the fossilized remains of a more complex and dynamic Indian culture they left behind.

For many immigrant parents, the real successes of their dreams, and the wisdom of their decisions to move to the United States, are felt to be contingent upon the behavior of their children. In raising their children in the United States, in creating a new generation, the immigrant parents struggle to keep their dreams alive and try to retain or regain the cultural or moral aspects they fear they have lost or may still lose. In order to fulfill their parents' dreams, Indian American children are often expected to do the same as their parents: to achieve financial success and security in the United States, while also still maintaining an Indian culture and identity. The parents' hopes are that their children will grow up in America, without becoming fully "Americanized." If the children are successful in school and career and are seen to still maintain an Indian identity, then the parents' anxieties over the potential costs of their decisions to immigrate are not realized, and the parents feel that they have achieved the material success of the West, without having lost what is perceived to be their Indian spiritual or moral essences.[20]

In order to maintain an Indian identity, the second generation is expected to have an attachment to India, things Indian, and other Indians, and most importantly, display what are considered to be "Indian values" or "family values." These values emphasize identification with and affinity for the family, as well as proper relations among family members according to generation and gender. Although these values are negotiated throughout the lives of the second generation, they have greatest salience with regard to marriage. It is at the point of marriage that the continuity of an Indian identity and its associated family values are most called into question.

At the point of marriage, both parts of the immigrant dream come together, as parents seek to have their children engage in proper marriages that reproduce their family status and class position as well as their ethnic identity. Second-generation Indian Americans generally grow up knowing that their parents consider one of their primary duties in life is to be seeing to their children's marriage. They know their parents would like for them to marry another Indian, and preferably one who is most like them according to the complexities of Indian identities. Marriage is in some ways the final scene in an immigrant's dream. It is the point at which it is determined whether the parents' immigration was a success and thus is the point at which the immigrant dream can most easily fracture.

Growing Up in "Two Worlds": Competing Discourses about Marriage

As the children of immigrant parents, most second-generation Indian Americans feel that they grow up in two worlds, a world of Indian culture and a world of American culture. Analytically, both historically and in the present, the boundaries between these worlds are quite porous; however, many second-generation Indian Americans experience these worlds as separate and distinct. They may feel that to "be Indian" and to "be American" are not easily reconcilable. The second generation often acts differently and feels differently in these worlds, and the people they know in either world may have only limited insight into the other.

The world of Indian culture is generally experienced as a more private world, primarily including the home and the family, but it also includes the public ethnic spaces that the parents have tried to create in American society. The Indian world can be a warm and familiar one, but it can also be experienced as unfair and restrictive. The world of American culture more typically includes their schools, their peers, shopping malls, and popular culture. The American world may be a more fun place for the second generation, and they may find their more American identities to be liberating. However, as discussed earlier, the American world can also be an alienating and racist one, a lonely world in which a young Indian American may sometimes be made to feel embarrassed about being Indian. In sum, the second generation may have ambivalent feelings about their more American world, as they may their more Indian one. They may find pleasures in both worlds, and desire each, but they may also feel that they do not always fit.

For most middle-class Americans generally, including Indian Americans, college is a time for gaining independence from parents and exploring and reworking their identities in preparation for adulthood. However, for many second-generation Indian Americans college is a time when they can try to reconcile their Indian and American worlds, when they can create Indian communities, culture, and identities on their own terms, rather than through their parents. One of the primary ways in which college may provoke a renegotiation of identity for some second-generation Indian Americans (particularly those who grew up in the South) is that it may be the first time they are around a large group of other Indians their age and are not supervised by their parents. The interactions of Indians on campuses are enabled by the presence of Indian or South Asian student organizations at most larger colleges and universities.[21] These student organizations provide a space for the second generation to forge distinct identities and cultures relevant to the complexity of their experiences as Indians and Americans. As I have previously discussed, the cultural programs put on by these organizations provide an important opportunity for the second generation to bring together their different worlds by performing their identity for themselves, their parents, and their Indian and non-Indian peers.[22] Rhetorically at least, many second-generation Indian Americans claim that in being Indian and in being American, in growing up in "two worlds," they benefit from having the best of both worlds. Following from their parents' dreams, they often claim that they are able to seamlessly mix that which is Indian and that which is American, and this is sometimes the explicit focus of their cultural programs. However, their struggles with the issue of marriage betray the ease with which this can be done.

While certainly not all second-generation Indian Americans feel conflicted about their identities or their experiences, at some point in their adolescent or early adult lives they are likely to experience conflicts with their parents, their peers, or within themselves, which brings them to question their identities as Indians and as Americans. This questioning is most likely to be prompted by conflicts over dating, sexuality, and gender. These conflicts arise from the different models for behavior offered by their Indian and American worlds.

As they are growing up, second-generation Indian Americans are presented with two dominant cultural models of the marriage process.[23] These models offer competing views about marriage, dating, and sexuality and different ideas about whom they should marry and how they should marry. These models are conveyed through the discourse of their parents, relatives, Indian peers, non-Indian peers, religious figures, as well as American and Indian media. Although the messages conveyed are in fact quite complex, both their Indian and American social worlds tend to essentialize them into oppositional discourses that are the basis of these competing models. Among Indians, American marriages are often viewed as selfish, frivolous, and risky, while among non-Indian Americans, Indian marriages are often viewed as oppressive, unfeeling, and unfair. These dominant discourses on the marriage process place the second generation in the difficult position of having to mediate conflicting cultural models of the marriage process in terms of their ethnic identity.

According to this dominant discourse, dating, premarital sex, and relationships with non-Indians are associated with being "Americanized"; while not dating, abstinence prior to marriage, and having relationships with other Indians are considered to be more appropriately "Indian" behaviors.[24] Indian Americans learn that according to an American model of marriage, couples date and become sexually involved, and while getting to know each other may somewhere along the way fall in love and may or may not decide to marry.[25]

According to the Indian model of the marriage process a couple ideally trusts the judgment of their parents in choosing a mate for them. An Indian married couple is supposed to come to know each other more intimately after marriage and learn to love each other after much compromise. The second generation learns that according to the Indian model, marriage is about relations between the spouses' families, about the creation of new networks of relationships. According to the American model, marriage is primarily about a relationship between husband and wife, a relationship between two individuals. Finally, according to the Indian model, marriage may be a lifelong commitment, while with the American model marriage may be a more temporary affair.

Marriage is thus the site where Indian and American identities, values, and cultural models most directly conflict and thus is a key point of struggle in the lives of young people raised as both Indians and Americans. These dichotomous constructions of the marriage process are the basis of the second generation's struggles in negotiating their identities and cultures but also provide the second generation with diverse imaginative resources and cultural options not available to many other American youth. These dichotomous cultural models often cluster around the issue of having an "arranged" marriage, which is considered to be distinctly Indian, as opposed to a "love" or "choice" marriage, which is considered to be more American.

Arranged Marriages: Conflicting Models, Conflicting Attitudes

Arranged marriages are such a site of struggle and conflict for the second generation because they have implications for how one marries, whom one marries, and when one marries. They are tied to Indian ideas about self, family, and community—ideas that the second generation often does not embrace. Arranged marriages are fundamentally a way of protecting group boundaries through controlling the selection of who is and is not a member of a family or a community. However, arranged marriages are also a symbolic ethnic boundary marker because the popular discourse of Indian Americans and other Americans arranged marriages are constructed as distinctly Indian.

The struggle over arranged marriages in the Indian American community is basically a struggle over what are perceived to be key Indian and American values that comprise the different models of marriage and reflect different notions of self. According to Indian notions of family values, children should respect the wisdom and authority of their parents on all matters, and parents and children should act dutifully toward each other. Parents are believed to know best and are expected to act with their children's best interests in mind. Parents are considered to have more experience with marriage and are supposed to be able to better choose a suitable match for their child. This understanding of the arranged marriage process is revealed in the story told by an Indian mother who was participating in a forum on arranged marriages held by a student organization at a local university:

> I'm all excited I'm coming to America, and Daddy goes, "You can't go to U.S. until you get married." . . . And it was one of those things, me and my daddy talked for several hours and he explained to me one thing, and I will share this with you. He said, "You didn't choose your parents, you didn't choose your brothers and sisters. So why do you want to choose him!" And he goes, "Did you like the school you went to?" I said, "Yeah." He goes, "Who choose that?" I said, "You did." He goes, "Did you like the college you went to?" I said, "Yeah." "Who choosed it?" I said, "You did." He goes, "Then what's the problem with this husband policy?" And I said, "Dad, I have to spend the rest of the time with him." He goes, "That's o.k., you can spend some with him and some with us, we'll do fine." "Dad! I can't do that!" But eventually mine was an arranged marriage, and I saw him once and I got married. To me arranged marriages have meant a

> lot. I think they are very good. And, it's basically, it's involvement of the families which I think makes a big difference because, a child, the kind of family atmosphere, the kind of environment he grow up or she grow up makes a big difference. And basically arranged marriages is knowing the two families together.

This model of arranged marriage stands in direct contrast with the traditional American model of marriage and associated values of choice, self-fulfillment, and self-determination. Growing up in America, children are generally raised to believe that they are the authors of their own lives, that they create themselves based on the choices that they make, and that they should be guided in those choices primarily by their own desires. This is seen most clearly in the American model of romance and marriage, in which one is supposed to make choices about a partner based on how desirable they are and how effectively they satisfy one's self-interest. According to the American model, marriage is primarily about a relationship between husband and wife. Certainly the concerns and interests of family can have a significant influence on the marriage process. However, it is the desire and will of the individuals that ideally are supposed to prevail. For second-generation Indian Americans who are raised with both sets of values—who wish to be good Indian children respectful of their parents, but who feel that their partner is someone whom they should choose based on quite different criteria—the arranged marriage process becomes a site where conflict and compromise are inevitable.

As they are growing up, second-generation Indian Americans generally do not accept an Indian model of marriage or hold their parents' criteria for marriage to be equally important. Typically, an American model of romance is embraced and they feel that their own desire, based on romantic love and mutual interest, is what will determine their marital choice—not their parents or other relatives, and not specific criteria like religion, caste, or profession. Many young Indian Americans feel that their parents have much stricter criteria than they do about whom they should marry, leading to much of the conflict surrounding marriage.

In the immigrant context a parent's greatest fear is often that their child will marry an American. Many parents fear that if their child marries the "wrong" person, the family will be dishonored and their culture will be lost. Given the dichotomous construction of Indian and American culture, parents feel that if their child marries an American, they have lost their Indian child (and potential grandchildren), and their immigrant dreams are lost with him or her. Furthermore, since non-Indians are viewed as not having Indian family values, any marriage to a non-Indian is also considered a particularly risky venture because it may end in divorce, potentially bringing further suffering for their child and difficulty and shame for the family. However, for some Indian Americans, some marriages outside of the group are worse than others. While Indian American parents would generally prefer their children not marry any American, many in the second generation know that their parents would more easily accept them marrying a white European American than a black African American.

For some parents, marrying an Indian of another religion is as objectionable, if not more so, than marrying an American. Several Hindu Indians I spoke with said that their parents told them explicitly that they should never consider marrying a Muslim. Seema, a Muslim, said her parents would also react strongly if she married a non-Indian or non-Muslim. She said, "That would probably be the worst thing I could do to my parents. . . . Basically, my Mom's told me that if I ever think about doing anything like that to wait until after she's dead." These concerns about maintaining the boundaries of a marriage group make arranged marriages so important.

When second-generation Indian Americans discuss the marriage process, their negotiation of Indian and American models, and identities, is apparent. As Jai discussed, for many second-generation Indian Americans, parental concerns about proper marriages, and particularly according to caste, can seem quite foreign. Exasperated, he explained, "It's just bizarre to me. . . . Like our parents are still caught up in this whole ideology that you got to marry within your caste. . . . I'm like 'I live in America, how am I going to find a girl who's from that part of the world who's living here who's my kind of'—ya know it's like they're still caught up in this fantasy that our children will marry the people from within our caste just like they did. And caste system is something that I can understand the ideology behind it, but certainly can't apply it to my life." Jai expressed a sentiment common to many second-generation Indian Americans, a sentiment that may extend to the boundaries of region, religion, and race as well. Importantly, Jai, like many young Indian Americans, attributes his criticisms of his parents' criteria to living in and having been raised in America. However, competing with this American attitude and model of marriage is a strong attachment to family, which is associated with their Indian identity. The second generation recognizes and may be seriously concerned about how their choices will affect the happiness of their parents and perhaps other relatives. The second generation grows up seeing their parents' interests in their marriages as a central part of the family values they are raised with, and they generally grow up seriously concerned about having a marriage that would make their parents happy.

Mohan, in his mid-twenties and in graduate school, thought a lot about marriage as he saw his friends, cousins, and even his younger sister getting married. He wanted to choose his own spouse, and he said that his mother even emphasized that he had to marry someone he loves. However, Mohan said that it was important for him to marry someone who made his parents happy, and he felt that finding such a person had not been easy. Mohan explained that he once dated a Brahmin girl, and his father and grandmother were not happy with the relationship because of their different caste. Mohan regarded their thinking as superstitious and was reluctant to let these ideas keep him from marrying another person whom he saw only as an Indian American like himself. Mohan knew that his parents would prefer him to marry the daughter of a friend who is of the right caste and marriage group but whom he did not find particularly attractive. Mohan thought that she would make a good daughter for his parents, but he had no strong feelings for her. He said he was not really sure what he wanted in a wife, and he was increasingly questioning whether he could find someone who would make him and his parents happy. Like many second-generation Indian Americans, Mohan's attachment and sense of obligation toward his family generally lead him to want to meet and marry another Indian whom his parents approve of; however, he has limited opportunity to meet someone whom he would desire that would also meet their criteria.

In a forum on arranged marriages an undergraduate named Prateek discussed how he viewed arranged marriages and how he felt he would become married. He said, "I currently believe now that the best thing for a student like myself—I'm from America—I think that I'm capable enough to find somebody on my own. . . . There are some students, I guess who need that help or that direction, or that guidance from their parents, or grandparents or what have you." In his construction of arranged marriages he positions it as something that is for people who are not "capable" enough, who are not independent or self-determining. Importantly, he associates his being "capable" with his being raised in America. However, in this same discussion he added that his family's approval is still terribly important, thus displaying the importance of "family values," and thereby his Indian identity too. He said, "I do also believe that whoever I would like to choose as my wife, I would like to have the approval of my mom, and my immediate family especially, before I committed to anything seriously such as marriage. For several reasons, because, family is always going to be first. . . . The best way for me to please myself is always to please my immediate family."

What most differentiates second-generation Indian Americans from other young Americans is that they know that in their future an arranged marriage is a possibility, and viewed more positively, is an option. The second generation grows up knowing that most of their parents, aunts and uncles, or even their cousins had such marriages, and they associate them with Indian culture. As a result, they grow up with an opinion or an attitude about the process and its relationship to their lives. They grow up at least having considered whether they could or might have an arranged marriage. Among the second generation there is quite a range of attitudes about the issue of arranged marriages and about parental involvement in marriage more generally. Arranged marriages may be viewed as burdensome vestiges of a backward culture or as a valued cultural resource in the modern world.

For many second-generation Indian Americans, if their parents had an arranged marriage and they view the marriage positively, then they are more likely to have a positive view of arranged marriages, even if they do not want one for themselves. Seema based her view of arranged marriages on her view of her parents' marriage. Seema said of arranged marriages, "I mean it has all these really bad connotations I guess to it, but . . . I don't think it's a bad thing. It's worked for my parents really well, so." A young woman who spoke at a student forum also voiced her support for arranged marriages. In doing so, she contrasted Indian marriages with American ones, saying that divorce occurs too quickly and frequently in the United States. She saw arranged marriages as a more effective alternative to the American marriage process, saying, "I just find it so refreshing that people . . . don't have to be in love, but they can get married and can make it work for years and years. And I think it's great that people can learn to grow and learn to love each other instead of trying to be in love first."

However, another young woman in the audience expressed ambivalent feelings about arranged marriages that are common among the second generation. While she viewed her parents' marriage favorably, she questioned whether it is a process that she could go through. She explained, "My mom and dad are basically like night and day, like they're so different, they have totally opposite personalities. . . . If I was a person like my mom and I met someone like my dad, I don't think it would work, for me. You know, like I don't know if I could make like the kinds of compromises that they've made." For young Indian Americans who do not view their parents' arranged marriages so favorably—who see the marriages as unhappy and particularly as oppressive to women—then they are even more likely to have misgivings about arranged marriages.

For most second-generation Indian Americans, arranged marriages are undesirable because they mean giving up control over their choice of a spouse and over the marriage process. Even those who may defend such marriages in the abstract, as a symbol or artifact of Indian culture, will at the same time be likely to resist it in their own lives. They feel that without such control, there is too much risk. As Manish discussed, "If you think about it, so many people have different preferences to what they want in a person. And how do you know if you haven't experienced it? If you find something in a person that you don't like, then you get married and that happens, I mean what are you going to do? You need to find it out before. And that's the problem with this arranged marriage thing. You don't know until after the fact, and then you're screwed."

While formally arranged marriages are not likely to occur for the second generation, the conflicts over parental/familial and individual interests, central to arranged marriages, still play themselves out in the marriage process of the second generation. The degree of parental involvement that the second generation does accept varies widely and may change as the children get older and seek more assistance with finding a spouse. While not typically agreeing to have "arranged marriages," in the most traditional use of the term, as will be discussed below, many second-generation Indian Americans agree to negotiate some sort of compromise.

Negotiating the Marriage Process and Creating New Models

Fischer, in his article "Ethnicity and Post-Modern Arts of Memory," suggests that the struggle of American ethnics is a struggle for self-identity.[26] The basis of this struggle is that there is no model for behavior, no existing image of how to adopt a pluralist or mutlifaceted concept of self, no model for being at the same time both an Indian and an American. This problem is especially true for the second generation and particularly if they are challenging the Indian marriage model. Several young people I spoke with said that they felt alone, lost, or confused in negotiating the terrain of dating and marriage since they felt there was no example to follow, no model for them to draw upon in constructing their behavior.

Fitting an American cultural model and the meanings associated with it, most second-generation Indian Americans I spoke with viewed dating as the appropriate way for people their age to explore emotional and physical intimacy. Some viewed dating simply as something fun to do, a way to experience and experiment without any thought toward long-term relationship or marriage, and most viewed dating as the best way to figure out whom it is they will want to marry. In viewing dating as the appropriate means to experiment with relationships prior to marriage, young Indian Americans, unlike most other Americans, position dating in relation to what they see as an undesirable Indian alternative; they view dating as an antidote to the dangers of an arranged marriage.

For several young people I spoke with, dating was discussed as a way to try to negotiate their own identities as Indians and Americans, a way to satisfy, through a relationship, an interest in feeling more or less Indian. For some, they found satisfaction in dating a non-Indian because they felt that they were able to satisfy and develop an aspect of their selves that they saw as different and separate from the pressures of Indian community and culture. For many, however, dating was a way to feel more Indian through dating another Indian. For example, if they dated another Indian they can more easily enjoy the language, food, and music that they feel is a significant part of their Indian identity. Suresh explained, "I pretty much only date Indian girls. And it's not like an active choice that I've made a long time ago, it was just something that seemed to develop over time. I can see, like non-Indian girls as being attractive, but not being attracted to them, so I make that distinction. . . . You know as you get further in, and think about it more and more, it seems that I'd probably be more into somebody that was Gujerati, that's Hindu or something like that, than I would not." Another young woman said that she likes dating Indian men because she feels a connection with them that she does not feel with other men. She feels they have been brought up in a similar way and "both want similar things out of life." More specifically, she said that she prefers dating men of her same region and caste group. In these examples of dating, we see the second generation adopting a more American model of the marriage process, but one that reproduces many of the boundary criteria important to an Indian model of marriage. However, even if they are dating Indian Americans whom their parents might approve of as potential marriage partners, they are still likely to keep the dating a secret from their parents duc to its conflict with the Indian marriage model.

As was discussed earlier, the cultural programs of Indian student organizations provide the second generation with an important forum to negotiate their identities and experience, and in doing so, to construct alternative models for behavior. Like the organizations of the Indian American community dominated by their parents, the second generation often chooses to place marriage issues at the center of their own public displays of Indian ethnicity. However, rather than simply trying to re-create displays of "traditional" culture as is typically done in the first generation's representations of the marriage process, the second generation often uses these programs to challenge a traditional model of the marriage process and to negotiate the dichotomous constructions of Indian and American identity.

One young woman I interviewed, Rani, told me that the first cultural program that the Indian student organization at her university ever performed centered on a skit about an Indian wedding in which she was the bride. She said that the students chose to simulate a traditional wedding ritual so that they could learn more about what they might expect in their own lives. At the time, few of the students had ever attended an Indian wedding, and few second-generation Indian Americans had yet reached marriageable age or had experiences that would serve as an example for their younger peers to follow. The students consulted the local Hindu priest in putting together the staged ritual and tried to present it as a "traditional" one. However, Rani said that the students scripted the wedding couple to meet each other on their own, without their parents' assistance. In this on-stage depiction of a traditional Hindu wedding, the students were struggling to negotiate a compromise with their parents' expectations. In doing so, they created a model for their parents and themselves, a mixing of traditional weddings with self-selected spouses, which in time came to reflect the actual experiences of many second-generation Indian Americans.

In another skit that was performed at a university cultural program, the Indian American students contested the criteria for marriage emphasized in the

Indian marriage model and the arranged marriage process. In the skit, a young man and woman stood on opposite sides of the stage with their backs turned to each other and then strolled backward to the center of the stage, taking turns speaking. The young woman began by reading Indian marital ads placed by parents for their children, speaking with a stereotypical Indian accent. The young man followed, doing the same. Then having dropped the accent, the young woman talked about what qualities she wanted in a mate, saying that an MD was not important, but that he should believe in her and help her to become whom she wants to be. The young man then read a poem, saying that he desired a "soul mate" to make him complete. The two then bumped into each other, apparently finding their soul mates. Through the skit, the students challenge parental expectations and interests in the marriage process and replace them with their own. They took the criteria that they associate with an Indian model of marriage and replaced it with an American one. At the same time, they provided a new romantic model for second-generation Indian Americans that they hoped was acceptable to their parents. It is significant that in stumbling along they found another Indian, since off the stage the second generation often stumbles into non-Indians while resisting their parents' expectations, a drama that would have been far more disturbing to their Indian parents.

Through these skits the students were expressing and dealing with their own anxieties about their futures. As college students, they were already aware of the significance of their marriages, and they were aware of what was expected of them in the near future. They were concerned about what will be their experience of the process, and they were actively trying to pose alternatives to their parents and themselves. They were trying to create something that is Indian and that is American, reflecting their own experiences and concerns, and they were hoping that they were doing so in a way that would satisfying their parents and their community. However, while Rani was eventually able to become the Indian bride in a "traditional" wedding ceremony in which she selected the spouse, the spouse she selected was not an Indian one.

Of course, many second-generation Indian Americans recognize that finding one's own spouse is not easy. Seema, a Muslim, second-generation Indian American college student, was concerned about how she would fit finding a spouse into her plans for becoming a doctor. She explained, "Well I guess the thing would be to meet him pretty soon. Like, hopefully like some time while I'm in med school. And then having maybe a couple of years to get to know him and stuff like that, and then get married. . . . Cause I want to, you know, be married when I'm young . . . and also like to have a family and stuff I think it's better to get that started, you know, at least in your early thirties at the latest." Realizing Seema's predicament, I asked her how she thought she would meet her husband. She replied, "That's like the really tricky part, because, I mean like I said, it's really hard to, you know, meet people. So I haven't really thought that much about it. . . . I was actually even considering this when I was applying to med schools. You know, do I want to go to like a bigger place because I'll have a better chance of, like, meeting a guy? [laughter] . . . But I didn't end up doing that. . . . So I guess I kind of hope it'll just happen. I don't really have a plan for it." In struggling to fulfill both her parents' and her own interests in her marriage, Seema, like many of her second-generation Indian American peers, felt that she was without a clear "plan." While not likely to accept an arranged marriage that would provide her with a "clearer plan," Seema, like many of her peers, said she would eventually be willing to accept a modified version of the more "traditional" marriage process.

Negotiating Compromises through Arranged Meetings

> What it comes down to is that each family has to make their own decisions and there is nothing that's generalizable. It's good to know that you're not alone with having to come up with a kind of compromise. But, you can't come up with a solution applicable for everyone.
>
> (Anne)

Most second-generation Indian Americans do not expect to have an arranged marriage. They either feel that their parents would not try to arrange a marriage for them, or they feel that if their parents did, they would successfully resist it. However, nearly all second-generation Indian Americans grow up with the knowledge that their parents could want to find someone for them, if they are interested. Although more traditional arranged marriages do occur, sometimes with and sometimes without the children's consent, most Indian American parents do not try to force an arranged marriage on their children. Instead, parents and children may negotiate their own compromise of Indian and American models of the marriage process. Parents may let their children know that when they feel they are ready to be married their parents will find someone for them. Or, they may tell their children that they are free to find someone on their own but that they should let their parents know when they do, so that they can offer their approval. However, as their children grow older, the parents may take a more active interest in trying to find a match for them, and the pressure to marry may increase.

As discussed earlier, most second-generation Indian Americans want to meet and marry another Indian with their parents' approval, but they have limited opportunities to do so. They may have known few other second-generation Indian Americans whom they could date and may simply not consider those whom they know to be eligible partners for varieties of reasons. Some may have devoted themselves to their academic or career successes and avoided dating experiences that would have allowed them to meet a spouse. Others may have had relationships with other Indian Americans that were unsuccessful or simply did not lead to marriage. They may also find that after their undergraduate years, they have fewer opportunities to meet other Indians in their workplace or graduate school. If by the end of their schooling second-generation Indian Americans have not found someone on their own that they want to marry, either Indian or non- Indian, then great pressure is placed on them to allow their parents to take advantage of existing social networks to find a partner for them.

Given the difficulties in finding someone to marry on their own, and due to their parents' pressures to marry, many second-generation Indian Americans eventually agree to a kind of negotiated compromise. While the nature of these compromises varies, one version that has become quite common is for the second generation to agree to what are often referred to as "arranged meetings," leading to a kind of modified arranged marriage. These arranged meetings are a way for parents and children to try to satisfy each other's interests. The parents are given the opportunity to introduce their children to potential spouses, whose backgrounds and families they find suitable, while the second generation is given a degree of choice in agreeing to the match and some time to get to know the person. These "meetings" are not typically viewed as "arranged marriages" by the second generation and are therefore viewed more favorably. As Suresh explained while participating in a small group discussion on dating and marriage, "But I think arranged marriage is not an arranged marriage, I think it's—for a lot of us it's going to be arranged introductions. Here's somebody whom you might be interested in talking to, but if you're not, then fine we'll move on. . . . I think that's something that's in the realm of possibilities, I think that's o.k." However, in these compromised arranged marriages the degree of choice and the length of time in making a decision are still a matter of negotiation between parents and their children, and even between potential spouses themselves. In negotiating the arranged meetings there may still be conflict over the models of marriage, the interests of the parents and children, and the identities of the second generation.

The different models of the marriage process held by the parents and children shape how the arranged meeting process is handled. Whereas parents tend to view the arranged meetings as a modification of the arranged marriage process, young Indian Americans may want it to be more of a modified dating process. A second-generation Indian American may agree to a meeting, seeing a great deal of flexibility in the situation. Having a negative view of arranged marriages, they are likely to view the meeting as a more formal way of going about dating. Young Indian Americans may see meeting someone through their parents (or through conferences or other networks) as a smarter, more reliable alternative to meeting someone through the less formal social situations more typical of the American model. They may see agreeing to an arranged meeting as a safe, effective, lower-risk way to begin a dating relationship and may still expect to have satisfactory time to get to know the other person and to make their own decision about whether or not to marry.

When Prateek was asked how he would respond if his parents told him that they wanted him to meet someone to consider for marriage, he responded, "I'd have to take it step by step. Um, well I'd like to definitely meet this person. [laughter] . . . And I guess get to know that person. I think getting to know the person is a big step in communication. . . . If my mom came up to me and said, 'I have this person lined up for you and I'd like you to meet this person,' I'd say that's fine, because, first of all because I trust my mother. . . . I mean I trust my family, it doesn't hurt to meet anybody. So, I like meeting people everyday [laughter]." Again, Prateek was showing the key Indian values of respect for and trust in parents, while also struggling to make the encounter a more casual "everyday" experience, directed at meeting and getting to know the person without an explicit consideration of marriage. Prateek was rhetorically struggling to negotiate a compromise that he and many other second-generation Indian Americans are called upon to make when considering marriage.

Alternatively, young Indian Americans may more cynically agree to participate in the arranged meeting process and may simply try to appease their parents and quiet their inquiries about marriage. Several second-generation Indian Americans I spoke with even decided to have arranged meetings while they were engaged in serious dating relationships with someone else. This was likely to occur if the young person was dating someone their parents would not approve of them marrying. Either the parents may not have known about their children's dating, or the parents did know and wanted to create the opportunity for their child to marry someone else.

However, some second-generation Indian Americans I spoke with who were already in long-term relationships also participated in the arranged meeting process but took it more seriously. Although feeling strongly committed to their partner, they were aware that their parents would not be happy with their marriage, and they knew that marrying another Indian whom their parents approved of would make their lives much easier. They agreed to meet with people their parents selected, curious about the prospects of finding someone who could make both them and their parents happy.

The criteria used in the selection process may also reflect differences in the children's and the parents' interests in marriage. The young person may see the meetings as a way to simply meet another Indian American spouse, while the parents may see the process as a way of ensuring that their child marry into the appropriate group . While young Indian Americans may agree to go along with a process simply in order to find a specifically "Indian American" spouse, through their parents' involvement in the process they may end up meeting with people selected from more narrowly defined marriage groups. Endogamous boundaries may then be reproduced through the marriage of young people who have little interest in maintaining those specific boundaries.

The mechanisms of the arranged meeting/marriage process vary. Ideally, parents draw upon their own social networks, utilizing relatives and friends in trying to find a spouse for their child. This network is most likely to provide a suitable spouse, whose background is similar to the family, and who is known to come from "a good family." The potential spouse may be a young person from the local community whom their son or daughter has grown up with, someone living more distantly in the Indian diaspora whom their son or daughter may have met only occasionally, or children of friends or more distant relatives whom the child has never met. In exploring their child's interest in a potential spouse, the parents may casually mention the person's name to their son or daughter, looking for a reaction, or may ask their child's sibling or more directly ask their child. Some parents, however, do not have an adequate social network to enlist in helping to find a spouse for their children, or after a few suggestions to a son or daughter the individuals in that network may be exhausted and the parents may turn to other means.

There are more and less formal means by which a parent might try to locate a spouse for their child. They may simply try to encourage their child to attend more community organizations and events or bring them to social gatherings such as weddings, all in the hope of their child meeting someone they might like who is part of the parents' social network. More formally, however, the parents may try to place a marital ad for their child, bring their children to conferences specifically for marriage, or enlist the assistance of marriage brokers. Ads can be placed in the US in immigrant publications such as *India Abroad* and *India West*, as well as in newspapers in India. With the development of the Internet, there are now a wealth of electronic ads and marriage services available to Indian Americans.[27] These are more likely to be used by the second generation themselves as a way of meeting and possibly marrying another Indian.[28] The use of marital ads is a particularly valuable resource for many Indian Americans in the South who live outside of centers of Indian American community.

The ads are generally viewed negatively by the men and women with whom I spoke. They are sometimes seen as a resource for those who are "desperate," as a last resort for those who have otherwise been incapable of finding a spouse. The ads are also seen to represent the worst of the arranged marriage process in the criteria they emphasize and the nature of the medium, and the child may only reluctantly agree to meet with people after their parents have placed an ad.

However, the ads are also a resource some second-generation Indian Americans embrace, putting them in contact with many more potential spouses than they would otherwise be able to meet. For those second-generation Indian Americans who used the marital ads, they were only one means in the complex process of trying to find a spouse. For example, one woman I spoke with, Sarita, had used an ad in *India Abroad* to meet her spouse. She is a Hindu and had dated an Indian Muslim for five years while in college. The relationship ended because of his family's objection to his marrying a Hindu, and his reluctance to go against his family's wishes. She then decided to have a marital ad placed in *India Abroad*. She met with about ten men and chose one as her husband.

Arranged marriages or arranged meetings, whether set up through social networks or marital ads, are directed at establishing a more proper match that is satisfactory to the parents' generation. However, it bears repeating that many second-generation Indian Americans do date and eventually marry people whom they have met on their own without their parents' involvement. Some of these relationships result in what would be considered proper marriages and some do not. Many second-generation Indian Americans find themselves dating and falling in love with non-Indians or the "wrong" kind of Indian. The issue of marrying the wrong person was brought up at a student forum on arranged marriages. Rajiv felt that the parents on the panel were oversimplifying the discussion about marriage. He challenged the parents on the panel by saying, "A lot of talk was given about, 'if you instill proper values, if you trust,' but um, sometimes circumstances happen where, where a deviation occurs from the path. . . . So what would be the scenario if one of your children came to you and said, 'I'm marrying someone who is not South Asian. I'm marrying someone who is not of the same religion. I'm marrying someone who doesn't fit the ideals that you set forth for me.' Because a lot of times, from our side . . . we go through a lot of pain thinking our parents . . . are not going to be happy with this. And it's a tough decision whether to say, I'm going to stick with it 'cause it makes me happy, or to end it because it makes my parents happy." For second-generation Indian Americans, the decision to marry a non-Indian is a very difficult one not just because their parents might object, but also because it raises questions about their identity. In marrying a non-Indian their Indian identity may be called into question not just because of their choice of spouse but also because they are making a major life decision that may go against their parents' wishes and thus against the family values they learned are so central to their Indian identity.

Second-generation Indian Americans are making diverse choices about marriage that have implications for their identities. There are undoubtedly many factors that come together in shaping the choices they make about whom and how they marry and the identities they create through this process. As has been discussed, their choices are shaped perhaps most obviously by their negotiation of their own desires and their parents' immigrant dream. In the next section I will explore how some of their choices are shaped by their class and racial positioning in the United States, and perhaps more significantly, by their gender.

Marriage Choices: Gender, Class, and Race

The Indian identity that is made available to the second generation, by their parents, by their community, and by themselves, is deeply gendered. This gendering of ethnic identity has very different implications for how each gender conceives of, constructs, performs, and feels about an Indian identity, and it can also have implications for the choices that each gender makes about whom they marry and how they go about getting married. The second generation grows up acutely aware of differences in gender roles and status in their families and in Indian society more generally.

For many Indian immigrants and their children, the family is seen as the nucleus of their culture and identity, and the thin membrane of the household protects the family from the polluting effects of American society. For the young Indian American who grows up in such families, the Indian identity is likely to be primarily located within that home, and the Indian mother becomes the primary caretaker of the Indian identity in the home. For the second generation, this construction of family, household, and gender has serious implications for the choices they will make about marriage. Many young Indian American women, and some men, come to feel that Indian "family values" place an unfair burden on women in maintaining Indian culture in America.[29] The location of an Indian identity in women has some expectedly very serious implications for their experiences with dating and marriage. They may be given less freedom to date, to have male friends, and to even go out with mixed gender groups. For many second-generation Indian women then, it is difficult to talk about being Indian without talking about the challenges of their gender.[30]

Second-generation Indian American men are generally raised as a privileged gender, raised to feel that they deserve respect, service, and devotion from women. However, while second-generation Indian American men enjoy certain gender privileges, many of them are not satisfied with the strongly segregated gender roles they saw their parents enact. They instead seek a wife with whom they share more interests, who is comparably educated, and with whom they expect to share more domestic responsibilities. Additionally, many second-generation Indian American men do not find the stereotypical subservience of Indian women to be desirable. As one undergraduate I spoke with said, "I want a girl who has some sense of independence . . . and not one who would just like do everything . . . when I want it."

While most second-generation men tend to want less segregated marriage roles than their parents had, most also desire a wife who will reproduce some of the behaviors of their image of a good Indian woman. They want a wife who will offer some of the devotion to them and their families that their mothers showed, and most importantly, they want a wife who will eventually make raising children her primary duty. Indian American young men may be more likely to seek a wife who, like their own mothers, will largely be responsible for creating an Indian household in which they feel their Indian identity will reside. Importantly, given the gendered constructions of an Indian identity, young men are less likely to feel that they embody an Indian identity, and so in order to maintain that identity they may feel that they will have to marry an Indian woman. Sanjay, an undergraduate I spoke with, explained this well, saying that he felt that he was "pretty culturally diluted," and so he wanted to marry a woman whom he felt knew the culture well, in order to help him preserve it in himself. Neel, a professional in his twenties, similarly located his identity in an Indian partner. He said, "I did at one time have an Indian American girlfriend whom I was very, very close with and whom you know, for the most part my identity was carried out with her."

The experiences of Indian American men and women are shaped by their gendered ethnic identities in other ways. The gender roles that young men and women are called upon to embrace as part of their Indian family values shape how young men and women view each other as potential spouses. Generally, men are raised to fill more of a provider role and women more of a domestic one. For many second-generation Indian Americans, fulfilling these roles is a dubious proposition, and their struggles with these roles shape whom they marry and how they marry.

While young Indian American women may be raised to enact the domestic role of the good Indian woman, as the children of class-aspiring immigrants they are also generally raised to be academically successful and to pursue a career. In thinking about marriage, some young Indian American women struggle with trying to integrate their interests in career and family. They may see this as a struggle of identity—a struggle to reconcile what they imagine to be the Indian and American aspects of themselves. Mary, who was unmarried and in medical school, explained, "You know I think that we have the dilemma that most of our mothers have wanted us to . . . be educated, more educated than they were. And at the same time they've taught us, you know, the domestic things, that they have been so good at—cooking, and you know whatever—woman things that they've done in the home. And, so we have . . . all of these conflicts of, you know we're supposed to be doctors, we're supposed to cook, we want families, but you know we're supposed to be the most successful engineer. . . . So, all of the different values we've been taught as growing up here in this culture, and you know what our mothers taught us growing up about, you know, what it is important to be when you are an Indian woman—they conflict."

Because of how gender is constructed among Indian Americans, many second-generation Indian American women hold negative views of Indian American men. Rani felt that some Indian American men have a "Raja syndrome," that they are looking to marry someone "just like mom," that is, someone who treats them like a "raja" or king and fulfills the Indian ideal of the devoted housewife. Rani explained that when she met other Indian American men for "arranged meetings," "the thing that was interesting is that the guys were a lot like [pause] my father. [laughter] . . . They had the traditional expectations of Indian women, and I did not intend to fulfill those expectations." As a result of their negative views of the women's gender role and of men's expectations that they fulfill it, some second-generation Indian American women tend to be less desirous of, and less desirable to, Indian American men. Some Indian American men I interviewed saw Indian American women as too "Americanized," "confused," or "not knowing what they want" because of their resistance to embrace their gendered ethnic identity.

Kavita, who was seeking her PhD in the sciences, felt that Indian men, even educated ones, will not want to marry her. She said that they want wives with PhDs, but they still also want wives to be home to cook and clean for them. Another highly educated woman, Parinda, echoed Kavita's concerns. Parinda said that she thinks some Indian men raised in the United States will say that it is OK for their wives to have an education and a career, but that they want the career to be more of a hobby. As an undergraduate woman named Shilpi explained, "I sometimes think that no matter how equal I was to them . . . if I was a doctor and he was an engineer, I'd still be the one coming home and cooking. And I don't know if I'm willing to do that." These young women struggled with balancing both parts of the immigrant dream: the moral, tied to gender and family, and the material, tied to their education and career. The expectations placed on them as Indian women and as the successful children of immigrant parents can lead to struggles over marriage choice.

Mary expressed a common resistance toward the segregated gender roles considered more typical of Indian families. She said, "It would be just great to have somebody that I could be a friend with, rather than somebody to take care of—somebody who has equal interest in child rearing and those kind of things." For some Indian American women, their interest in avoiding reproducing the role of "the good Indian woman" leads to an interest in marrying a non-Indian. As Anne continued, "I think that if I married somebody who is Indian I would just fall into the same pattern that my parents are in and I guess I could get used to it, but, it's not really what I want. I think that I'm young enough that I still think that there's something better out there." For Anne and for other young Indian American women, marrying a non-Indian, though not without its difficulties, may be seen as an attractive alternative to fulfilling the expectations of her gendered ethnic identity.

Given the various issues surrounding a gendered ethnic identity, some second-generation men and women have a difficult time finding an Indian American spouse who satisfies their Indian and American identities. Men may have difficulty finding someone who they feel is the right mix of "American" and "Indian" qualities, someone to whom they can relate in attitude and lifestyle as Americans, and who at the same time performs a more traditional gender role. Women may have difficulty finding someone who is of Indian descent whom they can disassociate from their negative perception of Indian gender roles. Finding a wife who embraces the gender roles of Indian family values is important to second-generation men as it may be necessary for them to satisfy their identity as Indian men. For a young Indian American woman, finding a husband who rejects the more gendered aspects of Indian family values may be important because it allows her to maintain her more "American" aspect of her identity.

Among the second-generation Indian Americans I encountered in my research in North Carolina two key patterns were evident, arising from these issues surrounding gender. The first is that in order to satisfy their identities, Indian American men may be more likely to look to India for a wife and consent to an arranged marriage; and, the second is that Indian American women may be more likely to marry a non-Indian, and because of the intersections of class and race in the South, typically white Americans.[31]

Regardless of whom second-generation Indian American women marry, it is important for them that both the Indian and American aspects of their self-identities are accommodated. Contrary to the dichotomous dominant discourse among Indian Americans, as well as sociological theories of assimilation, most of the women I interviewed who married non-Indians did not feel that their Indian identity was going to be compromised by their marriage choice.[32] One of the unexpected implications of the location of an Indian identity in women is that they did not necessarily feel that they had to marry another Indian American to maintain a secure sense of their Indian identity. Furthermore, all of the young women I spoke with who were dating or married to non-Indian men said that one of the key reasons they were attracted to them was because of the men's active interest in and openness to their culture. One woman commented that she felt that her children were going to be just as Indian being raised by a non-Indian who has an interest in Indian culture, as by an Indian who might not. Certainly these marriage choices can and do lead to conflicts for Indian American women that can have serious implications for their identities. However, in the cases I encountered the conflict was resolved prior to the wedding, so the women did not have to make the difficult choice between their spouses and their families.

However, for another young woman I spoke with, her decision to marry a white American raised questions about her identity that still lingered. Shilpa was engaged to a white American but struggled over her decision. Shilpa said that her parents do not seem concerned that she is marrying a non-Indian and that her mother was just happy that she was getting married. Shilpa was happy that her fiancé has cooked with her mother and had learned some Gujerati; however, she wished that her fiancé was Indian and had told him so. She is concerned that because she did not marry another Indian American her children will not grow up feeling proud of being Indian, will not speak Gujerati, and will not want to visit India. Shilpa has a younger sister who was engaged to another Indian American, and she seemed envious of their relationship. She recognized that her sister and fiancé had a shared language and shared experiences that she and her husband will never have.

Some Indian American women I interviewed also expressed concern about the educational ambitions and career positions of the men whom they would date and marry. In expressing these concerns, these women conflated professional success with being Indian. Mary, who was in her late twenties, suggested that she and some of her friends who had earlier dated non-Indian American men were now dating and marrying Indian American men, and she framed the change as a choice about class. She said, "You know actually I can tell you all of the women friends that I have—Indian women friends— . . . stopped dating American guys, and are dating or marrying Indian men who are, you know, doctors, or lawyers, engineers, teachers, you know, like of equal educational background." She explained, "We may complain about Indian men and everything, but none of us would marry anyone of a lower educational status." While Mary and her friends clearly wanted husbands who shared their education and class status, whom they assumed would be good providers for their families, they were also not simply willing to accept traditional gender roles. For Mary and her Indian American friends, now that they were older and had achieved their own careers, they felt that they were more ready to accept their roles as Indian wives, but they saw those roles as ones they will have to continue to negotiate with their husbands.

As discussed earlier, many second-generation Indian American women of course do choose to marry other Indian Americans for issues other than class and career, and of course, many Indian American men do find other second-generation Indian American women to marry. This is not surprising and calls for little explanation, except for the fact that the simple demographics of their lives brings them in contact with more non-Indians, and their opportunities for meeting many other Indians as they are growing up tend to be limited. For Indian American men and women marriage to another Indian is something which is often very self-consciously done in an attempt to strongly maintain an Indian identity by satisfying their own sense of their Indian and American identities, and by satisfying their parents.

There is very little that is normative or that can be taken as a given in the marriages of second-generation Indian Americans. The marriage choices of second-generation Indian Americans lie at the nexus of class, race, and gender issues faced by second-generation Indian Americans coming of age in the American South. Their experiences highlight the complexity, flexibility, and contingency of identity and culture in late modernity. However they marry, or whomever they marry, the marriages of second-generation Indian Americans are typically choices self-consciously taken from a variety of other imagined possibilities, and the result of choices based on personal histories that could have had different outcomes.

Conclusion: Challenging Fixed Identities

Raised as Indians in an American context the second generation grows up with different models of the marriage process. These models are seen to be in competition and cause conflicts for the second generation—conflicts between themselves and their parents and between their Indian and American aspects of their self-identities. These conflicting models create a tricky terrain for the second generation to negotiate, while at the same time offering a diversity of resources for them to draw upon. In negotiating this terrain and drawing on these resources, second-generation Indian Americans are creating new cultural models and creating more complex identities than the dominant discourses American and Indian society offer. By seeing second-generation Indian Americans as actors negotiating their cultures and identities through marriage, we can understand how in a complex society in late modernity culture and identity are not determining forces, but rather are a matter of choice, an option constrained in various ways. Thinking in this way appropriately gives agency to second-generation Indian Americans constructing their lives in such contexts and helps to challenge the dichotomous conceptions of culture of identity arising out of the dominant discourses that shape their lives.

Finally, the experiences of second-generation Indian Americans do not just have implications for their identities, but for the identities of the places they inhabit, and for the people whose lives they intersect. While some may still try to promote an identity of the South that is largely white and Christian, claims to such an identity are challenged by the presence of second-generation Indian Americans, of a variety of religions, forming relationships and creating new families in North Carolina. While some in the South struggle to hang onto an identity that is still local, small-townish, and nativist, this identity is disrupted by the presence of Indian Americans who are firmly located in the South but who are shaped by and participate in global diasporic cultures. As this chapter has shown, the South has shaped the experience of Indian American youth, as Indian American youth shape a new South, making traditional representations and understandings of the South more problematic in an increasingly complex and diverse world.

Notes

Epigraph. All of the names used in the chapter have been changed.

1. I use the term Indian Americans to describe those people living in the United States who have immigrated from India or who are of Indian descent, paralleling other ethnic identities in the United States, such as African American, Italian American, etc. I am using the term because it is a label most accessible to the people with whom I spoke. However, many identified themselves simply as "Indian," and some primarily by their religion (Hindu, Muslim, Sikh). The more inclusive term "Desi" is often used by and for South Asian Americans, though it had little salience in my research area. Occasionally, the term "brown people" was used, suggesting a racialized identity that parallels other color category terms for race in the United States, and that crosses national and religious lines among South Asians. The term "Asian Indian" is the official term used in the US census to distinguish people of Indian descent.

2. This chapter is based on ethnographic fieldwork I conducted in a metropolitan area in North Carolina most intensively during the late 1990s, with occasional follow-up research conducted since.

3. There are some second-generation Indian Americans who are engaged in same-sex relationships, and who are living adult lives without marriage. In doing so, they struggle to create an alternative vision of an Indian identity in the United States. For most second-generation Indian Americans, heterosexual marriage is felt to be compulsory. For a discussion of same-sex relationships among South Asian Americans see Rakesh Ratti, ed., *Lotus of a Different Color: An Unfolding of the South Asian Gay and Lesbian Experience* (Boston: Alyson Publications, 1993, Surabhi Kukke and Svati Shah, "Reflections on Queer South Asian Progressive Activism in the U.S." *Amerasia* 25, no. 3, (1999/2000), and Monisha Das Gupta, *Unruly Immigrants: Rights, Activism, and Transnational South Asia Politics in the United States* (Durham, NC: Duke University Press, 2006).

4. Stuart Hall, "Cultural Identity and Diaspora," In *Identity: Community, Culture and Difference*, ed. Jonathan Rutherford (London: Lawrence and Wishart, 1990), 235.

5. George Brown Tindall, *Natives and Newcomers: Ethnic Southerners and Southern Ethnics* (Athens: University of Georgia Press, 1995).

6. Arjun Appadurai, "Global Ethnoscapes, Notes and Queries for a Transnational Anthropology," in *Recapturing Anthropology*, ed. R. Fox (Santa Fe, NM: School of American Research Press, 1989); Carol Breckenrdge and Arjun Appadurai, "On Moving Targets," *Public Culture* 2, no. 1 (1989); Akhil Gupta and James Ferguson, "Beyond Culture: Space, Identity, and the Politics of Difference," *Cultural Anthropology* 7, no. 1 (1992).

7. Anthony Giddens, *Modernity and Self Identity, Self and Society in the Late Modern Age* (Stanford, CA: Stanford University Press, 1991).

8. Linda Basch, Nina G. Schiller, and Cristina S. Blanc, *Nations Unbound: Transnational Projects, Postcolonial Predicaments, and Deterritorialized Nation-States* (London, UK: : Gordon and Breach, 1994); Jonathan Friedman, *Cultural Identity and Global Process* (London: Sage, 1994); Ulf Hannerz, "Cosmopolitans and Locals in World Culture," in *Global Culture: Nationalism, Globalisation, Modernity*, ed. M. Featherstone (London: Sage, 1990).

9. The most notable collections of this research are *Ethnicities* (Ruben G. Rumbaut and Alejandro Portes, *Ethnicities, Children of Immigrants in America* [Berkeley: University of California Press, 2001]) and *Legacies* (Alejandro Portes and Ruben G. Rumbaut, *Legacies: The Story of the Immigrant Second Generation* [Berkeley: University of California Press, 2001]), based on the Children of Immigrants Longitudinal Study conducted in the 1990s, which focused on the experiences of Mexicans, Cubans, Nicaraguans, Filipinos, Vietnamese, Haitians, Jamaicans, and other West Indians in America.

10. Harry H. L. Kitano and Roger Daniels, *Asian Americans: Emerging Minorities* (Englewood Cliffs, NJ: Prentice Hall, 1988).

11. The Indian American community in my particular study area grew similarly, from about three thousand in 1990 to nearly eleven thousand in 2000, and about twenty thousand by 2010. Statewide, Indian Americans represent less than .5 percent of the total population, while in my research area they represent as much as 5 percent (www.census.gov).

12. For more on the Indian immigrant experience in the United States, see Jean Bacon, *Life Lines: Community, Family, and Assimilation among Asian Indian Immigrants* (New York: Oxford University Press, 1996); John Y. Fenton, *Transplanting Religious Traditions: Asian Indians in America* (New York: Praeger, 1988); Maxine P. Fisher, "Creating Ethnic Identity: Asian Indians in the New York City Area." *Urban Anthropology* 7, no. 3 (1978), and *The Indians of New York City* (New Delhi: Heritage, 1980); Arthur Wesley Helweg and Usha M. Helweg, *An Immigrant Success Story: East Indians in America* (Philadelphia: University of Pennsylvania Press, 1990); Johanna Lessinger, *From the Ganges to the Hudson: Indian Immigrants in New York City* (Boston: Allyn and Bacon, 1995); Raymond Brady Williams, *Religions of Immigrants from India and Pakistan: New Threads in the American Tapestry* (Cambridge: Cambridge University Press, 1988); Karen Isaksen Leonard, *Making Ethnic*

Choices, California's Punjabi Mexican Americans (Philadelphia: Temple University Press, 1992); and Parmatma Saran, *The Asian Indian Experience in the US* (Cambridge, MA: Schenkman, 1985). For more specifically on the experience of second-generation Indian Americans in other contexts, see Sunaina Marr Maira, *Desis in the House: Indian American Youth Culture in New York City* (Philadelphia: Temple University Press, 2001) and "Identity Dub: The Paradoxes of Indian American Youth Subculture (New York Mix)" in *Cultural Anthropology* 14, no. 1 (1999); Shalini Shankar's (*Desi Land: Teen Culture, Class, and Success in Silicon Valley* [Durham, NC: Duke University Press, 2008]) and Priya Agarwal's (*Passage from India: Post 1965 Immigrants and Their Children* [Palos Verdes, CA: Yuvati Publications, 1991]) studies located in California.

13. Paul D. Escott, "The Special Place of History," in *The South for New Southerners*, ed. P. D. Escott and D. R. Goldfield (Chapel Hill: University of North Carolina Press, 1991).

14. William S. Powell, *North Carolina: Through Four Centuries* (Chapel Hill: University of North Carolina Press, 1989), 531.

15. Ibid., 530.

16. Kenneth T. Jackson, *Crabgrass Frontier: The Suburbanization of the United States* (Oxford: Oxford University Press, 1985); Douglas S. Massey and Nancy A. Denton, *American Apartheid: Segregation and the Making of the Underclass* (Cambridge, MA: Harvard University Press, 1993).

17. As Portes and Zhou ("The New Second Generation: Segmented Assimilation and Its Variants," *Annals of the American Academy of Political and Social Science* 530 [November 1993]), Zhou ("Segmented Assimilation: Issues, Controversies, and Recent Research on the New Second Generation," *International Migration Review* 31, no. 4 [Winter 1997]), and Rumbaut and Portes (*Ethnicities*, 303) have shown in discussing the concept of "segmented assimilation," the race ascribed to the immigrant group and the racial formations of the area in which they settle can have a significant effect on the experiences of the immigrants.

18. According to the 2000 census North Carolina included 72 percent white/European Americans, 21.6 percent black/African Americans, 4.7 percent Hispanics/Latinos, 1.4 percent Asians and Pacific Islanders, 1.2 percent Native Americans, and .3 percent Asian Indians. The 2010 census revealed that the number of Latinos and Asians in North Carolina has skyrocketed, with Latinos now making up 8.4 percent of the total population and Asians 2.2 percent, with Asian Indians now at .6 percent (www.census.gov).

19. M. Gibson, *Accommodation without Assimilation: Sikh Immigrants in American High Schools* (Ithaca, NY: Cornell University Press, 1988).

20. See Chatterjee ("Colonialism, Nationalism, and Colonialized Women: The Contest in India," *American Ethnologist* 16, no. 4 [1989]) for a discussion of how a similar opposition was constructed by Indian nationalists struggling with the prob-

lem of how to achieve independence and become a modern nation without reproducing the Western state.

21. The South Asian bhangra club scene has exploded since I conducted my research (Ajay Nair and Murali Balaji, eds., *Desi Rap: Hip Hop and South Asian America* [Lanham, MD: Lexington Books, 2008]; Natasha Timar Sharma, *Hip Hop Desis: South Asian Americans, Blackness, and a Global Race Consciousness* (Durham, NC: Duke University Press, 2000. As discussed by Maira (*Desis in the House* and "Identity Dub"), the club scene is an important context for second-generation Indian Americans to explore and construct their identities and cultures. However, it is focused in larger cities and does not yet seem to have the same kind of presence in North Carolina.

22. Vincent H. Melomo, "'I Love My India': Indian American Students Performing Identity and Creating Culture on Stage," in *Asian American Literary Studies*, ed. Guiyou Huang (Edinburgh: Edinburgh University Press, 2005).

23. The concept of cultural models is drawn from the work in cognitive anthropology of D'Andrade and Strauss (*Human Motives and Cultural Models* [Cambridge: Cambridge University Press, 1992]), Holland and Quinn (*Cultural Models in Language and Thought* [Cambridge: Cambridge University Press, 1987]), and Strauss and Quinn (*A Cognitive Theory of Cultural Meaning* [Cambridge: Cambridge University Press, 1997]). These authors suggest that through interactions with others we learn cultural models or schema, which in turn motivate and guide our behavior.

24. Bacon, *Life Lines*; Anannya Bhattacharjee, "The Habit of Ex-Nomination: Nation, Woman, and the Indian Immigrant Bourgeoisie," *Public Culture* 5, no. 1 (1992); Karen Isaksen Leonard, "The Management of Desire: Sexuality and Marriage for Young South Asian Women in America," in *Emerging Voices: South Asian American Women Redefine Self, Family, and Community*, ed. S. R. Gupta (Walnut Creek, CA: AltaMira Press, 1999).

25. Dorothy C. Holland, "How Cultural Systems Become Desire: A Case Study of American Romance," in *Human Motives and Cultural Models*, ed. R. G. D'Andrade and C. Strauss (Cambridge: Cambridge University Press, 1992); Naomi Quinn, "Convergent Evidence for a Cultural Model of American Marriage," in *Cultural Models in Language and Thought*, ed. D. Holland and N. Quinn; Ann Swidler, *Talk of Love, How Culture Matters* (Chicago: University of Chicago Press, 2001).

26. Michael M. J. Fischer, "Ethnicity and the Post-Modern Arts of Memory," in *Writing Culture*, ed. James Clifford and George E. Marcus (Berkeley: University of California Press, 1986), 196.

27. Sandhya Nankani, "Bride Shopping on the Net." *Little India*, February 5, 1999.

28. Reena Jana, "Arranged Marriages, Minus the Parents," *New York Times*, August 17, 2000.

29. Sanyantani DasGupta and Shamita Das Dasgupta, "Women in Exile: Gender Relations in the Asian Indian Community in the U.S.," in *Contours of the Heart,*

South Asians Map North America, ed. S. Maira and R. Srikanth (Asian American Writers Workshop, 1996).

30. The existing scholarship on Indians in America, of the first and second generation, is overwhelmingly by and about women.

31. Two statistical studies of Asian American intermarriage based on census data reveal that unlike most other Asian groups, more Indian American men are marrying outside of their group than women (S. Hwang, R. Saenz, and B. E. Aguirre,. "Structural Assimilationist Explanations of Asian American Intermarriage," *Journal of Marriage and the Family* 59 (1997); Zai Liang and Naomi Ito, "Intermarriage of Asian Americans in the New York City Region: Contemporary Patterns and Future Prospects," *International Migration Review* 33, no. 4 (1999). Nevertheless, my own observations and that of others I spoke with while doing my research were that the opposite was true in my study area, and DasGupta and Dasgupta ("Women in Exile") also suggest this is true for Indian Americans more generally.

32. Jasbir K. Puar in "Resisting Discourses of Whiteness and Asianness in Northern England: Second Generation Sikh Women and Constructions of Identity," (*Socialist Review* 24, nos. 1 and 2 [1995]: 49) discusses how having a white partner, though read as assimilation, need not indicate such.

Works Cited

Agarwal, Priya. *Passage from India: Post 1965 Immigrants and Their Children*. Palos Verdes, CA: Yuvati Publications, 1991.

Appadurai, Arjun. "Global Ethnoscapes, Notes and Queries for a Transnational Anthropology." In *Recapturing Anthropology*. Edited by R. Fox, 191–210. Santa Fe, NM: School of American Research Press, 1989.

———. *Modernity at Large, Cultural Dimensions of Globalization*. Minneapolis: University of Minnesota Press, 1996.

Bacon, Jean. *Life Lines: Community, Family, and Assimilation among Asian Indian Immigrants*. New York: Oxford University Press, 1996.

Basch, Linda, Nina G. Schiller, and Cristina S. Blanc. *Nations Unbound: Transnational Projects, Postcolonial Predicaments, and Deterritorialized Nation-States*. London UK: Gordon and Breach, 1994.

Bhattacharjee, Anannya. "The Habit of Ex-Nomination: Nation, Woman, and the Indian Immigrant Bourgeoisie." *Public Culture* 5, no. 1 (1992): 19–44.

Breckenrdge, Carol, and Arjun Appadurai. "On Moving Targets." *Public Culture* 2, no. 1 (1989): i–iv.

Chatterjee, Partha. "Colonialism, Nationalism, and Colonialized Women: The Contest in India." *American Ethnologist* 16, no. 4 (1989): 622–33.

D'Andrade, Roy, and Claudia Strauss. *Human Motives and Cultural Models*. Cambridge: Cambridge University Press, 1992.

Das Gupta, Monisha. *Unruly Immigrants: Rights, Activism, and Transnational South Asia Politics in the United States*. Durham, NC: Duke University Press, 2006.

DasGupta, Sanyantani, and Shamita Das Dasgupta. "Women in Exile: Gender Relations in the Asian Indian Community in the U.S." In *Contours of the Heart, South Asians Map North America*, edited by S. Maira and R. Srikanth, 381–400. New York: Asian American Writers Workshop, 1996.

Escott, Paul D. "The Special Place of History." In *The South for New Southerners*, edited by P. D. Escott and D. R. Goldfield, 1–17. Chapel Hill: University of North Carolina Press, 1991.

Fenton, John Y. *Transplanting Religious Traditions: Asian Indians in America*. New York: Praeger, 1988.

Fischer, Michael M. J. "Ethnicity and the Post-Modern Arts of Memory." In *Writing Culture*, edited by James Clifford and George E. Marcus. Berkeley: University of California Press, 1986.

Fisher, Maxine P. "Creating Ethnic Identity: Asian Indians in the New York City Area." *Urban Anthropology* 7, no. 3 (1978): 271–85.

———. *The Indians of New York City*. New Delhi: Heritage, 1980.

Friedman, Jonathan. *Cultural Identity and Global Process*. London: Sage, 1994.

Gibson, M. *Accommodation without Assimilation: Sikh Immigrants in American High Schools*. Ithaca, NY: Cornell University Press, 1988.

Giddens, Anthony. *Modernity and Self Identity, Self and Society in the Late Modern Age*. Stanford, CA: Stanford University Press, 1991.

Gupta, Akhil, and James Ferguson. "Beyond Culture: Space, Identity, and the Politics of Difference." *Cultural Anthropology* 7, no. 1 (1992): 6–23.

Gupta, Sangeeta R., ed. *Emerging Voices: South Asian American Women Redefine Self, Family, and Community*. Walnut Creek, CA: AltaMira Press, 1999.

Hall, Stuart. "Cultural Identity and Diaspora." In *Identity: Community, Culture and Difference*, edited by Jonathan Rutherford, 222–37. London: Lawrence and Wishart, 1990.

Hannerz, Ulf. "Cosmopolitans and Locals in World Culture." In *Global Culture: Nationalism, Globalisation, Modernity*, edited by M. Featherstone, 237–53. London: Sage, 1990.

Helweg, Arthur Wesley, and Usha M. Helweg. *An Immigrant Success Story: East Indians in America*. Philadelphia: University of Pennsylvania Press, 1990.

Holland, Dorothy C. "How Cultural Systems Become Desire: A Case Study of American Romance." In *Human Motives and Cultural Models*, edited by R. G. D'Andrade and C. Strauss, 61–89. Cambridge: Cambridge University Press, 1992.

Holland, Dorothy, William Lachiotte Jr., Debra Skinner, and Carole Cain. *Identity and Agency in Cultural Worlds*. Cambridge, MA: Harvard University Press, 1988.

Holland, Dorothy C., and Naomi Quinn. *Cultural Models in Language and Thought*. Cambridge: Cambridge University Press, 1987.

Hwang, S., R. Saenz, and B .E. Aguirre. "Structural Assimilationist Explanations of Asian American Intermarriage." *Journal of Marriage and the Family* 59 (1997): 758–72.

Jackson, Kenneth T. *Crabgrass Frontier: The Suburbanization of the United States*. Oxford: Oxford University Press, 1985.

Kitano, Harry H. L., and Roger Daniels. *Asian Americans: Emerging Minorities*. Englewood Cliffs, NJ: Prentice Hall, 1988.

Kukke, Surabhi, and Svati Shah. "Reflections on Queer South Asian Progressive Activism in the U.S." *Amerasia* 25, no. 3, (1999/2000): 129–37.

Leonard, Karen Isaksen. *Making Ethnic Choices, California's Punjabi Mexican Americans*. Philadelphia: Temple University Press, 1992.

———. "The Management of Desire: Sexuality and Marriage for Young South Asian Women in America." In *Emerging Voices: South Asian American Women Redefine Self, Family, and Community*, edited by S. R. Gupta, 107–19. Walnut Creek, CA: AltaMira Press, 1999.

Lessinger, Johanna. *From the Ganges to the Hudson: Indian Immigrants in New York City*. Boston: Allyn and Bacon, 1995.

Liang, Zai, and Naomi Ito. "Intermarriage of Asian Americans in the New York City Region: Contemporary Patterns and Future Prospects." *International Migration Review* 33, no. 4 (1999): 876–900.

Maira, Sunaina Marr. *Desis in the House: Indian American Youth Culture in New York City*. Philadelphia: Temple University Press, 2001.

———. "Identity Dub: The Paradoxes of Indian American Youth Subculture (New York Mix)." *Cultural Anthropology* 14, no. 1 (1999): 29–60.

Maira, Sunaina, and Rajini Srikanth, eds. *Contours of the Heart, South Asians Map North America*. New York: Asian American Writers Workshop, 1995.

Massey, Douglas S., and Nancy A. Denton. *American Apartheid: Segregation and the Making of the Underclass*. Cambridge, MA: Harvard University Press, 1993.

Melomo, Vincent H. "'I Love My India': Indian American Students Performing Identity and Creating Culture on Stage." In *Asian American Literary Studies*, edited by Guiyou Huang. Edinburgh: Edinburgh University Press, 2005.

———. *Immigrant Dreams and Second Generation Realities: Indian Americans Negotiating Marriage, Culture and Identity in North Carolina in Late Modernity*. PhD dissertation in anthropology, Binghamton University, 2003.

Nair, Ajay, and Murali Balaji, eds. *Desi Rap: Hip Hop and South Asian America*. Lanham, MD: Lexington Books, 2008.

Nankani, Sandhya. "Bride Shopping on the Net." *Little India*, February 5, 1999.

Portes, Alejandro, and Ruben G. Rumbaut. *Legacies: The Story of the Immigrant Second Generation*. Berkeley: University of California Press, 2001.

Portes, Alejandro, and Min Zhou. "The New Second Generation: Segmented Assimilation and Its Variants." *Annals of the American Academy of Political and Social Science* 530 (November 1993): 74–97.

Powell, William S. *North Carolina: Through Four Centuries*. Chapel Hill: University of North Carolina Press, 1989.

Puar, Jasbir K. "Resisting Discourses of Whiteness and Asianness in Northern England: Second Generation Sikh Women and Constructions of Identity." *Socialist Review* 24, nos. 1 and 2 (1995): 21–54.

Quinn, Naomi. "Convergent Evidence for a Cultural Model of American Marriage." In *Cultural Models in Language and Thought*, edited by D. Holland and N. Quinn. Cambridge: Cambridge University Press, 1987.

Ratti, Rakesh, ed. *Lotus of a Different Color: An Unfolding of the South Asian Gay and Lesbian Experience*. Boston: Alyson Publications, 1992.

Rumbaut, Ruben G., and Alejandro Portes. *Ethnicities, Children of Immigrants in America*. Berkeley: University of California Press, 2001.

Saran, Parmatma. *The Asian Indian Experience in the US*. Cambridge, MA: Schenkman, 1985.

Shankar, Shalini. *Desi Land: Teen Culture, Class, and Success in Silicon Valley*. Durham, NC: Duke University Press, 2008.

Sharma, Natasha Timar. *Hip Hop Desis: South Asian Americans, Blackness, and a Global Race Consciousness*. Durham, NC: Duke University Press, 2000.

Strauss, Claudia, and Naomi Quinn. *A Cognitive Theory of Cultural Meaning*. Cambridge: Cambridge University Press, 1997.

Swidler, Ann. *Talk of Love, How Culture Matters*. Chicago: University of Chicago Press, 2001.

Tindall, George Brown. *Natives and Newcomers: Ethnic Southerners and Southern Ethnics*. Athens: University of Georgia Press, 1995.

Williams, Raymond Brady. *Religions of Immigrants from India and Pakistan: New Threads in the American Tapestry*. Cambridge: Cambridge University Press, 1988.

Women of South Asian Descent Collective, eds. *Our Feet Walk the Sky: Women of the South Asian Diaspora*. San Francisco: Aunt Lute Books, 1993.

Zhou, Min. "Segmented Assimilation: Issues, Controversies, and Recent Research on the New Second Generation." *International Migration Review* 31, no. 4 (Winter 1997): 975–1009.

9
Resilient History and the Rebuilding of a Community

The Vietnamese American Community in New Orleans East

Karen J. Leong, Christopher A. Airriess, Wei Li, Angela Chia-Chen Chen, and Verna M. Keith

As the floodwaters receded from New Orleans and rebuilding began, new stories of race relations emerged and new histories were written. One is the history of a predominantly Catholic Vietnamese American community located in eastern New Orleans. Before Hurricane Katrina, Vietnamese Americans constituted fewer than 1.5 percent of the city's population. Since Katrina, the small Vietnamese American community in eastern New Orleans has received significant press coverage due to its members' high rate of return and the rapid rebuilding of their community. This essay will explore how shared refugee experiences, the leadership role of the Catholic Church, and the historically specific circumstances of Vietnamese immigrant settlement in eastern New Orleans contributed to this community's mobilization and empowerment. Some might attribute the community's ability to recover so quickly to a strong work ethic and an innate identity—both features of the myth of Asian Americans as "model minorities." That myth is a 1950s and 1960s construction that has since been deployed to justify racist assumptions about African Americans, Hispanics, and American Indians. It also obscures historical processes. This essay argues that the eastern New Orleans Vietnamese American community's response to Katrina is clearly rooted in its particular history and collective memory. As the experience of the Vietnamese American community in Village de L'Est demonstrates, history and memory are more than analytical artifacts—they are political resources.[1]

Ever since Hurricane Katrina left a path of destruction through the central Gulf states, and particularly through the city of New Orleans, popular and scholarly discourse on race and Katrina has emphasized black and white. Initial media coverage viewed the disaster through a historical lens of United States black-white relations. That is not surprising because New Orleans prior to Katrina was a majority black city, with African Americans constituting 68 percent of the population. The city's early Afro-Creole culture had a major impact on the development of African American culture, and even today, according to the historian Gwendolyn Midlo Hall, New Orleans "remains, in spirit, the most African city in the United States." During the first weeks of flooding, much media attention focused on the extreme devastation endured by the Lower Ninth Ward, a primarily African American neighborhood with concentrated poverty in eastern New Orleans, and to a lesser extent on Lakeview, an affluent Euro-American neighborhood. Except in independent ethnic media, Latinos and Asian Americans of New Orleans were largely absent from the national post-Katrina discussions about race, class, and social justice in the United States. Obviously not impacted in the same numbers as African Americans, certain subpopulations in New Orleans—immigrants from Southeast Asia, Mexico, and Central America—also endured disproportionately high rates of poverty and suffered great losses and upheaval as a result of the flooding. Although some national media outlets addressed Katrina's impact on the Vietnamese refugee shrimpers along the Gulf Coast, many people still are not aware that New Orleans was home to one of the largest concentrated settlements of Vietnamese Americans in the nation.[2]

This particular Vietnamese American community, a legacy from the refugee resettlement beginning in the 1970s, is located in a residential suburb known as Village de L'Est in easternmost New Orleans. In the aftermath of the Vietnam War, the US government relied on nongovernment and faith-based organizations to help relocate refugees from Vietnam in the United States across 821 zip codes. The Associated Catholic Charities of New Orleans, for example, relocated Vietnamese in New Orleans and found federally subsidized, low-income housing for one thousand refugees in 1975 at the Versailles Arms Apartments. Chain migration—in which initial immigrants attract further migration of friends and family from the same place of origin—resulted in two thousand more Vietnamese moving into the neighborhood near the apartments from their initial settlement locations. The Vietnamese population grew to nearly five thousand by 1990.[3]

The influx of Vietnamese refugees and the white flight that began in the 1980s significantly changed the complexion of the neighborhood. By 1990, the neighborhood's population was almost equally divided between African Americans and Vietnamese Americans. Its poverty rates were higher than the city's pre-Katrina average of 18 percent, at almost 35 percent for African Americans and 31 percent for Vietnamese Americans. By 2000 in Village de L'Est, African Americans constituted 78 percent of renters of the Section 8 apartments (whose owners accept government subsidies in return for charging low income tenants below-market rates). One-third of the Vietnamese American community was foreign born. Even so, many African Americans and most Vietnamese Americans in the neighborhood were middle-class homeowners. In 1999 the average household income there was $20,753 for African Americans and $32,000 for Vietnamese Americans. The median housing value for Vietnamese American households in Village de L'Est was in the mid-$80,000 range. Although the neighborhood experienced tensions during the 1970s and 1980s, in the two decades prior to Katrina there was little public interaction, positive or negative, between the two groups.[4]

Due to Katrina, the dynamics of eastern New Orleans have been altered yet again. By spring 2007, over 90 percent of the Vietnamese American residents but fewer than 50 percent of the African Americans had returned to Village de L'Est. For African American renters the unavailability of affordable rental housing has constituted a barrier to return; three apartment complexes had housed nearly 40 percent of the African American population in the neighborhood. During the first year of recovery, the Vietnamese American survivors' early and high rate of return heightened their visibility and political leverage. By early December 2005, two months after Mayor Ray Nagin declared New Orleans safe for return, church leaders estimated that about six hundred individuals had returned and had begun cleaning and repairing Vietnamese American–owned homes in the neighborhood. The visible turnout of residents forced the city to provide dumpsters, and a petition signed by residents who stated their commitment to return to the neighborhood persuaded the utility company to restore power in mid-October 2005.[5]

To survive after Katrina, residents in this eastern New Orleans community had to establish themselves as active stakeholders both in their community and in the city. Fears that the city would not support efforts to rebuild its eastern part seemed confirmed in February 2006 when the mayor authorized the opening of a hurricane debris landfill less than two miles from Village de L'Est. Already faced with the burden of rebuilding their lives, residents had to organize quickly and collaboratively to oppose the landfill. Protest against the Chef Menteur landfill united Vietnamese Americans, African Americans, environmentalists, other social justice advocates, and elected officials in the multiethnic Coalition for a Strong New Orleans East, which brought such pressure to bear on the city that the mayor chose not to renew the landfill contract in August 2006. The coalition's political success, coupled with the relatively rapid repopulation of the isolated suburb with little city government assistance, became a highly popular Katrina story for national media outlets including the *New York Times*, CNN, and NBC Nightly News.[6]

National media coverage of the "Vietnamese Versailles community" generally presented a narrative that fit the stereotypical Asian American model-minority myth[7]: in less than three generations the New Orleans Vietnamese refugees had seemingly mastered the political system and overcome Katrina through the self-sufficiency and hard work associated with Asian Americans in general. One New

Orleans blogger observed in February 2006, "The story of this community is being touted across the city and region as an example of the power of 'anchoring' in the redevelopment of New Orleans neighborhoods." Media reports emphasized individual choice and community cohesion without noting the lack of rental units, racial discrimination, or differences in environmental impact that prevented others from returning. Participants in online discussion boards drew comparisons between the Vietnamese American community and "the African American community in New Orleans," even if media reports did not. One online participant stated, "These vietnamese folks are self-starters. The last thing they want is more governmental interference. NOLA's blacks, on the other hand, would rather sit around and wait for the government to save them." The *New Orleans Louisiana Weekly*, a local African American newspaper, in January 2006 hailed "The Miracle of Versailles: New Orleans Vietnamese Community Rebuilds" and ultimately concluded, "perhaps the most important key to their success is that the Vietnamese community refused to place its salvation into the hands of the government. They simply came home." Such emphasis on self-sufficiency ignores the voices of some members of the Vietnamese American community who have stated—echoing some African American community members—that federal government assistance is critical to rebuilding. Indeed, in separate interviews held in early 2006, Vietnamese American and African American residents of New Orleans East agreed that their community had received inadequate assistance in rebuilding from the state and city.

This immigrant story is not simply one of resolve and initiative nor of the faith and community emphasized in media reports, but of a cultural hybridity and historically specific transformation that preceded migration. A historical perspective on the Village de L'Est Vietnamese American community's faith and cohesion demonstrates how collective history and memory, in addition to the spatial concentration of this small Vietnamese American community, contributed to the ability to rebuild so quickly after Hurricane Katrina.[8] Father The Vien Nguyen, the pastor of Mary Queen of Vietnam Church, explained that the central role of the church in the community was not a postmigration phenomenon; it grew out of a pattern of church leadership that had developed in Vietnam over several hundred years. Catholicism, a foreign faith, was introduced into certain villages and transformed over time into a form of local leadership, subsequently motivating villagers to flee their homeland for fear of religious and political persecution. Spanish and Portuguese colonizers brought Catholicism to Vietnam in the sixteenth century. Vietnamese suspicion of foreign influences resulted in the persecution of Catholic Vietnamese in the early nineteenth century, and the persecution resulted in increased French intervention. After French colonial rule was established in the late nineteenth century, Vietnamese Catholics were free to worship. Initially, when Ho Chi Minh's resistance army overthrew

Japanese forces in 1945, the Catholics strongly supported his government, which benefited from nationalist sentiment that united the Vietnamese populace. That unity, however, soon unraveled after the formation of the second Ho Chi Minh government following national elections in 1946, as divisions increased between the Communists (Viet Minh) and non-Communists. This split fully manifested itself with the third Ho Chi Minh government, formed in November 1946, in which Communists dominated an overwhelming majority of the offices. By the 1950s, Vietnamese Catholic leaders increasingly and openly condemned the Communist government of Ho Chi Minh.[9]

The 1954 Geneva agreements split the country into two—with Communists governing the north and the non-Communists the south. Many Vietnamese Catholics had moved north, and now, under Clause 14d of the agreements, had a limited period—the time the troops took to assemble in their respective locations—to move to the opposite zone if they so chose. As a result, some nine hundred thousand refugees, mostly Catholics, fled from their villages in the Red River delta diocese of Bui Chu to the south. In rural areas the priest was often the only source of leadership and assistance for a community. After the siege of Saigon in 1975, many Vietnamese in South Vietnam attempted to flee, and some of those who succeeded found shelter in refugee camps lining the South China Sea coast and processing centers in Guam or the Philippines. Of those who arrived in the United States, research suggests that at Camp Pendleton half the refugees (55 percent) were Roman Catholic and that at Fort Indiantown Gap 40 percent were. The majority of refugees who left the camps were sponsored by families or groups. The US Catholic Conference accounted for 35 percent of the group sponsorships.[10]

After visiting the refugee camps, Archbishop Philip M. Hannan of New Orleans invited priests he met there to establish resettlement communities in New Orleans. He asked the Associated Catholic Charities of New Orleans to assist in finding Section 8 housing for the refugees. Vietnamese refugees in Village de L'Est originated from villages in the vicinity of Vung Tau city or the nearby village of Phuc Tinh, both located in the Ba Ria-Vung Tau Province some 120 kilometers southeast of Saigon. In 1985 the community founded its own ethnic parish, centered on Mary Queen of Vietnam Church. The religious faith, church leadership, and social organization that informed the migration decisions of these Vietnamese refugees and immigrants have contributed to a strong community identity.[11]

The concentrated settlement pattern of Vietnamese Americans in Village de L'Est, 75 percent of whom are Catholic, facilitated the implementation of the leadership structure and village-based community in the New Orleans neighborhood. The primary adaptation among the immigrant community has been that "the involvement of laypeople in meeting the needs of the community has increased since migration to the United States." As he did in Vietnam, the priest serves as the primary leader not only of religious life but also of the parish community. He is supported by a council that makes parish decisions, with each member representing a specific zone within the parish (in Village de L'Est, there are seven designated zones). Each zone, in turn, is divided into street units called "hamlets," with their own representatives and saints. The celebration of feast and saints' days facilitates community building among neighbors. The representatives have increasingly brought the political and social concerns of their constituents to the attention of the council. The council has responded by organizing committees to take care of specific community needs, including raising funds for burial expenses or assisting newcomers.[12]

The preexisting leadership structure was one of the most important community resources in the rebuilding process, allowing the church to keep track of its members' locations in Katrina's diaspora. Community members largely relied on their own social networks to evacuate with family and friends and to locate temporary housing in shelters or in other Vietnamese communities throughout the nation. The church choir, for example, caravanned as a group out of New Orleans days before the hurricane. The parish priests cared for the remaining elderly and those unable to evacuate on their own until they were all able to evacuate the flooded neighborhood. The community's limited size allowed Father Nguyen to visit parish members scattered throughout various states and set up a recovery network. He recalled, "My people were scattered in Austin, San Antonio, Dallas, Houston, and Arkansas. . . . My people were in California, Georgia, Florida, Washington, Minnesota, Michigan, and the Carolinas. They even went so far as New Hampshire and Connecticut." The pastor asked available council and hamlet representatives to meet in Houston to plan for the return to the parish as soon as permission was granted for people to reenter New Orleans. According to Nguyen, on October 5, the first day people could return to the city to begin the cleanup, more than three hundred parish members did so. It must be noted that the pastor has been a prominent source of information about the community. His role in narrating the Vietnamese community's collective dispersal and return to New Orleans serves to define both a cohesive faith identity for the Catholic Vietnamese Americans and a broader refugee identity of survival and sociocultural adjustment that includes all Vietnamese American residents regardless of religion.[13]

The Vietnamese American community in New Orleans East possesses social and cultural capital that is based on its members' lived experiences and historical memories. Because migration occurred within the past three generations and under the conditions of war, the community has sustained the strong social networks that operated during the refugee and migration experience as well as confidence in the efficacy of those networks. Members of the community exhibit a sense of strength derived from their experiences as war refugees or as recent immigrants. When asked about the difference between leaving Vietnam and evacuating from New Orleans, one person—who had just arrived in the United States in 2004 and had not yet returned to New Orleans from Houston by March 2006—noted that the former was much more dangerous: "It is harder leaving from your culture. Hurricane is nothing. In the hurricane, you have your family with you all the time." Observing that "our life is not as hard as it was before," this individual, like many others in the community, perceived the evacuation and rebuilding of New Orleans as less difficult than complete relocation from one's place of origin. That memory, along with the experience of adjusting to the United States, is shared by Catholic and Buddhist Vietnamese Americans and further contributes to a collective community identity.[14]

In addition to the role of religious faith in shaping immigrant life and ethnic community, the particular timing of Katrina also afforded the Vietnamese American community certain resources. Local activists had been working within the community to develop homeowner associations in response to concerns about community safety and had been attending city council meetings to articulate those concerns. National networks that had originated with the first waves of Vietnamese refugees arriving in the United States, such as Boat People SOS, also offered their assistance to evacuees as they negotiated the bureaucracy of the Federal Emergency Management Agency (FEMA) claims, insurance claims, and food stamps. Although those networks did not limit their assistance to Southeast Asian Americans, they built on their knowledge of those communities, familiarity in guiding recent immigrants through paper work, and ability to speak in various Asian languages, and they operated mainly in locations with high concentrations of Southeast Asian evacuees. In other words, having as refugees developed a community with limited (but not insignificant) federal and local government assistance, community members were able to draw on their relatively recent experience in rebuilding yet again.[15]

New patterns of interethnic interaction and spatial distribution may yet emerge in the aftermath of Katrina as New Orleans rebuilds. Katrina's enormous impact appears to have decreased the African American population while attracting Latino workers who are taking construction jobs. By November 2006, a few Latina-owned businesses, including restaurants and remittance offices, had opened up to serve the growing Latino population along the primarily Vietnamese business strip off Chef Menteur Highway. Early that month some individuals standing outside those businesses—from Mexico, Guatemala, and Honduras—indicated that they labored in construction and that many of them relied on social networks to locate work. In an interview about the new Latino presence in this area, Martin Gutierrez of Catholic Charities stated, "There will be some friction, but at the same time we all believe diversity is a strength." According to Nguyen, Latino immigrants had begun to attend services at Mary Queen of Vietnam even though they do not understand the Vietnamese language.[16]

Over the two years since Katrina made landfall, the community gained confidence as it successfully leveraged its newly found political power. Neighborhood Catholic and Protestant churches worked together since the hurricane to forge multiracial cooperation in the rebuilding of the community. The *Oakland Tribune* reported that Mary Queen of Vietnam provided volunteers to assist the primarily African American churches in the neighborhood with their cleanup. In May 2006 the Vietnamese American and African American Village de L'Est community joined with representatives of the Southern Poverty Law Center, a civil rights organization, to demand the closing of the Chef Menteur landfill. All those efforts appear to have created a new, more extended form of community. One African American focus group participant recalled that "those Vietnamese spent like 20 hours came to our church, clean our church and prepare for us" and that the priest had visited the service to talk about the Vietnamese American community. Another observed of the Vietnamese American community that "these people can teach us different things, they can teach us things . . . like I'm saying . . . they'll all become the real community." When asked if the possibility for Vietnamese Americans and African Americans to work together had increased, focus group participants agreed that Katrina "brought us closer." The April 2007 rebuilding plan proposed by Mayor Nagin and Dr. Ed Blakely, director of the city's Office of Recovery Management, listed the area among the top seventeen neighborhoods that would receive further assistance as a result of the recognized high return and rebuilding rates. Local Vietnamese American leaders considered the community making the list as a collective victory in deciding the fate of the community.[17]

The newly forged history of working together to survive sudden change and uncertainty provides a shared hope for this neighborhood, and even for the city. Cynthia Willard-Lewis, an African American member of the city council who represents the neighborhood (and in April 2006 hired a Vietnamese American to work in her office), suggested that the cooperation and rebuilding exhibited by the Vietnamese American community "can be a model for other communities. They are fighting to stay united and connected." In late August 2007 this community unity was already being mobilized to face a new challenge. Two weeks of deadly shootings and robberies suggested that Village de L'Est had become a target for violence, perhaps as a result of the publicity surrounding the community's success in rebuilding. Willard-Lewis, Father Nguyen, and other community leaders responded by working to increase police response time and protection for residents.[18]

Historians are well aware that historical memory can be, and has been, mobilized in dangerous ways. Yet the experience of this Vietnamese community in eastern New Orleans in the aftermath of the catastrophe of Hurricane Katrina is a powerful reminder that memories and knowledge of the past can also function as a significant source of community resilience and transformation.

Notes

1. US Census Bureau, American FactFinder, http://factfinder.census.gov/; Mari Matsuda, "Looking to the Bottom: Critical Legal Studies and Reparations," *Harvard Civil Rights-Civil Liberties Law Review* 22 (Spring 1987): 322–99; Ronald Takaki, *Strangers from a Different Shore: A History of Asian Americans* (New York: Little, Brown, 1989), 474–84. On the model-minority myth in the context of Hurricane Katrina, see Eric Tang, "Boat People," *ColorLines Magazine* 32 (Spring 2006), http://www.colorlines.com/article.php?ID=28.

2. Gwendolyn Midlo Hall, "Africans in Colonial Louisiana: The Development of Afro-Creole Culture in the Eighteenth Century," in *Creole New Orleans: Race and Americanization*, ed. Arnold R. Hirsch and Joseph Logsdon (Baton Rouge: Louisiana State University Press, 1992), 58–87, esp. 59. The US census for 2000 listed nearly forty thousand Hispanics in New Orleans alone prior to Katrina; see Grace Kao, "Where Are the Asian and Hispanic Victims of Katrina? A Metaphor for Invisible Communities of Color in Contemporary Racial Discourse," *DuBois Review* 3 (March 2006): 223–31, esp. 223–25.

3. "Exit Saigon, Enter Little Saigon," exhibition, January 19–March 31, 2007, Vietnamese American Heritage Project, Smithsonian Asian Pacific American Program, Concourse Gallery, S. Dillon Ripley Center, Smithsonian Institution, Washington, DC; Christopher A. Airriess and David L. Clawson, "Versailles: A Vietnamese Enclave in New Orleans, Louisiana," *Journal of Cultural Geography* 12 no. 1 (1991): 1–13, esp. 3; Min Zhou and Carl L. Bankston III, *Growing Up American: How Vietnamese Children Adapt to Life in the United States* (New York, Russell Sage Foundation, 1998), 78.

4. Carl L. Bankston III, "Vietnamese American Catholicism: Transplanted and Flourishing," *U.S. Catholic Historian* 18 (Winter 2000): 36–53, esp. 46. By 1990 the Vietnamese American rate of homeownership was above 37 percent. See Carl L. Bankston III and Min Zhou, "De Facto Congregationalism and Socioeconomic Mobility in Laotian and Vietnamese Immigrant Communities: A Study of Religious Institutions and Economic Change," *Review of Religious Research* 41 (June 2000): 453–70, esp. 459. On poverty rates among African Americans and Vietnamese Americans in Louisiana, see Wei Li et al., "Katrina and Migration: Evacuation and Return in an Eastern New Orleans Suburb by African Americans and Vietnamese Americans," paper delivered at the conference "Disaster and Migration: Hurricane Katrina's Effects on New Orleans's Population," Tulane University, April 2007 (in Wei Li's pos-

session), 5–7; Christopher A. Airriess, "Creating Vietnamese Landscapes and Place in New Orleans," in *Geographical Identities of Ethnic America: Race, Space, and Place*, ed. Kate A. Berry and Martha L. Henderson (Reno: University of Nevada Press, 2002), 228–54. The median house value for Vietnamese households in New Orleans East can be found at US Census Bureau, American FactFinder, http://factfinder.census.gov/home/saff/. On early interaction between African Americans and Vietnamese Americans in New Orleans, see Rawlein Soberano, "The Vietnamese of New Orleans: Problems of America's Newest Immigrants," 1978, ED173525 (microfiche), ERIC Clearinghouse (Teachers College, Columbia University, New York, NY).

5. US Census Bureau, American FactFinder, http://factfinger.census.gov/home/saff/. In addition to finding higher rents and fewer rental units than pre-Katrina, the Greater New Orleans Fair Housing Action Center in a post-Katrina rental study conducted between September 2006 and April 2007 "found a 57.5% rate of discrimination in metro New Orleans rental housing searches" for African Americans. "For Rent Unless You're Black: An Audit Report of Race Discrimination in the Greater New Orleans Metropolitan Rental Market," 2007, Greater New Orleans Fair Housing Action Center, http://www.gnofairhousing.org; Father The Vien Nguyen interview by Wei Li, December 5, 2005, notes (in Li's possession); Wei Li, field notes, February 5, 2006, field notes, Mary Queen of Vietnam Church, New Orleans, Louisiana, in Li's possession.

6. See for example, "Hurricane Katrina One Year Later," INSIGHT (CNN International, August 29, 2006); "Katrina through a Different Lens" (CNN, September 1, 2005), http://www.cnn.com/2005/US/09/13/katrina.ethnic.media.ap; "New Orleans Residents Protest Landfill Site," Associated Press, April 7, 2006; Greg Allen, "In New Orleans, Versailles Resurfaces," *All Things Considered* (NPR, March 27, 2007), http://www.npr.org/templates/ story/story.php?storyId=9163113; Cheryl Corley, "Immigrant Neighborhood Fights Dump" (NPR, May 12, 2006), http://www.npr.org/templates/story/story.php?storyId=5400944; Leslie Eaton, "New Orleans Debris Fuels a Political and Ethnic Fight," *New York Times*, May 8, 2006, p. A1; Christine Hauser, "Sustained by Close Ties, Vietnamese Toil to Rebuild," *New York Times*, October 20, 2005, p. A22; John King, "Keeping Them Honest," Anderson Cooper 360 Degrees (CNN, December 16, 2005), http://transcripts.cnn.com/TRANSCRIPTS/0512/16/acd.02.html; Marrin Savidge, "East New Orleans' Unshakeable History: Residents Vow to Return to Obliterated Communities," *NBC Nightly News* (NBC, November 4, 2005); and David Shafrel, "The Ninth Re-Ward: The Vietnamese Community Rebuilds after Katrina," *Village Voice*, December 27, 2006, http://www.villagevoice.com/generic/show_print.php?id=72328.

7. On the model-minority myth, see Sucheng Chan, *Asian Americans: An Interpretive History* (New York: Twayne Publishers, 1991), 167–69. For online discussions of Vietnamese Americans in New Orleans East, see "Out of It, into It," *N.O. Way: A*

Blog from New Orleans, February 6, 2007, http://noway.typepad.com/colin/2006/02/out_of_it_into_.html; and post by Chauncey, May 16, 2005, http://www.blackprof.com/archives/2007/05/new_orleans_a_continuing_natio.html. Lance Hill, "The Miracle of Versailles: New Orleans Vietnamese American Community Rebuilds," *New Orleans Louisiana Weekly*, January 23, 2006; New Orleans Vietnamese Americans evacuees focus group interview by Karen J. Leong, March 18, 2006, transcript, p. 11 in Leong's possession; New Orleans African American evacuees focus group interview by Christopher A. Airriess, June 24, 2006, transcript, p. 13, in Leong's possession.; Cynthia Nguyen and Thu Nguyen interview by Airriess, Angela Chia-Chen Chen, and Wei Li, December 3, 2005, notes by Wei Li in Li's possession; Cynthia Nguyen interview by Airriess, February 4, 2006, transcript, p. 7 in Leong's possession; Charles interview by Airriess, February 4 , 2006, transcript, pp. 6–7, in Leong's possession

8. For one take on the role of faith and immigrant experience in the Vietnamese community's successful return, see Stone Phillips, "The Vietnamese-American Community Recovers after Katrina," *NBC Dateline* (NBC, June 15, 2007).

9. The Vien Nguyen interview by Leong et al., November 5, 2006, notes, in Leong's possession; Le-Thi-Que, A. Terry Rambo, and Gary D. Murfin, "Why They Fled: Refugee Movement during the Spring 1975 Communist Offensive in South Vietnam," *Asian Survey* 16, no. 9 (1976): 855–63, esp. 859 and 863; Piero Gheddo, *The Cross and the Bo-Tree: Catholics and Buddhists in Vietnam* (New York: Sheed and Ward, 1970) 15–19, 23, 30–40.

10. Gheddo, *Cross and the Bo-Tree*, 58–59, 99; Nguyen Van Canh, *Vietnam under Communism, 1975–1982* (Stanford, CA: Hoover Institution Press, 1983), 164–65; Harry Haas and Bao Long Nguyen, *Vietnam: The Other Conflict* (London, UK: Sheed and Ward, 1971); Darrel Montero, *Vietnamese Americans: Patterns of Resettlement and Socioeconomic Adaptation in the United States* (Boulder, CO: Westview Press, 1979), 24, 37.

11. "Father Vien Nguyen, Interview with Charles Henry Rowell," *Callaloo* 29, no. 4 (2006): 1071–81, esp. 1080–81; Airriess, "Creating Vietnamese Landscapes and Place "; Bankston, "Vietnamese American Catholicism," 47.

12. Dorothy Vidulich, "Religion Central for Vietnamese in US," *National Catholic Reporter*, October 14, 1994, pp. 12–13, esp. 13; The Vien Nguyen interview by Leong et al.; Bankston, "Vietnamese American Catholicism," 50. The church-centered council is similar to other immigrant associations like *mutualistas* (mutual aid, or friendly, societies). Airriess and Clawson, "Versailles," esp. 5–6; Airriess, "Creating Vietnamese Landscapes and Place."

13. Karen J. Leong, field notes, November 5, 2006, New Orleans, Louisiana (in Leong's possession); "Father Vien Nguyen, Interview with Charles Henry Rowell," 1076–77.

14. New Orleans Vietnamese American evacuees focus group interview, p. 11. Journalists reported similar responses from Vietnamese American community members. On the role of refugee experience in shaping a collective identity, see Zhou and Bankston, *Growing Up American*, 232.

15. Cynthia Nguyen interview, p. 7. With the passage of the Refugee Act of 1980, the federal government provided short-term assistance in the form of food stamps and Social Security benefits.

16. Leong, field notes; Sara Catania, "From Hot Sauce to Salsa-New Orleans Vietnamese Adapt to Influx of Latinos," *New American Media*, October 16, 2006, http// news.newamericanmedia.org/news/view_article.html?article_id=3e0ffe22ee7a7bcb d9a2e1d4fb79f676; The Vien Nguyen interview by Li, April 14, 2007, notes (in Li's possession).

17. Momo Chang, "East Bay Volunteer Swept Up in Storm Relief," *Oakland Tribune*, November 16, 2005, http:// calbears.findarticles.com/p/artidcs/mi_qn4176/is _20051116/ai_nl5834992. On *NBC Dateline* a couple of African American homeowners in Village de L'Est credited the Vietnamese American community with leading the rebuilding of the neighborhood. See Phillips, "Vietnamese-American Community Recovers after Katrina," *NBC Dateline*. New Orleans African American evacuees focus group interview, pp. 10–11; The Vien Nguyen interview by Li, April 14, 2007.

18. Hauser; "Sustained by Close Ties "; April Capochino, "Why Stay? Vietnam Evacuee Helps Displaced New Orleanians Find the Answer," *New Orleans City Business*, July 3, 2006, http://www.neworleanscitybusiness.com/viewStory.cfm? recID =16023.

Works Cited

Airriess, Christopher A. "Creating Vietnamese Landscapes and Place in New Orleans." In *Geographical Identities of Ethnic America: Race, Space, and Place*, edited by Kate A. Berry and Martha L. Henderson, 228–54. Reno: University of Nevada Press, 2002.

———. "Versailles: A Vietnamese Enclave in New Orleans, Louisiana." *Journal of Cultural Geography* 12, no. 1 (1991): 1–13.

Bankston, Carl L., III. "Vietnamese American Catholicism: Transplanted and Flourishing." *U.S. Catholic Historian* 18 (Winter 2000): 36–53.

Bankston, Carl L., III, and Min Zhou. "De Facto Congregationalism and Socioeconomic Mobility in Laotian and Vietnamese Immigrant Communities: A Study of Religious Institutions and Economic Change." *Review of Religious Research* 41 (June 2000): 453–70.

Canh, Nguyen Van. *Vietnam under Communism, 1975–1982*. Stanford, CA: Hoover Institution Press, 1983.

Capochino, April. "Why Stay? Vietnam Evacuee Helps Displaced New Orleanians Find the Answer." *New Orleans City Business*, July 3, 2006. http://www.neworleanscitybusiness.com/viewStory.cfm? recID=16023.

Catania, Sara. "From Hot Sauce to Salsa-New Orleans Vietnamese Adapt to Influx of Latinos." *New American Media*, October 16, 2006. http//news.newamericanmedia.org/news/view_article.html?article_id=3e0ffe22ee7a7bcbd9a2e1d4fb79f676.

"Exit Saigon, Enter Little Saigon." Exhibition. January 19–March 31, 2007. Vietnamese American Heritage Project, Smithsonian Asian Pacific American Program, Concourse Gallery. S. Dillon Ripley Center, Smithsonian Institution, Washington, DC.

"Father Vien Nguyen, Interview with Charles Henry Rowell." *Callaloo* 29, no. 4 (2006): 1071–81.

"For Rent Unless You're Black: An Audit Report of Race Discrimination in the Greater New Orleans Metropolitan Rental Market." Greater New Orleans Fair Housing Action Center. 2007. http://www.gnofairhousing.org.

Gheddo, Piero. *The Cross and the Bo-Tree: Catholics and Buddhists in Vietnam*. New York: Sheed and Ward, 1970.

Haas, Harry, and Bao Long Nguyen. *Vietnam: The Other Conflict*. London: Sheed and Ward, 1971.

Hall, Gwendolyn Midlo. "Africans in Colonial Louisiana: The Development of Afro-Creole Culture in the Eighteenth Century." In *Creole New Orleans: Race and Americanization*, edited by Arnold R. Hirsch and Joseph Logsdon. Baton Rouge: Louisiana State University Press, 1992.

Kao, Grace. "Where Are the Asian and Hispanic Victims of Katrina? A Metaphor for Invisible Communities of Color in Contemporary Racial Discourse." *DuBois Review* 3 (March 2006): 223–31.

Le-Thi-Que, A. Terry Rambo, and Gary D. Murfin. "Why They Fled: Refugee Movement during the Spring 1975 Communist Offensive in South Vietnam." *Asian Survey* 16, no. 9 (1976): 855–63.

Leong, Karen J. Field notes. November 5, 2006. New Orleans, Louisiana. In Leong's possession.

Li, Wei. Field notes. February 5, 2006. Mary Queen of Vietnam Church, New Orleans, Louisiana. In Li's possession.

Matsuda, Mari. "Looking to the Bottom: Critical Legal Studies and Reparations." *Harvard Civil Rights-Civil Liberties Law Review* 22 (Spring 1987): 322–99.

Montero, Darrel. *Vietnamese Americans: Patterns of Resettlement and Socioeconomic Adaptation in the United States*. Boulder, CO: Westview Press, 1979.

Nguyen, The Vien. Interview with Wei Li. December 5, 2005, notes. In Wei Li's possession.

Takaki, Ronald. *Strangers from a Different Shore: A History of Asian Americans*. New York: Little, Brown, 1989.

US Census Bureau. American FactFinder. http://factfinder.census.gov.

———. *American FactFinder. http://factfinger.census.gov/home/saff/.*

Vidulich, Dorothy. "Religion Central for Vietnamese in US." *National Catholic Reporter*, October 14, 1994.

Zhou, Min, and Carl L. Bankston III. *Growing Up American: How Vietnamese Children Adapt to Life in the United States*. New York: Russell Sage Foundation 1998.

Contributors

Christopher A. Airriess is professor of geography at Ball State University. Among his many and wide-ranging research publications on human geography are "Spatial Liminality as Moral Hazard and Boat Squatter Toleration in Post World War Two Hong Kong," *Habitat International* (2014), and "The Geographies of Secondary City Growth in a Globalized China: Comparing Dongguan and Suzhou" in the *Journal of Urban History* (2009).

Daniel Bronstein is assistant professor in the History Department at Paine College in Augusta, Georgia. His publications include "La Cubana City: A Cuban Cigar Manufacturing Community near Thomasville, Georgia during the 1890s" in the *Georgia Historical Quarterly* (2006), and "Segregation, Exclusion, and Chinese Communities in Georgia, 1880–1940" in *Asian Americans in Dixie: Race and Migration in the South* (2013).

Angela Chia-Chen Chen is associate professor in the College of Nursing and Health Sciences and an affiliate faculty member of Asian Pacific American Studies at Arizona State University. She has authored and coauthored many studies on Asian Pacific American health issues, including "Perceived Discrimination and Its Association with Mental Health and Substance Use among Asian Americans and Pacific Islanders Undergraduate and Graduate Students" in the *Journal of American College Health* (2014), and "Chinese American Adolescents: Perceived Parenting Styles and Adolescents' Psychosocial Health," in *International Nursing Review* (2013).

John Howard is professor of American studies at King's College London. He is the author of *Concentration Camps on the Homefront: Japanese Americans in the House of Jim Crow* (2008), and *Men Like That: A Southern Queer History* (1999).

John Jung is professor emeritus of psychology at California State University, Long Beach. He is the author of four works on Chinese Americans, including *Chopsticks in the Land of Cotton: Lives of Mississippi Delta Chinese Grocers* (2008), and his memoir of growing up in Georgia, *Southern Fried Rice: A Chinese Laundry in the Deep South* (2005).

Verna M. Keith is professor of sociology and director of Race and Ethnic Studies at Texas A&M University. She is author, coauthor, and coeditor of many works, including *In and Out of Our Right Minds: The Mental Health of African American Women* (2003), and *Skin Deep: How Race and Complexion Matter in Color Blind America* (2004).

Karen J. Leong is associate professor of Asian Pacific American studies and women and gender studies at Arizona State University. Among her several publications are, *The China Mystique: Pearl Buck, Anna May Wong, Mayling Soong Chiang, and the Transformation of American Orientalism* (2005), and "Allure and Anxiety: Gamblers, Glamour Girls, and New Women in East Asia Commentary," in *Intersections: Gender and Sexuality in Asia and the Pacific* (May 2012).

Wei Li is professor of Asian Pacific American studies and geography at Arizona State University. She has authored, coauthored, and coedited several works on ethnic and immigrant studies, including *Ethnoburb: The New Ethnic Community in Urban America* (2009), and *Immigrant Geographies in North American Cities* (2012).

Vincent H. Melomo is associate professor of anthropology at William Peace University in North Carolina. His research interests on the South Asian diaspora and gender, family, and marriage have resulted in several research presentations and publications, including "I Love India: Indian American Students Performing Identity and Creating Culture on Stage" in Guiyou Huang, ed., *Asian American Literary Studies* (2005).

Raymond A. Mohl, who sadly passed away just as this book was going to press, was Distinguished Professor of History at the University of Alabama-Birmingham. He published numerous books and articles on American urban and ethnic history, including *South of the South: Jewish Activists and the Civil Rights Movement in Miami, 1945–1960* (2004), and *The Making of Urban America*, 3rd ed. (2012).

David M. Reimers is professor emeritus of history at New York University. He is the author and coauthor of several works on immigration and ethnic history, including *Still the Golden Door: The Third World Comes to America* (1992), and *The World Comes to America: Immigration to the United States Since 1945* (2012).

Greg Robinson is professor of history at the Université du Québec À Montréal. He is the author of several works on Japanese American history, including *By the Order of the President: FDR and the Internment of Japanese Americans* (2001), and *After Camp: Portraits in Japanese American Life and Politics* (2012).

Chizuru Saeki is associate professor in the History and Political Science Department at the University of North Alabama. She is the author of *Perry and the Blackships Festival* (2014), in addition to articles in the *Japan Review* and the *International Social Science Review Journal.*

Wenxian Zhang is professor and head of Special Collections and Archives at Olin Library at Rollins College in Winter Park, Florida. He is the author and coauthor of many works on Chinese business and entrepreneurs, such as *Entrepreneurial and Business Elites of China: Chinese Returnees Who Have Shaped Modern China* (2011), and coeditor of *A Trip to Florida for Health and Sport: The Lost 1855 Novel of Cyrus Parkhurst Condit* (2009).

Index

"accommodation without assimilation," 203
Adkins, Carl, 38–39, 42–43
Adkins, Homer (governor), 62
African Americans, xiii, 5, 16, 18–19, 21–22, 30, 39, 55, 61, 76, 78, 110, 113–115, 135, 155–157, 163–4, 170, 178–179, 201, 209, 234–237, 240–241
Alabama Development Office (Tokyo), 43
alien land laws, 3, 13–14, 62, 84
Alvin Nursery Company, 30
America First: Chinese Americans and the Second World War, 166
American Legion, 52
anti-immigrant laws, xii
antimiscegenation laws, 113, 174–175, 178–179
Arab Americans, xiii
Arimura, Akira, 21
arranged marriages, 207–220, 224
Asian American Chamber of Commerce of Central Florida, 92
Asian American Federation of Florida, 91–92
Asian American Hotel Operators Association, 88
Asian American Movement, The, 91
Asian Spectrum, 92
assimilation, 223
Associated Catholic Charities of New Orleans, 238
atomic bombs, 37–38, 41
Augusta Chronicle, 178

Bangladesh Association of Florida, 90, 92
Barbour, George M., 76
Barker, Rodney, 38
Bengali Cultural Festival, 90
Bessho, Koh, 14
Bessho, Namyo, 14
Birmingham Botanical Gardens, 43
Birmingham Museum of Art, 43
Bishop, Max, 40
Blakely, Ed, 241
"Blueprint for a Slum," 53
Bow, Leslie, 2
Bowl of Rice Movement, 167
Burlingame, Anson, 78, 121
Burlingame, Fanny, 117, 121
Burlingame Treaty (1868), 75, 78

Café du Monde, 21
Camp Livingston, 4, 16
Camp Savage, 56
Camp Shelby (Mississippi), xii, 16, 55
Caribbean immigration, 73
caste system, 209–210
Catholic Church, 9, 17, 56, 93, 234, 237–238, and Vietnamese, 234–238
Chan, Geraldine. *See* Sieg, Geraldine Chan
Chef Menteur landfill, 236, 241

Chen, Frank, 119; Josephine, 119
Chicago Sun Times, 120
China Travel Service, 119
Chinese American Benevolent Association of Miami, 118
Chinese Consolidated Benevolent Association (CCBA), 165–167
Chinese Exclusion Act, xii, 7, 75, 84, 110–113, 115, 134–135, 148
Chinese farmers, 78
Chinese grocery stores, 7, 78–79, 114, 135, 142, 144, 146–147, 149–150, 156, 170
Chinese immigration, 6, 75–78, 81, 108–111, 115–116, 136–137
Chinese laundries, 6, 77, 111–114, 135, 144–145, 147, 157
Chinese question, 110
Chinese Relief Association, 168
Chinese Six Companies, 133
Chinn, Frank A., 124
Chon, Tuck, 144
Choong, Bing, 142
Chow, Charlie, 113
Chow, Wah, 168
Christianity, Chinese, 159–160, 180
Chuang, Yao, 38–39
Chu family, 145–146
Civil Rights Act (1964), 30
Confucian philosophy, 115
"coolies," 1, 109–111
Cotton States Exposition (1884), 11
cotton trade, 12
Cousins, Norman, 38, 40–42
Crain, J. H., 61
Crowley, Louisiana, 13
Crumpler, Frances, 113
Crumpler, Herbert, 113
Cuban exiles, 73
Cuban Revolution, 94

Daikin Festival, 43
Dakuzaku, Julia, 56–58
Dakuzaku, Kame, 49, 56–58
Dakuzaku, Taro, 49, 56–58
Daniels, Paul, 12
Daniels, Roger, xi, 51, 75
Daoist gods, 1
Date, Hideo, 21
Dauphin Way Methodist Church, 32, 38–39
Demon Tribune, 51
Desh-Videsh, 90
Dixon, Governor Frank, 31
Doshisha College, 80
Drinnon, Richard, 60
Dyer, Arnice, 55

economic development, xiii, 6, 42–43, 125, 201
education, 8, 14–15, 162–166, 173, 205, 216, 224
education status, 224
Encyclopedia of Southern Culture, xi
Eng, George, 118
Enola Gay, 38
European immigration, 81
Executive Order 9066, 17, 31

Federal Bureau of Investigation (FBI), 16, 31, 41, 81
Federal Emergency Management Agency (FEMA), 240
Filipinos, 6, 87
Filipino sailors ("Manilamen"), xi, 2, 11
Finch, Earl, 54–55
Finch homes, 56
Finn, Richard B., 41
First Baptist Church of Augusta, 160
Flager Street Baptist Church, 118
Florida, Asian population, xi, 6, 81–89, 93
Florida Agriculturalist, 76, 110
Florida Chinese News, 89
Florida East Coast Railway, 80
Florida Hindu Parishad, 90
Florida Muslim Alliance, 90
Florida Splendid China, 108–109, 118–121, 124
Florida Viet Bao, 89
Floridians for Immigration Control, 94
Fort McClellan (Alabama), 4, 33–34

442 Regimental Combat Team, xii, 21, 33, 55, 57
Fourteenth Air Service Division, 167
Fujita, Scott, 21

gender identity, Indian Americans, 222–224
Geneva agreements (1954), 238
Georgia, Asian population, xi
Gong, Edmond J., 109, 115, 117, 122–123
Gong, Joe Fred, 78–79, 114–115, 122
Gong, Lue Gim, 78, 109, 116–117, 121–122, 124
Gong Company, 145
Gong Lum v. Rice, 163
Granada, Colorado, internment camp, 17
Guangdong Province, 132, 138–139, 143, 148
Guay, Joe, 139, 141

Hall, Gwendolyn Midlo, 235
Hamako, Tokumi, 14
Hannan, Philip M. (archbishop), 238
Harada, Jiro, 13
Harry Wing's laundry, 113
Hasegawa, Clara, 54
Hata, Masami, 18
Hattiesburg, 55–56
Hattori, Frank, 19
Hattori, Yoshihiro, 21
Hawaii, xii, 4
Hearn, Lafcadio, 11
Heart Mountain, Wyoming, 50
Hieshima, George Asaichi, 20
Higake, Akiko, 54
Hinata, Katsue, 14, 17
Hinata, Tomehitsu, 14
Hirohito, Emperor, 34, 36
Hiroshima, 37
Hiroshima maidens, 38, 41–42
Hiroshima Peace Center, 38
Hispanic Americans, xiii, 234
Hispanic immigrants, xiii, 88
Hitch, Caroline, 11
Ho Chi Minh, 237–238
Honda Manufacturing of Alabama, 43
"honorary white," 8, 155, 159, 161–162, 170, 174, 176, 179–181
House Un-American Activities Committee, 52
Houston Chronicle, 121
Hurricane Katrina, 8–9, 22, 234–241

Ickes, Harold, 52
Iijima, Kaz, 55
Ijuin, Tetsuo, 20
Imahara, James, 20
Immigration Act (1924), xii, 9, 15
Immigration and Naturalization Act (1965), xii, 86–87, 199
Imura, Saeki, 30
Inagaki, George, 16
"in between people," xiii. *See also* a "third race"
India Abroad, 218–219
India Festival of Gujarati Samaj, 90
Indian Americans, 3, 8
Indian Popular Culture Forum, 90
"Indian values," 204–205, 209–210, 217
India West, 218
intermarriage, 15, 113
International Asian-American, 91
internment camps, 50, 179
internment of Japanese Americans, 16, 33–34
Inumaro, Tetsutaro, 12
Ishikawa, Kay, 55–56
Islamic School of South Dade, 90
Isomoto, K., 14
Issei, 4–5, 12–15, 30, 51, 57, 61, 64–65
Italians, 73, 75

Jacoby, Tamar, 94
Japan America Society of Alabama, 43
Japanese American Citizens League (JACL), 16, 21–22, 57–58, 60
Japanese Americans, 5, 51–52, 54–55, 57–59, 61–65
Japanese American soldiers, xii
Japanese companies, 4

Japanese immigrants, 4, 29–31, 79, 81
Japanese surrender at end of World War Two, 34, 36
Japan Society of New Orleans, 12, 14
Japan-US Southeast Association, 43
Jerome (Arkansas), xii, 4, 49, 54, 56–57, 59, 63
Jim Crow, 5, 9, 30, 39, 43, 61, 161–163, 174, 178, 181
Joe, George, 168
Joe Gow Nue Grocery Store, 140–141, 143–144
Joe's Market, 79, 111, 114–115, 117, 122, 124
Johnson, Lyndon, 30
Johnston, Ray, 63
Jung, John, 2
Jung, Wing Fook, 168

Kanazawa, Tomi, 20
Kato, Michio, 12
Kee, Bean, 116
Khyati, Joshi Y., 3
Kimura, Minoru, 15
kinship networks, 9
Kiyono, Tsukasa, 32
Knapp, Seaman A., 12
Knight, Ray, 17
Kohara, Kay, 15
Kohara, Manabu, 15
Kohara, Saki, 15
Koo, Dominic, 117
Koopmanschap, Cornelius, 75
Korea, xii
Korean American Journal of Florida, 89
Korean War, xii, 84, 164, 170
K. T. Manufacturing Company, 20
Ku Klux Klan, 55
Kun, Chuck, 138
Kwan, Joe, 118
Kyushu rice, 12

Lake Arthur Herald, 13
Lam, C. H., 165
language barrier, 116, 158
language schools, 165–166
Lau, Kwong-Wah (minister), 93, 118
Leach, Neal A, 12
Lee, Charley P., 113
Lee, Samuel, 117
Lee's Corner Market, 172
Lewis, Robert A., 38
Li, Hop Lung, 113
Life Magazine, 32
Little Chinese Bird, 112
Little India, 90
Loo, Evelyn Woo, 164, 166, 172
Louisiana Distributing Company, 13
Louisiana League for the Preservation of Constitutional Rights, 19
Louisiana Purchase Exhibition, 12
Louisiana State University, 14–15, 21
Loving v. Virginia, 178
Low, Gow, 124
Low family, 145–147
Loyola University, 14
Lucky Dragon incident, 41
Lue Gim Gong orange, 122

MacArthur, General Douglas, 37
Mandarin Plaza, 124
Manila Times, 86
Manzanar, California, internment camp, 17
Marutani, William, 22
Mary Queen of Vietnam Church, 237–238, 241
Masaoka, Mike, 16
McAndrews, Mimi, 92
McCarran-Walter Act (1952), 84
McIlhenny, Edward A., 20
Meyer, Dillon, 52, 63
Miami Herald, 120
Midway, battle of, 34
Mississippi Delta, 7, 22
Miyao, Walter H., 33
Mobile Infirmary, 40
"model minority," 51, 118, 170, 234, 236
"Mongolian race," 110
Moon, Jew Guey, 143

Morai, Masaji, 43
Morikami, George Sukaji, 81
Morikami Park and Museum, 81
Myer, Dillon, 60, 63

Nagasaki, 37, 58
Nagasaki maiden project, 38–42
Nagata, Joe, 15
Nagata, Sam, 15, 21
Nagin, Mayor Ray, 236, 241
Nakahara, Mary, 56
Nakamura, Ayako Noguchi, 58
Nakano, Katsuto, 54
national origins quota system, xii, 87
Native Americans, 2, 19, 108, 201, 234
New Encyclopedia of Southern Culture, xi
New Orleans Louisiana Weekly, 237
New Orleans Times Picayune, 120
Nisei, 5, 14–15, 18, 49, 51, 55, 57–58, 61
Nomasa, Hisashi, 14
Nue, Joe Gow, 140–141
Nguyen, The Vien (minister), 237, 239–241
Nguyen, Luyen Phan, 92

Odate, Michiko, 54
Okamoto, Kikuha, 65
100th Infantry Battalion, 4, 16, 33. *See also* 442nd Regimental Combat Team
On Leong Association, 117
Organization of Chinese Americans, 93
Overseas Chinese News, 89

Pacific Citizen, 58
pan Asian movement, 91–92
"paper sons," 137, 139
Peairs, Rodney, 21–22
Pearl Harbor, xii, 4, 16, 29–31, 33
Perez, Leander, 19
"perpetual foreigner," 8, 155, 174, 179–180
Peru, 16
Pettus Museum, 34
Philippines, xii
Philips, John W., 12
Pinkerton, Elizabeth, 59
plantation life, 60–62, 75
"probationary whites," 22
Puerto Ricans, 73

Quan, Robert Seto, 2

racial prejudice, 2, 13–16, 19, 22, 31, 33, 36–37, 39, 56, 77
"Raja syndrome," 222
Reconstruction, 1, 6, 11, 76
Red Stone Arsenal, 34
Reimers, David, 85
Rice Belt Journal, 13
rice cultivation, 12–13, 29
Robertson, Walter, 41
Robinson, Greg, 52
Rohwer, Arkansas, xii, 4, 50, 53–54, 56, 59–60, 63–65
Rohwer Outpost, 51, 53–54, 65
Roosevelt, Franklin, xii, 4, 30–31, 52
Rufo, Raymond, 171
Rufo family, 164, 172
Russo-Japan War, 80

Sady, Rachel Reese, 50
Saibara clan, 14
Sakai, Kamosu Jo, 79–81
Sasaki, Herbert, 55
Satsuma, Alabama, 29–30
Satsuma orange, 3, 29, 31
Satsuma United Methodist Church, 30
Saturday Review of Literature, 38
Sawada family, 15, 32
Sawada, Kosaku, 3, 29–30
Seabrook Farms, 50, 53, 58
secondary migrants, 88, 125
"selective acculturation," 94
serial migration, 138
Seven Eleven Minit, 171
Shimano, Eddie, 52
Shindo, Charles H., 21
Sieg, Geraldine Chan, 161, 172, 175

Sing, Loo Yet, 158
Sing, Wah, 117
Siu, Paul, 77
slavery, 6, 61, 76, 110
sojourners, 115
Sons of the Golden West, 54
Sony Magnetic Products of America, 43
southern governors, xiii
Southern Pacific Rail Road, 134
Spangler, Frank M., 34
Splendid China (Shenzhen), 119
split household, 155–156
Strangers from a Different Shore, 84
Sugahara, Roku (Dairoku), 17–18, 20
sugar plantations, 2, 11
Sukyo Mahikari, 2
Suzuki, Yoko, 38–39

Tajiri, Larry, 52
Takaki, Ronald, 84
Takamine, Jokichi, 3, 11–12
Takayama, Kay, 39
Takeda, Bean, 50–51, 53–55, 66
Tampa Tribune, 120
Tanimoto, Kiyoshi, 37–38, 42
Tashima, Robert, 17, 19
Texas, Asian population, xi
"third race," xiii, 2, 30, 39, 155. *See also* "in between people"
This Is Your Life, 38
Tokunaga, Mike, 16
Tomoda, Kyokuzo, 20
Towne, J. Mac, 112
Toyota Motor Manufacturing of Alabama, 43
True Democrat, 13
Truman, President Harry, 34, 41, 123
Tsukamoto, Al, 56
Tsukamoto, Mary, 56–59
Tulane University, 20–21
"two worlds," 205

Uchida, Sadatsuchi, 12
United States immigration, 81, 85
University of Florida, 87
Urdu Times, 90
US Catholic Conference, 238
US census: **1870**, 75, 136; **1880**, 136; **1900**, 136; **1910**, 136; **1920**, 136; **1930**, 157; **1940**, 79; **1950**, 79; **1960**, 86; **1990**, 73, 113; **2010**, xi, 82–83, 127
US Congress, xii, 1
Uyeda, Clifford, 15–16

Van Valkenberg, Robert, B., 29
Viet Minh, 238
Vietnamese Americans and immigrants, 9, 22, 235–240
Vietnamese refugees, 86, 235, 238–240
"Vietnamese Versailles Community," 236–237
Vietnam War, xii, 84–85
Village de L'Est, 9, 234–239, 241
Virginia, Asian population, xi

Wah, Quong, 116–117
Wah Sing's laundry store, 113
Wah-Young, Joe, 141
war brides, 81, 84–85
War Brides Act (1945), 84
War Relocation Authority (WRA), xii, 4, 17–20, 50–53, 59–61, 63–65
war relocation camps, 4
wartime propaganda, 37
Watanabe, Iris, 58
Wei, William, 91
Weichang, Qian, 119
We the People, 59
Willard-Lewis, Cynthia, 241
Wilson, Harry L., 19
Wilson Dam, 31
Wilson Plantation, 5, 60–62, 64
Wing, Chester Chin, 113
Wing, Joe, 78–79, 114, 124
Wing, Jung, 161
Women's Army Corps, 57–58
Wong, Henry, 142
Wong, Jew, 142

Wong, K. Scott, 166–167
Wong, Margaret, 164, 172
Wong, Ruby Lum, 171–172
Wong, Tommy, 169, 171
Wong Dai, 134
Wong family, 145–147, 172
Wong On, 134
Woo, Evelyn. *See* Loo, Evelyn Woo
World Exhibition (1904), 29
World War Two, xii, 4, 8, 16, 81, 85, 166–170
Yamato Colony, 80–81, 85
Yawata, Roger, 14
Yee, George Quong, 144
"yellow peril," 77
Yenari, Hajime, 20
Yenari, Katsu Oikawa, 20
Yenari, Ted, 20
Ying, Nelson, 109, 123
You, Xiaozhen, 126
Yuke, Joe, 139, 141